The
Simon and Schuster International Pocket Food Guide

by
Quentin Crewe

Simon and Schuster/New York

The Author

Quentin Crewe is a general writer and journalist who finds himself in the curious position of having become an expert eater, always asked to write about food, rather in the way that an actor might always get cast as the butler. He has, however, written the two books, *A Curse of Blossom* and *Frontiers of Privilege*, as well as Mitchell Beazley's *Great Chefs of France*. He has been a regular contributor to various national newspapers and to *Queen* and *Vogue* magazines. He finds time to run a dairy farm and a small hotel with an excellent restaurant in Cheshire. He has been married more than once and has five children.

★ Denotes dishes with Quentin Crewe's personal recommendation and dishes not to be missed by the adventurous gourmet in search of new gastronomic experiences

---

How to use the book

All entries are in alphabetical order by cuisine. Chapters on major cuisines are sub-divided according to the classifications commonly found on a menu. Words which may help you in ordering can be found in the useful word lists at the end of each chapter or section.

Edited and designed by
Mitchell Beazley Publishers
87–89 Shaftesbury Avenue, London W1V 7AD
© Mitchell Beazley Publishers 1980
Text © Quentin Crewe 1980
All rights reserved including the right of
reproduction in whole or in part in any form
Typeset by Typesetting Services Ltd., Glasgow
Printed in Hong Kong by
Mandarin Offset International Ltd.
A Fireside Book
Published by Simon and Schuster
A Division of Gulf & Western Corporation
Simon & Schuster Building
Rockefeller Center
1230 Avenue of the Americas
New York, New York 10020
Library of Congress Cataloging in
Publication Data 80–5767
ISBN 0–671–41789–4

Editor Bobbi Mitchell
Designer Ray Smithwhite
Chief researcher Sandy Carr
Map illustrator Eugene Fleury
Executive Editor Susannah Read
Art Editor Douglas Wilson
Production Julian Deeming

Contents

Introduction

Phrase books, it has always seemed to me, are the product of a transparent fallacy. No matter how perfectly you pronounce some carefully rehearsed Portuguese sentence on the lines of "Could you please reassure me as to the likelihood of my laundry, which consists of two pairs of grey-blue underpants, a sleeveless nightgown and a starched evening shirt, being returned before sundown?" you will be quite unable to understand the stream of chatter you will have unleashed from the Brazilian housemaid, whom you have lulled into thinking that you are a fluent speaker of her language.

Similarly if you ask a Yugoslavian waiter what something on a menu is, his explanation will merely compound your confusion. Moreover, while a little mime might help you with a Rio de Janeiro housemaid or a lightning-struck Bavarian postillion, no-one can easily act out "liver and bacon".

Hence this book. The hope is that, wherever you may be in the world, you will be able to look at a menu, and, with the minimum of research, find on it something which you would like to eat, or, at any rate, something which does not offend either your religion or your stomach.

For me there have been both happy and sad discoveries in the compiling of this book. The happy ones have been in the realization that in so many countries, notably America, Indonesia and Yugoslavia, there is such a fund of traditional cookery surviving in the face of varying onslaughts. The sad ones have been the cases where those onslaughts have succeeded. Whereas in Poland, before the war, people hunted in the woods for berries and mushrooms to enliven their food, today the young people do not know one plant from another and have literally never heard of three-quarters of the dishes which filled a cookery book of fifty years ago. They eat tinned muck. The same is gloomily true of every country where the deadening hand of communism has fallen. A denial of the spirit embraces the denial of the fun of eating. In some cases, therefore, I have included dishes which I hope you will find, but fear you may not.

Obviously it would be impossible to include every dish from every country. One Chinese restaurant alone may have as many as four hundred dishes on its menu. I have tried to list as many of the standard and classic dishes of each cuisine as space would allow and also to include a number of interesting or unusual dishes for adventurous eaters. In the end, the decision to put in or leave out a dish has to be a personal one and I must ask you to accept this arbitrary approach.

At the same time, this book contains some 10,000 entries. Obviously I do not carry in my head the precise recipes for so huge a variety of dishes. Equally my knowledge of some cuisines is better than it is of others. Indeed, I have little doubt that my enthusiasm for one or two may shine through with unjustified bias. What I hope is that you will write to argue with me and to plead the cause either of whole cuisines or of particular dishes. There will be revised editions of the book and I would like those who know a country and its cooking well to help improve upon this first edition.

It turned out to be impossible to treat each country in exactly the same way. In France, *à la périgourdine* always means the same thing, no matter what ingredient it may be applied to, though this is by no means true of all such phrases. In Italy, *alla fiorentina* is applied to half-a-dozen different methods, meaning in each case how a particular thing is cooked in Florence. Different peoples follow different patterns of eating, so that sometimes the order of courses is rigid, whereas sometimes it is quite haphazard.

The style of entries therefore varies. Sometimes they are simply alphabetical, while elsewhere they may be divided into courses or other categories. If you cannot find a dish, it is worth looking in the brief list of useful words, which may tell you at least what the main ingredient is.

I have put stars against some dishes. This does not mean that if you see them on a menu they are bound to be good. It means either that the dish is so typical of the cuisine that, if you want to understand the cooking of the country, you should try it, or it means that this is something I can never resist. If you have it and don't like it, it plainly falls in the first category. If you like it, we can agree on our good taste.

This is a book about food, so there is but scant reference in it to drink. I have, however, put in the most important drinks of each country and provided a short list of wines for the great wine producing countries.

Happily the different nations of the world have preserved their individual cuisines, for in the matter of food all human beings are deeply conservative. I hope that this book may help people to enjoy these differences.

> Alas! What various tastes in food,
> Divide the human brotherhood!
> Birds in their little nests agree
> With Chinamen, but not with me.
> Colonials like their oysters hot,
> Their omelettes heavy—I do not.
> The French are fond of slugs and frogs,
> The Siamese eat puppy-dogs . . .
> The Spaniard, I have heard it said,
> Eats garlic, by itself, on bread . . .
> In Italy the traveller notes
> With great disgust the flesh of goats
> Appearing on the table d'hôtes:
> And even this the natives spoil
> By frying it in rancid oil.
> In Maryland they charge like sin
> For nasty stuff called terrapin . . .
> In Massachusetts all the way
> From Boston down to Buzzards Bay
> They feed you till you want to die
> On rhubarb pie and pumpkin pie,
> And when you summon strength to cry,
> "What is there else that I can try?"
> They stare at you in mild surprise
> And serve you other kinds of pies . . .
> I dare not ask abroad for tea;
> No cannibal can dine with me;
> And all the world is torn and rent
> By varying views on nutriment.
> And yet upon the other hand,
> De gustibus non disputand—
> um.

Hilaire Belloc *On Food*

Africa
(South, east and west)

Africa, once contact with the Mediterranean Sea is lost, does not provide much comfort for the greedy. Apart from Ethiopia, the food depends largely upon who happened to colonize the area, and Ethiopia's national dish *injera na wat* (a sort of grey unleavened bread, resembling thin sheets of foam rubber with dollops of searing pepper-hot stew) is not a cause for regret that there are no other survivals from pre-European days.

In nearly every country the food you find in hotels is international stuff. With a bit of luck in ex-French colonies it may be quite well cooked, in ex-British ones it may at least provoke merriment. In Nairobi I have had suet pudding, in Blantyre Irish stew, in Salisbury Lancashire hotpot. No matter how hot the climate, the British clung to their nursery food.

The one country where you can eat well is South Africa, although outside the big cities you may only get the Brown Windsor soup syndrome. The produce is superb, the fish quite beautiful. South Africa is almost the last place on earth with an abundance of lobsters.

As they are the only people to have created something from what they found in their adopted country I list a few truly South African dishes. They may not be much to your taste but they are Boer.

The best thing to drink in every African country is the beer (unless in Ethiopia you care to try the local mead, *Tej*). South Africa once more is the only place to produce drinkable wine. Some names to look for: *Backsberg, Constantia, Grunberger, Montpellier, Paarl, Roodeberg, Rustenberg, Simansulei* and *Verdun.*

Biltong strips of beef (sometimes ostrich meat) seasoned, hung and dried. Eaten raw

Bobotie ground meat casserole flavoured with curry powder, lemon, sugar and almonds and thickened with beaten eggs

Koeksisters doughnuts served cold in a spiced syrup

Mealiepap porridge of corn meal usually served with meat and gravy. Also eaten as a breakfast dish, with milk and sugar

Melktert cinnamon-flavoured milk pudding baked in a flan case

Poffertjies enriched batter fried as little cakes and eaten hot, dredged with sugar

Sosaties lamb kebabs soaked overnight in a curry-flavoured marinade, grilled and served on a bed of rice with the thickened, cooked marinade used as a sauce

Tomato brede neck of mutton simmered very slowly with sliced tomatoes, onions, chilli, a little sugar and water. Beans or cabbage often replace the tomatoes as a main ingredient in the dish

---

And so three goats were slaughtered and a number of fowls. It was like a wedding feast. There was foo-foo and yam pottage, egusi soup and bitter-leaf soup and pots and pots of palm-wine. . . . Yam pottage was served first because it was lighter than foo-foo and because yam always came first. Then the foo-foo was served.
Chinua Achebe *Things Fall Apart*

Africa, north—*See* Arab food
Algeria—*See* Arab food

Arab food

In the depths of the Empty Quarter of Saudi Arabia I came to understand the point of Middle Eastern dietary laws. We killed a sheep one day and cooked a bit of it. Tough. Next day we had a bit more. Tender and delicious. The third day it was high. By the fifth day it was green and revolting, and I was overjoyed when some strangers appeared over the dunes and the laws of hospitality dictated that we must give them our food. They and my Bedu companions gobbled down the rotting meat. Nobody suffered any ill effects. The main reason, then, that any meal in the desert countries includes mutton or lamb is that it is safe, whatever its condition.

The limited character of the national cooking of Saudi Arabia, Syria, Jordan, Iraq and the United Arab Emirates is due to the extremely short time that the majority of their populations have been anything but nomadic tribesmen, eating only transportable foods such as rice and dates or ambulatory food like sheep and camel (the latter is delicious when young).

In the more fertile coastal regions such as Oman and the Yemen there are fruit and vegetables and fish, which relieve somewhat the monotony of the diet of the interior. Naturally oil riches and air transport have improved the availability of ingredients in the larger inland cities, so that hotels provide an international menu of the deep-freeze order.

It is, however, when the Arab world reaches the Mediterranean that its food becomes really interesting. Egyptian and Lebanese cooking combine the sophistication of European cuisines with the excitements of eastern spices, making it enjoyable rather than just a way of staving off hunger. Farther west the food changes still more, so that I have devoted a separate section to North Africa.

As for drink, in the stricter Arab countries you will get only fruit juices. In less pious areas you will find *arak*, imported wines and various sickly liqueurs. Beer is often the best bet.

Atayef, gatayef or **katayef** pancakes folded around a mixture of crushed walnuts, sugar and flower-water or around clotted cream with syrup

★ **Baba ghannoug** (Egypt) purée of baked peeled eggplants with sesame paste (*tahine*), dressed with lemon juice, crushed garlic and olive oil

Falafel mixture of minced fava beans, parsley, coriander, onions and garlic, shaped into balls and deep fried. Eaten hot with *tahine*

Fatayer pastry filled with chopped spinach, onions and olive oil. Baked

Fatta (Egypt) soup of calf's or lamb's feet garnished with toasted bread, chick peas and yoghurt

Fattoush "peasant salad"; toasted croûtons are added to a salad of cucumber, tomatoes, parsley and mint

Ferique whole wheat kernels cooked with meat or squab and flavoured with spices

Fu'l medames (Egypt) cooked brown beans, dressed with lemon juice and olive oil, seasoned with crushed garlic

Hamman meshwi grilled squab

★ **Hummus bi tahine** chick peas mixed with sesame paste, garlic, lemon juice and olive oil. Eaten with bread as an hors d'oeuvre

Kafta ground meat, chopped onions and parsley mixed with spices and grilled on skewers

mabrouma ground meat mixed with onion and parsley, rolled around pine nuts and baked

Kawareh bil hummus see *Fatta*

Kharouf mehshi whole lamb stuffed with rice, meat, pine nuts, almonds and spices. Strictly for banquets

★ **Kibbeh** a popular Middle Eastern dish with many

variations. Cracked wheat (burghol), ground meat, onions and spices are wrapped around a mixture of cooked ground meat, chopped onions and pine nuts and deep fried. May also be eaten raw (*naye*) with a mint, olive oil and black pepper dressing

Lahm bil ajeen type of Arabian pizza

Samak meshwi fish first marinated then grilled over charcoal

Sambousek small pies similar to Turkish *börek*. The usual filling is chopped onions, parsley and cheese

Sayyadiya poached or fried fish fillets on a bed of highly seasoned rice with a brown onion sauce

---

The commonest myth about Arab food is that a sheep's eye is always offered to the guest of honour. A more likely event is that a whole sheep's head will be put in front of you. When it happened to me, I asked the Emir who was giving me lunch whether the eye was a special delicacy. "I don't think so," he said, gouging one out and popping it into his mouth. I tore off a bit of ear by way of a diversion. He gouged out the other eye. "Do you want it?" he asked. "Against my religion," I said, in a moment of inspiration. "Ah, yes," he said and gobbled that one down as well.

Mehshi means "stuffed". Any of the following—eggplants, zucchini, vine leaves or cabbage —may be stuffed with a mixture of ground meat, rice and onions, cooked in their own juices or in tomato juice

★ **Moulokhiya** (Lebanon, Egypt, Jordan) green mellow leaves of the *moulokhiya* bush, cooked in lamb or chicken stock, flavoured with garlic and coriander and served on a bed of rice, croûtons, chicken and/or lamb chunks

Mutabbel (Lebanon, Syria, Jordan) see *Baba ghannoug*

Salata salad of fresh cucumbers, lettuce and tomatoes in lemon juice and oil or dressed in yoghurt or *tahine*

Seleek (Saudi) chunks of lamb stewed with chopped onions, milk and rice

Sfeeha pastry rolled around a mixture of ground meat, chopped onions, pine nuts and spices

★ **Shawarma** slices of lamb, marinated overnight and then packed on to a vertical skewer and rotated in front of a charcoal fire. The meat is shaved off

Ta'amiya (Egypt) see *Falafel*

Tabbouleh (Lebanon) cracked wheat (burghol) soaked and rinsed before mixing with chopped onion, tomatoes, parsley, mint, lemon juice and olive oil. Eaten with lettuce, cabbage or vine leaves used as spoons

Useful words

Aish bread
Arak aniseed spirit
Bira beer
Bouza dondurma ice-cream
Haleeb milk
Hisab bill
Jibn cheese
Kahwa coffee
Khubz round, flat bread
Khudar vegetables
Laban zabadi yoghurt

Lahm meat
Lista menu
Mai water
Mezza hors d'oeuvre
Nibid wine
Shai tea
Shourba soup
Sukkar sugar
Tahine sesame-seed paste
Taklia garlic and coriander sauce
Zubda butter

Sahitain! bon appétit!
Sohitak! cheers!

Iran

At the time of writing, it is hard to say how anyone would fare in Iran. Perhaps the steaks, beef stroganoff and chicken Kiev which used to be provided for foreigners have been declared unworthy or unholy. On the other hand, it was always in the little restaurants in side streets that real Iranian food was found.

The one thing to avoid is ice. Ice is usually stacked on the pavements and the Iranians are great spitters.

Abdug a yoghurt drink

Abgusht Iranian soup-stew

Adas polo rice with lentils, beef or lamb, raisins and onion

Ash sak thick soup with meat balls, yoghurt, spinach, walnuts, parsley and dill

Bastani keshi ice-cream flavoured with rose-water

Borani chogondar yoghurt and beet cold soup

Chelo plain boiled rice usually served with a nut of butter and a raw egg yolk (*tokhmeh morg*) in a half shell. A golden, crispy crust should form at the bottom

★ kabab many Iranian restaurants serve only this dish. It consists of rice and marinated charcoal-grilled meat. The rice is served with the usual accompaniments together with a bowl of sumac (sharp and sour edible red berries) and a bowl of yoghurt mixed in with it. The meat may be lamb, chicken or game

Dolmeh barg stuffed vine leaves

kalam stuffed cabbage leaves

Eshkeneh shirazi a yoghurt soup from Shiraz, flavoured with onions, walnuts and fenugreek

Fesenjan braised duck or chicken in walnut and pomegranate sauce

Gormeh salzi meat and vegetable stew

Jujeh kabab chicken kebab

Khoresh thin stews used as sauces for *chelo*, made from whatever is in season at the time. The meat is usually lamb but may be chicken, game or fish with vegetables

Kufteh tabrizi ground lamb or beef rolled into a ball with split peas, cinnamon, onion and lemon juice with a whole prune or hard-boiled egg in the middle

Kuku a kind of omelette cake made with a mixture of beaten eggs, vegetables and herbs, baked

Malassol type of caviar

Morg polo a delicious festive dish with chicken, raisins, rice, apricots and saffron

Panir white goat's-milk cheese

Polo rice cooked with a variety of ingredients—chicken, lamb, vegetables and sometimes fruit and nuts. The rice is frequently coloured with saffron. Like many Iranian meat dishes, it may be flavoured with sugar and thin strips of orange or tangerine rind

Rishta a kind of Iranian pasta

Sabzi polo rice with lamb, onions and green vegetables

Shir berenj rice pudding flavoured with rose-water

Shirini polo sweet rice with chicken, orange, almonds, saffron, raisins and onion

Sholezard saffron-, lemon- and cinnamon-flavoured rice pudding

Useful words

Abijau beer
Chai tea
Ekuck, nan bread
Gusht meat
Hesap bill
Kahveh coffee

Karah butter
Ma water
Mahi fish
Menü menu
Sharab wine
Sukkar sugar

Afiyet olsun! bon appétit!
Serefa! cheers!

North Africa

Despite influences ranging from the Phoenician to the French, the cooking of the Maghreb—as Morocco, Algeria and Tunisia are known collectively—is basically a desert people's style of cookery.

It is a style dictated quite as much by utensils as by ingredients or taste. Nomadic people were limited in their cooking by what pots they could carry with them or, in some cases, build out of the earth where they camped. What goes into a dish is not a matter of great importance. A *tajine* (*tagine*) is really the name of a pot, which is equally applied to whatever is cooked in it. Even *couscous*, which is the national dish of all three countries (and incidentally the only one ever to be adopted anywhere else), can be made with almost any grain, on to which can be piled meat or chicken or vegetables or any combination of these. Recipes in the Maghreb are sketches not formulae. This imprecision, characteristic of all Arab countries, prevents North African cooking from being anything more than a pattern of eating.

At the same time the people of North Africa attach great importance to the fun of eating. They love feasts and ceremonies. They serve food with a flourish, for instance pouring tea out of the pot from a height, like a fountain. They enjoy dances and people balancing glasses on their heads by way of diversion during meals. They are weavers of romance and spectacle and these are as much a part of a formal meal as is the food itself.

The specific differences between the three countries are not great, but can perhaps be summed up by the sauces most commonly served with *couscous* in each one. Morocco, which has certainly the most varied and subtle repertory of them all, uses a saffron sauce. Tunisia, which has a highly spiced taste, uses chilli peppers and ginger. Algeria, which lacks the fertile variety of ingredients of the other two, uses tomato.

The pattern of a North African meal is not rigid. It will start with a soup or a savoury pie. Then comes a chicken dish or a *couscous*. Finally a dish of unbelievable stickiness and sweetness. There are many of these sweet dishes but I have included only a few, simply because they can be easily identified and are usually selected visually. The meal ends with mint tea rather than coffee. Quite a performance is made of the preparation of this tea, which may have rose petals, special brown sugar or other delicacies put into it. Once, in Tangier I asked for a spoonful of the "jam" the people at the next table were having in their tea. The waiter obliged. I felt a trifle odd after drinking it. It was explained later that the jammy substance was a form of hashish, called *maajoun*.

The only trouble with North African menus is that they may be written in Arabic, French or Spanish (or indeed any language that comes to hand). The spelling may take any form, but I have tried to be as consistent as possible. Where I have found a particular dish in one country I have said so, using the abbreviations Alg., Mor. and Tun. for Algeria, Morocco and Tunisia respectively, but you may find many dishes interchangeable.

Assida bil bufriwa (Tun.) a thick hazelnut and flour cereal covered with a sweet egg sauce and decorated with nuts

Baghrir (Alg.) semolina pancakes

★ **Barkoukess** (Alg.) steamed semolina with a fava bean and tomato sauce (really a vegetable *couscous*)

Boufawar (Alg.) a vegetable *couscous* with green beans and potatoes

Bouza (Tun.) sorghum and hazelnut cake, very sticky and rich

★**Brik bil lahm** (Tun.) little parcels of ground lamb and an egg wrapped in infinitely thin pastry fried in oil. This is a masterpiece of pastry-making and legerdemain in wrapping the raw egg in with the stuffing. It also requires careful eating in your fingers if the egg is not to trickle down your chin

Chakchouka (Tun.) sweet peppers, onions and tomatoes stewed together with whole eggs added to the pot at the last minute

Chetit'ha djedj (Alg.) chicken and chick pea stew, served at weddings

Chorba beidha (Alg.) chicken soup with vermicelli, thickened with egg yolk

   frik (Alg.) lamb soup with green wheat

★ **Couscous** this dish is cooked in a special kind of double boiler. The meat and vegetables are boiled in the lower half. The top half has holes in the bottom through which the steam rises to cook the grain which is in this part. The grain thus acquires the flavour of whatever is below. The grain, most commonly semolina, is then piled on a dish and the meat and vegetables put on the pile. A sauce is poured over it before serving

Djeje bilbasla (Mor.) chicken with raisins and onions

   bilooz (Mor.) casseroled chicken served with a sauce of onions and almonds

   m'ammar (Mor.) roast chicken stuffed with almonds and carrots

   m'faowar (Mor.) chicken steamed with saffron

   ul garagh hamara (Mor.) chicken smeared with a coriander, mint and saffron paste, finally grilled and served with the braising sauce

   ul garagh hamara (Mor.) chicken with pumpkin purée

El briouat (Mor.) crescent-shaped pastry filled with almond paste

   sane bilooz (Mor.) casseroled tongue with almond and spice sauce

Felfel mahchi (Tun.) sweet peppers stuffed with meat, onions, coriander and egg, fried in oil and served with a tomato and *harissa* sauce

Fkoss (Mor.) sweet kind of bread flavoured with caraway, poppy and aniseed

Guenaoia (Tun.) stew with chunks of ground lamb and an egg *harissa*, chillis, sweet peppers and okra, flavoured with coriander

Halwa ditzmar (Alg.) a block of chopped dates, figs, walnuts and a little aniseed bound together with honey

★**Hareera, harira** (Mor.) a chicken soup with rice or noodles and chick peas. In Fez it is served with a flour paste instead of rice. Hareera is traditionally eaten at sundown during Ramadan

Harissa a violently hot red pepper sauce used with almost any main dish

Hoot bcharmeela (Mor.) sautéed fish steaks with a hot tomato sauce

   muklee (Mor.) fish cut with deep gashes (filled with a spicy paste) floured, dipped in paprika and fried

   shkfah (Mor.) baked fish

Kabda m'charmla (Alg.) pieces of liver stewed with herbs and served with tomato sauce

Kadi wa djmaatou (Alg.) casseroled chicken cut in pieces and put in the oven with an egg on each piece until eggs are cooked

Kawarma (Mor.) casserole of lamb first cooked with spices, then smothered in onion rings and cooked until the onions are dark brown

Kefta, kifta (Alg.) spicy meat balls

Kharchef mahchi (Alg.) cardoons stuffed with ground meat and spices

Khfaf (Alg.) another semolina cake

Kifta bi stumatish (Mor.) ground beef fashioned into meat balls, boiled with tomatoes and hot spices and topped with eggs poached with the meat

Kotban (Mor.) meat pounded into a paste, mixed with onions, spices and herbs and sometimes chilli peppers, fashioned into small pieces, skewered and cooked over charcoal. Usually served with a hot sauce

Koucha (Tun.) whole baby lamb baked in a clay case with lots of rosemary

Krafas bil djedj (Alg.) chicken casserole with celery, saffron and potatoes

Lablabli (Tun.) rich garlicky soup made with chick peas

Lafdaosh (Mor.) spaghetti with saffron

Lahm el m'qali (Mor.) lamb stewed with lemon and olives

Masfouf (Alg.) see *Mesfouf bil anib*

★ **Mechoui** (Mor.) a whole lamb roasted in a mud oven or sometimes roasted whole over a fire. The oven is usually built specially out of doors for a feast; North Africans love huge picnics. Now the word means roast lamb

Mechouia (Tun.) an hors d'oeuvre of grilled sweet peppers, tomatoes and onions, mixed with oil, lemon, tuna fish and hard-boiled egg

Mesfouf bil anib (Tun.) sweet *couscous* mixed with raisins

It is always risky to assume anywhere that one cannot be understood. Some friends of mine lunching at Zagora, a desert town in Morocco, had not been impressed by the service. The waiter looked a bit like a horse. "Don't give him a tip, let's give him a lump of sugar," they said. The waiter bowed and said in perfect English, "I would regard that as a great honour. In my country it is the custom for a bridegroom to give his bride sugar, which used to be a rare commodity, in recognition of her worth and beauty."

---

lhalou (Alg.) casserole of lamb cooked with almonds and prunes and flavoured with cinnamon and orange-flower water. Like so many dishes in the Maghreb this is rather sweet and sickly

ma'assel (Mor.) mutton or any other meat casseroled with spices. Shortly before it is ready, honey is added. Served with ground toasted almonds

Lekleeya dzireeya (Alg.) casserole of squab with eggs poached in the casserole at the last minute

Mahdjouba (Alg.) semolina envelopes stuffed with tomatoes and sweet peppers

Mah harh (Mor.) clams cooked with spices

Makroud (Tun.) semolina cake stuffed with dates, cinnamon and grated orange peel, served soaked in syrup

el louse (Alg.) lightly baked almond biscuits dipped in syrup and rolled in icing sugar

Malsouka (Tun.) wafer-thin pastry used for many dishes

Markit ommalah (Tun.) veal, onions, white beans, chillis and *harissa* stewed slowly together and flavoured with coriander. Mixed pickles and vinegar are added before serving

Mhalbya (Tun.) cake made with rice, nuts and geranium water

M'kuli (Mor.) chicken with lemon and olives

Mosli (Tun.) stew of lamb or beef and potatoes

Mrozeea (Mor.) fried meat pie

M'tewam (Alg.) lamb meat balls garnished with almonds, simmered in a runny mixture of the same ingredients

Pastila (Mor.) layers of wafer-thin pastry filled with slices of squab and an oily mixture of the cooking juices from the squab and raw eggs. It is like a large crispy envelope and is served with cinnamon and sugar

Qarnoun mahchi (Alg.) artichoke hearts stuffed with ground meat and onions

Rechta (Alg.) casseroled chicken with semolina noodles

Rjla del ranmee (Mor.) leg of lamb covered with a spicy paste and cooked in a casserole

Rrumen bjbn (Mor.) pomegranate with cheese and honey

Ruzill l'kadi (Mor.) baked turban-shapes of noodles soaked in honey

Salatat batata (Tun.) a hot (in every sense) potato salad flavoured with caraway

★**Samsa** (Tun.) layers of gossamer-thin pastry alternated with ground roasted almonds and sesame seeds baked, covered with lemon and rose-water syrup

Schlada salad. Salads are often cooked and sometimes served warm. They are made of sweet peppers, tomatoes and carrots and take many forms

Sfanje (Mor.) doughnuts

Sferia (Alg.) chicken cooked in a casserole with chick peas, served with an egg, lemon and parsley sauce and garnished with croquettes

Shakshouka see *Chakchouka*

Shorba bil allouch (Tun.) a lamb and vegetable winter soup

Skhina (Mor.) a Jewish dish eaten every Saturday by the orthodox. It is a casserole of beans cooked with calf's foot and shank and some hot spices

Sstrmbak (Mor.) mussels cooked with spices, served out of their shells with a lot of lemon

Taffah (Mor.) apples; often stewed with cinnamon, lemon and orange-flower water

Tajine stew of anything, *tajine* being the name of the pot

dial elkbda (Mor.) liver casserole with black olives

el dj'ben (Alg.) fried cheese and lamb meat balls simmered in a lamb and onion sauce

ez zitoun (Alg.) veal and olive casserole

j'bin (Tun.) cheese *tajine*, made as below, but without spinach

maadnus (Tun.) spinach *tajine*; meat, onion, tomato, chilli and white beans are stewed slowly together, then mixed with breadcrumbs, cheese, cooked spinach and half a dozen beaten eggs and baked in the oven. The dish is served cut in slices with some of the original meat sauce

Tammina (Alg.) semolina and honey cake

Tcharak (Alg.) croissants filled with almond paste, known as *cornes de gazelle*

Temar mahshe (Tun.) dates stuffed with a mixture of almond sugar and rose-water, coated in sugar

Tsfaia (Mor.) casseroled chicken served with a sauce of onions and almonds

Torshi (Tun.) turnips marinated with lime juice and served with *harissa*

Yahni (Alg.) fried chicken

★**Yo-yo** (Tun.) doughnuts made with orange juice; deep fried and then dipped in a honey syrup

Useful words

Anchouwa anchovies

Baklava sweet cake with nuts and spices between layers of thin pastry covered with syrup

Boukha brandy distilled from figs, a Jewish drink

Brewat, briwat almond paste, rice and honey mixture for sweets

Diffa feast

Djeja chicken

Etzay mint tea—green tea with a handful of mint leaves

Fattura, hissab bill

Hout fish

Kaki flour and salt biscuit, rather like a pretzel

Kemoun cummin

Kesra(h), ksra round, flat bread

Khobz bread

Kleowee kidneys

Lahmoun meat

Merguez small, oily spiced sausages

Mhammes sweet patties

Mogh brains

Msir preserved lemons

Mslalla pickled olives

Pita kind of flat bread

Quadid dried meat

Roze rice

Shorba soup

Smen rancid butter

Zitoun olives

Ala sahatik! cheers!
Chaha likom! Chaha tayiba! bon appétit!

Argentina — *See* South America

Australia and New Zealand

A fine cuisine takes centuries to establish and I fear that it probably requires an indolent aristocracy to refine it from the orgies of a gross oligarchy. Australians have superb produce—marvellous beef and lamb, wonderful fish, first-class vegetables and exotic tropical fruit. Nevertheless, these democratic people have never been much concerned with food. There was no native cuisine to build on, the aborigines being nomadic and given to half-roasting whole kangaroos and eating them dripping with blood. The settlers themselves were too busy settling to bother with anything but solid food to give them energy. Yet, since the war, there has been a wave of immigrants from Europe and things are looking up.

The only famous Australian dish is carpet-bag steak—a giant piece of thick rump steak slit down the middle and stuffed with a few oysters, seasoned with salt, pepper and lemon juice and baked. In New South Wales try the huge Sydney rock oysters; in Queensland mud crab is particularly good. Snapper is very good in southern Australia, where you will find it stuffed and baked. In the west, try Barramundi fish.

Plain steaks are nearly always good, as is the roast lamb. You will constantly encounter Pêche Melba, invented in England by Escoffier for Dame Nellie Melba, the great Australian soprano. You will also see the meringue and passion-fruit cake made for Anna Pavlova.

Wine labels in Australia are packed with information and it is well worth reading them. The ones to look for are: *Bilyara, Brand, Brown Brothers, Leo Buring, Château Tahbilk, Gramp, Kaiser Stuhl, Lake's Folly, Lindeman, McWilliams, Mildara, Morris, Penfold's, Reynella, Rothbury Estate, Saltram, Smith's Yalumba, Tyrell* and *Wynns*.

New Zealand settlers, unlike their Australian counterparts, managed to graft on to the dreary "home" cooking which they brought from the less well fed houses of Britain a little of the livelier tradition they found in the land they took over.

Again their produce is superb when fresh (rather than shipped, chilled or frozen, half-way round the world)—especially the dairy produce and the lamb. As in Australia, it is at its best when simply prepared.

The Maori influence, however, produces lots of interest. Marinated raw fish is common. *Paua* (abalone), *pipis* (which taste like cockles) and *toheroas* (like clams) are excellent shellfish. The whitebait in batter patties are good. In April and May, the young *titi* (muttonbird, a type of petrel) is well worth trying. Maori vegetables are unusual—*puha* and *rauriki* (sow-thistle) are a little like spinach. *Kumara* is the sweet potato.

The Maori way of cooking meat, fish and root vegetables is in an earth oven or *hangi*. A hole is dug in the ground. The food is wrapped in flax leaves and placed on fiery stones, on top of *manuka* or tea-tree wood which gives a special flavour. Water is poured in to produce steam, and then the oven is sealed with special mats and earth. Several hours later the food is, supposedly, cooked to perfection.

The climate guarantees an extensive range of fruit, the most exotic being the *kiwifruit* (Chinese gooseberry), *tamarillos* (tree tomatoes), and passion-fruit.

Austria—*See* Germany

Belgium and Luxembourg

Belgian food, for many people, especially those with large appetites, is something of a comfort. While it is not such a serious undertaking as it is in France, it has far greater delicacy than Dutch or German food. It is also more of a mixture, because quite apart from the fact that the Belgians are two peoples—the Flemish and the French-speaking Walloons—the south of the country was governed by the Spanish for two centuries.

There are problems about language, for although in northern Belgium both Flemish and French appear on the menu, the Flemish often affect not to understand either French or German. If you have this difficulty it is worth referring to the Dutch section of this book, as Flemish and Dutch have many similarities, or the French section.

On the whole you are more likely not to have trouble but to enjoy yourself, because the Belgians, of all parts, are very fond of eating, and even have a phrase for looking after one's interests which is "defending one's beefsteak".

You must be prepared for long waiting in restaurants, as everything is cooked to order and it is considered very rude to hustle the waiters. Allow about two hours for a meal.

The usual drink is beer, but you will find both German and French wines in most restaurants. There are some unexpected, quite strong, sour beers—*faro*, which is made from wheat and *gueuze lambic*, the national, very strong, draught beer made from a mixture of wheat and barley. *Kriekenlambic* is cherry-flavoured beer.

★ **Anguilles au vert** a spring and summer dish of baby eel sautéed in butter with sorrel, mint, verbena, sage and other herbs, then simmered in white wine with more herbs. The liquor is enriched with egg yolks to make a sauce. Served hot or cold
   à l'escavèche pickled eel fried, then jellied and served cold
   en matelote eel stewed in fish stock and white wine, served in a white sauce
Asperges à la flamande boiled or steamed asparagus served with a sauce of hard-boiled eggs crushed in melted butter
Bifteck et frites steak and chips
Boudin de Liège savoury sausage made with herbs
★ **Carbonnade à la flamande** beef stewed in beer with onions, brown sugar and herbs. Bread spread with mustard is often added towards the end of the cooking to give a special texture to the sauce, or it may be put on top and grilled
Chicorée de Bruxelles see *Witloof*
   et volaille bruxelloise chicory stuffed with chicken and rolled in ham, covered with a cream sauce

Choesel au madère small slices of meat such as oxtail, sweetbreads or other offal, with bacon fat, pig's ear and trotter, served in a Madeira sauce with onion, garnished with mushrooms
Civet de lièvre hare casseroled in wine and "jugged" in its own blood with onions and herbs
   à la flamande *or* **du pays de Liège** hare casseroled as above with prunes added
Couques de Dinant gingerbread
Ecrevisses à la liégeoise crayfish poached in fish stock, thickened with cream or butter and flavoured with parsley
Escavèche fish marinated in aromatic herbs and fried
Estouffat de marcassin à la bière young wild boar marinated and cooked in beer
Filet de sole St Arnould fried sole dressed with hops and small squares of toast
Fricadelles bruxelloises sausage-shaped rissoles of ground meat, usually pork or beef or a mixture of the two, with herbs and spices
Gaufres waffles baked in cast-iron moulds

Gense hutsepot Flanders casserole. Contains all sorts of local meats and vegetables

★ **Grives à la liégeoise** casserole of thrushes stuffed with juniper-berry butter. Served with croûtons

Hochepot (*or* **hutsepot**) **gantois** casserole as above. From Ghent

Huîtres d'Ostende oysters baked with shrimps, white wine and cream, topped with cheese and breadcrumbs

Jambon d'Ardennes smoked Ardennes ham

Kletskoppen macaroons

Konijn met pruinen *or* **lapin à la flamande** rabbit casseroled with bacon and onions and served with raisins and prunes soaked in brandy

Limburger a semi-hard fermented cheese with chives, parsley and tarragon

Loose-tinken thin slices of beef rolled round a slice of bacon and braised in beer with sugar and onions

Marcassin young wild boar

Mokkes cinnamon macaroons

★ **Moules à l'anversoise** mussels poached in white wine with shallots, onions and herbs

Nœuds sugared toffee biscuits

★ **Oie à l'instar de Visé** goose boiled with garlic and vegetables, then cut up, fried and coated with a cream, butter and garlic sauce

Pain à la grecque a type of bread

Paling in't groen Flemish name for *anguilles au vert*

Remondou sharp-flavoured cheese also called *fromage piquant*

Rognons de veau à la liégeoise roast veal kidneys with juniper berries and a dash of gin

Salade liégeoise meat stew with string beans, potatoes, onions and bacon

Saucisson d'Ardennes salami

Soupe à l'ardennaise soup made with chicory, leeks and potatoes

Tarte al djote tart made with beet leaves and cheese for dessert

Truite à l'escavèche trout poached with herbs, then jellied

Vlaamse karbonaden Flemish name for *carbonnade à la flamande*

★ **Waterzooi** (**waterzootje**) fish soup with carp, eel, perch and pike stewed in white wine with thyme, bay leaf, sage and parsley

   à la gantoise a more sophisticated version of the chicken soup above in which the stock is thickened with cream and flavoured with lemon juice

Witloof chicory or Belgian endive. Served in a variety of ways, but the Belgians prefer it lightly fried (*poêlé*) or raw

Luxembourg

The Luxembourgeois are given to Teutonic appetites, tempered by a modicum of French finesse. They are an unusually industrious people, so that they need a lot to eat and think nothing of four- or five-course meals.

Much of their food comes either from the rivers or the woods—trout, pike, crayfish, hare and wild boar. In the summer they like to eat out of doors, preferably with a brass band pompeting away beside them.

The menu is usually in French with a sprinkling of German, so that most dishes will be found in the French section. Look out for *Geheck* (a soup made with pork, calf's lungs and plums) and *tarte au quetsch* (an open tart filled with small blue plums soaked in *quetsch*). The most common drink in Luxembourg is rather frothy beer, but there are some local wines—a fruity kind of Moselle, some sparkling *vin mousseux*. The *eaux de vie* made from plums—*quetsch*, *mirabelle* and *prunelle*—are all good and can be drunk as "chasers" to beer or after dinner. There is also a blackcurrant liqueur (*cassis*) made at Beaufort.

Bolivia, Brazil—*See* South America
Bulgaria—*See* Eastern Europe

Canada

The origins of Canadian food differ little from those of the United States. The same adaptations were made by the British and French settlers, making use of the new foods they found and absorbing some of the Indian customs. In both countries, life for the newcomers was extremely hard and the fare of the pioneers, particularly in Canada, was of necessity very simple and often did not differ very much from the corn-based diet of the indigenous people.

Perhaps the most important natural produce Canada has is superb fish. The salmon, albeit famous, never seems quite so good as Scotch salmon, but there are one or two wonderful fish peculiar to the country. The Winnipeg goldeye, often cured in willow smoke, tastes like a cross between Dover sole and trout. The *cisco*, from Lakes Ontario and Erie, is somewhat similar. The Arctic char, found nowhere else, the trout, the different cods, the *doré*, the crabs, lobsters, mussels, the Malpèque and Buctouche oysters, are all excellent.

My favourite Canadian product is the wild rice from Manitoba, which is the best in the world. Then from the Maritimes comes a special kind of fern, the fronds of which are boiled and called *fiddleheads*. In New Brunswick there is an excellent seaweed called *dulse*.

Canada has a remarkable range of game. Besides the obvious kinds there are: buffalo, often eaten as *pemican* which is a mixture of meat and berries, bear and groundhog.

I have not made a separate list of dishes because most of the traditional regional foods have self-explanatory names, or can be found in the United States, Britain or France sections. Some of the more interesting dishes are mentioned below.

In Quebec, the French-Canadians have their distinctive style of cooking, but most dishes have straightforward French names—for instance, the well-known Brome Lake duck is usually served *à l'orange*, though it may come stuffed with wild rice in a hot green-olive sauce. A few names may be unfamiliar: *creton français* is rather like *pâté de foie gras*, *beignes* and *coquignoles* are doughnuts, *crêpes et sucre d'érable* are pancakes with maple sugar, *ragoût de pattes et boules* is a stew of pig's feet and meat balls. Perhaps the most famous French-Canadian dish is *tourtière*, a very substantial pie filled with a mixture of ground pork and beef, onions and breadcrumbs, flavoured with garlic.

In parts of Ontario, you may find a German influence, but the names are clear. In Newfoundland, *brews* is a dish of cod cooked in milk with broken biscuits and *flipper pie* is made of seal.

Finally, of course, there is the most famous Canadian contribution to food—maple syrup. There are innumerable dishes made with this, and you might, in the spring when the sap starts to rise, find yourself at a "sugaring off" party, where the boiled syrup is dribbled on the snow and wound round popsicle sticks.

The Canadians are considerable imbibers, producing every known kind of drink. Canadian whisky is made of corn, rye, barley, malt and blending agents which make it drier than the American bourbon. They also make a type of Scotch, brandy, various liqueurs and a straight alcohol called *whisky blanc*.

There are Canadian wines, even a champagne. The names to look for are *Brights* (including *Chelois* and *Baco noir*), *Château Gai, de Chaunac* and *Inniskillin* (*Maréchal Foch*).

17

The Caribbean

Most people who go to the Caribbean stay in large hotels, where they eat expensively imported, poorly cooked versions of what they eat at home. This is a pity, partly because it does nothing for the economies of the islands they are visiting, and partly because they miss an amazing variety of dishes made with local ingredients, differently adapted according to the customs of the nation which colonized each island.

If you cannot find a particular dish in this section it is worth referring to South and Central America and to the cuisines of the major colonizers.

Accra, acrat de morue, acra l'en morue see *Stamp and go*

Akkra (Jamaica) pea or bean fritters

Arroz y habichuelas see *Peas and rice*

Asopao (Puerto Rico) thin rice stew with chicken and possibly shrimp, crab or lobster

Bacalaitos see *Stamp and go*

Bakes (Trinidad) sweet scones fried or griddle baked

Calaloo, calalou, callaloo, callau, callilu this most famous of Creole soups, usually associated with Trinidad but also found on several other islands, is related to New Orleans crab gumbo. It contains *callaloo* leaves and possibly crab, salt pork, okra, eggplant, onions, tomatoes, coconut milk, garlic, spices, herbs and hot pepper sauce

Chicharrón, chicherón fried pork rind—crackling—sold in several Spanish islands as a street snack

Colombo (Martinique, Guadeloupe) curry, also known as *kerry* in the Dutch islands

Crabes farcis (Martinique, Guadaloupe) the backs of land crabs (or *jueyes*) stuffed with crabmeat cooked with herbs, sweet peppers and breadcrumbs

Crapaud (Montserrat, Dominica) large delicately flavoured frogs, usually fried or braised and served with wedges of lime. Also called "mountain chicken"

Diri et djon djon (Haiti) rice with special tiny black mushrooms

Escabèche, escovitch fillets of fried or grilled fish in a piquant marinade

Floats sweet yeast dough balls fried in hot oil

Flying fish (Barbados) a moist succulent fish, usually fried

Foo foo mashed plantain dumplings, poached or fried

Funchi (Dutch Antilles) a savoury cornmeal pudding cut into chunks and served with fish stews and meat dishes

Goat a favourite meat throughout the Caribbean and the main ingredient of such specialities as curried goat flavoured with coconut milk and lime juice (Jamaica), and *stobá*, an elaborate stew packed with herbs and spices (Curaçao)

Griots de porc (Haiti) cubes of pork marinated in onion, herbs, orange juice and garlic and fried in hot oil. Served with *ti malice*, fried plantain and sweet potatoes

Hop 'n' John, hoppin' John (Bermuda) see *Peas and rice*

Java honden povtie (Dutch Antilles) a mound of rice topped with two fried eggs and surrounded by meat and vegetables seasoned with curry powder, soy sauce and spices

Kerry see *Colombo*

Keshi yena (Dutch Antilles) a whole Edam cheese hollowed, stuffed with meat or fish, olives, onions and tomatoes, and baked

Lambi conch, also known as *concha* and *conque.* The flesh must be marinated and pounded to tenderize it. Used in chowders, salads, fritters, or sometimes sliced, marinated and eaten raw

Langosta criolla (Cuba) lobster fried with tomatoes, onions, sweet peppers, hot pepper sauce and lime juice or white wine

Marucou (Trinidad) possum stew

Matete (Trinidad) crabmeat marinated in onions, herbs and wine and cooked in coconut oil thickened with cassava flour

Matrimony (Jamaica) fruit salad of star apples and sometimes oranges, with milk and sugar

Morcilla blood sausage

Pain patate (Haiti) sweet potato pudding

Pasteles (Puerto Rico) like Mexican *tamales*

Peas and rice the peas used in this famous Jamaican dish are pigeon peas, also called goongoo, gunga, gungo or Congo peas, pointing to their African origin. Usually cooked with rice, coconut milk, pieces of salt pork or bacon and seasoning, but eaten everywhere with many variations. The dish occupies an important place in Caribbean folklore

Pepperpot an ancient Amerindian stew of whatever is available—chicken, pork, beef, oxtail, a calf's head or foot—with cassareep, a juice prepared from cassava roots. Like a stockpot, it is often kept going indefinitely. Some claim to have eaten *pepperpot* a hundred years old

   soup (Jamaica) soup of salt pork or beef with okra, *callaloo* or spinach leaves, yams and kale cooked in coconut milk

Pescado Santo Domingo (Dominican Republic) sea bass, served cold as an hors d'oeuvre

Piment oiseau hot Haitian sauce

Pork souse (Trinidad, Barbados) pig's head, feet and tongue cooked and steeped overnight in lime juice and hot peppers, usually served with *morcilla*

Roti (Trinidad) bread pancake filled with curried fish or meat

Saltfish and ackee (Jamaica) salt cod shredded in a sauce of garlic, onions, sweet peppers, bacon bits and butter, with *ackee*

Sans coche, sancocho (Trinidad) stew of various meats and many other ingredients including onions, split peas, yams, *callaloo*, cassava, chillis, plantains, green peppers, coconut milk, okra and pumpkin

Sea egg sea urchin

Sopa hamaca (Dominican Republic) stew of lobster, fish, rice, potatoes, onions, garlic, sweet peppers and cabbage

Sopito (Dutch Antilles) fish stew made with coconut milk

Stamp and go (Jamaica) codfish fritters usually served as an hors d'oeuvre or with drinks

Stobá see *Goat*

Tassot de dinde (Haiti) dried turkey

Tatoo (Trinidad) fried iguanas

Ti malice (Haiti) tart onion and herb sauce

Tum-tum (Trinidad) mashed plantains

Tropical fruit and vegetables

Ackee brought to Jamaica by Captain Bligh of the *Bounty*; a dramatic scarlet fruit which splits into three when ripe, revealing large, shiny black seeds. Its edible pulp looks like scrambled egg. Used as a vegetable

Baddo see *Taro*

Bamie see *Gombo*

Boniato sweet potato

Boonchi yard-long beans, originally from Asia, very popular in the Dutch Antilles

Calabaza calabash

Callaloo edible leaves of the *taro* plant. Also Chinese spinach

Carrossol, guanábana see *Soursop*

Chayote, chocho, christophene, cristofina tropical squash with a prickly skin and single seed

Chou coco, chou glouglou, chou palmiste heart of palm. Usually sliced, boiled and served in sauce, or stewed, scrambled with eggs, frittered or used in salads

Coco, eddo see *Taro*

Gombo, molodron okra

Naseberry avocado-shaped fruit with greyish skin and pink flesh

Palmista see *Chou coco*

Quimbombo see *Gombo*

Sapodilla see *Naseberry*

Soursop dark green knobbly fruit with delicious edible pulp tasting like spicy purée

Star apple looks like a round eggplant. Has a star-shaped core when cut, and sweet flesh

Taro tuberous root vegetable with rather indigestible flesh

Chile—*See* South America

China

USSR

SINKIANG-UIGHUR

KANSU

TSINGHAI

TIBET

SZECHWAN

NEPAL

LHASA •

BHUTAN

BANGLADESH

INDIA

YUNNA

BURMA

LAC

A Chinese menu is one of the most confusing in the world. I have long had a fantasy by which all those numbers should be made uniform, so that Number 14 would always be Spring Roll and Number 256 Eight-jewel Duck, no matter whether you were in Wigan or Valparaiso.

However, it is never going to be as simple as that, for the complexities are enormous. Chinese cuisine was already sufficiently an art for it to be written about 4,000 years ago. Such a tradition has produced enough dishes to fill this book many times over.

The next problem is the size of the country. China is vast and its climate quite different from province to province, so that the variety of its cooking is at least as great as that of Europe from Scandinavia to Spain and across to Turkey.

MONGOLIA

INNER MONGOLIA

HEILUNGKIANG

KIRIN

LIAONING

HOPEH

PEI-CHING •
(PEKING)

T'IEN-CHING •
(TIENTSIN)

KOREA

NINGSIAHUI

LAN-CHOU
(LANCHOW)

SHANSI

SHANTUNG

YELLOW SEA

SHENSI

HONAN

KIANGSU

NAN-CHING •
(NANKING)

• SHANG-HAI

HUPEI

ANHWEI

CHEKIANG

• CH'UNG-CH'ING
(CHUNGKING)

• NAN CH'ANG-HSIEN
(NANCHANG)

Lu-chou
(Luchow)

HUNAN

KIANGSI

KWEICHOW

FUKIEN

EAST
CHINA SEA

KWANGSI
CHUANG

KWANGTUNG

KUANG-CHOU
• (CANTON)

TAIWAN

ETNAM

Macau

HONG KONG

SOUTH
CHINA SEA

Despite its size, only about 11 per cent of its land area can be cultivated. One might expect this to be a limitation when compared with the abundance of France or Italy. The reverse is true. Chinese cuisine is a cuisine of necessity and thus of invention. No other nation cooks the webbed feet of birds, bears' paws, snakes, dogs and mice.

Chinese cooking, largely because of its cheapness, has been exported to almost every country of the world. Necessarily it has been adapted to the taste of the countries which have adopted it—so that a classical Chinese dish in India may be spiced in such a way as to be unrecognizable as the dish with the same name in New York. Possibly the most famous "Chinese" dish—chop suey—isn't Chinese at all but American.

Another bar to the reading of a Chinese menu is that the Chinese name of a dish may be in one of several languages transliterated in one of several ways.

Nobody should be put off by any of these considerations, because Chinese food is the equal of any and not to adventure in it is a tragedy.

Naturally, I do not claim that this list is comprehensive, but it covers the basic dishes and it will also help you to understand the fundamental patterns of Chinese cooking. Finally, it will enable you to ask for something which you would particularly like to eat.

The listings make no differentiations between the regional styles of Chinese cooking, because few restaurants stick rigidly to one category. Furthermore, many dishes of one region are cooked in the others with only minor variations.

The three big divisions are these. Cantonese food is usually steamed. Alternatively, it is parboiled before quick frying in a light oil. Every meal includes rice. Northern food (which is often called Peking) is generally more substantial and concentrates more on deep frying. The emphasis is on crispness, as in Peking duck. Wine is used a lot in cooking and a fair amount of spice. Bread, baked, steamed or fried, often replaces rice. Shanghainese food is starchier and fatter. More oil is used, especially sesame-seed oil for frying. Food is cooked longer, whether stewed or steamed. More spices, garlic, ginger and pepper are used and allowed to penetrate the usually diced ingredients during the longer cooking. Noodles often take the place of rice.

In Manchuria and Inner Mongolia there is much more use of meat, in particular lamb, which is rarely found farther south. Szechuan is famous for highly spiced food and there is now a fashion for this region's cooking in the West.

In the listings I have used primarily the Cantonese names for dishes, as this is the best known of the various cuisines. The Cantonese transliteration appears in bold type. Where appropriate, I have also provided the Mandarin transliteration in italics. The alphabetical order generally follows the Cantonese, except where the Mandarin dish is more important or where there is no Cantonese equivalent. As Chinese menus are more inclined to give descriptions of dishes, rather than titles, the order of words may vary. If you cannot find a dish under the first word, it may be worth looking under any of the others in the name of the dish.

Soups

The Chinese do not start a meal with soup. Indeed in a simple meal it comes last. In some meals there may be two soups. The first will be served possibly as the second course and will be an important soup such as shark's fin or bird's nest. Most soups are a clear broth in which meat and vegetables have been briskly cooked.

Baak choy tang, *bai tsai tang* cabbage soup with pork and ginger

Bart jun dow foo gung meat, vegetable and bean curd thick soup

Bart jun dung gua lup tang, *ba jen dung gua la tang* melon, meat and vegetables in a clear soup

Bow yu ghuy peen tang, *bao yu ji pian tang* sliced chicken, abalone and vegetables in a clear soup

Bow yu tang, *bao yu tang* abalone soup, with Chinese mushrooms and celery

Ching dun hua gu tang slow-simmered mushroom soup

Ching jeng ya-z tang clear duck soup

Ching tong yu to, *ching tang yu du* chicken broth with spongy "buns" of baked fish innards

Cho goo ghuy peen tang sliced chicken and mushrooms in a clear soup

Chuen gnau peen tang, *juan niou pian tang* sliced beef and vegetables in a clear soup

Dan hua tang clear soup with an egg stirred in

Doong gwaah hoong, *dung gua jung* winter melon soup made with chicken broth

Dou fu bo tsai tang bean curd and spinach soup

Dung bakk gup, *dun bai ge* squab broth with winter melon and Chinese mushrooms

Dung goo ngarp jeong tang boned webbed foot of duck and mushrooms in a clear soup

Dung gu ji pian tang, *dung goo ghuy peen tang* sliced chicken and mushrooms in a clear soup

For toi dung gwa tang, *huo tuei dung gwa tang* sliced Chinese ham and melon in a clear soup

Fung jau dung goo tang, *feng gua dung gu tang* steamed chicken feet and mushrooms in a clear soup

★ **Ghuy tong wun tun,** *ji tang hun tun wun tun,* put into a rich chicken soup made with mushrooms and celery. Often served as a whole lunch. Not to be confused with the wan ton, wan tan or wun tun soup restaurants serve in the West

Ghuy yoong low sun tang, *ji yung lu sun tang* asparagus soup thickened with minced chicken and egg white

Ghuy yoong sook mai tang minced chicken with corn soup

★ **Ghuy yoong yien wan,** *ji yen wo tang* bird's nest soup, made with chicken broth

Ghuy yung yuen dow tang minced chicken and green beans in a clear soup

Guy gon tang, *ji gan tang* chicken liver, heart and gizzard and cabbage soup

Gwaah jee choy tang, *gua-z tsai tang* Chinese watercress soup with minced pork and ginger, thickened with eggs

High par dung gwa yung thick soup of crabmeat and melon

High yuk dow foo gung, *hsieh rou dou fu geng* crab, vegetable and bean curd thick soup

Hsieh rou yu jr tang shark's fin soup with crabmeat

Huang gua juan ji tang chicken and cucumber soup

Hwang yu geng, *wong yu gung* thick soup of yellow fish and bean curd

Ja tsai ju sih tang, *jar choi yuk* see *tang* pork and Szechuan pickle in a clear soup

Jarp kum dung gwa lup tang, *shr jin dung gua la tang* similar to *Bart jun dung gua lup tang*

Jarp kum sar wor mixed meats and vegetables in a soup, served in a pot

Jeng bai tsai duan steamed Tientsin cabbage soup, garnished with ham

Ji ju chicken soup with rice cooked in the stock

Ji pian tang, *ghuy peen tang* sliced chicken and vegetables in a clear soup

Juh gerk fooh jook tang, *ju jiao fu ju tang* pig's feet and bean curd soup flavoured with oysters and wine

Ko mo dou fu tang mushroom and bean curd soup

Kuo mu guo ba tang, *how mor wor bar tang* Peking mushroom soup with crispy rice

Lien ngow tang, *lien ou tang* lotus root soup, flavoured with tangerine peel, beef and dried Chinese dates

Rou szu tsai tang shredded pork and green vegetable soup

Rou wan-z tang fairly clear soup with meat balls and a little wine

Saang choy yu tang, *shen tsai yu tang* lettuce and fish soup

San hsien tang chicken, mushroom and bamboo shoot soup

★**Sarm see tang,** *san sih tang* sliced chicken, abalone and shrimp in a clear soup

Shuet choi dung sun tang, *hsueh tsai dung sun tang* bamboo shoots and salted vegetables in a clear soup

Sook muy daahn faah tang, *su mi tang* corn soup flavoured with onion, garlic and ginger, thickened with eggs

Sook my low shun tang asparagus and corn soup

★ **Suan la tang, shuen lart tang** a thick "hot and sour soup" of shredded meat, bean curd, vegetables and mushrooms, with vinegar, pepper and chilli

Tang mian noodle soup, but it includes mushrooms, chicken, pork, ham, bamboo shoots and watercress. Meant to be a meal or a large snack

Tong, *tang* soup

Tsing done but goo tang, *ching dun bei gu tang* double-boiled mushrooms in a clear soup

Tsu jiao yu pian tang, cho jiu yu peen tang sliced fish, quick boiled and served in a clear soup with pepper and vinegar

Ya she tang duck's tongue soup made with meat stock and wine

Yim seen tong, *yen hsien tang* shredded fresh and salt pork in a clear bamboo shoot soup

★ **Yu jr tang** shark's fin soup

Yuk peen choi sum tang, *rou pian tsai shin tang* sliced pork and vegetables in a clear soup

Yuk peen harm darn tang, *rou pian hsien dan tang* pork, salted egg and vegetables in a clear soup

As well as ordinary soups there are hotpots, which are roughly like fondues. A pot of simmering stock is put on the table and a variety of ingredients given to each diner. You pick up what you want with chopsticks and cook it in the stock-pot. Once it is cooked you dip it in a little sauce and eat it. When everyone has finished, they are given a bowlful of the now very rich stock. Finally, noodles and vegetables are put into the remaining stock and served as a last course. As almost anything can go into a hotpot of this kind, I list only three to give an idea of the variety.

Ju hua guo chrysanthemum hotpot. The stock is a simple chicken stock. The slices of food are chicken, pork, beef, shrimp, fillet of sole and oysters. The vegetables are usually spinach, cabbage and bean curd. The sauce is soya sauce, sesame-seed oil, wine and eggs

★ **Shih jin nuan guo** "ten varieties of hotpot". In this case the main ingredients—beef, pork, ham, shrimp balls, bamboo shoots, steamed pancake rolls with pork filling, spinach, cabbage and noodles—are all put into the pot

and the stock poured over them. They are then boiled for a short while and the diners pick out the pieces they want. The sauce is soya and sesame-seed oil

Shua yang rou Mongolian hotpot. The stock is chicken with ginger, onion, garlic and parsley. The main ingredient is lamb and the main vegetable, spinach. The sauce is soya, sesame-seed oil, sugar, peanut-butter, mashed fermented bean curd and cayenne pepper. With this fire pot go steamed bread rolls flavoured with sesame

Rice and noodles

Baak faahn, *bai fan* boiled rice

Cha shieu chao mien fried noodles served with braised roast pork, cabbage and bamboo shoots in a rich sauce

Cheung sao mien fried noodles with vegetables, chicken and pork

Chow fan, *chao fan* fried rice

Hsia ren chao mi fen rice-stick noodles quick fried with celery and shrimp

Huo tuei dan chao fan boiled rice quick fried with egg, diced ham and peas

Ieh fooh mien fried thread-like noodles with pork and tomato

Ja jiang mian boiled egg-noodles with a rich minced pork sauce and shredded vegetables

Juh yook jook, *ju rou tso* boiled rice simmered with minced pork, onions and pickled cabbage

Sieu ngaap jook, *shao ya tso* rice simmered with duck, dried scallops and scallions

Tong mien, *tang mian* noodles in chicken broth, with chicken, mushrooms, spinach and ham

Eggs

Cha yeh dan hard-boiled eggs with their shells cracked all over but kept on, simmered for ages in water with aniseed, soya sauce, tea leaves and salt. They have a pretty marbled appearance when peeled

Chien ji dan jie tiny omelettes filled with minced beef

Dan juan rolled egg pancakes with pork filling flavoured with wine. Served cold, cut in diagonal slices

Foo yoong tan little omelettes, fried with pork (or other meat or fish), lots of scallions, mushrooms and pea sprouts

Fu rung hsieh rou crab omelette

Fun see juh yook (daahn), **fen tse ju rou chao dan** eggs lightly scrambled with pork, ham, vegetables, a little sugar and a fistful of powdered silk (**fun see**)

Ghuy tan gow tiny omelettes, almost like pancakes, filled with pork, scallion and ginger stuffing and steamed and covered with oyster sauce

Haw bow (daahn) fried eggs folded in half

High yuk foo yung tan little omelettes stuffed with crabmeat

Hsun dan boiled eggs with slightly soft yolk, marinated in soya sauce, sesame-seed oil, sugar and hickory-smoked salt

Jeng ji dan beaten raw eggs steamed over water with stock and wine in it. Sometimes chopped spinach, beef or pork is added

Ji dan chao hsi hung shr tomato omelette

Jing (daahn), **jeng dan** steamed egg custard, more like smooth scrambled eggs with stock and soya sauce mixed in

Liou huang tsai eggs mixed with chopped mushroom, shrimp, water chestnut, ham and cornstarch, stir fried with ample lard until you get a smooth puddingy effect

Muk sui yuk shredded pork omelette

Pay tan, **pi dan** "thousand-year-old" eggs. Duck eggs preserved for about three months in a clay made of pine ash, charcoal ash and other wood ash, lime and salt bound with strongly brewed tea. I find them awesome to look at—their whites purply-brown and transparent, their yolks an earthy green-brown. But their appearance is delightful compared with their taste

Woon dow chow tan, **wan dou chao dan** scrambled eggs with peas and ham

Fish and shellfish

Baak faahn yu, **bai fan yu** "white upside-down fish"; herring fried with egg yolk all over and egg white on one side

Baak yu, **bai yu** herring

Bao yu tsai hsien quick-fried cabbage braised with abalone and soya sauce in chicken stock

Bark cheuk har poached shrimps served with chopped garlic, onion, chilli and soya sauce

Bark fa yeung high kim deep-fried crab claw with shrimp and pork stuffing

Bau yu dung goo, **bao yu dung gu** cold abalone with mushrooms

Been yu porgy

★Bi yu shan hu literally "green jade and red coral". Actually crab eggs fried with the stems of green vegetables

Bor lay har kow quick-fried shrimp balls

Bow yu, **bao yu** abalone

Cha sung shu yu fried mandarin fish, with a sweet-sour sauce

Chao haah look stir-fried shrimps with scallions in a sweet-sour sauce

Chao hsia ren shrimp quick fried with peas

Chao lung hsia see **Dow see loong haah**

Chao shan hu, **chow seen woo** boned eel quick-fried, with a garlicky soya sauce

Chao yu pian fillets of sea-bass, quick fried with ginger and onions

Chao yu sung fried minced fish on a bed of fried shredded turnips, garnished with ground peanuts

Chieh yu, *jie yu* shad

Chien hsia bing shrimp fishcakes made with water chestnuts and ginger, served with fried cabbage

Chien yu bing fishcakes of mixed fish and shrimps, fried with mushrooms and ham

Ching chao hsia ren, **tsing chow har yan** quick-fried freshwater shrimps

Ching dou hsia ren, **tsing dow har yan** quick-fried freshwater shrimps with peas

Ching jing doong gwooh, *ching jeng dong gu* minced fish on Chinese mushrooms, steamed

★ **Cho kiu yu tang**, *suan jiao yu tang* fried whole black carp, simmered in soup with vinegar

Choi yuen har kow quick-fried shrimp with green kale

Chow bow yu pien, *chao bao yu pian* abalone braised with cabbage, ham, ginger and other vegetables

Chow yu, *chao yu* fish browned in the frying pan and then braised with ginger, scallions, parsley and a little wine

Chun cheung yu, *jin chiang yu* tuna fish

Daai haah, *da hsia* shrimp

Daai tao yu, *da tou yu* catfish or porgy

Dou shr hsia ren shrimp fried with fermented black beans

Dou shr jeng hsien yu sea-bass steamed with fermented black beans

★ **Dow see loong haah** lobster fried and quick braised with minced pork and fermented black beans. A positively Cantonese dish

Dung yu white fish steamed with wine, onion and ginger, served cold in its jelly

Fan jie hsia ren guo ba, **farn care har yan wor bar** quick-fried freshwater shrimps simmered in tomato sauce, served on hot crackling rice

Feng wei hsia large shrimp with their tails left on, fried in batter

Fu yung har yan quick-fried freshwater shrimps with egg white

Gan shao hsia ren shrimp quick fried with hot red pepper and simmered in wine, soya sauce, tomato paste and cornstarch to glaze them

Gan shao yu fried sea-bass simmered in a hot bean sauce and a sweet-sour garlic and ginger sauce

Geong chung guk high fried crab braised with ginger and chopped onion

Ghuy yau sarm bark, *ji yiou san bai* stewed sliced abalone, asparagus and Tientsin cabbage in a white chicken sauce

★ **Ghuy yow lay yu**, *ji yiou li yu* carp fried in chicken fat with chilli, oyster sauce, ginger and scallions, then braised in chicken broth and served with bean curd cakes

Gon yiu chee scallops

Gone siu yee sung scallops boiled and shredded, then deep fried with broccoli leaves

Gup ghaai, *ge li* clams

Gwuy yu, *gua yu* perch

Haah, *hsia* shrimp

Haw lo yu, *he yu* river bass

Heung wat san yu kow quick-fried freshwater fish ball with sliced vegetables

High par sin goo crabmeat and stewed mushrooms with an egg-white sauce

Ho, *mu li* oysters

Ho yow bow yu pien, *chao bao yu pian* braised abalone with oyster sauce

Hoong yu, *hung yu* red snapper

Hoy lo yu, *hai yu* sea-bass

Hoy sum, *hai shen* sea-slugs

Hsieh rou ban huang gua crabmeat and cucumber salad with a sesame-seed oil, soya sauce and vinegar dressing

Hsieh rou dou fu quick-fried bean curd simmered with crabmeat in chicken stock

Hsien gan bei yao hua quick-fried scallops and pork kidneys

Hsun yu marinated fish, deep-fried and slowly braised in stock with soya sauce and sugar until dried. *Hsun yu* means "smoked fish". It used to be smoked but no longer is

Hung shao duei hsia fried shrimp with a julienne of ginger and onions simmered in a soya and wine sauce

Hung shao guei yu fried mandarin fish, braised with mushrooms, fat pork and bamboo shoots in a meat stock

Hung shao yu fried sea-bass with a ginger and onion julienne simmered in a soya and wine sauce, sometimes stuffed with a pork stuffing
Hung siu bau chee shark's fin stewed in meat and soya sauce
Ja hsia chiu fried shrimp balls
Jiem yu sole
Jing jeng shr yu shad steamed with ham, pork fat, mushrooms, bamboo shoots and wine
Jing yu, jeng yu steamed sole with a julienne of mushrooms, golden needles (*gum jum*), dates and ham
Keh jup chow haah kow shrimp balls braised with sweet peppers and pulped tomatoes
Kung bau ming har, *gung pao ming hsia* deep-fried shrimp simmered in a soya and chilli sauce
Lay faah yu, li hua yu mandarin fish
Lay yu, li yu carp
Lo yu, min yu cod
Loong haah, *lung hsia* lobster
Ngaah choy chow haah, *ha tsai chao hsia* shrimps braised with snow peas and bean sprouts

garlic and soya sauce and then with smoking lard
Tang tsu hwang yu, tong cho wong yu deep-fried whole yellow fish in a sweet-sour sauce
Tiem shun yu, tian suan yu sweet-sour pungent fish. See *Ngung lao yu*
Tsing jing sek barn grouper steamed with ginger and onion
Waung faah yu, hwang hua yu mullet
Wu liou yu see *Ngung lao yu*
Wu liu guei yu braised mandarin fish with a ginger and sweet-sour sauce
Wuy waung yu sturgeon
★**Yang chow haah kow** balls of minced shrimp bound together with pork fat and egg-white and deep fried. This quite simple dish is a good example of the hours of preparation Chinese food demands. Blending the three ingredients by hand, which has to be done with moments of gentleness and moments of savagery, can take a good half-hour

You may think it odd that Chinese restaurants pile the food into the same bowl, regardless of what has been in it before. It is odd. In China a dinner service for ten consists of 148 pieces.

Ngun yu whitebait
Ngung lao yu, wu liou yu meaning "five willows fish". Boiled red snapper, with a julienne of cucumber, carrot, ginger and sweet pickle (made with vinegar)
Ping jee yu turbot
Pong haai, pang crab
Rang hai ge li minced clams and pork baked in clam shells with ginger, onion and soya sauce
Saah mun yu, *sha men yu* salmon
Sai kun sin yau quick-fried squid with celery
Sar wor yu tau, *shao guo shr-z tou* fish heads, bamboo shoots, bean curd and mushrooms stewed in soya sauce
Sieu waung gwaah yu, shiao hwang gua yu minnow (little yellow melon fish)
Sung shu yu fried sea-bass served with an elaborate sweet-sour sauce of vegetables. See *Cha sung shu yu*
Szu tu yu boiled sea-bass covered with a sauce of onion, ginger,

Yau pau dai ji quick-fried scallops with vegetables
Yeung gwaar, rang gua squash stuffed with minced fish, fried then braised with a little wine
Yeung yu, rang yu fish skinned and mixed with shrimp, water chestnuts, mushrooms, ham and scallions, then put back into the skin and fried. Served with a ginger and wine sauce
Yin chong yu fried and smoked pomfret
Yu chee, *yu chr* shark's fin
Yu pien choi yuen see *Chao yu pian*
Yu sun wor bar stewed fish lips in white sauce, served on rice
Yu yeung fooh gwaah, yu niao gu gua bitter melons stuffed with minced fish, fried and then braised with crushed black beans
Zao liou hwang yu, chow lo wong yu small pieces of yellow fish fried in fat and braised in wine
Zao liou yu pian, cho lau yu peen see *Zao liou hwang yu*

Poultry

★ *Ba bao ya* literally "eight treasure duck": boned duck stuffed with rice, pork, shrimps, mushrooms, water chestnuts, ginkgo nuts and chestnuts and roasted. When served it is cut in eight pieces

Baak ghuy, *bai ji* cold chopped chicken served in bite-size pieces

Baak jaahm ghuy, *bai tsan ji* chicken boiled with wine, rubbed with sesame-seed oil, chopped and served with a ginger and sesame-seed oil sauce

★ *Bei jing kao ya* "Peking duck": the duck is first inflated so that the skin separates from the body and is then dried in the wind after which it is smeared with honey, dried again, then roasted. Served with slices of cucumber, scallion, hoisin sauce and little pancakes. The diners roll up the shredded duck and vegetables in the pancake, which they have covered with sauce, and eat it in their fingers

Bei jing tien ya, **buck kin teen ngaap** see *Bei jing kao ya*

Chang cha hsiung ya camphor-wood- and tea-smoked duck

Chao ji gan quick-fried chicken livers and snow peas

Chao sarm seen, *chao san hsien* quick-fried sliced chicken, abalone, shrimp and vegetables

Chao shui ya pian breast of wild duck fried with mushrooms and bamboo shoots

Chao ya gan duck liver stir fried with bamboo shoots and mushrooms

Ching jew chow ghuy pien, *ching jiao chao ji pian* braised sliced chicken, sweet peppers, scallions and red bean sauce served with a soya sauce

Ching jiao ji sih see *Tsing jiu ghuy see*

★ *Ching jing baak gup,* **ching jeng bai ge** squab steamed with golden needles (*gum jum*), mushrooms, red dates, ginger and scallions

Choi pay ghuy quick-fried chicken chopped and served with *hua jiao yen*

Choi yuen chow ghuy pien see *Ching jew chow ghuy pien*

Choi yuen geong chung ghuy chicken steamed with ginger and onion, chopped and served with kale

Dung gu pa ya fried duck and fried mushrooms steamed together with ginger and scallions

Fu yung pian minced chicken breasts mixed with egg white, sugar and wine into a sort of batter, quick fried in slices with water chestnuts and bean sprouts

Fung gone choi darm quick-fried chicken livers and vegetables

Fung gone gup peen quick-fried chicken and squab livers and vegetables

Gaah heung ngaap, *jia hsiang ya* boned duck stuffed with onions, garlic, ginger and mushrooms, browned, then simmered in a sauce of the stuffing and served with braised spinach

Ge-z sung coarsely minced squab, fried with water chestnuts, served on a bed of thin fried noodles

Geong chung dow see ghuy quick-fried chopped chicken with ginger and black bean sauce

Ghuy gwat jeung, *ji gu jiang* small pieces of chicken stewed with soya sauce and sugar

Ghuy see dow mew see *Yin ya ji tsu*

Gow far ghuy, *jiao hua ji* chicken stuffed with meats and vegetables wrapped in lotus leaves and baked in clay

Guo shao ji boiled chicken, boned, covered in a paste of cornstarch, soya sauce and wine and deep fried

Gwai gei ghuy, *guei fei ji* quick-fried chicken and bamboo shoots simmered in soya sauce and sugar

Haap to ghuy, *he tao ji* fried chicken with ham and walnuts

Hao yu ge sung chopped squab quick fried with oyster sauce, mushrooms and peas. Eaten rolled up in a lettuce leaf

Har yee kai "beggar's chicken"— whole chicken stuffed with mushrooms, pickled cabbage, herbs and onions, wrapped in lotus leaves, encased in clay and baked. The guest of honour breaks the clay with a mallet

He tao ji ding see *Haap to ghuy*

He yeh ju ji split chicken, fried and then simmered with wine, tomato and soya sauce, covered in a sauce of *faah jiu*, scallions and ginger, wrapped in a lotus leaf and roasted

Hsiang gu chun ji chicken steamed with mushrooms

★*Hsiang su ya* "crispy and aromatic duck": duck rubbed with seasoning, pressed with onion and ginger. Left. Rubbed with soya sauce and *heung new fun.* Steamed. Brushed off and left again. Finally deep fried, chopped up and served with roasted pepper and salt (*hua jiao yen*) and steamed rolls

braised duck" is simmered with ginger, sesame-seed oil, onion and mushrooms

Jaah baak gup, chao bai ge deep-fried squab

Ja ba kwai, ja bart fie chicken marinated and deep fried, served with a dry mixture of roasted, crushed Chinese red pepper and salt browned over the heat (*hua jiao yen*). The chicken for this dish is cut in eight pieces, which is what the name means

Ja bai ge deep-fried squab. See *Jaah baak gup*

Ja la-z ji ding, chow lart ji ghuy deng quick-fried diced chicken and green peppers with soya and chilli sauce

---

Given extensive leisure, what do not the Chinese do? They eat crabs, drink tea, taste spring water, sing operatic airs, fly kites, play shuttlecock, match grass blades, make paper boxes, solve complicated wire puzzles, play *mahjong*, gamble and pawn clothing, stew *ginseng*, watch cock-fights, romp with their children, water flowers, plant vegetables, graft fruits, play chess, take baths, hold conversations, keep cage-birds, take afternoon naps, have three meals in one, guess fingers, play at palmistry, gossip about fox spirits, go to operas, beat drums and gongs, play the flute, practise on calligraphy, munch duck-gizzards, salt carrots, fondle walnuts, fly eagles, feed carrier pigeons, quarrel with their tailors, go on pilgrimages, visit temples, climb mountains, watch boat races, hold bull fights, take aphrodisiacs, smoke opium, gather at street corners, shout at aeroplanes, fulminate against the Japanese, wonder at the white people, criticize their politicians, read Buddhist classics, practise deep-breathing, hold Buddhist seances, consult fortune tellers, catch crickets, eat melon seeds, gamble for moon cakes, hold lantern competitions, burn rare incense, eat noodles, solve literary riddles, train pot-flowers, send one another birthday presents, kow-tow to one another, produce children, and sleep.

Lin Yutang

Hua sheng-z ji diced chicken leg quick fried with peanuts, *faah jiu* and chilli

Hueng so chuen ghuy, hsiang tsu chuan ji marinated chicken deep fried three times

Hueng so chuen ngaap, hsiang tsu chuan ya marinated duck fried three times

Hueng so ghuy toi, hsiang su ji tuei marinated chicken legs, deep fried

Hung par teen ngaap duck fried, then simmered with soya sauce and sugar

Hung shao pa ya this "soya

Jar chun gone, ja jen gan deep-fried chicken gizzards and duck livers with vegetables

★*Jee bow ghuy, jr bao ji* literally "paper-wrapped chicken". Slices of chicken and ham, dipped in sugar, soya sauce, cornstarch, oil and wine, wrapped in paper and fried

Jeung bau gai deng see *Jian bao ji ding*

Jeung bau hup to ghuy deng, jiang pao he tai ji ding see *Haap to ghuy*

Ji yiou ba huo tuei tsai shin, ghuy yao pa for toi choi sum steamed

Tientsin cabbage with chopped chicken and ham glossed with chicken fat

Ji yiou jin bai, **ghuy yao jun bark** steamed Tientsin cabbage with chicken sauce

★*Jian bao ji ding* stir-fried chicken cubes (sometimes with nuts) in a hoisin and yellow bean sauce (typical of Peking)

Jiang yu ji chicken simmered in a traditional red sauce based on soya sauce

Jiao ma ji boiled breast of chicken, sliced and served with sesame-seed oil and wine sauce

★*Jin chiang ji* "gold-coin chicken": it is the shape of the chicken rather than how it is made which is important. Sometimes round pieces of chicken, ham, mushroom and pork are skewered and roasted. Sometimes a boned leg of chicken is stuffed with ham and steamed. Then it is coated with egg and flour, roasted and cut in round slices.

Jing jiang ya, **ging jeung ngaap** "home-cooked duck": same as above with red bean sauce included in the stuffing. This is Peking sauce duck, as opposed to Peking duck

Ju hua ji shun chicken marinated in wine, fried and dipped in sesame-seed oil and chilli sauce

Kao rang ji boned chicken, stuffed with pork, ginger and onion, and roasted

★**Kay jee ghuy** diced chicken, ham, mushrooms and bamboo shoots, stuffed into a pig's intestine to make a very lengthy, savoury fat sausage, and roasted. The sausage is chopped in thin slices, which gives the dish its name—chicken draughtsmen

Kung bao ji ding, **kung po ghuy deng** quick-fried diced chicken with soya sauce and chilli

La yu ji ding chicken and spinach stir fried and served with fried chilli

Li zu men ji fried chicken and chestnuts

Low hon pa ngaap braised duck in soya sauce with vegetables

Lung yan ya chuan duck breasts in conical rolls covered with chilli peppers, steamed and served surrounded with green vegetables

Ma yiou ji, **ma yau ghuy** deep-fried chicken, chopped and served in sesame-seed oil sauce

Maw gwoo mun baak gup squab casseroled with ham, mushrooms, sugar and *heung new fun.* Served with snow peas

Maw gwooh chow ghuy pien, *mo gu cha ji pian* thinly sliced chicken fried with mushrooms and garlic. Known as "velvet chicken"

Mo gu ji pian quick-fried chicken breasts with mushrooms and snow peas

Sai kun chow gup peen quick-fried sliced squab and celery

San chao gup peen, *sheng chao ge pian* quick-fried sliced squab and bamboo shoots

See jew ghuy peen quick-fried sliced chicken and vegetables in chilli and black bean sauce

Shwun ji chicken smoked over burning sugar and tea in a sealed pot. Served hot or cold

Sieu ghuy, *shao ji* roast chicken

Sieu ngaap, *shao ya* roast duck

Siu guk yu gup chopped squab, fried then baked

★*Sung-z ji tsu* shredded chicken breasts quick fried with chillis, covered with roasted pine kernels. These are served with lettuce leaves. Diners spread the chicken on a leaf, roll the leaf up and eat it in their fingers

Tiem shun ghuy gon, *tien suan ji gan* fried chicken livers, hearts and gizzards braised with vegetables

Tsing jiu ghuy see, *ching jiao ji sih* quick-fried shredded chicken and green peppers

★**Tsui ghuy,** *tsui ji* literally "drunken chicken": chicken cooked in stock, cut up, heavily salted and soaked for two or three days in its stock and wine. Served cold

Tsui pi ya-z this "crispy skin duck" is simmered with onion, garlic, ginger and aniseed, then deep fried

Waaht ghuy, *jing tsen ji* chicken casseroled with mushrooms, cloud ears (*wun yee*) and golden needles (*gum jum*). Known as braised satin chicken

Wang bao ji chicken marinated in ginger, scallions, wine, cloves, etc., then wrapped in a net of fat and roasted

★**Yim guk ghuy** "salt baked chicken": chicken literally buried in salt, and served in small pieces
Yin ja ji tsu shredded chicken breasts, quick fried with bean sprouts
Yiu lin ji split chicken marinated in ginger, wine and soya sauce, "splash fried". It is then served with a dipping bowl of hot pepper sauce (*lah jew jeong*), garlic and soya sauce
Yu lang ji simmered chicken, cut small with alternate layers of smoked ham. Served with broccoli
Yum yeung ghuy chicken and ham rolled on a skewer and roasted

Meat

Chaah gwaah jing juh yook, *cha gua jeng ju rou* sliced pork steamed with tea melons
Chaah sieu, *cha shao* fillet of pork marinated in spices, rubbed with wine and soya sauce and roasted. Served cut in slices
Chao ju gan quick-fried sliced liver, onions and spinach leaves with a soya and wine sauce
Cha yao hua deep-fried kidneys served with roast pepper and salt (*hua jiao yen*)
Choi sum see ji tau see *See jee tao*
★**Choi yuen hoy au ngau yuk, *tsai ba hao yu niou rou*** quick-fried shredded beef with vegetables and oyster sauce
Chow kun choi ngau yuk see, *gwang dung chao niou rou szu* shredded beef, deep fried with celery and onion, mixed with a soya and wine sauce
Chow ngau yuk see yeung chung, *chao niou rou sih yang tsung* quick-fried shredded beef with braised onions in soya sauce
Chow yook soong, *chao rou sung* minced pork braised with diced water chestnuts and other vegetables and sprinkled with fried peanuts
Chung sik ngau lau "Chinese beef steak": sliced steak quick fried, with soya sauce and tomato sauce and vegetables
Dou shr pai gu spare-ribs braised with fermented black beans
Dow chow juh yook, *dou shao ju rou* lima or fava beans, braised with diced pork
Dow gock chow juh yook, *dou jia chao ju rou* sliced pork braised with runner beans
Dung shun harm choi yuk see quick-fried sliced pork braised with bamboo shoots and other vegetables in soya sauce
Dung sun yuk see, *dong sun rou sih* quick-fried shredded pork and bamboo shoots
Dung yang rou lamb in aspic
Faahn gwaah chow ngow yook, *hsiang gua chao niou rou* sliced beef with crushed black beans braised with vegetable squash
Fu ju rou pian quick-fried pork braised with mushroom and bean curd skin
Gaai laan chow chaah sicu, *jie lan chao cha shao* roasted pork fried with braised broccoli
★*Gan shao niou rou tsu* quick-fried shredded beef with green peppers and transparent noodles
Geong chung ngau yuk quick-fried beef with ginger and onion
Gone giu ngau yuk see, *gan chao niou rou sih* quick-fried shredded beef with chilli sauce
Goo lo yuk "sweet and sour pork": diced pork in batter with a sweet and sour sauce, with sweet peppers and pineapple
Guo shao niou rou beef boiled with onion, aniseed, ginger, etc. Then covered in cornstarch, egg and gravy paste and deep fried
Ho yau ngau yuk, *hao yiou niou rou* thinly sliced beef, marinated in wine, oil, cornstarch and baking soda, quick fried, with oyster sauce
Hoong sieu juh yook, *hung shao ju rou* casserole of diced pork with leeks and onions, served on a bed of braised spinach
Hua jiao rou wan-z pork balls made with spices and wine and deep fried
Hung men wu hua ju rou see *Ngung faah yook mun sun*
Hung shao du-z braised tripe with alum quick fried with greens and a wine, soya and sugar sauce
Hung shao niou rou stewed shin of beef simmered with soya sauce and wine

31

Hung shao ti bang braised shoulder of pork, simmered with soya sauce, anise and wine with mushrooms added

Hung siu yuen tai, *hung shao yu pian* see *Yuen taai*

Hup toe yuk deng, *he tao rou ding* quick-fried diced pork with walnuts

★ **Jaak taai** pig's feet, stuffed with sliced pork, simmered with garlic, ginger, anise and *heung new fun*, served on spinach

Jap kum ping poon, *shr jin bing pen* mixed sliced cold meats and cold vegetables

Jar yuen ji, *ja wan-z* quick-fried pork balls, served with roasted pepper and salt (*hua jiao yen*)

Jarp kum sar wor see *Soups*

Jen ju rou wan pork balls made with egg, soya sauce, ginger, mushrooms, water chestnuts and onions, rolled in rice and steamed

Jeung ngau yuk yau bau har, *jiang niou rou yiou* slices of beef stewed in soya sauce, sugar and aniseed mixed with quick-fried freshwater shrimps. Served cold

dung chao niou rou sih see *Chow kun choi ngau yuk see*

Laat jew jeung, *la jiao jiang* sweet peppers and dried shrimps braised with chillis

Law baak chow ngow yook, *lo bo chao niou rou* beef and turnips braised with garlic, ginger and scallions

Liang ban yao pian pork kidneys sliced and quick fried with spices and served cold

Mi fen rou layers of braised pork cut thin with a paste of ground fried rice, soya and sesame-seed oil, onion and ginger between each slice, steamed with ginger and onion

Mooi choy jing yook bang, *mai tsai jeng rou bing* minced pork steamed with pickled cabbage, water chestnuts and mushrooms

Mu hsu rou shredded pork quick fried with beaten eggs, scallions and *wun yee*, served with the same pancakes as Peking duck in which the diners roll up the pork mixture and eat with their fingers

---

Rules from the Chinese classic *Book of Etiquette* (1000 BC)
1. Do not roll your rice into a ball
2. Do not gobble your food
3. Do not swill your soup
4. Do not eat noisily
5. Do not crunch bones in your teeth
6. Do not put back fish and meat you have tasted
7. Do not throw bones to the dog
8. Do not snatch
9. Do not spread your rice out to cool
10. Do not suck bits of food out of the soup bowl into your mouth
11. Do not add condiments to the communal soup
12. Do not pick your teeth

Jiang bao rou ding stir-fried pork cubes in soya bean jam sauce (*min seeh*)

★ *Jiang rou* large chunks of pork braised with wine, ginger, anise, cinnamon, *gwaah pay*, cloves and soya sauce. Served without sauce

Jiu yim pai gwat, *jiao yen pai gu* deep-fried diced pork served with roasted pepper and salt

Kao pai gu see *Sieu pi gwut*

Keh chow juh yook, *chieh chao ju rou* sliced pork and spices braised with eggplant

Kun choi ngau yuk see, *gwang*

Ng heung ngau yuk, *wu hsiang niou rou* dried beef stewed with soya sauce and sugar. Served cold

Ngaah choy chow juh yook, *ya tsai shao ju rou* sliced pork quick fried and then braised with snow peas, bean sprouts, celery and *wun yee*

Ngung faah yook mun sun, *wu hua rou men sun* sliced pork braised with bamboo shoots

Niou rou jiang la jiao green peppers stuffed with minced beef

Pa jou-z rump of pork sealed in

the frying pan, boiled and served with soya gravy

★*Rou sih chao ching jiao* sliced pork, quick fried, added to quick-frying green peppers together with a soya and wine sauce, so that all are braised together. This is the standard way all meat-and-vegetable dishes are cooked

Sai kun ngau yuk, *shi ching niou rou* see *Chow kun choi ngau yuk see*

Sai kun yuk deng quick-fried diced pork with celery

San chow pai gwat, *sheng chao pai gu* fried pork rib in sweet-sour sauce

Sar wor see ji tau, *shao guo shih-z tou* see *See jee tao*

★*See jee tao,* *shr-z tou* "lion's head meat balls": made with fat and lean pork, mushrooms, onion, ginger and wine, cooked with cabbage hearts. There are many variations of this dish. Often crab or shrimps are added to the balls. Some fry them before long braising

See jiu ngau yuk quick-fried sliced beef in chilli and black bean sauce

Shen hsien rou pork cubes steamed with soya sauce and wine. Served plain

Sieu juh, *shao ju* roast pork

Sieu pi gwut, *shao pai gu* barbecued spare-ribs

Tang tsu pai gu sweet-sour pork spare ribs. Complain if the pork

is not crisp or the sauce not made with red haws (*shan cha ping*)

Tiem shun jug gerk, *tian suan ju jiao* sweet-sour pig's feet

Tiem shun pi gwut, *tien suan pai gu* sweet-sour spare-ribs

Tien suan gu lao rou see *Tang tsu pai gu*

Tong cho lay jek deep-fried diced pork with chilli and tomato sauce

Tsing jar lay jek quick-fried diced pork, served with roasted pepper and salt

Tsing jiu yuk see, *ching jiao rou sih* see *Rou sih chao ching jiao*

Tsung bao yang rou quick-fried sliced mutton with braised scallions

Wan dou jiang pork coated in soya sauce and flour, quick fried with braised peas

Wu hsiang niou rou beef braised with "five-spice"

Wui war yuk, *hui guo rou* quick-fried sliced pork with chilli and soya sauce

Yang tsung pai gu quick-fried pork chops, braised with shredded onion

Yiu gwor yuk deng quick-fried diced pork with cashew nuts in soya sauce

Yuen taai, *yuan ti* round piece of hock and leg of pork sealed in frying pan and then long simmered in soya sauce and wine, served on a bed of seaweed, which is cooked with it

Vegetables

Bai jr wo sun boiled water bamboo shoots covered in a gravy and garnished with minced ham

Chao dou ya tsai bean sprouts stir fried with mushrooms and celery hearts

Chao hsueh dou quick-fried peas, mushrooms and bamboo shoots

Chao jie lan tsai quick-fried mustard and cress

Chao jie tsai quick-fried broccoli

Chao ou pian quick-fried sliced lotus root, braised with mushrooms and bamboo shoots

Chao sih ji dou quick-fried french beans and water chestnuts

Chow to jiu pai tsai quick-fried string beans and braised Tientsin cabbage

Fei tsui geng chopped quick-fried spinach, served with minced chicken

For tor nye yau choi sum, *huo tuei nai yiou tsai shin* steamed vegetables with creamy sauce garnished with minced ham

Ghuy yau choi sum, *ji yiou tsai shin* steamed mixed vegetables covered with white sauce made of chicken fat

Gone siu dung sun, *gan shao dung sun* fried bamboo shoots and salted vegetables

Gone siu yee dung, *gan shao er dung* mushrooms and bamboo shoots boiled and quick fried

Ho yau sin goo stewed mushrooms with oyster sauce

Ho yow dow fooh, *hao yiou do fu* fried bean curd with oyster sauce

Hsien tsai tsan dou fried fava beans and mustard and cress braised in chicken stock

Hui kou mo yiou mushrooms braised with cabbage heart and bamboo shoots

Hui wan dou peas braised with mushrooms, bamboo shoots and a little ham

Hung shao dou fu, hung siu dow foo braised bean curd with soya sauce

Hung shao jie-z see *Jie-z hsiang*

Hung shao li tzu bai tsai stir-fried hearts of Tientsin cabbage, mushrooms and chestnuts

Hung siu bark kwan mushrooms braised in soya sauce

Ji yiou jin bai, ghuy yau jun bark, steamed Tientsin cabbage covered with white sauce made with chicken fat

Jie-z hsiang sliced eggplant deep fried with bamboo, chicken, shrimp and ham, covered with a soya and wine sauce and garnished with walnuts, peanuts and almonds

La bai tsai fried cabbage braised in a hot sweet-sour sauce. Served cool

Lo bo hsien ge fried white Chinese radishes

Ma po pou fu bean curd braised with thick soya sauce and hot peppers, mixed with minced pork and chopped mushrooms

Men yiou tsai fried cabbage hearts, mushrooms and bamboo shoots

Nai yiou tsai hsin quick-fried Tientsin cabbage, simmered in a white sauce of chicken stock, served with a milk and bean flour sauce

Nye yau jun bark braised mixed vegetables in white sauce

Nye yau par sin goo, *hai yiou ba hsien gu* stewed mushrooms and vegetables in a creamy sauce

Po jup guk say so baked asparagus, Chinese endive and bamboo shoots served with a spicy sauce

So jap kum fried mixed vegetables braised in soya sauce

Suan la bai tsai Tientsin cabbage heart and chillis fried in fat in which *faah jew* has previously been fried

Wu hsiang dou fava beans cooked with "five spice" and *faah jew*

Yiou men sun bamboo shoots braised in soya sauce, wine and sugar

Sweets

The Chinese do not eat many sweets. My own view is that this is hardly surprising, because the ones they do have are particularly nasty. They have less need of them as their ordinary cooking involves considerable use of sugar. As a rule an everyday Chinese meal will not include a sweet. They do appear on the elaborate festival or banquet menus which you sometimes find in traditional restaurants.

Ba tsu tu dou fried potato fritters served in a hot syrup of sugar and peanut oil

Ba tsu ping guo apple fritters glazed in a covering of brittle sugar. Also known as "toffee apples"

Baat bo faahn, *ba bao fan* "eight treasure rice": layers of glutinous rice and suet alternating with layers of lotus seeds, dates, cherries, plums and various dried fruits

Cha yang wei sweet pastry balls wrapped in beaten egg white and deep fried

Chuy mow faah knotted ribbon of dough made with flour, suet and sugar, deep fried

Hsing ren dou fu curd made with sweet and bitter almonds and rice covered with syrup, decorated with sliced cherries

Jieh maah bang, *jr ma bing* sesame-seed biscuits

Li-z dan gao meringue covered with powdered chestnut—sometimes served on whipped cream instead of meringue, also known as "Peking dust"

Mei guei guo ja, mei kuei kuo cha flour, egg and sugar made

into a pasty mixture that is deep fried and sprinkled with rose sugar. Served with rose petal syrup
San bu jan egg yolk, flour and sugar mixture, fried

Wan dou huang boiled pea, sugar and flour mixture. Allowed to set, cut in cubes, served cold
Zao ni hun tun deep-fried *wun tun* with date and walnut and orange peel filling

★ Dim sum

There are various Cantonese dishes that properly appear only at lunchtime or as snacks at odd times of the day or even just at bedtime. They are known collectively as *dim sum*. In China they would not be eaten at a main meal, although their popularity in the West has made many occidental restaurants bend the rules.

Dim sum means "little heart". Mostly the dishes are tiny steamed dumplings with various fillings. They come to the table in round wooden or bamboo containers piled one on top of another. In Hong Kong there are restaurants devoted solely to *dim sum*. Waitresses carry round trays, calling out the name of the variety they have. Ordering is done by beckoning the waitress with the dish you want. Bills are totted up by counting the number of dishes on your table. I have listed here the principal dumplings and included a few other appetizers.

Cha chu kuen fried spring roll
Cha shao pao steamed buns stuffed with pork
Fen kuo crab dumpling
Fun gwor vegetable and shrimp dumpling
Ham sui kok fried dumpling
Har kau shrimp dumpling
Hsia jen tu ssu deep-fried shrimp toast
Kai bau tsai steamed buns stuffed with chicken
Ngau yuk mai steamed beef ball
Pai kwat steamed spare ribs
Shiu mai pork dumpling
Tsing fun kuen steamed shredded chicken
Tsing ngau yuk steamed beef ball in lotus leaf

Tung ku ning jou braised mushrooms stuffed with pork and water chestnuts
Woo kok fried Taro puff. Taro is an edible root

There are also some sweet dishes, for example:

Daan tat custard tart
Ma lai goe steamed sponge cake
Ma tai goe fried water chestnut sticks
Ma yung bau steamed sesame bun
Shui tsing gou white fungus sweet dumpling
Tou sha pao steamed date bun
Tse chup goe sugar-cane juice roll
Yeh chup goe coconut pudding

Wine

Chinese "wine" varies in strength from fierce spirits that fry the soles of your feet from the first sip, to quite delicate wines with flower flavours.

The toughest comes from the far north and is called *Kaoliang*. It is distilled from *sorghum* and is stronger even than Russian vodka, though it may be flavoured with rose petals. From central China comes *Shaoshing*, a "wine" of ordinary strength (though distilled) made from rice. This is the commonest Chinese "wine". In the south they make *Liao pan*, which means half-strength. Often it includes orange blossom. Chinese wine is served warm.

Rice wine is now comparatively rare and even the Chinese often cook with sherry. Sherry is probably the nearest substitute for rice wine one can find for drinking with a Chinese meal. There are many schools of thought as to what goes well with Chinese food—ranging from Chablis to rich Burgundy. I am very happy to drink either, but quite often I have lager, particularly with Cantonese food.

Useful words

Baak gup, *ge* squab
Bark choy, *bai tsai* Chinese white cabbage
Bart gok Chinese star anise
Bing pen the first four cold dishes of a meal
Bow yu, *bao yu* abalone
Chaah gwaah, *cha gua* tea melon

Haw laahn dow snow peas
Heung new fun spices of five fragrances—anise, clove, fennel, cinnamon and Chinese red pepper
Ho see dried oysters
Hoong joe Chinese dates
Hoy sieu jeung, *hoi sin jiang* the red bean sauce

The best green tea (*chang*) comes from Fukien. It is called *Wu I Ch'a.* The best varieties of black tea (*hoong*) are *Kee-mun, Liu-an, Wu-loong* and *Po-erh.* Never put milk or sugar in real China tea.

Chao tsai the four stir-fried dishes after the cold hors d'oeuvre
Char, *cha-z* fork
Choong, *tsung ya* onions. The Chinese mostly use scallions
Chow, *chao* stir frying
Daahn, *dan* egg
Ding heung clove (tree)
Doo, *dao-z* knife
Doong gwooh, *dung gu* the usual dried Chinese mushroom with browny-black cap
Dow ngaah, *dou ya* bean sprouts
Dow see black bean sauce
Dung gu winter mushrooms, thin variety. Dried
Dunn, *dun* cooking in a double boiler
Faah jew (*or* jiu), *hua jiao* red pepper from the province of Szechuan. Both aromatic and hot
Faahn gwaah vegetable squash
Faai jee, *kuai-z* chopsticks
Faat choy a hairy kind of seaweed
Fooh gwaah balsam pear or bitter melon
Gar fair, *ka fei* coffee
Geong, *jiang* ginger root
Ghuy, *ji* chicken
Gnapp, *ya* duck
Gon yu chee dried scallops
Gum jum, *jin jen* lily flowers dried, known as golden needles
Gwaah jee choy Chinese watercress. This plant has leaves shaped like water melon seeds which taste somewhat vinegary
Gwaah pay dried tangerine peel

Hua gu dried winter mushrooms
Hua jiao yen roasted pepper and salt
Jeong yow, *jiang yiou* soya sauce
Ji'aah, *ja* deep frying
Jien sautéeing
Jing, jeng steaming
Jook sun, *ju sun* bamboo shoots
Ju, *ju* pig, pork
Ju kuai-z bamboo chopsticks
Jup gravy (also laying out the dead, so the squeamish may prefer *wu-suey*, glue water)
Kao roasting
Kao lu roasting in an oven
Kuo mo button mushrooms. Fresh or dried
Lah jew jeong, *la jiao jiang* hot chilli sauce
Lien jee, *lian mi* lotus seeds, like little nuts
Lien ngow lotus stem
Maah tuy, *ma tie* water chestnuts (literally "horses' hooves")
Maw gwooh, *kuo mo* button-mushroom
Mei jing monosodium glutamate. A white crystalline salt. It brings out the flavour of things, but is not much loved by health faddists
Min seeh, *hwang jiang* soya bean jam
Ming lu cooking on open fire
Mun, *men* stewing
My dan, *jang dan* bill
Naahm yu bright red cheesey bean curd sauce

"Tsou fung hei, ng seh fei." (The rising of the autumn winds is fair warning that the five snakes are fat enough to eat.)

Snakes are considered a delicacy in China. They are primarily a winter food and the Chinese eat almost any kind—pythons, cobras, kraits, rat snakes—certainly more than five. There are many snake dishes—fried snake, snake's liver in soya sauce, deep-fried snake skin. In Hong Kong you can buy packets of snake fillets and instant snake soup. There is also snake bile wine, *sarn seh*. The most popular snake dish is snake broth. It is also probably the one you would like to try first.

Ngaah choy pea sprouts. What most people think are bean shoots

Ngow, *niou* beef

Po, *ao* simmering

Saang see jeung, *hei dou jiang* a sauce of aromatic red beans

Shao see *Kao*

Shui, *shoei* water

Tan dan, *tsai dan-z* menu

Tien wan, *yen wo* bird's nest. This really is the nest of a small species of swift or swallow which the birds make with their saliva. The soup originated in the Shanghai and coastal region

Tsao gu dried straw or grass mushrooms, black in colour

Tse gan, *chr-z* spoon

Wok round-bottomed round cooking pan

Wong dzao, *mi jiou* yellow-coloured rice wine

Wooi heung fennel

Wun tun, *hun tun* fine dough envelopes, filled with chicken, pork or shrimp and parsley or spinach with spring onions, soya sauce and ginger. They should look like wispy fish

Wun yee, *yun er* cultivated mushroom known as cloud ears

Yeung, *gong gi* cock

Yeung, *gong* sheep

Yien say, *hsiang tsai* Chinese parsley. Flatter, paler than ours

Yook gwuy cinnamon

... a tea-pot, the inevitable prelude in these countries to every meal, was set before each of us. You must swallow infinite tea, and that boiling hot, before they will consent to bring you anything else. At last, when they see you thus occupied, the Comptroller of the Table pays you his official visit, a personage of immensely elegant manners, and ceaseless volubility of tongue, who, after entertaining you with his views upon the affairs of the world in general, and each country in particular, concludes by announcing what there is to eat, and requesting your judgement thereupon. As you mention the dishes you desire, he repeats their name in a measured chant, for the information of the Governor of the Pot. Your dinner is served up with admirable promptitude; but before you commence the meal, etiquette requires that you rise from your seat, and invite all the other company present to partake. "Come," you say, with an engaging gesture, "come, my friends, come and drink a glass of wine with me; come and eat a plate of rice"; and so on. "No, thank you," replies everybody; "do you rather come and seat yourself at my table. It is I who invite you"; and so the matter ends. By this ceremony you have "manifested your honour", as the phrase runs, and you may now sit down and eat it in comfort, your character as a gentleman perfectly established.
Huc and Gabet *Travels in Tartary, Thibet and China, 1844–1846*, translated by William Hazlitt

Czechoslovakia—*See* Eastern Europe
Denmark—*See* Scandinavia

Eastern Europe

Bulgaria

Bulgarian cooking may seem to some of us to lack that last touch of refinement and delicacy. The first two dishes I list, for instance, contain lamb's intestines. The second one is boiled and baked, then smothered in tomato paste *and* thick béchamel. We should not be put off—every Bulgarian seems to live to be a hundred and attributes his longevity to the food.

In the matter of wine, if you find a red bottle with the word *Cabernet* on it or a white one with *Chardonnay* go for those. Otherwise I have put a few names in the useful word list that may guide you if you have a difficult choice.

Bulgarian alphabetical order is: А, Б, В, Г, Д, Е, Ж, З, И, Й, К, Л, М, Н, О, П, Р, С, Т, У, Ф, Х, Ц, Ч, Ш, Щ, Ъ, Ы, Ь, Э, Ю, Я
а, б, в, г, д, е, ж, з, и, й, к, л, м, н, о, п, р, с, т, у, ф, х, ц, ч, ш, щ, ъ, ы, ь, э, ю, я

Агнешка шкембе чорба (agneshka shkembe chorba) soup of lamb's intestines with eggs and vinegar added

Агнешки чревца с пресен лук на фурна (agneshki chrevtsa s presen luk na furna) lamb's intestines, boiled with vegetables, then baked with onions, tomato paste and garlic, covered with a thick béchamel sauce

Агнешко – магданозлия (agneshko magdanoslija) cubes of lamb, simmered with onions, parsley and slices of lemon

★Баница (banitsa) very thin flaky pastry figure-of-eight rolls stuffed with *sirene* cheese, yoghurt and egg

Градинарска чорба (gradinarska chorba) "gardener's soup"; a vegetable soup of onions, carrots, celery, beets, green beans, peas, cabbage and yoghurt

★Гювеч (giuvech) a spicy stew of vegetables and meat baked with a top layer of yoghurt and eggs

Дроб сърма (drob sarma) boiled lamb's liver and intestines with rice and onions wrapped in caul fat and baked in the oven. Served with a thick egg sauce

Зелен фасул (zelen fasul) sliced green beans, carrots, onions, tomatoes and sweet peppers simmered together

Каварма (kavarma) cubes of meat stewed with lots of onions and oil

Карвавица (karvavitsa) black pudding with pork lung, heart, kidneys, liver and caraway seed

Кебабчета (kebabcheta) sausage-shaped ground meat and spices grilled over charcoal

Курбан чорба (kurban chorba) a sour soup of boiled lamb with liver, scallions, tomatoes, paprika, sweet peppers, chillis, rice and marjoram. A beaten egg is added before serving

Кьопоолу (kiopoolu) eggplant chopped and puréed with green peppers, tomatoes, garlic, chillis, olive oil, lemon juice and chopped parsley. Served deep fried

Кюфтета (kiufteta) grilled meat balls made of veal, pork, bread, onions, eggs and parsley

Луканка (loukanka) dry, spicy sausage, like salami

Лютеница (liutekitsa) mashed red finger peppers, tomato paste *(saltsa)* and chillis, finely chopped onions, tomatoes and garlic, garnished with chillis

Лютива салата (liutiva salata) green peppers and chillis mixed with finely chopped onion, oil, vinegar and garlic, chilled

Манастирска чорба (manastirska chorba) soup of navy beans, carrot, celery, onions, tomatoes, chillis and marjoram

Мешана салата (meshana salata) mixed salad

Мляко с ориз (mliako s oris) a thick, chilled, milk and rice pudding with cinnamon

Печен фазан (pechen fasan) baked pheasant

Печено прасе (pecheno prase) roast suckling pig

★ **Пилаф с пъдпъдъци и стафиди (pilaf s padpadatsi i stafidi)** quail pilaff, baked with onions, garlic, rice, currants and white raisins

Пълнени чушки (palneni chushki) sweet peppers stuffed with ground meat and rice

Пълнено агнешко бутче (palneno agneshko butche) leg of lamb stuffed with butter, soaked bread, ground meat, scallions, parsley and egg and simmered with vegetables. Served in slices

Пържени чушки със сирене (parzheni chushki s sirene) peppers stuffed with cheese and eggs, egg-and-breadcrumbed and fried

Пържоли от сърна (parzholi ot sarna) fried slices of venison

Рибена чорба (ribena chorba) fish soup with vegetables poured over a yoghurt and egg base

Сърми (sarmi) ground meat, boiled rice, carrots and sweet peppers wrapped in cabbage leaves and baked

★ **Таратор (tarator)** a soup of diced cucumber, yoghurt, chopped walnuts, dill, garlic and oil. Served chilled

Фасул (fasoul) white beans, garlic, onions, oil, carrots, lemon juice, sugar and parsley mixed together and served cold

★ **Хляб "Райска птица" (hliab "raiska ptitsa")** bird-of-paradise bread with *sirene* cheese, yoghurt, flour and eggs with triangles of cheese, cubes of ham, olives and red peppers on top

Шаран пълнен с орехи (sharan palnen s orehi) carp stuffed with onions, walnuts, cooked rice and red peppers, baked in the oven

Шопска салата (shopska salata) peppers, tomatoes, cucumbers, onions, abundant chillis, oil and vinegar, sprinkled with *sirene* cheese

Яхния (jahnija) stew of any meat, vegetables, garlic, paprika and white wine simmered slowly

Useful words

Бира (bira) beer
Вино (vino) wine
Вода (voda) water
Гроздова (grozdova) brandy
Гъмза (gamza) a light red wine
Димят (dimiat) a dry white wine
Захар (zahar) sugar
Кафе (kafe) coffee
Мавруд (mavrud) a dry red wine
Масло (maslo) butter
Мелник (melnik) a dry red wine
Месо (meso) meat
Мляко (mliako) milk
Ориз (oriz) rice
Палачинки (palachinki) pancakes

Пиле (pile) chicken
Питка (pitka) flat white bread
Риба (riba) fish
Свинско (svinsko) pork
Сирене (sirene) white crumbly cheese
Сливова (slivova) plum brandy
Сметка (smetka) bill
Телешко (teleshko) veal
Тракия (trakia) a dry or medium white wine
Хляб (hliab) bread
Чай (chai) tea
Шунка (shunka) ham
Яйца (jaitza) eggs

Наздраве! (nazdrave) cheers!
Добър апетит! (dobar apetit) bon appétit!

Czechoslovakia

As Czechoslovakia was not invented until 1918, it can hardly have a cuisine of its own. Furthermore, each of its component parts had been subjected to separate influences. Slovakia to the east had been greatly influenced by Hungary, Bohemia and Moravia were closer to Austria. The result is a jumble typical of the Balkans.

Czech alphabetical order is: a, b, c, č, d, e, f, g, h, ch, i, j, k, l, m, n, o, p, r, ř, s, š, t, u, v, w, x, y, z, ž

Bramborová polévka potato soup
Bramborové knedlíky potato dumplings
Bramborový salát potato salad
Debrecínska pečínka smoked roast pork, served cold
Dušena roštěnka braised slices of beef in a brown onion sauce
Houskový knedlíky fist-sized dumplings, made from a mixture of flour, eggs, milk and cubes of white bread. Served in slices
Hrachova polévka pea soup
Jablkový závin apple strudel
★**Kapr na černo** a traditional Christmas Eve dish. Poached carp is served with a black sauce made from fish stock, raspberry juice, beer, lemon rind, sugar, honey cake, raisins and almonds
Karbanatky a type of hamburger
Kmínová polévka a thick white soup flavoured with caraway
Koláčky tarts made of yeast dough, filled with plum jam, cottage cheese or almond paste
Koprová omáčka a dill sauce made with flour, fat and sour cream. Served with boiled beef
Kuře na paprice chicken in a paprika sauce
Makový dort poppy-seed cake
Míchana zelenina mixed vegetables
Míchaný oyocný kompot mixed fruit compote
Nadívaná (Plněná) rajská jablíčka stuffed tomatoes
Okurkový salát cucumber salad
Oukrop garlic and potato soup
Pajšl na smetaně tripe in cream sauce

Pečená husa se zelím roast goose with sauerkraut
Pečená kachna roast duck
Pečené kuře roast chicken
Plněné papriky peppers stuffed with ground meat and served with tomato sauce
Polévka s jatrovými knedličky beef bouillon with dumplings made from liver, garlic, lemon rind, egg and breadcrumbs
Povidlový koláč plum jam flan
Pražska šunka Prague ham
Pražský klobás Prague sausage
Rajská polévka s rýží tomato soup with rice
Segedinský guláš Hungarian goulash
Sekaná pečené roast ground meat
(Smažený) řízek veal escalope or pork fillet dipped in flour, egg and breadcrumbs and fried
Svíčková na smetaně beef tenderloin marinated and then roasted. Served with a sour-cream sauce
Švestkové knedlíky plum dumplings
Telecí pečeně roast veal
Tlačenka s cibulí head cheese and onions
Tvarohový koláč cheese cake
Uzená šunka smoked ham
★**Vepřova pečeně** pork roasted with caraway seeds. (Traditionally served with dumplings and sauerkraut)
Zadělavané žaludky stewed goose gizzards
Zajíc na smetaně hare in cream sauce
Zavináč rollmops

Useful words

Chléb bread
Cukr sugar
Čaj tea
Hovězí maso beef
Jehněčí lamb
Jídelní lístek menu
Káva coffee
Máslo butter
Maso meat
Mlíko milk
Plzeňské pivo Czech beer from

Plzen (Pilsner)
Ryba fish
Syr cheese
Štika pike
Šunka ham
Telecí veal
Účet bill
Vejce eggs
Vepřove pork
Víno wine
Voda water

Na zdraví! cheers!
Dobrou chut! bon appétit!

Hungary

There is something different about the Hungarians, an inventiveness and an ingenuity possibly, which elevates them in many ways above their neighbours. It may have something to do with their language which belongs in a different group from all the other Balkan states. Or it may be that their geographical position has placed them at the furthest reaches of all the influences that have affected the area.

Hungarian cooking can embrace, as does French cuisine, delicacy and rough perfection. The contrast between a rich Hungarian meaty soup, which can be a whole meal, and one of their delicate fruit soups makes the point in the first course. The pressed boar's head is the match of any French head cheese; this and such dishes as *vese velö tojással* make the hors d'oeuvre so unusual. Fish is all freshwater as Hungary has no sea coast, but the carp, pike-perch and sterlet are traditionally excellent. Goulashes need no introduction, but you may well be surprised at their delicacy in their native country—none of that oily, orange fire-water which people elsewhere try to pass off as goulash. And the vegetables can be superb. I have a particular favourite called *tökfözelek*, which elevates the vegetable squash from a watery banality to a gastronomic surprise.

Hungarian alphabetical order is: a, á, b, c. cs, d, dz, dzs, e, é, f, g, gy, h, i, í, j, k, l, ly, m, n, ny, o, ó, ö, ő, p, r, s, sz, t, ty, u, ú, ü, ű, v, z, zs

Hideg izelitö — Hors d'oeuvre

Bulgar saláta a delicious mixed vegetable salad named after Bulgaria as a tribute to the prowess of its gardeners

Csuka csiki mártással cold pike with beet sauce

★Diszno sajt pressed boar's head

Házi pástétom pâté maison

Herz szalámi Hungarian salami

Kaszinótojás "casino eggs"— hard-boiled egg whites stuffed with anchovies, egg yolks, sour cream and mustard served on a bed of cubed vegetables with mayonnaise

Liptói körözött cottage cheese spread with cream, caraway seeds, butter, paprika and chives

Tojásétlek — Egg dishes

Debreceni rántotta omelette with green peppers and smoked sausage

Gombás vese tojással scrambled eggs, kidneys and mushrooms

Kolbászos rantotta scrambled eggs, diced bacon and sausage

Rántotta zöldpaprikával green pepper omelette

Tükör tojás parajjal fried eggs with creamed spinach

★Vese velö tojással calf's brains, kidney, onions and eggs, scrambled together with paprika

Levesek — Soups

Soup is an important part of a Hungarian meal, both in summer and winter. They are often thickened with a *roux*, and are usually substantial. The Magyar herdsmen used to carry packs of dried meat, which they could then easily convert into soups and stews on their expeditions. Fruit soups are very popular and are almost always served cold. Basically, they consist of boiled fruit with sugar, flavoured with cloves, cinnamon, lemon and thickened with sour cream.

Bableves csipetkével dried bean soup made from smoked ham stock with sour cream. Served with small noodle pieces

Barackleves apricot soup

Borleves white wine soup with egg yolks, clove, sugar and lemon

Burgonya leves potato soup

Céklaleves beet soup mixed with sour cream and egg yolk

Erdélyi leves a Transylvanian soup of beef stock, sour cream, egg yolks, dill and chives

Gombaleves mushroom soup

Gulyásleves a filling soup like *bográcsgulyás* but with less meat

Hal leves clear fish soup

★ **Kaporleves** fresh dill soup with milk, sour cream and egg yolk

Kelvirágleves cauliflower soup

Korhely leves a curative soup particularly recommended for hangovers. It is made with sour cabbage, slices of smoked sausage, caraway seeds and sour cream

Köménymagleves a medicinal soup which is supposedly excellent for the stomach, made of caraway seeds with onion and egg

Lebbencsleves pieces of *lebbencs* (thin dough), diced bacon, onion and paprika, fried and then simmered in water with added potato slices

★ **Meggyleves** sour-cherry soup

Palócleves a huge soup from the Paloc region with mutton, bacon, onions, paprika, garlic and caraway seeds, potatoes, green beans and sour cream

Paradicsomleves tomato soup with rice, sprinkled with sugar

Salátaleves lettuce soup with dill, garlic, whey, sour cream and vinegar

Spárgaleves asparagus soup

Zellerkrémleves celery soup

★ **Zöldbableves** a tart green bean soup with vinegar, paprika and sour cream

Tészták, palacsinták— *Dumplings, pancakes and noodles*

Hungarians use many different soup garnishes (*Levesbevalók*) in the form of dumplings, noodles and even pancakes.

Csipetke tiny pinched flour and water dumplings for soup

Daragaluska semolina and egg dumplings

Darás metélt semolina noodles

Galuska egg dumplings

Gránátos kocka squares of cooked dough mixed with potatoes, onion and paprika and then baked

★ **Hortobágyi palacsinta** pancakes stuffed with ground veal, onion, paprika and sour cream. Served with a sour cream sauce

Májgombóc dumplings made from liver, bread, onions, egg and flour

Palacsintametélt pancake strips for soup

Szalonnás gombóc bacon dumplings

Tarhonya a Magyar staple made by kneading flour and eggs into dough, breaking it and drying it (the Magyars left it in the sun). The ensuing egg barley pellets are boiled in water and used in soup

Tojáskocsonya squares of egg custard for soup

Turós csusza noodles sprinkled with sour cream, smoked bacon crackling, cottage cheese, baked

Vajgaluska dumplings made with butter, flour and egg

Zsemlegombóc bread, flour, egg, milk and parsley dumplings

Hal — *Fish*

★ **Halászlé** this Magyar speciality is a very fiery fish stew. Chunks of carp and other freshwater fish are poached slowly with onion, sweet peppers, tomatoes and whole cherry paprika

Halpaprikás cubes of carp, cooked in sour cream with onion and

paprika. Served with *galuskas*

Rácponty a Serbian dish. Carp steaks are laid on sliced potatoes, covered with onion, sweet peppers and tomatoes and baked with a sour-cream sauce

Rántott ponty carp steaks egg-and-breadcrumbed and fried

Föetelek — Main dishes

There are four different Hungarian basic stews:

Gulyás: thin stew always with beef, onion, paprika, potatoes and *csipetke* in it. No cream

Paprikás: stew with a thick pink sauce of paprika and sour cream

Pörkölt: literally means "singed"; a stew with cubed meat, a very thick sauce, onions and paprika. No cream

Tokány: long, thin strips of beef or veal cooked in their own juice, with a little onion and black pepper. Originally paprika was never used, but most modern *tokány* dishes include it

Bácskai rízses hús a rice dish of cubed pork, onions, green peppers, tomatoes and paprika

★**Bográcsgulyás** "gulyás" means herdsman and this famous goulash dish dates back to the early Magyars. It is still often prepared in large cauldrons or *bogrács*. Beef cubes, chopped onion, sliced sweet peppers, tomatoes, potatoes, paprika, chilli powder, garlic and caraway seeds are stewed with tiny egg dumplings

Borjú pörkölt braised veal cubes

Csángógulyás a goulash with braised beef cubes, onion, garlic, caraway seeds, paprika, sweet peppers, sour cabbage and rice

★**Csikós tokány** pork braised slowly with bacon, onion, sweet peppers, tomato and black pepper. Served with sour cream and dumplings

Erdélyi marhatokány a beef stew with white wine, bacon, onion, tomato paste and garlic

★**Fatányéros** this Transylvanian dish of different meats served on wooden platters is reminiscent of the ancient Magyars who used to eat out in the open off slabs of wood from fallen trees. Similar to a mixed grill, it consists of grilled pork chops, bacon, beef and veal fillets with fried potatoes

Gundel tokány braised strips of fillet steak, goose liver, beans, scrambled egg and onions

Hagymás rostelyos sirloin steak fried with onions

Herány tokány a Transylvanian dish of braised strips of beef and pork with sour cream

Hétvezér tokány named after the Seven Chieftains who first led the Magyars into Hungary. Braised strips of beef, pork and veal, with onions, *lecsó* and sour cream

★**Magyaros szuzérmék** a very fiery

dish of pork—originally veal— médaillons fried in pork dripping and covered with fried chopped onions, potatoes, chilli powder and paprika

Marhapörkölt a thick beef stew served with dumplings

Nyárson sült csirke spit-roasted chicken

Pacalpörkölt a thick tripe stew with paprika, onion, garlic, caraway seeds, green peppers and tomatoes

Paprikás csirke chicken braised with onions, garlic, paprika and cream. Served with egg dumplings

Pirított máj magyarosan braised chicken livers with onions, paprika, sweet peppers and tomatoes. Served with rice

Pörkölt csirke chicken stew with tomatoes, green peppers, garlic, paprika and onions

Rablóhús "robber's meat"— kebabs on skewers, roasted with onions over an open fire

Rántott sértes borda pork chops breadcrumbed and fried

Serpenyös rostelyos pot roast of beef steaks, green peppers, tomatoes, onion, garlic, potatoes, caraway seeds and paprika

Sertésborda parasztosan braised pork chops with diced fried onion, bacon and potatoes

Székelygulyás a Transylvanian goulash with pork and sour cabbage

Székely sertésborda pork chops simmered with onions, paprika, garlic and caraway seeds, then braised with sour cabbage and sour cream and sprinkled with dill

Temesvári sertésborda a dish of pork chops with tomatoes, onion, bacon, sweet peppers and green beans simmered together

Zsiványpecsenye "bandit's meat" —barbecued or spit-roasted meat

43

Köretek — Főzélekek — Vegetables

Gombapaprikás braised mushrooms with sour cream, paprika and onion

Káposztás kocka shredded white cabbage fried in lard, sugar and black pepper with squares of flat cooked dough

Kelkáposztafőzelék boiled savoy cabbage with caraway seeds, garlic and diced potatoes

Lecsó a colourful mixed dish of sweet peppers, streaky bacon, onion, paprika and tomatoes

Liptó burgonya cooked potato mixed with grated *liptói* cheese, bacon crackling and dill. Baked

Paprikás burgonya boat-shaped potatoes simmered with fried onion, garlic, paprika, chilli powder and caraway seeds with circles of smoked sausage

Paraj főzelék spinach purée

Párolt vörös káposzta braised red cabbage

Rakott burgonya alternate layers of cooked potato slices and hard-boiled egg, sprinkled with sour cream and breadcrumbs and baked

Rakott káposzta alternate layers of braised sour cabbage and a mixture of cooked ground pork, chopped onion and smoked sausage, sprinkled with sour cream and heated in the oven

Ropogos hagyma fried onions

Savanyú káposzta sour cabbage

Sólet baked beans and barley mixed with onion and paprika, with some smoked meat added

★ **Tökfőzelék** strips of squash sautéed with onion and mixed with sour cream, dill and vinegar

Töltött káposzta cabbage stuffed with ground pork or pork and beef, onion and rice. It is simmered with smoked pork ribs and sour cabbage, served with sour cream

Töltött paprika sweet peppers stuffed with ground pork, rice and onion

Töltött paradicsom tomatoes stuffed with crayfish

Saláták — Salads

Burgonyasaláta potato salad with sugar, salt, vinegar, chopped parsley and onion rings

Céklasaláta beet salad

Fejes saláta lettuce salad

Káposztasaláta a salad of chopped cabbage, onion and caraway seeds

Karfiolsaláta cauliflower salad

Paprikasaláta sweet pepper salad

Paradicsomsaláta tomato salad with onion

Töksaláta a squash salad of fried squash strips in yoghurt and lemon juice

Uborkasaláta cucumber salad with garlic, sugar and pepper

Vegyes saláta mixed salad

Zöldbabsaláta green bean salad

Édességek — Desserts

Csúsztatott palacsinta layered pancakes with sugar and apricot preserve filling

Diós metélt walnut noodles

★ **Dobostorta** named after its inventor, this famous speciality is a thin layered sponge cake with chocolate filling and a caramel glaze

Indiána fánk chocolate covered chou pastry filled with chocolate cream

Lekváros derelye dough pockets filled with jam and boiled, then sprinkled with sugar and cinnamon or golden breadcrumbs

Mákos metélt poppy-seed noodles

★ **Rakott metélt** noodles with a mixture of beaten eggs, sour cream, vanilla, cottage cheese, white raisins, nuts and jam, baked

palacsinta sweet filled layered pancakes

Rétes paper-thin pastry with various fillings

Rigó jancsi chocolate-filled chocolate sponge squares

★ **Somlói galuskas** a delicious speciality of three layers of sponge — one vanilla, one walnut and one chocolate — soaked with rum and filled with egg custard, cream, nuts and white raisins, served with cream and a chocolate sauce

Szilvás gombóc plum dumplings

Torta diós walnut gâteau

Túrós gombóc cottage cheese dumplings
Túróscsusza pieces of cooked dough mixed with melted butter, cottage cheese, sour cream and bacon crackling. Although not a sweet dish, this is nevertheless served as dessert in Hungary

Hungarian wine

Alföld region the largest region in the sandy Great Plain
Badacsony a hill village on the side of Lake Balaton
  Badacsonyi Kéknyelü: excellent dry white wine
  Szürkebarát: "grey friar"—rich white wine
  Zöldszilváni: "green Sylvaner"
Balaton producing white wine from the Italian Riesling grape
Balatonfüred-Csopak a mixed region of good wines, the *Füred* being sweeter and less sharp than the *Csopak*
Bársonyos-Császár a northern region producing agreeably sharp, fresh white wines. Mór is its most famous town
  Móri Ezerjó: dry white wine
Eger known for its red wines
  Egri Bikavér: "Bull's Blood" is made with a blend of grapes—Kadarka to make it strong, Médoc noir (Merlot) and Oporto to make it smooth and dark
  Egri Leányka: medium-sweet white wine of high quality
Mátra hegyalia the southern slopes of the Mátra mountains provide very good table wines
  Mátraalja Debröi Hárslevelü:

rich table wine
  Mátraalya Muskotály: muscatel
Mecsek in southern Hungary. The town of Pécs is famous for its sparkling white wines
  Pécsi Olaszrizling: a delightfully dry wine
Somló small vineyard district
  Furmint: dry white wine
Sopron western town on the border with Austria
  Soproni Kékfrankos: light red
  Soproni Leányka: dry white
Szekszárd south central Hungary
  Szekszárdi Kadarka: ruby in colour and lovable, if a bit harsh
Tokaj-hegyalia: region producing outstanding quality wine and classic grapes. Sweetness in Tokaji wine is measured in *puttonyos*. The higher the number the sweeter the wine
  Tokaji Furmint: classic Tokaji grape
  Tokaji Szamarodni: dry Tokaji
  Tokaji aszú: dessert wine
Villány-Siklós southern wine centre
  Villányi Kadarka: very strong red, inclined to be pale
  Villányi Burgundi: first-rate red

Useful words

Baracklikor a sweet apricot liqueur
Barackpálinka a dry apricot spirit
Bárány lamb
Bor wine
Csirke chicken
Cukor sugar
Étlap menu
Hus meat
Káve coffee
Kenyér bread
Maj liver
Marha hus beef

Paprika probably introduced by the Turks—a generic word for all types of vegetable peppers, both fresh and the dry powders
Rizsa rice
Sajt cheese
Sonka ham
Sör beer
Számla bill
Tea tea
Tej milk
Vadas game
Vaj butter
Viz water

Isten éltessen! egeszsegedre! cheers!
Jó étvágyot kivánok! bon appétit!

Poland

Polish food, half a century or more ago, was known for its grandeur. With the exception of a few dishes like the *bigos* hunting stew, its reputation was based on the work of haughty chefs, often French, who worked for the aristocracy.

What you may find today in Poland is the traditional peasant food which the grandees scorned. It is not wildly exciting, but there are considerable delights—like *barszcz* and its summer equivalent, *chłodnik*, excellent carp and pike dishes, glorious sausages and beautiful mushrooms, superb breads and cakes. As befits the country which has provided us with a Pope, much of its food is affected by religious considerations—the suckling pig served at Easter, the herrings for fast days, the special cakes for feast days.

As for drink, there is nothing to touch Polish vodka. My own favourite is the one flavoured with mountain ash berries, but they are all worth trying. The Poles like mead, even flavoured with strawberries. I think it is revolting and would advise you to stick to beer or imported wine.

Polish alphabetical order is as follows: a, ą, b, c, ć, d, e, ę, f, g, h, i, j, k, l, ł, m, n, ń, o, ó, p, r, s, ś, t, u, w, y, z, ź, ż

Babka literally "grandmother"; a rounded pastry

★**Barszcz** a famous soup, always served on Christmas Eve (when it is meatless) and at Easter. It is based on meat or fish, vegetable stock, dried boletus mushrooms and fresh beets. *Kwas* is added to taste, as well as garlic crushed with salt and sugar

Befsztyk tatarski steak tartare

★ **Bigos** this national dish used to be a favourite during hunting expeditions. It is a stew with a sauerkraut base, with sausages, bacon, dried mushrooms, red wine and any meat, usually venison. It may contain fresh white cabbage

Bliny fried buckwheat pancakes served with butter or sour cream

Botwina summer soup of young beets, including leaves and stalks, veal stock, vegetables, lemon, cream, béchamel sauce and *kwas*. Served with finely chopped beets, hard-boiled eggs, dill, parsley and chives

Buraki cooked, grated beets with cooking apples, béchamel sauce and cream. Served hot

Chłodnik a delicious cold summer *barszcz* of beets, cucumbers, scallions, radishes and dill in sour cream, lemon, beet juice and vinegar

Ciastka drożdżowe tea brioches

Comber sarni saddle of venison

Cwikła grated boiled beets with added sugar, salt, horseradish, caraway seeds and lemon juice

Flaki po polsku cooked tripe slices mixed with cooked vegetables and simmered in stock. Sprinkled with cheese and breadcrumbs

Galareta z nóżek cielecych calf's feet in aspic

Golonko hand of pork cooked in water with vegetables. Served with puréed peas or horseradish and malt vinegar

Gołąbki "little squab": cabbage rolls stuffed with pork, rice and onion and baked

Kalafior z masłem cauliflower with butter and breadcrumbs

★ **Kapuśniak** pork and pork ribs simmered in stock with smoked sausage, vegetables, including onion and sauerkraut, dill and caraway seeds

Karp po żydowsku literally "in the Jewish fashion"; carp cooked in water with vegetables and served cold in aspic

w szarym sosie carp simmered in vegetable stock and wine, served in a grey sauce. See *Szary sos*

Kasza gryczana buckwheat groats

Kisiel fruit-jelly dessert

Kluski śląskie noodles made from potatoes, eggs and potato flour

Knedle z wiśniami dumplings stuffed with cherries

Kotlet schabowy pork chop egg-and-breadcrumbed and fried

Kotlety mielone hamburger steak

Krem whipped cream dessert

Krupnik beef, vegetable and barley soup with sour cream. Also means a hot honey liqueur

Kurczęta nadziewane chicken stuffed with bread, butter, egg and dill and roasted

Lane ciasto thin egg and flour noodles boiled in soup

Łazanki small squares of dough boiled in water and served with fried bacon and grated cheese

Makownik poppy-seed roll

Mazurek very thin, rich, short pastry covered with dates, white raisins, nuts, jam, etc., baked and covered in icing sugar

Mizeria cucumbers in a sour cream and dill sauce

Móżdżek cielęcy calf's brains

Nerki cielęce duszone w winie calf's kidneys stewed in wine

Ozór wołowy w szarym sosie cold ox-tongue sliced and served in hot *szary sos*

★ **Paczki** rum doughnuts filled with rose jam

Paprika nadziewana sweet peppers stuffed with ground meat, rice and onions and baked in the oven

Pieczeń huzarska stewed joint of beef, braised in the oven with an onion, egg and bread stuffing

Piernik honey cake and spices

★ **Pierogi leniwe** cottage cheese, egg and flour dumplings

   ruskie ravioli stuffed with cheese, potatoes and onions

   z miesem meat ravioli

Placki ziemniaczane grated potato fritters

Polędwica wołowa z rusztu grilled sirloin of beef served with dill and horseradish

Schab pieczony roast loin of pork studded with cloves and served with onions

Sernik cream cheese cake with white raisins

Śledź w oliwie herring in oil

Szary sos a sweet-sour grey sauce with spices, honey cake, sugar, lemon juice, almonds, white raisins, wine and stock

★ **Sztuka mięsa zapiekana** boiled beef and vegetables covered with a thick horseradish sauce

Tort makowy poppy-seed cake

Uszka "little ears"—tiny parcels of dough filled with mushrooms, onions and breadcrumbs and boiled

Włoszczyzna any vegetable which can be boiled in water

Zraziki w sosie veal steaks fried in a caper sauce with cream and lemon juice

★ **Zrazy** thin beef, veal or lamb escalopes, fried, then simmered in a sauce of onions and mushrooms

Zupa grzybowa mushroom soup

Useful words

Bryndza ewe's milk cheese

Chleb bread

Chrzan horseradish

Cielęcina veal

Cukier sugar

Dziczyzna game

Geś goose

Grzyby mushrooms

Herbata tea

Jajko egg

Kaczka duck

Kawa coffee

Kurczę chicken

Kwas sour beet juice ferment

Masło butter

Mięso meat

Mleko milk

Or karta menu

Owoce fruit

Piwo beer

Rachunek bill

Ryba fish

Ryż rice

Ser cheese

Szczupak pike

Szynka ham

Śmietana cream

Wątroba liver

Wieprzowina pork

Wino wine

Woda water

Wołowina beef

Sto lat! Na zdrowie! cheers!
Smacznego! bon appétit!

Romania

The Romanians are, despite Dracula, probably a jollier lot than the Bulgarians, although they both suffered equally from some five hundred years of Turkish domination.

As far as food goes, Romania certainly has the edge over Bulgaria, perhaps because of its closer contact with Hungary. Indeed Transylvania was a part of the Austro-Hungarian empire and Romania has therefore literally drawn nourishment from both directions—east and west.

Romanian wine is light and fresh, though often inclined to be too sweet for our taste. The names to look for are *Tirnave*. *Cotnari* (a little like a bright *Tokaj*), *Fetească*, *Babească*, *Focsani* and *Murfatlar* (though this is very sweet).

Romanian alphabetical order is: a, ă, b, c, d, e, f, g, h, i, î, j, k, l, m, n, o, p, q, r, s, ş, t, ţ, u, v, w, x, y, z

Ardei copt românesc peeled green peppers, served cold with a sauce of vinegar, olive oil, garlic and a little red paprika

    umplut cu carne green peppers stuffed with pork, veal, rice and egg and baked in tomato sauce

Biftec la grătar grilled beef steak

Budincă de ficat liver pudding

★**Carne de miel** baby lamb roasted in the oven with wine and herbs

    de vacă prăjită roast beef

    de viţel stil ţărănesc veal "peasant style": cubes of veal fried with a lot of onions and chillis, then simmered in stock

★**Ciorbă** sour soup, traditionally made with the soured fermented juice of wheat bran

    de burtă sour soup of tripe, egg, cream and vegetables

    de perişoare a sour soup with veal and pork meat balls, vegetables, sour cream, egg yolks and dill

Cotlete de porc la gratar grilled pork chops

★**Crap marinat** pieces of carp cooked with oil, celery, parsley, wine and vinegar, then left to marinate for several days

    umplut whole carp stuffed with chopped olives, fennel, parsley, garlic, lemon and oil, baked

Creeri de viţel fripţi veal brains egg-and-breadcrumbed and fried

Ficat de pui cu ceapă chicken livers simmered with onions and parsley in white wine

Ficat de viţel umplut calf's liver stuffed with bacon, onion, egg and breadcrumbs, stewed

Foi lica cu cremă de ciocolată chocolate layer cake

Frigărui mixed grill of various cuts of pork, liver, kidneys, onions, mushrooms and tomatoes

Fursecuri small biscuits made with walnuts and chocolate

Găscă prăjită roast goose

★**Ghiveci (cu zarzavaturi)** this vegetable stew is one of Romania's national dishes—a colourful affair of various mixed vegetables baked in the oven with oil and stock. Can also be made with additional fish or meat

Grătar amestecat an enormous mixed grill of various cuts of pork, liver, kidneys, brains, etc., and *mititei*

Limbă de vacă afumata smoked beef tongue, served usually with a sauce of tomatoes, onions, oil and olives, hot or cold

Mămăligă (de aur) the national Romanian staple, eaten in a variety of ways. It is a cornmeal mush which thickens as it cools

★**Mititei** homemade beef sausages, grilled

Musaca cu pătlăgele vinete a traditional dish of a layer of ground pork and veal, onions and rice, alternating with layers of fried eggplants and tomatoes, baked

★**Pastramă** smoked, salted mutton, grilled and served with *mămăligă*

Pâtlăgele vinete tocate eggplant and oil paste

Perişoare de carne amestecată small fried pork and veal meat balls. Served as an hors d'oeuvre

Peste fript în hîrtie small fish grilled in greaseproof paper over an open fire

Plăcinta cu carne tocată thin strudel pastry stuffed with a ground-meat filling and baked

Pui gătit tărăneste "peasant style" chicken casseroled with onions, chilli and sour cream

Pui prăjit la tavă casseroled chicken, with a cream and dill sauce

Purcel mic la grătar roast suckling pig

Rață ăla Romania casseroled duck baked in the oven with sauerkraut

Salată de cartofi potato salad with onions, oil and vinegar

Sarmale (Varză umplută cu carne) small cabbage rolls stuffed with ground meat, onions and rice, on a bed of sauerkraut, baked

Șatou delicious custard with lemon and white wine

Scrumbie marinată marinated herring served as an hors d'oeuvre

Supă de cartofi potato soup with vegetables, bacon, egg yolk, sour cream and dill

Tocană de carne de oaie lamb stew with garlic

de carne de vacă beef stew, served with dumplings

ciobanului cu varză a stew of sauerkraut, onions, pork ribs, with sour cream and dill, served with *mămăligă*

de porc cubes of pork stewed with onions, wine and tomatoes

de pui cu tarhon chicken stew with wine and tarragon

de vițel cubes of veal stewed with garlic, onions and sour cream

Torta cu ciocolată chocolate cake made with quantities of egg yolks

cu nuci walnut cake

★ **Vacă prăjită ăla Bucuresti** roast beef basted during cooking with stock and cream. Cream and lemon are added to the juices

Varză ăla Cluj a Transylvanian dish, consisting of layers of sauerkraut, rice and onions, ground pork, beef and ham, with sour cream poured over each layer. Covered with cream and dill and simmered slowly

Vinete cu carne eggplants stuffed with onions, garlic, eggplant pulp and ground meat and baked, covered with tomatoes

Useful words

Apă water		**Notă de plată** bill	
Bere beer		**Orez** rice	
Brînză white goat cheese		**Ouă** eggs	
Cafea coffee		**Pîine** bread	
Carne meat		**Suncă** ham	
Ceai tea		**Tuică** plum brandy	
Clătite sweet pancakes		**Unt** butter	
Galuște, gogoase dumplings		**Vin** wine	
Lapte milk		**Zahar** sugar	

Noroc! cheers!
Poftă bună! bon appétit!

Yugoslavia

When one speaks of Yugoslavia one is really talking of six Socialist republics—Bosnia-Hercegovina, Croatia (including Dalmatia), Macedonia, Montenegro, Serbia (including two autonomous provinces of Vojvodina and Kosovo) and Slovenia. Owing to the numerous conquerors—Slav, Austrian, Venetian, Turkish, French—who have occupied different parts of the country at different times, each area has its distinctive style of cooking. I have therefore noted in brackets, after each dish, the region it comes from (i.e. Bos., Cro., Dal., Kos., Mac., Mont., Serb., Slov. and Voj.). The general language of the country is Serbo-Croat and I have used this throughout, rather than plunging into Macedonian, Slovenian, or even Albanian for much of Kosovo. Wherever regional variations in Serbo-Croat are very marked, I have given alternatives.

Both the Roman and Cyrillic alphabet are used in Yugoslavia. I have used the Roman alphabet here. The order is: a, b, c, č, ć, d, dž, dj, e, f, g, h, i, j, k, l, lj, m, n, nj, o, p, r, s, š, t, u, v, z, ž

★ **Alaska čorba** (Serb.) this famous "fishermen's soup" is made all along the Danube. It contains chunks of white fish and is thickened with egg and lemon

Bakalar na mornarski način (Dal.) pounded smoked cod brought to the boil and then shaken up with oil, stock, parsley and garlic

Barbun u pergamentu (Dal.) red mullet barbecued in greaseproof paper

Bečka šnicla veal cutlet egg-and-breadcrumbed and fried

Bosanska kalja od kupusa (Bos.) mutton or pork stew with cabbage

Bosanske ćufte (Bos.) ground meat balls baked with an egg, yoghurt and caraway seed sauce

Bosanski lonac (Bos.) cubes of meat, bacon, vegetables, vinegar and white wine stewed together

Brodet na dalmatinski način (Dal.) fish stew, often made with mackerel, onions, tomatoes and wine. Served with rice

Crni risoto black rice dish made with squid and its ink sac

Crvene paprike sa suvim mesom i jajima (Mac.) a very hot dish. Smoked spare ribs and chilli peppers first stewed, then chopped, mixed with oil and beaten eggs, and baked

★ **Čevapčići** (Serb.) grilled meat balls, a popular Yugoslav snack. Served with finely chopped onions or chillis

Čulbastije (Serb.) grilled pork cutlets

Djuveč (Serb.) an expansive casserole of many vegetables, cubes of mixed meats, and rice

Flekice s kupusom (Voj.) boiled noodles mixed with sautéed, shredded cabbage

Gibanica (Serb.) cheese and paper-thin pastry slices, *kajmak* and eggs

★ **Istarske fritule** a popular Istrian dessert. Spicy fritters made with white wine and liqueur

Jabuke u rumu (Slov.) whole apples stewed in rum and sugar

Jagnjeća sarma u maramici (Serb) ground lamb, lamb's liver. heart, etc., rolled up in lamb's intestines and baked

Lički kupus (Cro.) layers of sauerkraut and smoked pork, casseroled, with boiled potatoes

Medenjaci (Mont.) honey cakes

Mešano meso mixed grill

Ohridska jegulja pečena na pepelu (Mac.) eel from Lake Ohrid, baked in hot embers

Palačinke (Serb.) pancakes. The best are honey and walnuts or cream cheese with raisins

Paprikaš od suvog ovčeg mesa (Mont.) smoked mutton stew with bacon, cabbage and vegetables

Paprike sa sirom (Serb.) green peppers stuffed with eggs and ewe's milk cheese, sprinkled with *kajmak* and baked

Pečena divlja plovka (Voj.) roast wild duck

Pečenje od srnećeg buta (Voj.) roast haunch of venison

Pečeno prase roast suckling pig

Pijani šaran iz skadarskog jezera (Mont.) carp from Lake Skadar, baked with wine and garlic

Pileći paprikaš sa noklicama (Voj.) chicken stew with egg dumplings

Pile se jufkom (Kos.) pieces of cooked chicken and tiny bits of *jufka* pastry (made from flour, eggs and milk) baked in the oven with onions, parsley and paprika

Pljeskavice (Serb.) grilled ground pork and veal rissoles

Plučica na kiselo (Cro.) chopped calf's lung and vegetable soup, served with yoghurt and lemon

Podvarak (Serb.) chopped sour cabbage baked with a whole duckling and pork chops

Pogača (Serb.) hot bread, sometimes filled with *kajmak*

Pohovan file od smudja (Voj.) perch fillets dipped in egg and fried

Potica nadevena orasima (Slov.) kind of swiss roll with a rich butter cream and walnut filling

Punjene paprike-babure (Serb.) baked green peppers stuffed with onion, rice and ground meat

Punjeni plavi patlidžani (Mac.) eggplants stuffed with onions, tomato, green peppers, rice and eggplant pulp and baked

Ražnjiči (Serb.) veal or pork kebabs

Riblja čorba fish soup

Ričet (Cro.) a stew of white beans, smoked pork ribs and oat flakes

Sarma od kiselog kupusa (Serb.) small rolls of sour cabbage leaves stuffed with meat, onions and rice, layered alternately with smoked pork ribs and stewed slowly

Skuše kuvane (Dal.) boiled mackerel served cold with a sauce made from sardines, onion, parsley, oil and vinegar

Sogan-dolma (Bos.) stuffed onions

Srpski ajvar (Serb.) side salad of baked eggplants and green peppers, puréed and beaten with oil and lemon juice

Šiš-čevap (Bos.) skewers of cubed beef or lamb, green peppers, onions, tomatoes and potatoes, fried

Štajerska kisela čorba (Slov.) soup of pig's feet and tails with vegetables. Vinegar is added to taste before serving

Tarator od krastavaca (Mac.) cucumber and yoghurt salad

Tavče (Mac.) a casserole of white beans, onions and chilli peppers

Zeljanica (Serb., Bos.) spinach pastry. See *Gibanica*

Yugoslav wines

Čviček (Slov.) a pale red

Dingač (Dal.) a heavy sweet red

Fruškogorski biser (Voj.) white, sometimes sparkling

Grk strong white, sherry-like

Lutomer full-flavoured Riesling

Posip (Dal.) a good white wine

Postup (Dal.) a full-bodied red

Prokupac (Serb.) full-bodied red

Prošek (Dal.) dessert

Ruzica dark rosé

Traminac (Slov., Voj.) white

Vranac (Mont.) red

Žilavka (Bos.) dry white

Useful words

Cenovnik, jelovnik menu

Čaj tea

Govedina beef

Hleb (Serb.) bread

Hren horseradish

Jaja eggs

Kačkavalj hard cheese, usually made from ewe's milk

Kafa coffee

Kajmak (Serb.) salty, sour cream cheese

Kruh (Cro.) bread

Kunić rabbit

Malinovac raspberry liqueur

Meso meat

Mleko milk

Patka (Serb.) wild duck

Piletina chicken

Pirinač rice

Pivo beer

Plovka (Cro.) wild duck

Puter butter

Račun bill

Riba fish

Salata salad

Sir cheese

Supa (Serb.) soup

Šaran carp

Šećer sugar

Šljivovica plum brandy

Teletina veal

Vino wine

Voće fruit

Voda water

Prijatno! bon appétit!
Živeli! cheers!

Egypt — *See* Arab food
Finland — *See* Scandinavia

France

ENGLISH CHANNEL

Cherbourg

LE HAVRE
ROUEN
Bayeux
Deauville
Caen

Dieppe

Boulogne

Cal

NORMANDY

Brest

St Malo

Chartres

BRITTANY

Rennes

MAINE
Le Mans

Loire
Angers

St Nazaire
Nantes
ANJOU
Tours

TOURAINE

POITOU
Poitiers

MARC

La Rochelle

ANGOUMOIS
Lim

Cognac

LIMOUSI

Bay of Biscay

MEDOC

Périgueux

Dordogne

BORDEAUX
GUYENNE

LANDES

Garonne

GASCONY
TOULOUSE

Biarritz
Bayonne

BEARN
Pau

Lourdes

Pyrenees

SPAIN

ANDORR

There is no single reason why France has the best food in the world. Much of it is due to her geographical position, giving her a greater variety of produce than any other country. Political accident has played its part, sustaining her in an industrial age, yet keeping her, so much longer than Britain for instance, a rural nation. Then temperament must have its share of the credit.

52

However many causes one adduces, the fact is that France is the only Western country where cooking, and indeed eating, is an art.

French cooking, based though it may be on a long tradition, combines qualities of energy and imagination. It is a constant search for perfection, reflecting the changes of human behaviour and the immutability of human nature.

53

Of course it has its ups and downs. Escoffier, the great chef of the turn of the century, for all that he did in the way of improving the lives of chefs and sorting out much of the confusion which had overcome nineteenth-century cuisine, went too far in codifying the methods of cookery. He had rather the effect that Henry Irving must have had on the acting profession.

It is only since the war that the strait-jacket he put on cooking has been broken out of, so that now we are seeing a revolution in French food which matches the changes in every other sphere of life.

There is much talk of the *nouvelle cuisine* and, in one sense, it is a reality. Food is lighter, there is more concentration on the taste of the ingredients, their freshness and quality. Never, in fact, has produce been so good. At the same time *nouvelle cuisine* is something of an illusion. There is no new food, there are no new methods, no new implements. All that is happening is that the art of cooking is living, searching and responding to our needs.

The chefs whose names have become as well known in France as those of film or pop stars—Bocuse, Vergé, Guérard, etc.—are great practitioners, but practitioners in a direct line of inheritance from all the other famous names of French cuisine over the centuries.

This might be the point to clear up another confusion. *Cuisine minceur*, invented by Guérard, is not a new style of cooking. It is simply a slimmer's diet made somewhat more palatable. It is true that some of the dodges he devised to eliminate fattening things from his weight-watchers' dishes could have a general application in the lightening of food, but mostly it is drab stuff and was never intended to be anything other than less drab than plain steak and shredded carrots. It will not find a place in this book. Nor will Complan.

All that said, I am conscious that the listings of French dishes err on the side of the conventional. This is deliberate. The range of French food is so vast that I have thought it best to concentrate on the classic dishes which will survive almost whatever happens. The young chefs experiment, but they do so within a framework which varies very slowly. The truffles which seemed to cover every great dish fifty years ago may have gone but the basic principles are always there, settled some 150 years ago by Carême, the greatest French chef of all.

Where to eat

This is largely a matter of how much you want to spend, but the question is made easier by the custom of restaurants posting their menus outside their premises. What we call a menu the French call *la carte*, whereas a *menu* is a fixed price meal. Often the notice outside will refer to three *menus* at varying prices, which usually include half a carafe of wine. Very often, when you get inside, you will find that the cheapest one (which lured you in) is only served on some days, or before 12.30, or some such device. If you pick and choose off the *carte*, the meal will be much more expensive. A *brasserie* has the great charm of allowing you to eat only one dish. In some sleepier provincial towns, in small commercial hotels, you may still find the real *table d'hôte* where, for a very modest sum, you will eat whatever the family are eating.

Meals

Petit déjeuner (breakfast): a modest business in France with coffee, croissants, butter and jam (they are coming round a bit to marmalade or black cherry, but it is usually the eternal apricot). When ordering this, ask for *café complet*.

Déjeuner (lunch): the French manage two huge meals a day.

Dîner (dinner): a serious business, though it must be said that although French manners are more formal than ours they are more easy-going about clothes than we are. You see people in flak jackets in the smartest restaurants.

The menu

This is quite simply laid out. Usually the *menus* will be on a separate card, offering a choice of only two things by way of a starter, main course and cheese for the cheapest, and probably three starters and main courses plus cheese and sweets for the more expensive. The *carte* will be divided into *hors d'œuvre, potages, poissons, volaille, viandes, gibier, légumes, fromages* (which are eaten before the puddings) and *entremets* (sweets and puddings). There may be *entrées*, which strictly means dishes served before the roast, but has come to mean the main course. In most restaurants there will be a *plat du jour* (dish of the day), which is often the best thing to eat, because it will be made from ingredients fresh that morning. In smarter restaurants there may be *spécialités de la maison*, which are what the chef thinks he does well.

Hors d'œuvre

Artichauts à la vinaigrette artichokes with an oil and vinegar dressing. Served cold

Asperges froides en buisson cold asparagus rolled in slices of ham, coated with jellied mayonnaise and decorated with spinach juice

Avocat Fermont halves of hot avocado filled with a poached egg, served with a *sauce béarnaise*

Beignets de laitances fritters of poached soft roe

   soufflés à la hongroise onion fritters

Bœuf en salade boiled beef salad

Bouchées aux truffes truffles simmered in Madeira, baked in small patty cases

Boulettes de viande small meat balls, fried

Boutargue see *Poutargue*

★ **Cèpes marinés** boletus mushrooms marinated in oil, garlic, herbs and spices and chilled for a few days. They have a wonderful spongy taste

Chou-fleur pimprenelle marinated cooked cauliflower served in a mustard and cream sauce

Choux au fromage cheese puffs

Cœurs de palmier palm hearts. These appear very frequently on French menus and can be served hot with various sauces or cold with a *sauce vinaigrette*

Confit d'oie preserved goose

Coquilles Saint-Jacques see *Fish and shellfish*

Cou d'oie farci goose neck stuffed with sausagemeat, goose flesh, *foie-gras* and truffles, cooked in a vast quantity of goose fat

Crabe froid à l'anglaise dressed crab

Croque-Monsieur hot toasted cheese and ham sandwich

Croquettes de volaille diced chicken, ham, truffles and mushrooms mixed with egg yolks and a *velouté* sauce, made into croquettes, egg-and-breadcrumbed and fried in oil

Croustade bressane pastry mould filled with a mixture of chicken breasts, truffles and mushrooms in a cream sauce flavoured with Madeira or port

Croûte landaise fried bread with a slice of *foie-gras* covered with *sauce Mornay* and baked

Croûte savoyarde slice of ham on a layer of puffed pastry, covered with a cheese sauce and grilled

Crudités a selection of raw sliced vegetables, often accompanied by a *sauce vinaigrette*

Cuisses de grenouilles frites frogs' legs egg-and-breadcrumbed and sautéed

Escabèche de sardines fried sardines marinated in a stock of onion, carrot, green pepper, wine, thyme and parsley, served chilled

★**Escargots à la bourguignonne** snails cooked in wine, replaced in their shells and returned to the oven with a mixture of butter, garlic, shallots, parsley and breadcrumbs

Fonds d'artichauts à la grecque artichoke hearts simmered with carrots and onions in wine and olive oil. Served chilled

★**Fromage de tête** literally "head cheese", a cold dish of pig's head, pork and veal shoulder, pork rind and tongue, first simmered and then baked with spices

Galantine boned poultry, meat or even fish, chopped up, pressed together with a stuffing to make a loaf or in the case of chicken, which was the original *galantine*, sewn up in its own skin. Usually coated in aspic. Served cold

★**Gâteau de foies blonds de poulardes de Bresse au coulis de queues d'écrevisses** very fine mousse of chicken livers with a crayfish tail sauce. It is pale, a little bitter and quite wonderfully delicate

Grenouilles frogs. See *Cuisses de grenouilles* and *Nymphes à l'aurore*

Mosaïque de légumes alternating layers of carrots, string beans, peas and artichokes, bound with a ham mousse

Mouclade steamed mussels served with a garlic, lemon and egg sauce

Moules marinière see *Fish and shellfish*

★**Nymphes à l'aurore** frogs' legs poached in white wine, then covered in a pink *sauce chaud-froid* and served with an aspic jelly. Sprinkled with tarragon

Oeil d'anchois raw egg yolk surrounded by circles of anchovy and minced onions

Paillettes aux anchois pastry straws covered with anchovy

Pâté everyone knows what a pâté is, but properly speaking if it is to be called a pâté, the mixture of meat, fish, poultry or their livers should be baked in a pastry case

Guillaume Tirel smooth-fleshed fish ground up and mixed with egg whites and cream to make a fluffy stuffing. Spread on pork fat in a mould, covered with fillets of John Dory and a layer of egg, tarragon, parsley, chives and cream paste, and then with a layer of asparagus. The whole process is repeated, ending with a layer of pork fat, and the pâté baked

Pieds de porc panés cooked pig's feet, egg-and-breadcrumbed and baked. Served with *sauce hollandaise*

Pissaladière French version of pizza without the cheese

Poutargue dried grey mullet roe, served in a *sauce vinaigrette*

Quiche lorraine open tart of creamy egg custard and strips of bacon. Modern practice allows a small amount of Gruyère

Ramequins au fromage tiny cheese flans

Ratatouille to my mind a nasty oily mush of onions, red peppers, tomatoes, zucchini, eggplants and garlic, simmered together, in which the merit of each is lost

Rillauds, rillons see *Rillettes*

Rillettes d'oie a potted mixture of goose and pork. *Rillettes* are sometimes made simply with pork

Rissoles deep-fried puff pastry turnovers or pies

Rôties galloises Welsh rarebit. See *Great Britain* (*Snacks*)

Salade salad. The French will make a salad from anything ranging from some unexpected weed plucked from a hillside to an elaborate combination of fish, meat and vegetables

   brésilienne rice and pineapple salad in a dressing of fresh cream and lemon juice

   Café de Paris lettuce and sliced cooked chicken in a light *sauce mayonnaise*, with anchovies, olives and hard-boiled eggs

   catalane rice, onions and sweet peppers with anchovies in a *sauce vinaigrette*

demi-deuil potato and truffle, served with a mustard sauce

des midinettes rice and green peas in a *sauce vinaigrette* with added chervil and tarragon

monégasque poached *nonats* (see *Fish*) and tomatoes on rice

niçoise jumble which may contain anything but nearly always includes tomatoes, onion, anchovies, olives, beans, rice or potatoes, tuna fish and herbs

Otero red pepper, tomato, anchovy and onions in a mustard *sauce vinaigrette*

quimperloise white fish fillets, shrimp, crab, hard-boiled eggs, capers and herbs in tomato-flavoured mayonnaise

Réjane rice, cucumber and sliced chicken breast in a *sauce vinaigrette*

riche modern salad of *foie-gras* lightly sautéed, served with spinach leaves in an oil and vinegar dressing

russe there are many variations, but it is usually a mixture of cooked beans, turnip, potato and raw carrots, cucumber, celery and mushrooms, all cut up small. Coated with mayonnaise

Saucisson chaud à la lyonnaise hot salad of poached sausage with potatoes

Soufflé d'écrevisses Léopold de Rothschild crayfish butter, crayfish slices, asparagus tips and black truffles in a soufflé

de jambon Alexandra ham, cheese and truffle soufflé, alternating with buttered asparagus tips

Tarte aux oignons onion tart

Terrine a terrine is an earthenware dish, usually oblong in shape and deep. It has come to mean the food which is cooked in it, that is to say, a loaf of chopped meat or fish or poultry or their livers, mixed with finely minced vegetables, a little pork fat, spices and herbs. It is usually flavoured with wine or brandy. Baked and served cold

Thon à l'huile tuna fish in olive oil, garnished with lettuce and hard-boiled eggs

Tomatoes à l'antiboise tomatoes stuffed with tuna fish, capers, egg mayonnaise and herbs

Tourte des gastronomes sweetbread and mushroom pie served with a Madeira sauce

★ **Truffe sous la cendre** whole truffle wrapped in layers and layers of paper (usually six), laid in a *terrine* and cooked in hot ashes. When the last layer of paper is burned, the truffle is cooked

Truites tyroliennes trout fried, marinated in tomato sauce

Potages—Soups

Soups of all kinds will be found on the menu under the heading *potages*. The different terms for soups are used pretty loosely. A *consommé* is always a clear broth. A *potage* was originally a big affair with meat and vegetables, but now means almost any kind of thick soup (though to confuse, you can have a *potage clair*). A *soupe* is again thick, usually rustic and often poured over bread.

Bisque shellfish soup of one sort or another. *Bisque de homard* (lobster) is the best, using the lobster shells ground up

★ **Bouillabaisse** the inspired jumble that is *bouillabaisse* would take three pages to describe. The essentials are that the fish—*rascasse, Saint-Pierre, lotte, vive* or any others—should be absolutely fresh, that the fish stock should be the best, made with no pepper, salt or spices, and that great care should be taken that no herb predominates. Lobsters, eels and leeks are imperative, as is the saffron. After that almost any variation is permissible. An honest, middle-ranking restaurant in or near Marseilles is the place to try it

Bourride a Provençal soup of mixed fish flavoured with *aïoli*. It has no shellfish

Consommé clarified broth

Borghèse chicken consommé with asparagus tips and strips of chicken breast

brunoise consommé with carrots, leeks, turnips and celery

Célestine consommé with pancake, parsley and chervil

Colbert the same as *printanier*, with a poached egg in it

double very strong consommé, flavoured with sherry or Madeira

en gelée jellied consommé

julienne consommé with matchstick slices of vegetables

madrilène an enriched consommé with tomatoes

printanier chicken consommé with finely chopped vegetables

à la royale consommé with tapioca and *royale*

de volaille chicken consommé. Properly speaking this is made with one whole chicken and the carcase of another; the sort of extravagance none but the French could quite bear

Cotriade de maquereaux mackerel, leek and mushroom soup

Crème cream soup

Agnès Sorel chicken and mushroom soup, with tongue

d'Argenteuil cream of asparagus soup

Fontanges cream of green pea soup with sorrel

Germiny rich consommé, with egg yolks and sorrel

à la reine thickened chicken consommé, served with diced chicken and fried croûtons

à la soissonnaise white haricot bean soup

Croûte-au-pot consommé with vegetables from a *pot-au-feu*

Ferrecapienne a fish soup made somewhat on the lines of a *bouillabaisse*, the fish being marinated in thyme, lemon and oil, but made with only one fish

Garbure béarnaise a very thick soup of vegetables of all sorts, especially cabbage, cooked with a large piece of ham or pork

Gratinée lyonnaise see *Soupe à l'oignon*

Miques du Périgord dumpling soup, but really more of a stew, with dumplings, sliced bacon and vegetables

Le mourtaïrol a saffron soup from Périgord. It mostly consists of bread, soaked in chicken broth

Ouillat a Pyrenean soup made with tomatoes, onions, garlic and goose fat, poured over bread

Panade bread and milk, thickened with egg yolk

Petite marmite (Henri IV) a chicken, beef and marrow bone are cooked in a consommé with vegetables. This is then strained and served with the chicken meat, the diced beef and some cabbage

Potage crème Saint-Germain usually a purée of fresh green peas, but can be made with dried peas and fresh vegetables

aux abatis giblet soup

à l'ambassadeur pea and sorrel soup thickened with rice

d'Artois white bean and vegetable soup

Bagration may be either a veal soup thickened with macaroni, or a rather good fish soup garnished with *quenelles* and crayfish tails

Balvet green pea soup, with other vegetables

Billy By cream of mussel soup, served hot or cold

à la bonne femme potato, leek and cucumber soup

Condé red haricot bean soup

Conti purée of lentil soup

Crécy carrot soup

Dubarry thick cauliflower soup

fréneuse purée of turnips and potatoes

Jubilé see *Potage Balvet*

mimosa a consommé garnished with minced green beans and sieved yolk of hard-boiled egg

Parmentier potato soup with leeks and cream

Pierre-le-Grand Peter the Great was a huge and hungry man, so I suppose it is reasonable that there are three soups called after him. One is plain mushroom, the next mushroom and grouse, and the last celeriac

Saint-Cloud green pea and lettuce soup

Solférino potato balls in a potato, carrot, leek and tomato soup flavoured with chervil

Potée toulousaine a *potée* is a thick soup usually made with pork and vegetables. This version also includes Toulouse sausages

à l'ail garlic soup

ardennaise endive, leek and potato soup. Poured over bread

auvergnate a thick soup of

pig's head, leeks, carrots, lentils, turnips, potatoes and cabbage

champenoise a huge soup drunk by harvesters in the Champagne region. Made with smoked pork, bacon and vegetables

dieppoise mussel, sole and freshwater fish soup

fermière soup of leeks, cabbage, turnips and potato, poured over bread

au gras-double tripe and vegetable soup poured over bread

limousine au pain de seigle vegetable soup poured over rye bread; the vegetables are separate

ménagère a homely vegetable soup with bacon, poured over bread

nîmoise leek, cabbage and celery soup with barley, flavoured with basil

normande vegetable soup, principally leeks and potatoes

à l'oignon onion soup. One of France's simplest but most excellent dishes. It has pieces of fried bread in it and is sprinkled with cheese and browned under the grill before serving

à l'oseille sorrel soup

paysanne leek, cabbage and potato soup poured over toast

au pistou a crushed paste of garlic, basil and oil (*pistou*) is put in the bowl and a soup of green beans, zucchini and potato poured over it

à la queue de bœuf oxtail soup

savoyarde leek, onion, celery and potato soup, poured over bread

tourangelle chicken, turnip, leek, cabbage and pea soup

aux truffes everyone now copies this truffle soup with *foie-gras* which Paul Bocuse made for President Giscard d'Estaing. It comes in a small bowl, covered with pastry and the moment of breaking it and releasing the aroma of truffles is a delight

Tortue claire real turtle soup

Tourin blanchi garlic soup, flavoured with thyme, poured over slices of bread

à la bordelaise onion soup, with thickened consommé

toulousain garlic soup, made with goose fat and egg

Tourri see *Ouillat*

Velouté aurore tomato and avocado soup

de volaille cream of chicken

Xavier cream of rice with shredded chicken and *royale*

Vichyssoise very creamy cold leek and potato soup

Oeufs—Eggs

Cromesquis d'œufs balls of chopped hard-boiled eggs, truffle, cream and egg yolks fried in batter

Oeufs à l'alsacienne poached eggs in a paprika *sauce chaud-froid*, set on a mousse of *foie-gras* and decorated with sliced truffles and chicken breasts

à l'andalouse poached eggs in a white *sauce chaud-froid* tinged with saffron, set on a chicken mousse, decorated with sliced truffles, all covered in aspic

à la d'Aumale same as *andalouse* but with ham not chicken

Bercy baked eggs with sausages and tomato sauce

Borgia poached eggs on baked tomatoes, covered with *sauce béarnaise*

brouillés scrambled eggs

châtelaine poached eggs on chestnut purée, with veal stock

Cluny baked eggs with chicken croquettes

(en) cocotte à la crème eggs poached in a cocotte with cream

à la coque soft-boiled eggs

à la diable fried eggs with a little mustard and vinegar

durs hard-boiled eggs

frits en aumônière fried eggs and small rounds of fried bread, cheese and ham enclosed in a pouch-shaped pancake. The case resembles a purse for alms

frits Cavour fried eggs on fried tomato halves served with Piedmont *risotto*

en gelée chilled poached eggs in aspic on a ham base

en meurette poached in a sauce of garlic, onion, red wine and chicken consommé, served on fried bread

Meyerber fried eggs with kidneys in a *sauce Périgueux*

Mireille steamed eggs with truffles and cream

au plat, sur le plat fried or baked eggs

pochés poached eggs

pochés bénédictine poached eggs on a creamy cod base, served with a cream sauce. Not to be confused with the Anglo-Saxon *Eggs Benedict*

pochés à la bretonne poached eggs with ham and artichokes

pochés grand-duc poached eggs with truffles and shrimps

pochés Henri IV poached eggs with artichokes

pochés à la d'Orléans tartlets of chicken in a *sauce suprême*, topped with a poached egg

pochés à la reine poached eggs on macaroni covered in a *sauce béchamel* and cheese

à la poêle fried eggs

à la tripe sliced, hard-boiled eggs and onions in a *sauce béchamel*

★ **à la Villeroy** poached eggs coated with a *sauce Villeroy*, rolled in egg and breadcrumbs and deep fried

Omelette if you do not think much of omelettes, you can never have eaten a French one

chasseur with chicken livers, onions and mushrooms

à l'espagnole strictly speaking just with onions although there are many variations

aux fines herbes with chopped parsley, chives, chervil and tarragon

grand'mère with croûtons and chopped parsley

au lard with fried bacon

limousine with bacon, mushrooms, parsley or chervil

lorraine with cream, Gruyère cheese, bacon and herbs

à la ménagère with macaroni or any pasta

mousseline a fluffy omelette

Pipérade a Basque speciality. A mixture of sliced sweet peppers, tomatoes and onions and sometimes ham, cooked until almost puréed, into which mush eggs are scrambled

Soufflé I defy anyone to think of a reasonable description of a soufflé. The French word *souffler* means "to blow" or "to puff"—a soufflé then is an airy affair in which the main taste is merely suggested in a froth of egg yolks, baked so that it rises. There are also cold soufflés, or, even more delightful, *soufflés glacés*—a cross between a soufflé and a cream ice. The best in the world is found in M. Pic's restaurant in Valence. See *Desserts*

Symphonie d'œufs an exercise in eggomania. This is an omelette with chopped hard-boiled eggs and whole poached eggs folded inside it

Poissons et crustacés—Fish and shellfish (see also *Sauces* etc., p.79)

Aiglefin haddock

Alose de l'adour shad stuffed with sorrel leaves and grilled, then baked on a little minced ham and garnished with sorrel leaves

Anchois anchovies

Anguille eel

à la flamande dite "au vert" pieces of eel simmered in white wine with onions, celery and green herbs, served in a sauce of the cooking liquor, egg yolks and cream

Barbeau barbel

Barbillon small barbel

Barbue brill

Baudroie angler fish, monk fish, rock fish, frog fish and assorted

dogfish names

Bigorneaux periwinkles

Blanchailles whitebait or similar, usually deep fried

Bouillabaisse see *Soups*

★ **Brandade de morue** a purée of poached salt cod mixed with oil, milk and garlic until it has the consistency of a purée. This is a Camargue dish and there they regard the addition of mashed potatoes as a miserly cheat

Brème porgy

Brochet pike. See *Quenelles de brochet*

à l'orléanaise baked pike served with a vinegar and shallot sauce

Cabillaud à la ménagère cod baked with new potatoes and onions, sprinkled with parsley

Capoum scorpion fish

Carpe à la juive a cold dish of carp in a jellied white wine sauce

  farcie à l'ancienne carp larded with salt pork and strips of truffle, stuffed with a mixture of pounded whiting, breadcrumbs, roe, brandy, butter, eggs and cream, baked in cheesecloth

Carrelet flounder or dab, usually filleted and fried

Colin hake

Congre conger eel

Coques cockles

Coquilles d'écrevisses cardinal scallop shells filled with *sauce béchamel*, shrimp butter, crayfish and sliced truffles. Sprinkled with cheese and grilled

Coquilles Saint-Jacques scallops, usually cooked in wine, lemon juice and butter with sliced mushrooms

  ★**Saint-Jacques havraise** sautéed in butter with chopped shallots and garnished with shrimp in a white wine, vermouth and cream sauce

  Saint-Jacques landaise sautéed with pine nuts, served with a little parsley and vinegar

★**Coulibiac de saumon** salmon sautéed with onion and mushrooms (and, traditionally, spinal cord of sturgeon), baked in pastry. Perfectly delicious

Crabe crab

Crevettes shrimps

  grises small shrimps

  roses large shrimps

Darne de saumon salmon steak

Daurade *or* **dorade** porgy

Écrevisses à la bordelaise crayfish sautéed with vegetables, herbs, brandy and wine

  en buisson literally "in a bush"; crayfish cooked in a *court-bouillon*, then hooked by their tails on to the appropriate dish and garnished with parsley

Éperlans smelts, generally fried

Escalope de saumon à l'oseille des frères Troisgros thin salmon escalopes quickly fried and served with a sorrel, stock, white wine, shallot and cream sauce

Escargots snails

Espadon swordfish

Esturgeon sturgeon. Rarely found

Filets de sole cardinal fillets of sole spread with a whiting forcemeat and poached, then served on croûtons, garnished with lobster tails and covered with *sauce béchamel*

  de sole châtelaine sautéed and served on a mixture of cooked macaroni, Parmesan cheese and sliced truffle with *sauce béchamel*

  de sole Doria fried in butter with lightly cooked cucumber

  de sole homardine poached sole served with a *sauce à l'américaine* (see *Homard*), lobster meat, cream and *sauce hollandaise*

  ★**de sole Marguery** basically, poached fillets of sole with cooked mussels and shrimps in a white wine sauce

  de sole Orly fried in batter, served with tomato sauce

  de sole en paupiettes rolled up with forcemeat, sometimes with truffles, and poached

  de sole Véronique poached, garnished with Muscat grapes, covered in a white wine sauce

  de sole Walewska poached and surrounded by sliced truffle and shrimp, with a *sauce Mornay*

Flétan halibut

Fruits de mer small shellfish

Goujonnettes from the word *goujon* (gudgeon, a tiny freshwater fish). Fillets of flat fish cut into *juliennes*, floured and deep fried

★**Gratin de queues d'écrevisses Fernand Point** one of the great dishes of the *nouvelle cuisine*. Crayfish shells are crushed and made into a sauce with onions, carrots, brandy, white wine, tomato purée, tarragon and cayenne pepper. The tails and claws are cooked in a little butter with brandy, cream and truffles and combined with the preceding sauce and a *sauce hollandaise*. The crayfish are then mixed in and the whole dish is lightly grilled

Grenouilles frogs. See *Hors d'œuvre*

Grondin gurnard

Harengs herrings

Homard lobster

  à l'américaine *or* **à l'armoricaine** there has been a long-running dispute as to the name of this dish, some maintaining that it was

invented in Brittany (Armorica),
others that it was called American
for varying reasons. Curnonsky
settled the matter by declaring
that it was invented in 1870 by
a chef called Fraisse who
produced it in an emergency for
some latecomers. He had just been
to America, so when asked the
name of the dish, said *homard à
l'américaine*. It is lobster sautéed
in oil and butter and then
simmered briskly in brandy, wine
and stock with shallots and
tomatoes, served with pilaff rice.
There are many wild variations

Clarence similar to *américaine*
but with curry powder and cream

à la Newburg sautéed lobster
with brandy and Madeira in a
cream and egg sauce

au porto lobster cooked in a
court-bouillon, warmed in a port,
butter, egg and cream sauce

Thermidor the lobster is halved,
grilled slowly and then replaced
in the halved shell which is lined
with *sauce béchamel* to which
English mustard has been added.
Browned with more sauce

Huîtres oysters

de Marennes excellent green
(vertes) and greyish-white
(blanches) oysters

Laitances soft roes

Lamproie à la bordelaise the poor
lamprey is done to death in the
cruellest possible manner—
steamed alive, revived, bled so
that its blood drips into a casserole
containing some *Sauternes* wine,
finally executed and marinated in
the casserole. It is then added to a
sauce of leeks, onions, shallots,
garlic, celery, carrots and
smoked ham. A subsequent
process of heating, reheating,
flaming, etc. takes ten hours or so

★**Langouste grillée aux deux
sauces** spiny lobster grilled and
served with *sauce Choron* and
sauce américaine

Langoustines large shrimp

à la valencienne served on a
mixture of cooked rice, diced ham,
peas and strips of sweet pepper

Limande lemon sole

Lotte eelpout. You will find this
rather a good fish. The chef Alain
Chapel has a dish made with its
liver which is unforgettable

Lotte de mer see *Baudroie*

Loup (de mer) sea bass

Maquereau mackerel,
traditionally served with a
gooseberry sauce

Matelote de petits Saint-Pierre
stew of John Dory with shallots
and garlic, in a *court-bouillon*
with added wine

Merlans frits en colère "angry"
whiting, so called because they
are deep fried with their tails
popped in their mouths

Morue à l'anglaise poached salt cod,
served with boiled potatoes and
hard-boiled egg in a cream sauce

à la bénédictine poached salt cod
blended with mashed potatoes, oil
and milk, and browned

Moules mussels

★**marinière** the best mussels
come only in a reduced mixture of
white wine, shallots, the liquid in
which the mussels were cooked
and breadcrumbs. Parsley, thyme,
butter and lemon juice are added

Mousse de merlan heavy cream
is added to pounded whiting,
mixed with egg whites and the
mixture put into a mould lined
with sliced truffles and baked

Mulet grey mullet

Nonats small Mediterranean fish

★**Omble chevalier** char, found in
France only in Lake Annecy

Oursin sea-urchin

Palourdes clams

Perche perch

Plie flounder

Poulpe octopus

Praires small clams, often raw

★**Quenelles de brochet** sieved
pike mixed with a *panade* and
beaten eggs, shaped into little
sausages and poached

Raie skate

Rascasse hog-fish, scorpion-fish

Rouget (strictly *rouget-barbet*) red
mullet. There is a *rouget-grondin*
(red gurnet) used in soups

★**à la nantaise** grilled red mullet
with a sauce of their livers,
chopped shallots, wine, meat jelly,
butter and parsley

Royans fresh sardines

Saint-Pierre John Dory

Sardines sardines, best simply
grilled or fried. Escoffier's friend
Caillat devoted a book of 150
recipes to them

antiboises fresh sardines baked

in an onion, white wine and tomato sauce

Saumon salmon. I'm not a great eater of salmon in France where the taste is for the Scandinavian rather than the Scottish variety and their smoked salmon is not up to much

Sole sole—in France the unfortunate sole is more often an excuse for a sauce than an interesting fish. Without blushing, restaurants produce an odious lemon sole smothered in a ghastly sauce made with bad white wine, paprika and mango chutney, set on artichoke hearts with a miniscule slice of truffle and one shrimp on the top, and call this rubbish *sole dame aux camélias*. I do not jest. I list only a few of my favourites and the very famous

arlésienne poached in white wine, with chopped onions, tomatoes, parsley and lemon juice

Bercy poached on a bed of shallots in white wine and served with parsley and lemon

au Chambertin baked in red wine on a bed of shallots, parsley and chopped mushrooms

Colbert egg-and-breadcrumbed and fried. The backbone is removed and the cavity filled with *beurre maître d'hôtel*

Dominique stuffed with a mixture of pounded whiting, mushrooms, cream, herbs, egg white and *sauce Mornay*, and baked in wine and stock

★ **dugléré** poached in white wine with butter, onion and tomatoes

hermitage sole, with their backbone removed, stuffed with breadcrumbs, butter, egg, shallots and herbs. Served in a sauce of the cooking liquor with butter and cream

Lutetia baked, garnished with sliced truffles and mushrooms in a little cream

Murat fried in butter and garnished with diced, sautéed artichoke hearts and potatoes

Saint-Germain breadcrumbed and grilled, garnished with potato balls cooked in butter and served with a *sauce béarnaise*

sautée aux pignons marinated in beer and anisette and sautéed with pine nuts

Tanche tench

Thon tuna fish

Truite au bleu trout poached in a *court-bouillon*

de rivière river trout

saumonée salmon trout

Ttoro a Basque stew of various fish and shellfish with onion, garlic, sweet peppers, chilli and tomatoes

Turbot braisé Maurice Chevalier turbot poached in champagne and served with a very creamy *sauce hollandaise* enriched with eggs

Richelieu poached turbot arranged with cooked lobster and served with a *sauce normande* to which sliced mushrooms, truffle, chopped lobster and crayfish butter have been added. Served with boiled potatoes

rôti aux primeurs larded turbot roasted on a bed of vegetables. Served with young glazed carrots, leeks, onions and potatoes

★ **soufflé** not a soufflé of turbot but a whole fish stuffed with a fish mousse (often pike). The fish is poached in the oven with sweet white wine and served with a smooth cream sauce mixed with lobster butter

Turbotin chicken turbot, a delicate fish

à l'amiral poached in white wine and covered in a *sauce normande* with a little crayfish butter and garnished with crayfish tails, oysters, carp roe or slices of truffle

Vive weever—an inferior dreary fish to be avoided

Volaille—*Poultry* (see also *Sauces* etc., p. 79)

Abatis de volaille chicken giblets

Aiguillettes de canetons Montmorency duckling breasts sautéed in butter, flambéed in cognac, cut into strips and served in a sauce of port, orange juice,

stock, redcurrant jelly and sour Montmorency cherries

Ailerons chicken wings

★ **Ballottines de volaille**

Curnonsky boned chicken pieces with the legs intact, marinated and spread with a little stuffing of ground veal, ham and pork, a slice of *foie-gras* and one of truffle, then rolled up into a parcel and wrapped in pork fat. They are then sautéed and simmered in wine and stock on a bed of vegetables. To serve, the pork fat is removed, and each roll placed on a croûton. Cream is added to the cooking juices to make a sauce and the dish garnished with artichoke hearts and potatoes

Blancs de volaille see *Suprêmes de volaille*

de volaille Angeline poached chicken breasts on semolina cakes, topped with a truffle, in a paprika *sauce béchamel*

de volaille Mireille poached chicken breasts with a sliced truffle on top, alternating with layers of spinach, grilled with *sauce béchamel* and cheese

Blanquette de volaille à la bourgeoise chicken pieces simmered with onions and mushrooms, served in an egg yolk and cream sauce

Canard duck

Claude Jolly slices of duck in stock and red wine, glazed with jellied stock and served with a slice of duck liver (previously marinated and cooked in port) also coated with the jellied stock

à la Margaux duck simmered with vegetables in Château Margaux and allowed to cool, then stuffed with a *mousse* of minced duck meat, duck livers and butter. Slices of cooked duck breast are "glued" on to the body with more of the mousse. The dish is decorated with more swirls of mousse, coated with jelly and chilled

à la suédoise duck completely covered and marinated in brine for five days, then poached with carrots, leeks and celery

à l'orange roast duckling served with a thick gravy of stock, orange juice and rind, garnished with orange slices

rouennais duckling stuffed with a mixture of duckling livers, onions and spices and roasted. Rouen ducks are killed by smothering, so that the blood spreads throughout the bird's meat making it dark and giving it a special flavour

rouennais à la presse the duckling is roasted, the legs discarded and the breast removed and cut into strips. The chopped carcase is crushed in a special duck press and sprinkled with red wine. The ensuing sauce is enriched with a little brandy and poured over the hot duck slices

★**Cassoulet languedocien** see *Meat*

Chapon capon

de Bresse gros sel slices of truffle are inserted under the skin of a Bresse capon which is completely buried in rock salt and cooked in the oven. The solid salt casing is broken open and the bird emerges wonderfully flavoured with an unexpectedly crisp skin. Hobo steak in the United States is cooked in the same way

Confit d'oie preserved goose

Coq à la bière chicken braised in dark beer with a little Dutch gin, cream and mushrooms

au vin à la bourguignonne one of the greatest French casseroles; sautéed chicken pieces, bacon, baby onions, mushrooms and garlic transferred to a casserole and simmered in red Burgundy. A sauce of the puréed chicken liver, its blood and a little cognac is mixed in at the end. Fried croûtons are sometimes added. In the Jura, they make a version with "yellow" wines called *coq au vin jaune* or *coq au vin de paille*

Crêtes et rognons Souvaroff cockscombs and kidneys are one of the oldest French dishes, having been the favourite of Catherine dei Medici. In this version the combs are braised with onions and carrots and then cooked quickly with sliced truffles, Madeira meat jelly and *sauce demi-glace*. The kidneys are sautéed separately and then warmed with the combs. Served with rice, a little purée of *foie-gras* and cheese

Émincé de volaille cooked chicken slices

de volaille Maintenon slices of poached chicken wing heated with Madeira, butter and sliced truffles and bound with *sauce allemande*

Foies de volaille chicken livers

Fricassée de poulet à l'angevine
chicken pieces simmered with
onions, mushrooms and dry white
Anjou wine, with a cream sauce

de poulet vallée d'Auge chicken
pieces simmered in stock, served
with mushrooms and baby onions
in a thick egg and cream sauce

Oie à l'alsacienne goose stuffed
with sausagemeat and roasted.
Served with sauerkraut and ham

Oison gosling

Pascalines de poulet chicken
forcemeat, cheese and *chou* pastry
mixed into oval shapes and
poached. Served on a thin layer
of *sauce béchamel*, topped with
truffles and more sauce

Poularde fat hen or roasting
chicken

Albuféra chicken stuffed with a
rice, onion, truffle and *foie-gras*
mixture and poached in stock.
Served with a *sauce allemande*
with added cream and meat jelly,
garnished with mushrooms,
kidneys, cockscombs and truffles

à l'aurore stuffed with rice,
onion, *foie-gras* and truffles,
served with a paprika *sauce
suprême* and mushrooms

belle aurore chicken pieces
cooked in white wine, served in
an egg, cream and lemon sauce

au blanc chicken poached in
stock, served in a *velouté* sauce
enriched with egg yolks and cream

**de Bresse truffée en vessie
Joannes Nandron** boned chicken
with truffles under its skin, stuffed
with chopped veal, cream and
cooked vegetables with a leek in
the middle, placed inside a pig's
bladder and poached in stock

chanteclair stuffed with savoury
rice, served with globe artichokes,
asparagus and *sauce allemande*

châtelaine chicken casseroled
in butter, served with stuffed
globe artichokes, chestnuts,
asparagus tips and a brandy and
white wine sauce

dauphinoise slices of truffle are
inserted under the chicken skin
and it is stuffed with its liver, *foie-
gras*, cognac and Madeira, cooked
in stock inside a pig's bladder

demi-deuil poached with slices
of truffle inserted beneath the
skin, served in a *sauce suprême*

Derby chicken stuffed with rice,

truffle and *foie-gras*, roasted and
served with croûtons of *foie-gras*
in a Madeira sauce

Diva stuffed as for *Derby*,
poached and served with a paprika
velouté sauce with added cream

favorite stuffed as for *Derby*
and poached in stock. Garnished
with cockscombs, kidneys and
sliced truffle and coated with a
sauce suprême

au gros sel simmered with
carrots, onions and leeks in stock.
Served with rock salt

impératrice poached chicken
garnished with lamb's sweetbreads
and brains, served in a *sauce
suprême*

à l'indienne poached, coated
with a *sauce suprême* mixed with a
little curry powder

Joinville boned chicken, its
wings and legs intact, stuffed
with a forcemeat of chicken,
cream and egg whites, chopped
cockscombs, diced sweetbreads
and black truffles. It is re-shaped
and casseroled in butter with a
little chopped ham and onion.
Served with a sauce of the juices,
verbena liqueur and brandy

maréchale stuffed with tongue,
truffle and *foie-gras*, poached and
served with *sauce suprême*.
Garnished with asparagus
tartlets, cockscombs, truffle and
mushrooms

Nantua boned chicken with the
leg and wings intact, stuffed with
chicken forcemeat, covered with
crayfish and truffles, re-shaped
and poached in stock. Served with
a *sauce suprême* enriched with a
purée of shallots, tomatoes and
white wine previously cooked in
the crayfish juices

au perles de Périgord stuffed
with truffles, braised in brandy
and white wine

pochée princesse poached
chicken in a *sauce suprême* with
truffles, served with artichoke
hearts and asparagus tips

poêlée châtelaine chicken
simmered with butter and
surrounded by poached chestnuts

régence poached, garnished
with *quenelles* of chicken
forcemeat, truffles, mushrooms
and *foie-gras* patties

sauce ivoire poached, served in

65

a *sauce suprême* with added meat jelly, rice and buttered cucumbers

Tosca stuffed as for *Derby* and poached in stock with sliced truffles and celery

Véronique poached, coated with a creamy *sauce béchamel* and garnished with calf's sweetbreads, lamb's brains, soft-boiled eggs and sliced truffles

Victoria stuffed with truffles and *foie-gras*, pot-roasted and finished in Madeira and stock. Garnished with diced potatoes and served with a brown sauce

Poule au pot chicken simmered with carrots, leeks and celery, flavoured with an onion stuck with cloves and a roasted onion. Served without the onions and with a dish of sea salt

Poulet young spring chicken

  aux aromates chicken pieces spiked with tarragon, basil and rosemary, sautéed in butter with onions and mushrooms

  de Bresse en soupière a whole chicken baked with vegetables in a tureen covered with a thin layer of flaky pastry

  cocotte bonne femme spring chicken stuffed with sausagemeat, its liver, breadcrumbs and parsley, cooked in butter with onions, bacon and potatoes

  de grain grillé à l'américaine small spring chicken cooked as below, but served with grilled bacon, tomatoes and mushrooms

  de grain grillé à la diable roast spring chicken halved and opened out flat, brushed with mustard, sprinkled with breadcrumbs and grilled. Served with watercress, potatoes and a *sauce diable*

  grand'mère chicken stuffed with onion, sausagemeat, breadcrumbs and its liver, casseroled with diced bacon, onions and potatoes

Marceron boned chicken with the legs and wings intact, stuffed with a mixture of ham, chicken *foie-gras* and brandy, re-shaped and braised on a bed of vegetables

  à la reine medium-sized roasting chicken

  sauté Beaulieu sautéed, garnished with chopped artichoke hearts, potatoes and black olives in a white wine and lemon sauce

  sauté bordelaise sautéed and garnished with sliced artichokes, potatoes and onion in a white wine sauce

  sauté bourguignonne sautéed, served in a red Burgundy, pork fat, mushroom and *demi-glace* sauce with glazed onions

  sauté a la bressane sautéed, served in a white wine and cream sauce with cock's kidneys and mushrooms

  sauté florentine one of the rare occasions when *florentine* does not involve spinach. In this case the chicken is sautéed and comes with Madeira, truffles and *risotto*

  sauté grenobloise chicken pieces sautéed with cloves of garlic and finished with white wine and tomatoes

  sauté hongroise sautéed with onions, paprika, white wine and tomatoes and served with a sauce of its juices and cream

  sauté Marengo sautéed, with mushrooms, garlic and white wine, served with a tomato *sauce demi-glace* and garnished with fried eggs, croûtons and crayfish

  sauté a la mode d'Auvergne sautéed and garnished with chestnuts and sausages. Served in a white wine, onion and tomato *demi-glace* sauce

  sauté Otero sautéed with mushrooms and shallots, served in a port and butter sauce with poached squab's eggs on croûtons

  vauclusienne chicken casseroled with chopped bacon, onion, tomatoes, garlic, parsley and white wine. Olives and fried eggplants are added at the end

  vivandière stuffed with *boudins blancs* and cooked in butter, then covered with Calvados and cream, and served with apple sauce

Poussins very small baby chickens

  à la bohémienne stuffed with breadcrumbs, their livers, herbs and paprika and cooked in butter with a little onion. Sprinkled with paprika and served in a white wine, cream and *foie-gras* sauce

  Cendrillon boned, halved and flattened and cooked in butter, then sandwiched between some truffled sausagemeat and wrapped in sausage skin. Grilled and served with *sauce Périgueux*

  châtelaine simmered with

onions, carrots, potatoes, shredded lettuce, peas and bacon

hermitage boned, flattened, halved *poussins*, egg-and-breadcrumbed and cooked in butter. Coated with a truffled *sauce chasseur* and garnished with potato balls

Véronique cooked in a casserole with Muscat grapes and covered with a white wine, meat jelly and cream sauce

à la viennoise cut in half and flattened, egg-and-breadcrumbed and fried in clarified butter

Salmis de canard partially roasted duck, jointed, then sautéed with mushrooms and truffles. Served with a strong wine gravy

Steaks de canard duck breasts, usually cooked in butter and served in a sauce of shallots, Armagnac and red Burgundy

Suprêmes de volaille breast and wing fillets from a (spring) chicken. There are some 250 variations of which I list the better-known and most interesting. The fillets are simply seasoned, dipped in flour and sautéed in butter, but what counts is the sauce. In some cases the sauce or garnish is the same as for a *poularde* with the same title but not always. Where they differ, I have included both dishes. They are also called *blancs de volaille*

de volaille Antonin Carême truffled chicken breasts cooked in butter, served on a bed of *pommes Anna* with a little truffle, and a rich port and cream sauce

de volaille favorite served on croûtons covered with a slice of *foie-gras* in a Madeira and truffle sauce. Garnished with asparagus

de volaille Françoise chicken breasts cooked in butter and served with a cream sauce, surrounded by asparagus tips

de volaille à la hongroise with a butter, paprika, white wine and cream sauce

de volaille Jeanette a cold dish of chicken breasts in *sauce chaud-froid* flavoured with tarragon and covered with aspic, surrounded by crushed ice. Escoffier names this dish after the polar exploration ship *La Jeanette* which stuck in the ice in 1881. Only one member of the crew survived

Pojarski minced chicken breasts re-formed with breadcrumbs, cream and butter

Timbale châtelaine *timbale* filled with cooked macaroni, cheese, braised sweetbreads and a *sauce demi-glace* mixed with cockscombs, kidneys, sliced truffles and Madeira

Maréchal Foch *timbale* with layers of macaroni, mixed with *foie-gras* and cheese and layers of sliced chicken in a Madeira, truffle, tomato and *demi-glace* sauce

Volaille au vinaigre chicken sautéed in butter, and then simmered in white wine, vinegar, stock and tomato paste

Viandes—*Meat* (see also *Sauces* etc., p. 79)

Meat in France is a very different affair from that in most countries, perhaps because it is treated in a way that makes beef beefier, lamb lambier, and so on. Partly this is due to their eating all meat far pinker than most other people would contemplate. The French, too, are a thrifty nation and eat much more offal and other bits of animals.

Agneau lamb

de lait baby milk-fed lamb

de pré-salé young lamb grazed in the fields bordering the sea

Alouettes sans tête à la brumaire slices of veal stuffed with ground veal, ham and pork, rolled up and sautéed. Served with a Madeira sauce

Aloyau beef sirloin

Amourettes Tosca poached veal marrow warmed with crayfish, truffles and a creamy *sauce béchamel*, served with shell-shaped pasta

★ **Andouilles, andouillettes** sausages made with finely chopped pig's chitterlings and stomach encased in a large pig intestine. Usually served cold

Bifteck steak. Ask for it *bleu* (almost raw), *saignant* (rare), *à point* (medium) or *bien cuit* (well done)

Blanquette de veau pieces of veal boiled with vegetables and served with mushrooms and small onions in a white sauce

Bœuf à l'arlésienne slices of boiled beef served with a sauce of onions, eggplants, tomatoes and red peppers

★ **à la bourguignonne** beef marinated with onions, carrots, herbs and red wine, and then stewed in a casserole with onions, garlic, bacon and mushrooms

à la ficelle beef boiled with vegetables, usually served with tomato sauce. The broth is served separately with croûtons

★ **à la mode** larded beef marinated in wine and brandy and then braised very slowly with vegetables, calf's feet and pork rind. Garnished with carrots and baby onions

à la tyrolienne slices of cold boiled beef served in a sauce of onions and tomatoes

Boudins white (*blancs*) and black (*noirs*) puddings. The white are sausages made with pork, bacon fat, *foie-gras*, onion, eggs and cream, poached, while the black are made with pig's blood, pig's kidney fat, onion and cream. Both types are grilled before serving

Carbonnade à la flamande slices of beef cooked in a casserole with onions, beer, brown stock and a little brown sugar

Carré d'agneau loin of lamb

d'agneau Mireille roasted with potatoes and artichoke hearts. This dish is called *mistral* when sliced truffles are added

de porc rôti roast loin of pork

★ **Cassoulet languedocien** a thick white haricot bean stew with pork, pieces of *confit d'oie*, garlic sausage, onions, garlic and tomato paste. The ingredients vary according to the town in which it is made. It may include mutton, salt pork, partridge or preserved duck

Cervelas pork garlic sausage

Cervelles brains

Béatrice poached calf's brains

mixed with truffled *foie-gras* and *sauce béchamel*, made into balls, egg-and-breadcrumbed and fried

à la génoise calf's brains, fried lightly in butter and layered with Parmesan and tomato sauce

royale calf's brain, puréed with egg yolks and cream, cooked *en cocotte* in a *bain-marie*

Chateaubriand porterhouse steak

Choucroute à la strasbourgeoise pickled white cabbage cooked in white wine and stock with pork fat, carrot, onion, juniper berries, goose fat, pork and sausage. Served with frankfurters

Cochon de lait Saint-Fortunat suckling pig stuffed with a mixture of cooked barley, its liver, herbs, chipolata sausages and braised chestnuts, roasted

Côte de bœuf ribs of beef, usually roasted

Côtelettes cutlets

d'agneau Tosca lamb cutlets covered with a purée of *foie-gras* and chopped ham, egg-and-breadcrumbed and fried. Served with asparagus tips and truffle

Champvallon mutton cutlets simmered with sliced onions, sliced potatoes and garlic in stock

Maintenon sautéed mutton cutlets served on fried croûtons spread with *foie-gras* and covered with *julienne* strips of mushroom, truffle and chicken in a little *sauce allemande*. Served with *sauce Chateaubriand*

Côtes de porc charentière sautéed pork chops served with a sauce of shallots, tomato paste, vinegar, white wine and stock mixed with a little sugar, mustard and pickles

de porc à la limousine sautéed pork chops served with braised red cabbage

de veau bordelaise sautéed veal chops served with artichoke hearts

de veau grand'mère large veal chops cooked in a casserole with mushrooms, bacon, glazed onions and Madeira

★ **de veau marquise** sautéed veal cutlets served in a Madeira sauce with truffle, cream and *foie-gras*

de veau Pojarski chopped veal cutlet meat mixed with breadcrumbs, butter and cream, re-shaped as cutlets, egg-and-breadcrumbed and sautéed

Couronne de côtelettes rôties crown roast of lamb

Crépinettes small flattish sausages

Cul de veau à la mode du vieux presbytère hind end of veal loin stewed in white wine and stock with morels, flavoured with a little curry powder and tarragon and served in a sauce of its juices thickened with eggs and cream

Culotte de bœuf topside of beef

Daube à l'avignonnaise same as below but using leg of mutton

à la provençale larded beef first marinated in red wine, vinegar and brandy with vegetables and then braised slowly in a casserole with onions, garlic and bacon fat

★ **Entrecôte marchand de vin** grilled steak with *beurre marchand de vin*

Mirabeau grilled entrecôte steak, criss-crossed with anchovy fillets and tarragon leaves. Served with olives and anchovy butter

Porteneuve grilled steak covered with minced shallots and served with a *sauce béarnaise*

Épaule d'agneau farcie landaise boned shoulder of lamb stuffed with ground veal, pork and chicken livers, breadcrumbs, parsley and brandy, roasted

de veau shoulder of veal

Épigrammes d'agneau braised boned breast of lamb cut into cutlet shapes, covered with a little *sauce béchamel*, egg-and-breadcrumbed and fried, arranged alternately with sautéed lamb cutlets

Escalope savoyarde fried veal escalopes covered with a cream, brandy, Madeira and morel sauce, sprinkled with cheese and glazed under the grill

vallée d'Auge a Normandy dish of veal escalopes sautéed with Calvados and cream and served with apple slices

de veau Brillat-Savarin veal escalopes sautéed in butter and flambéed in brandy, covered with a mushroom and cream sauce and glazed under the grill

de veau à la viennoise veal escalopes egg-and-breadcrumbed and fried

Filet de bœuf Régence larded beef fillet casseroled on a bed of vegetables with brandy

de bœuf Richelieu larded beef fillet roasted on a bed of vegetables, garnished with potatoes, braised stuffed lettuce, mushrooms and tomatoes, with a Madeira sauce

de bœuf sarladaise fillet larded with pork fat and truffles cooked in Madeira on a bed of carrots. Served with a *sauce Périgueux*

mignon small triangular fillet steaks, dipped in melted butter and breadcrumbs and grilled

Foie de porc pig's liver

de veau à l'étuvée larded calf's liver braised with onions, carrots, garlic and brandy

de veau vénitienne liver baked with bacon, parsley, shallots and mushrooms, sprinkled with breadcrumbs and browned

Fricandeau slice of veal from the topside, usually braised

Fricassée de veau pieces of veal first sautéed and then simmered in stock. Served with a sauce made from the stock, egg yolks, cream, nutmeg and lemon juice

Fritots d'amourettes slices of bone marrow, fried in batter

Fromage de tête de porc pork brawn or head cheese

Gigot when a menu says *gigot* without specifying *d'agneau*, it should be leg of mutton

d'agneau en chevreuil leg of lamb first marinated and then roasted. Served with a *sauce poivrade*

d'agneau aux primeurs leg of lamb coated with butter, roasted and then coated with breadcrumbs and *fines herbes* to give it a crispy skin. Served with spring vegetables

Gras-double tripe

Grenadins thick veal escalopes

Hachis hash of left-over meat

Haricot de mouton cubes of mutton simmered with bacon fat, onions, garlic and tomato paste

Jambon à la crème de Saulieu sliced ham with mushrooms in a cream sauce made with white wine, tomatoes and cheese

au foin you are unlikely to meet this, literally a ham boiled with hay. It has a remarkable taste but this may be just as much from the juniper berries and spices which are added

persillé a Burgundian dish of ham cooked in a highly spiced stock and then sliced and put in a terrine alternating with layers of a *persillade* made of chopped shallots, garlic, parsley, chervil, tarragon and butter. This is covered with a ham stock jelly flavoured with brandy and port. When it is cut, the ham has attractive green veins running through it and tastes marvellous

Jarrets de veau knuckle of veal

Langue de bœuf ox-tongue

Longe de veau loin of veal

Lonzu dried fillet of pork in a sausage skin. A Corsican dish

Médaillons de veau Alexandra small rounds of veal sautéed in butter, garnished with a slice of truffle, and with artichoke bases filled with morels in cream. Served in a brandy and Marsala sauce

Mignonnettes same as *noisettes*

Mouton mutton

Museau de bœuf ox muzzle

Navarin printanier spring mutton *ragoût* with onions, potatoes, carrots, turnips, peas and garlic

Noisettes small, round fillets

de pré-salé à la dauphine round *noisettes* of lamb sautéed in butter and served on round fried croûtons, with a wine sauce and *dauphine* potatoes

des tournelles lightly sautéed lamb steaks covered with a little onion purée, glazed under the grill and served with a vermouth and sherry sauce

Noix de veau topside of veal

Pain de . . . meat loaf

Palais de bœuf ox palette

Palets de bœuf rounds of boiled ground beef

Paupiettes thin slices of meat stuffed with a forcemeat, rolled up into a cork shape and wrapped in a bacon rasher. Braised in stock

Petit salé pickled pork

Pièce de bœuf à la mode larded beef topside braised in wine and brandy with boned calf's feet, onion, carrots and bacon

de bœuf à la royale beef larded with pork fat and ham, flambéed in brandy and simmered in champagne and beef stock with calf's feet, tomatoes and garlic. The beef is served cold in a jelly

Pieds de porc pig's feet

de veau Cendrillon boned, cooked calf's foot, cubed and mixed with chopped truffles and sausagemeat, shaped into cutlets, breadcrumbed and grilled

Poitrine de porc belly of pork

de veau farcie Gascogne breast of veal stuffed with sausagemeat, breadcrumbs, eggs, cream and *fines herbes*, rubbed with thyme and simmered with vegetables

de veau farcie niçoise breast of veal stuffed with ground salt pork and chicken livers, rice, breadcrumbs, chopped spinach, grated cheese, egg yolks and herbs, casseroled on a bed of vegetables. Served cold with tomatoes and black olives

Porc pork

★Queue de bœuf à l'auvergnate braised oxtail in white wine, served with glazed onions and chestnuts cooked in consommé

Quasi de veau bourgeoise casserole of veal hind end with vegetables, calf's foot and pork

Ragoût de mouton au riz à la française cubes of mutton stewed with onions and tomato paste Rice is added at the end

Ris d'agneau lamb's sweetbreads

de veau bonne maman calf's sweetbreads braised in veal stock on a bed of vegetables

de veau forestière braised calf's sweetbreads with shallots, white wine and *cèpes*

de veau poêlé larded calf's sweetbreads braised with onions, carrots and pork rind and served on croûtons of fried bread with a vegetable garnish

de veau Régence calf's sweetbreads braised in white wine and port on a bed of vegetables and served in a cream, mushroom and *foie-gras* sauce, garnished with truffles

de veau Taillevent calf's sweetbreads simmered with a *julienne* of carrots and mushrooms, diced truffle and white wine. The sauce is thickened with cream and the whole mixture poured into a puff pastry shell and served hot

Rognons d'agneau lamb's kidneys

★ sautés Turbigo sautéed kidneys with cooked mushrooms

and grilled chipolata sausages, served with a white wine and tomato sauce

Rosbif roast beef

Rôtis de bœuf à l'anglaise English roast beef

Rouelle de veau thick round of veal larded with anchovy fillets and marinated in vinegar, then sautéed and served with the juices

Saucisses sausages

Saupiquet du Morvan warmed ham escalopes covered with a *sauce béarnaise* to which Madeira and truffles have been added

dish got its name from the Tartar hordes who used to put pieces of young horsemeat under their saddles to make them tender. Ugh

Subrics de cervelle cooked calf's brains mixed with chopped spinach and pancake batter, fried in small spoonfuls

Tête d'aloyau rump steak

Tête de veau à l'anglaise boiled calf's head, served with boiled bacon and parsley sauce

Tournedos small, thick, round slices of beef fillet

Tell me what you eat and I will tell you who you are.
Brillat-Savarin

Sauté d'agneau à la navarraise cubes of lamb sautéed with onion and vinegar and then simmered gently with sweet peppers, chilli and garlic

★**de veau Marengo** veal casseroled with garlic, shallots, mushrooms, tomatoes, onions and white wine. Green olives are added, together with crayfish poached in wine and fried eggs

Selle d'agneau rôtie Mirabelle roast saddle of lamb garnished with colourful small vegetables

judic garnished with braised lettuce stuffed with rice, truffled *foie-gras* and sautéed lamb's sweetbreads

Orloff fillets of braised saddle of lamb, removed from the bone and sliced. The cavity in the saddle is filled with *sauce soubise* alternating with the meat slices and a slice of truffle. The saddle is then glazed with a sprinkling of Parmesan and more sauce

de veau Metternich braised saddle of veal in a *sauce béchamel* with paprika. Served with rice

Soufflé de jambon Alexandra pounded ham with Parmesan cheese, truffle and a rich *sauce béchamel* with eggs, alternating with asparagus tips, baked

Steak aux œufs au miroir hamburger with fried eggs

au poivre steaks with crushed peppercorns rubbed into them, sautéed in butter

tartare raw ground beef fillet mixed with a raw egg, capers, chopped onions and parsley. This

cordon rouge larded with Parma ham, stuffed with *foie-gras* and sautéed. Served on a fried croûton, criss-crossed with strips of red pepper, in a brandy and port sauce

★**Curnonsky** named after the famed gastronome; sautéed *tournedos* with grilled tomatoes and beef marrow, served in a brandy and port sauce with a little truffle

Henri IV grilled *tournedos* served on fried croûtons, with a *sauce béarnaise*, surrounded by sautéed potatoes and artichokes

tourangelle sautéed *tournedos* surrounded by prunes stuffed with *foie-gras* and served in a peppery Madeira sauce with chopped truffle

★**Tripes à la mode de Caen** tripe simmered with onions in salt water for at least six hours, then cooked with bacon, garlic and cloves for another eight hours. The actual preparation is enormously elaborate involving calf's feet and beef suet and possibly some Calvados and a great deal of skimming, straining and general activity. The result is undoubtedly the best kind of tripe one can ever eat

Veau veal

★**Vol-au-vent de ris de veau financière** braised, sliced calf's sweetbreads heated in a *sauce demi-glace* with some *quenelles*, cooked mushrooms, sliced truffles and olives. The mixture is then put in vol-au-vent cases

Gibier—Game (see also *Sauces* etc., p. 79)

The French eat game both fresher and rarer than we do. There is nothing you can do about getting them to hang it longer. You can, of course, ask them to cook it longer, in which case it will be tough. Irksome moral: you cannot have it both ways.

Alouettes larks
Bécasse woodcock
Bécassine snipe
Becs-figues blackcaps or "fig-peckers"
Biche doe
Canard sauvage wild duck
★**Cailles** quails
   Brillat-Savarin pot-roasted on a bed of diced vegetables with some bacon and veal, then casseroled with sliced truffles, slices of sautéed *foie-gras*, brandy, veal stock and wine
   à la Stanislas boned quails stuffed with *foie-gras* and truffles, flavoured with a little Madeira, wrapped in pastry, baked
Cerf red deer, stag
Chevreuil roe-buck, often used generically for venison
Civet de lièvre jugged hare
   de lièvre à la lyonnaise jugged hare with chestnuts
Coq de bruyère wood grouse
Daim fallow deer
Faisan à la bohémienne pheasant stuffed with *foie-gras* and its own liver, cooked in a casserole with goose fat and onions. Served with pilaff rice and a paprika, wine and cream sauce
   à la mode de Gascogne stuffed with chicken livers soaked in port and truffles, then marinated in port. Simmered in pork fat and butter with more truffles
★ **à la Sainte-Alliance** stuffed with woodcock forcemeat and roasted. Served on a croûton with slices of bitter orange
   à la vigneronne cooked in a casserole with butter. Served on croûtons covered with a paste made from the pheasant liver, brandy, *foie-gras* and butter and in a sauce of Alsatian wine, brandy and cream with stewed black and white grapes
Filets de levraut La Vallière fillets of young hare sautéed, then served in a *sauce chasseur* with truffles and tarragon added

de levraut Mornay young hare sautéed in butter and served in a Madeira and truffle sauce
Gelinotte hazel-grouse
Grives thrushes. Most usually turn up in pâté but very often served plain roasted. See *Belgium*
Lapereaux young rabbits
Lapin rabbit
   de garenne wild rabbit
   en gibelotte rabbit stew with mushrooms, onions, pork fat and white wine
Levraut leveret, young hare
★**Lièvre à la royale** boned hare stuffed with a mixture of its kidneys, minced liver, heart and lungs, veal, pork, ham, chicken livers, *foie-gras* and brandy. Then formed into a *ballottine*, wrapped in pork fat and casseroled with onions, carrots, garlic, shallots, celery, the hare trimmings, brandy and red wine
★**Marcassin** young wild boar
Mauviettes larks
Merles blackbirds
Ortolans ortolans
Palombe wild dove
Perdreau partridge
   bourguignon stuffed with its liver, bacon and breadcrumbs, pot-roasted and served in a brandy and wine sauce
   de grand'mère stuffed with its liver, pork fat and truffles, cooked in butter. Then halved, casseroled with sliced truffles in wine, brandy and veal stock. Served with chestnut purée
   à la limousine stuffed with *cèpes* and chicken livers, cooked in a casserole with more *cèpes*
Pigeonneaux tender young squab, usually bred for the table
   aux concombres spring dish of young squab roasted in butter and garnished with caramelized cooked cucumbers and onions. Served with a vermouth and cream sauce

crapaudine "squab dressed as toad"; spatch-cocked, dipped in butter and breadcrumbs and grilled. Served with a *sauce diable*

   à la polonaise stuffed with chopped squab livers, chicken livers, onions and shallots, cooked in butter and covered with fried breadcrumbs

   Prince Rainier III a marvellous dish of boned squab spread with a ground pork and veal mixture, truffle and *foie-gras*, its liver and heart, and reshaped. Roasted, served on fried bread slices with a wine, brandy and *demi-glace* sauce

Pilet pintail

Pintade, pintadeau guinea-hen, the former the older, the latter the younger bird

Pluvier golden plover

Râble de lièvre saddle of hare

   de lièvre à la cauchoise hind-quarters of hare, marinated in white wine and herbs, roasted and served in a Calvados, cream and mustard sauce and garnished with sautéed apples

   de lièvre saupiquet roasted saddle of hare served with a sauce of its liver and blood, shallots, vinegar, a *bouquet garni* and red wine

Sanglier wild boar

Sarcelle teal

Selle de chevreuil grand veneur saddle of venison first marinated and then roasted. Served in a *sauce poivrade* mixed with the marinade and heavy cream, and with a chestnut purée

   ★**de chevreuil Saint-Hubert** marinated saddle of venison, roasted in oil and served in a *sauce poivrade* with added raisins and almonds

Timbale de pigeonneaux La Fayette a *timbale* with macaroni, crayfish butter, truffles and squab breasts on top. Served with a *sauce béchamel*

Tourterelles turtle-doves

Train de lièvre rôti saddle and hind legs of hare, wrapped in pork fat and roasted in butter

Vanneau lapwing

Venaison venison

Légumes—Vegetables

Ail garlic. Many people assume that the French put garlic with everything. In fact, except in Provence, they use it rather sparingly. However, they are not frightened of it and on occasions, eat whole roasted cloves of it. When cooked for long enough, garlic loses its ferocity

★**Artichauts à la barigoule** globe artichokes stuffed with chopped shallots, mushrooms, parsley and nutmeg, with a little pork fat on top and stewed in white wine and stock on a bed of chopped onions and carrots

Asperges asparagus

Aubergines eggplants

   à l'égyptienne halved, stuffed with the pulp mixed with breadcrumbs, tomato sauce and garlic, browned in the oven and served topped with tomatoes

Betterave beetroot

Bironnes chayottes. In season from November to end of February, cooked like cucumbers or vegetable squash

Brocoli broccoli

Cardons cardoons

Carottes à la Vichy carrots boiled in very little water with a knob of butter and a little sugar so that the liquid becomes syrupy

Céleri celery

Céleri-rave celery root

Cèpes *Boletus edulis*: dark brown mushrooms with a delicious squashy consistency. Found in spring and autumn

Champignons mushrooms. The French use this term to cover not only what we think of as field mushrooms but also the enormous number of edible fungi which they use in cooking

Chanterelles *Cantharellus cibarius*: yellow, trumpet-shaped mushrooms

Chayottes same as *bironnes*

Chicorée curly endive

Chou cabbage

   de mai spring cabbage

   marin or **de mer** sea-kale

   rouge à la limousine red cabbage cooked with chestnuts

   vert farci en ballottine layers of cabbage leaves and ground meat

73

encased in pork fat and tied up in a rectangular bundle. Braised
Choucroute pickled white cabbage. (Sauerkraut is quite different in that it is fermented.)
Chou-fleur cauliflower
Chou-rave kohlrabi
Choux brocolis broccoli
  de Bruxelles brussels sprouts
Choux-navets turnip tops
Ciboules scallions
Concombre cucumber
Cornichons pickles
Courge squash
Cresson watercress
Duxelles minced mushrooms and shallots cooked in butter with a bouquet garni. Cream is stirred in at the end
Échalotes shallots
Endive chicory
Épinards spinach
Fenouil fennel
Feuilles de vigne vine leaves
Fèves fava beans
Flageolets kidney beans, green haricot beans
Fonds d'artichauts artichoke hearts
Gâteau au chou vert shredded cabbage rolled up in pastry and baked
Girolles same as *chanterelles*
Gombos okra
Gratin dauphinois thin potato slices put in a garlic-rubbed casserole with beaten egg, milk and grated cheese, and baked
  languedocien slices of cooked eggplant and tomatoes, layered, sprinkled with breadcrumbs, parsley and oil and baked
Haricots blancs white haricot beans
  d'Espagne runner beans
  panachés mixed string beans and green flageolets
  rouges kidney beans
  verts string beans
Jardinière de légumes mixed vegetables
Laitue lettuce, often braised
Lentilles lentils
Macédoine de légumes mixed diced vegetables
Mâche lamb's lettuce, excellent with a bacon fat and vinegar dressing
Maïs sweetcorn
Mange-tout mange-tout or snow peas

Marrons chestnuts
Morilles *Morchella esculenta*: morels. Grow in spring
Mousserons *Tricholoma georgii*: St George's mushrooms
Navets turnips
Oignons onions
Oronges *Amanita caesarea*: Caesar's mushrooms, found in late summer and autumn
Oseille sorrel
Panais parsnip
Patates douces sweet potatoes
Petits pois peas
  pois princesse same as *mange-tout*, snow peas
Piments doux sweet peppers
Pissenlit dandelion leaves, much used in salads
Poireaux leeks
Pois peas
  cassés split peas
  chiches chick peas
  à la française peas, lettuce, onions and parsley boiled together in a little water with a small amount of sugar and butter
Poivrons same as *piments doux*
Pommes (de terre) potatoes. Usually abbreviated to *pommes*, not to be confused with apples
  Anna sliced potatoes in layers, baked with butter and salt
  Byron potatoes first baked, then mashed and fried, placed in a flan ring, covered with cream, sprinkled with cheese, browned
  château cut in the shape of large olives and cooked gently in clarified butter until golden
  chips what we call potato chips
  à la crème boiled potatoes finished in cream and butter
  dauphine mashed potatoes mixed with egg and unsweetened *chou* paste, brushed with egg and baked
  duchesse mashed potatoes mixed with egg and egg yolk, flavoured with a dash of nutmeg, made into small balls and baked
  fondants potato balls cooked in a casserole with butter
  au four baked potatoes
  frites french fried potatoes
  frites allumettes matchstick potatoes, deep fried
  Macaire baked potatoes are scooped out and the mash fried in butter and put back in the

potato case. Sometimes the mash is merely fried like a pancake

maître d'hôtel sliced potatoes simmered in stock, covered with butter and sprinkled with parsley

noisettes walnut-sized potato balls roasted gently in butter

paille very thinly-cut long strips of potato, deep fried

Pont-Neuf genuine french fried potatoes

purée mashed with milk and butter

en robe des champs boiled potatoes in their skins

à la sarladaise layers of *Anna* potatoes and slices of truffles, with a few pieces of diced *foie-gras* in between

à la savoyarde same as *gratin dauphinois* but with consommé instead of milk

soufflées thickish slices of potatoes deep fried, allowed to cool, and then plunged again into *very* hot fat when the potatoes blow up into ping-pong balls

vapeur boiled potatoes

voisin same as *Anna* but with a layer of grated cheese between each potato layer

Potiron pumpkin

Radis radish

Ratatouille see *Hors d'œuvre*

Rutabaga turnip

Salsifis salsify

Scarole escarole, endive

Subrics d'épinards chopped, cooked spinach mixed with batter and fried in spoonfuls

Tomates tomatoes

Topinambours Jerusalem artichokes

Truffes truffles; the subterranean fungoid family of *Tuberaceae*. They are found at depths of up to a foot. Part of the magic of French cooking which came, in Escoffier's time, to be over-used. Their mystery lies not only in their own flavour, which they impart to other food, but also in their ability to enhance the actual taste of any ingredient. It is comparatively rare to find truffles on their own but it is worth eating them once in a lifetime. The best ways of eating them are:

au champagne simmered in champagne and veal stock and served with a sauce of reduced cooking liquids. When Madeira is substituted for the champagne, the dish is called *truffes à la serviette*

sous la cendre see *Hors d'œuvre*

Fromages—Cheese

The French cheeseboard is one of the most enchanting parts of the meal. There are at least four hundred cheeses and one can make a new discovery every day of the year. Cheese in France is eaten before dessert.

Banon Provençal soft cheese, usually of cow's milk. Comes wrapped in chestnut leaves and tied with raffia

Bondon Normandy cow's milk cheese, shaped like a cylinder

Bleu d'Auvergne from the Auvergne, a soft cow's milk cheese with internal mould, in the shape of a flattened cylinder

Bleu de Bresse soft cheese with blue veins made from pasteurized cow's milk, a long cylinder shape

Boursin soft cow's milk cheese, commercially made, sometimes flavoured with herbs and garlic

Brie a flat round of mildly fermented soft cheese

Brillat-Savarin soft triple-cream cheese in the form of a thick disc

Camembert mildly-fermented soft cheese, less delicate than *brie*. Should not be eaten runny (when a cheese is runny, it is undergoing a second fermentation)

Carré de l'Est soft, pasteurized, cow's milk cheese with a slight smell of mushrooms

Chabichou strong soft goat cheese shaped like a chopped-off cone

Chèvre colloquial term for goat's cheese

Coulommiers very soft, smooth cow's milk cheese with quite a tang, circular in shape

Demi-sel fresh Normandy cow's milk cheese, in a small square

Fourme de Montbrison firm and homogeneous cow's milk cheese, in the shape of a tall cylinder

Gérômé thick circle of soft cow's milk with a smooth reddish rind, spicy to taste. Also a *gérômé anise*, flavoured with caraway

Livarot soft Normandy strong-smelling and strong-tasting cheese, shaped like a cylinder. Wrapped up in marsh grass

Maroilles strong smelling and sharp soft cow's cheese in a flat rectangular shape. Invented about a thousand years ago by the monks of Maroilles

Monsieur a smaller, taller version of *camembert* with a much stronger taste, and strong smell

Mont d'Or Lyons cheese, of either goat's or cow's milk, or both, with a blue rind. Comes in a small, thin, flat circle

Munster soft and strong-tasting cow's cheese, shaped like a flat cylinder, sometimes flavoured with cummin

Neufchâtel see *Bondon*

Olivet from Orléans. A soft cow's milk cheese with a delicate blue rind. Sometimes coated with ash

Petit-suisse fresh unsalted cheese made all over France, in the shape of a small cylinder, often eaten with sprinkled sugar

Pont-l'Evêque soft cow's milk cheese with a yellow rind and a rather rubbery texture

Port-Salut pressed cow's milk cheese, in the shape of a thick round, smooth and mild

Reblochon soft, lightly-pressed cow's milk cheese in a flat round. It has a smooth, supple consistency and a mild taste

Roquefort soft blue sheep's milk cheese cured in a cave, shaped like a tall cylinder—an extremely ancient cheese

Saint-Marcellin soft cow's milk cheese in the shape of a small, flat round with a blue-grey rind. Used to be a goat's cheese

Tomme there are countless *tommes*, many of them pressed goat and sheep's milk cheeses and mostly from the south-east corner of France

Vacherin soft cow's milk cheese in a large, thin round. There are several varieties, nearly all having a balsam flavour, since they are wrapped in pine bark

Entremets— Desserts, *Glaces*— Ice-cream, *Fruits*— Fruit, *Pâtisserie*— Pastries, *Noix*— Nuts

I have not listed a huge number of sweets, puddings or desserts, because these are usually displayed on a trolley in French restaurants, so you will be able to see what you want.

Abricots Condé ring of rice cooked in milk and flavoured with vanilla, decorated with apricots and coated with an apricot and kirsch syrup

Amandes almonds

Ananas pineapple

Avelines hazelnuts. Also *noisettes*

Babas au rhum *savarin* dough cakes soaked in a sugar syrup and spread with apricot jam

Bananes bananas

Bavaroise cream dessert made in a mould with whipped egg yolks, sugar and milk, flavoured with vanilla and cooked, chilled

Beignets fritters

   favoris macaroons sandwiched together with apricot jam, dipped in a liqueur syrup, coated with batter and deep fried

Bombe a round mould lined with ice-cream, filled with various mixtures and frozen

   cardinal raspberry ice filled with vanilla ice-cream

   ★ **favorite** chestnut ice-cream filled with apricot mousse, flavoured with rum

   Monte-Carlo vanilla ice-cream filled with strawberry mousse, served with strawberries

   Nélusko chocolate ice-cream filled with vanilla mousse

Brugnons nectarines

Cassis blackcurrants

Cerises cherries

Charlotte de pommes apple charlotte

   à la russe sponge fingers encasing a vanilla and cream custard

Citron lemon
Clafoutis cherry flan
Coing quince
Coupe Adelina Patti vanilla ice-cream surrounded by brandied cherries, topped with *crème Chantilly*

clo-clo *marrons glacés* soaked in maraschino and mixed with vanilla ice-cream, surrounded by strawberry purée and *crème Chantilly*

favorite fresh pineapple cubes soaked in liqueur, covered with vanilla ice-cream. Small meringues filled with pineapple ice are arranged on top, covered with strawberry purée and *crème Chantilly*

Jacques crystallized fruit soaked in liqueur, covered with a layer of lemon and a layer of strawberry ice, topped with fresh peach slices and strawberries

Crème à l'anglaise custard

Chantilly sweetened whipped cream

renversée au caramel custard baked in a mould lined with caramel syrup

Crêpes Suzette pancakes sprinkled with sugar and served hot at the table with a sauce of butter, sugar and liqueur poured over them

Dattes dates

★**Saint-Honoré** a delicious cream cake created by the old Pâtisserie Chiboust, on rue Saint-Honoré, near the Palais Royal in Paris. It is a circle of *chou* pastry on a pastry base filled with *crème Saint-Honoré* (fluffy custard)

Gaufres waffles

Génoise a plain fluffy sponge cake made with numerous eggs

Glace ice-cream

Alhambra strawberry mousse in a vanilla ice-cream casing

Carmen apricot ice around a raspberry-flavoured *crème Chantilly* filling

Diane vanilla ice-cream around a chestnut mousse flavoured with kirsch and maraschino

Madeleine cubes of crystallized pineapple soaked in kirsch and maraschino, mixed with vanilla ice-cream and *crème Chantilly*

Granités water ices based on fruit juice, which when frozen have a gritty texture

Grenades pomegranates

Groseilles currants

à maquereau gooseberries

Jalousies small cakes made of flaky pastry

Kaki persimmon

Langues de chat "cats' tongues"; crisp flat biscuits

Macédoine de fruits fruit salad

. . . I raised to my lips a spoonful of the tea in which I had soaked a morsel of the cake . . . suddenly the memory returns. The taste was that of the little crumb of madeleine which on Sunday mornings at Combray . . . my aunt Léonie used to give me, dipping it first in her own cup of real or of lime-flower tea.
Marcel Proust *Swann's Way* (trans. Scott Moncrieff)

Éclairs strips of *chou* pastry, baked, split open and filled with coffee or chocolate-flavoured cream, iced on top

Figues figs

Flan aux pommes Jérôme flan filled with apple purée flavoured with kirsch, covered with slices of apple and baked

Fraises des bois wild strawberries

Romanoff strawberries soaked in orange juice and Curaçao and covered with *crème Chantilly*

Framboises raspberries

Friandises see *Petits fours*

Galettes flaky pastry cakes

Gâteau cake

Madeleines tiny, oval sponge cakes

Mandarines tangerines

★**Marjolaine** roasted ground almonds and hazel-nuts are mixed with sugar, flour and countless egg whites. When baked, four layers of the meringue are sandwiched together with a chocolate cream, a butter cream and a praline butter cream and dusted with chocolate and sugar

Marquises water ices made with pineapple juice, strawberries, kirsch and sugar

Mille-feuilles numerous thin layers of puff-pastry sandwiched together with cream and/or jam

★**Mont-Blanc** sieved cooked chestnuts with vanilla-flavoured *crème Chantilly* piled in peaks on top

Mûres blackberries, mulberries

Myrtilles bilberries

Nèfles medlars

★**Oeufs à la neige** soft, oval meringue shapes poached in boiling milk and served in a custard made with the milk

Omelette norvégienne *or* **en surprise** baked Alaska; *génoise* sprinkled with liqueur, covered with ice-cream and encased in meringue. It is baked very quickly so the meringue becomes golden and the ice-cream doesn't melt

Pain perdu *brioche* or toast dipped in sweetened milk and beaten egg flavoured with vanilla and fried. The British call this "Poor Knights of Windsor"

Pamplemousse grapefruit

Parfait au café frozen dessert of coffee, egg yolks, syrup and cream

Pastèque watermelon

Pêches à l'aurore fresh peaches soaked in kirsch syrup, arranged on strawberry mousse and covered with a Curaçao *sabayon*

impératrice rice cooked in milk, flavoured with kirsch and maraschino, covered with halved peaches poached in syrup, then a layer of apricot *compote*, and another rice layer. Served with liqueur-flavoured apricot sauce and crushed macaroons

Melba peaches arranged on vanilla ice-cream and covered with raspberry purée

Petits fours little biscuits and cakes served at the end of a meal, sometimes quite elaborately decorated. Includes sweets and sugared fruits

Poires Hélène pears poached in syrup, left to cool, served on vanilla ice-cream and covered with a hot chocolate sauce

Madeleine cooked pears and apricot jam piled into a *savarin*, and covered with *crème Chantilly*

Richelieu pears poached in claret flavoured with sugar, cinnamon and orange rind. Served cold with the wine which is thickened with redcurrant jelly and *crème Chantilly*

Pommes apples

Profiteroles little *chou* puffs usually filled with cream or custard, built up into the shape of a pyramid and covered with thick chocolate sauce

Pruneaux prunes

Prunes plums

Raisins grapes

Reine-claude greengage

Riz impératrice cooled cooked rice, flavoured with liqueur, mixed with whipped cream, custard and gelatine and moulded. Served with liqueur-flavoured apricot syrup

Sabayon whipped egg yolks, sugar, wine and liqueur

Savarin round yeast cake soaked in sugar syrup flavoured with rum

Sorbet water ice, usually made with fruit juice. Often served in the middle of a meal to clear the palate

Soufflé see *Eggs*

dame blanche soufflé made with almond milk and toasted almonds

Martine orange soufflé alternating with a layer of sponge fingers soaked in Grand Marnier

Palmyre vanilla soufflé alternating with a layer of sponge biscuits soaked in kirsch

★**Rothschild** cream soufflé mixed with chopped candied fruit soaked in kirsch. Served with *crème Chantilly*

Sarah Bernhardt vanilla soufflé alternating with macaroons soaked in Curaçao. Served with strawberries soaked in Curaçao and *crème Chantilly*

Suédoise de fruits layers of jelly alternating with stewed fruits

Tarte alsacienne flan pastry filled with *crème pâtissière* with slices of apples or pears on top and baked

★**tatin** a sublime apple tart, served when cool

Tivoli aux fraises ring of kirsch jelly filled with *bavaroise* mixed with strawberry purée and frozen. Served with strawberries soaked in kirsch and maraschino and vanilla-flavoured *crème Chantilly*

Trou normand lemon *granité* served in a cone half-filled with Calvados apple liqueur

Vacherin round meringue layers sandwiched together with cream, fruit and ice-cream. Sometimes liqueur is added

Sauces, butters, styles and garnishes

Foreigners are inclined to think of French food as being mucked about. This was always far from the truth, but now is even less true, as the whole spirit of the so-called *nouvelle cuisine* is dedicated to allowing the real taste of ingredients to show through. What is true is that the genius of French cooking lies in combinations of tastes which complement one another and the enhancement of a quality by the addition of something else.

Over the years the French have perfected these skills, so that styles and "marriages" have been given names. It would be wrong to imagine that the names are rigid descriptions, because this would deny the other great French talent of improvisation. I have attempted to clear some sort of path through the undergrowth of nomenclature.

First, sauces. Here we are on safer ground. While any chef may have his own variation of a sauce, the ones I have listed are almost always made in the same way.

Garnishes and styles are more complicated. There are fixed ideas as to what constitutes a particular garnish, e.g. *arlésienne, Godard*, etc., yet *arlésienne* may also mean the way in which something is prepared in Arles. So while the garnish will always be the same, the style of doing say, red mullet, and the style of cooking chicken in Arles may be two entirely different things, and different again from the garnish.

Names of people, e.g. Richelieu, attached to different dishes may not mean the same thing, whereas sometimes, e.g. Rossini, they do. My hope is that these lists may help you through the jungle. They also help to show that French cooking is by no means as codified as people suppose.

Sauces and butters

Ailloli *or* **aïoli** garlic mayonnaise

Beurre butter. French cuisine demands a number of butters which are butter pastes mixed with a variety of ingredients

    blanc vinegar and shallots gradually mixed with soft butter

    maître d'hôtel softened butter mixed with herbs and lemon juice

    marchand de vin minced shallots cooked with red wine, mixed with butter, meat glaze and parsley

    noir butter cooked until brown with parsley, capers and vinegar. Often used with brains and skate

Coulis d'écrevisses crayfish tails finely sieved and mixed with cream

Sauce Albert white sauce with horseradish, cream and breadcrumbs

Albuféra *sauce béchamel* with sweet pepper butter

allemande *velouté* sauce bound with egg yolks. Also called *sauce parisienne*

américaine *and* **armoricaine** see *Homard (Fish)*

andalouse *sauce mayonnaise* with tomato paste and chopped green peppers

aurore *velouté* sauce with tomato paste. Can also be made with paprika, cream and *sauce béchamel*

béarnaise white wine, tarragon, vinegar and shallots bound with egg yolks and lots of butter. Chopped tarragon is added

béchamel a white *roux* of butter and flour mixed with milk flavoured with nutmeg, onion and a *bouquet garni*

Bercy *velouté* sauce with fish stock, white wine, shallots and lots of butter

bigarade *sauce demi-glace* with oranges, wine and Curaçao

bordelaise *sauce demi-glace* with red or white wine, shallots, tomato sauce and beef marrow

bourguignonne red wine sauce with a little carrot, bacon, onion and flour used with fish and egg dishes

bretonne chicken or fish *velouté* with mushrooms, other vegetables, white wine and cream

cardinal *sauce béchamel* with cream, lobster butter and cayenne pepper

Chantilly whipped cream added to a hot white *sauce hollandaise* or a cold *sauce mayonnaise*

charcutière *sauce demi-glace* with white wine, chopped onion and gherkins

chasseur *sauce demi-glace* with mushrooms, white wine and a little tomato paste

Chateaubriand white wine sauce with shallots, thyme and mushrooms mixed with veal stock and *beurre maître d'hôtel*

chaud-froid jelly sauce which can be either brown (*brune*) or white (*blanche*), used to coat meat, game, fish or poultry

Choron *sauce béarnaise* with tomato paste added

demi-glace basic brown sauce, reduced and strengthened with meat jelly or strong veal stock

diable *sauce demi-glace* with white wine and shallots, sharpened with chilli or cayenne pepper

duxelles *sauce demi-glace* with mushrooms, shallots and white wine

espagnole basic brown sauce

gaillarde see *Sauce gribiche*

grand veneur red wine sauce with red-currant jelly and cream

gratin thick *sauce demi-glace* with mushrooms, shallots and lemon juice

gribiche hard-boiled egg yolks mixed with oil, vinegar, herbs, gherkins and capers

hollandaise rich sauce made with butter, lemon juice and egg yolks

italienne *sauce demi-glace* with tomato, finely shredded mushrooms and shredded bacon

ivoire *sauce allemande* with a lot of meat jelly

Joinville *sauce allemande* with shrimp butter and truffles

lyonnaise *sauce demi-glace* with minced onions, white wine and vinegar

madère *sauce demi-glace* with Madeira

marchand de vin same as *Bercy*, but with meat stock and red wine

mayonnaise egg yolks, vinegar and lemon juice with olive oil

Miroton *sauce lyonnaise* with more onions and white wine

moelle *sauce demi-glace* with diced beef marrow

Mornay *sauce béchamel* with grated Parmesan cheese

mousseline *sauce hollandaise* to which whipped cream is added

mousseuse light and fluffy sauce made with butter and egg yolks, flavoured with lemon juice

Nantua *sauce béchamel* with cream and crayfish or lobster butter and some crayfish tails or minced lobster mixed into it

nivernaise fish *velouté* with carrots, herbs and onions

normande fish sauce with a little oyster liquid and mushroom stock thickened with egg yolks and cream. Sometimes has white wine

paloise *sauce béarnaise* with added mint

parisienne see *Sauce allemande*

périgourdine same as *Périgueux* with sliced, not chopped truffles

Périgueux *sauce demi-glace* with chopped truffles and Madeira

piquante *sauce demi-glace* with vinegar, shallots and gherkins, flavoured with tarragon

au pistou an olive oil and herb (primarily basil) sauce

poivrade carrot, onions and celery mixed with game trimmings, vinegar and *sauce demi-glace*, seasoned with freshly ground pepper

portugaise tomato sauce with garlic and onion

poulette *sauce allemande* with mushroom stock

raifort horseradish sauce

ravigote *sauce vinaigrette* with capers, onions and herbs

rémoulade *sauce mayonnaise* with mustard, gherkins, capers, herbs and a little anchovy essence

Robert *sauce demi-glace* with onions, white wine and mustard

rouennaise *sauce demi-glace* with duck livers, shallots and a little red wine

saupiquet hare's blood and mashed liver, with shallots, red wine and vinegar. For venison

smitane white wine and sour cream with onion and lemon

soubise onion and rice sauce with butter and a lot of cream

suprême chicken *velouté* with cream and a little meat jelly

suédoise apple compote with *sauce mayonnaise,* mustard and grated horseradish

tartare *sauce mayonnaise* with hard-boiled egg yolks, oil, vinegar, chives and capers

Valois *sauce béarnaise* with added meat jelly

vénitienne *sauce allemande*

with vinegar, sieved spinach, chopped tarragon and chervil

verte spinach, watercress, parsley and herbs all pounded together with *sauce mayonnaise* and cayenne pepper added

Villeroy *velouté* sauce with essence of truffles and essence of ham

vinaigrette french dressing (oil and vinegar mixed)

Velouté basic white sauce made with *bouillon* and white *roux*

Styles and garnishes

à l'alsacienne the classical Alsatian garnish is with noodles, pieces of *foie-gras* and slices of truffle coated with a Madeira sauce. The term often means simply with *foie-gras*

andalouse the formal garnish includes sweet peppers stuffed with rice, eggplants *au gratin* and a *sauce demi-glace* with tomato. Anything with a Spanish undertone may be included

à l'anglaise when applied to fish means breadcrumbed and fried, served with *beurre maître d'hôtel*

arlésienne with stuffed tomatoes *à la provençale,* eggplants and pilaff saffron rice

à la bonne femme white wine sauce with shallots, mushrooms and lemon juice. Carrots, celery and herbs may be added

à la bordelaise usually means in a red wine sauce with beef marrow but can, particularly with fish, mean with vegetables, tomato paste, brandy and white wine

à la bourguignonne onions, mushrooms and diced bacon cooked in butter. Any sauce going with this garnish should have red wine, as opposed to *sauce bourguignonne* which has white wine

à la boulangère a braised onion and potato garnish

bouquetière with vegetables

à la bourgeoise a carrot, onion and diced bacon garnish

à la bretonne with an onion, white wine, garlic and tomato sauce

à la catalane with tomato sauce and pilaff rice

en chartreuse applied to game birds such as partridge or pheasant, this means that the bird

is braised with carrots, onions, turnips, peas, cabbage and bacon. Often arranged in layers or elaborate patterns

châtelaine the full garnish consists of artichoke hearts covered with a salpicon of ox-tongue, mushrooms, truffles and *foie-gras* covered with *sauce béchamel* and browned with a little cheese. In general, involves artichokes

choisi braised lettuce sprinkled with grated cheese and covered with *sauce moelle,* with some new potatoes covered with gravy

à la dauphine with *pommes dauphine*

à la dieppoise white wine, mussels, and mushrooms

à la dijonnaise usually means with a mustard sauce

à la duchesse with artichoke hearts, mushrooms and potatoes

dugléré with tomatoes, white wine, shallots and herbs

à l'espagnole usually involves red peppers, tomatoes and garlic

favorite *foie-gras* sautéed in butter with truffle and asparagus

financière mushrooms, cockscombs, truffles, olives, veal and poultry *quenelles* all covered with a *sauce madère*

flamande braised cabbage, carrots, turnips, bacon and sausage

florentine with spinach

forestière mushrooms and diced potatoes sautéed in butter, with sliced truffles and gravy

Gascogne or **Gasconne** usually involves Armagnac

à la génoise usually with tomato sauce and often with tuna fish

Godard same as *financière* with sweetbreads added

81

au gratin thin crust formed when browned under the grill or in the oven, often with breadcrumbs

à la grecque applies to vegetables cooked in water ideally with parsley, celery, thyme, bayleaf, coriander, fennel, peppercorns, lemon juice and olive oil, allowed to cool and served very cold

jardinière with diced vegetables in individual heaps

judic small braised lettuces with a *sauce demi-glace* and a fine *ragoût* of sliced truffles, cockscombs and kidneys

landaise usually means with *foie-gras* and truffles

lyonnaise always with onions

macédoine mixed diced vegetables

madrilène with tomatoes or tomato sauce

maréchale egg-and-breadcrumbed, sometimes with truffles and asparagus tips

Marie-Louise artichoke hearts, filled with mushroom purée, covered with grated cheese and browned, with thin slices of truffle and asparagus tips

marquise macaroni with Parmesan cheese, truffle and shrimps coated with a creamy *sauce béchamel* and shrimp butter

à la ménagère as a garnish, with peas, braised lettuce and *pommes Macaire* but hardly a very specific term. It's an indication of the spirit of improvisation expected of the housewife who looks for the best daily produce

à la meunière coated with flour, sautéed and served in hot melted butter with sliced lemon

milanaise egg-and-breadcrumbed

Mirabeau with anchovy and olives

Mireille usually with some wine, truffles and possibly asparagus tips

Mistinguette with herbs, *foie-gras* and white wine

Montpensier involves Madeira, asparagus tips and truffles

à la nage in a *court-bouillon* of white wine, carrots, shallots, onions, herbs and spices

normande often means with apples and Calvados. See also *Sauces*

à l'orientale usually means with saffron but can include anything with a hint of the East

Orloff with *sauce soubise* and *sauce Mornay*

Parmentier with potatoes

paysanne usually with onions and carrots or any simple combination

piémontaise the garnish consists of sliced mushrooms and tomatoes, fried, sprinkled with grated cheese and heated with garlic and parsley, accompanied by rice cooked in consommé with more Parmesan. The term otherwise usually means with white truffles and a risotto

à la polonaise usually involves breadcrumbs

à la portugaise the garnish is tomatoes and zucchini, fried with garlic and parsley, accompanied by pilaff rice. In general the term usually involves red peppers and tomatoes

à la poulette can mean with a *sauce allemande* or a *sauce normande*. This may seem somewhat confusing but a *sauce normande* was originally a *sauce allemande* with butter added. Nowadays *normande* is a white wine sauce with a fish flavour but the term *à la poulette* still covers both versions

printanier with spring vegetables

provençale the garnish consists of tomatoes, stuffed with the ingredients mentioned below, accompanied by *cèpes* or other mushrooms and parsley. As a general term it means with tomatoes, onions, garlic, breadcrumbs, olives and anchovies

renaissance spring vegetables arranged in piles round the dish

Richelieu as a garnish, grilled mushrooms, braised lettuce, new potatoes and stuffed tomatoes. With fish it usually involves *beurre maître d'hôtel*

Rossini the garnish means with noodles, Parmesan cheese, *foie-gras* and slices of truffle all coated with a Marsala sauce. In general it means all these things, but a Madeira sauce is often used

Saint-Germain usually with peas in some form or other

Sarah Bernhardt with *foie-gras* purée

à la savoyarde with cheese and potatoes

sicilienne with sweetbreads and truffles on flat, round, semolina

cakes. Served with more
sweetbreads and covered in *sauce
béchamel*
Souvaroff when applied to birds,
usually means cooked with
brandy, *foie-gras*, truffles and
flavoured with Madeira
Talleyrand the garnish is with
macaroni, cheese, truffles and

foie-gras all mixed together. In
general it includes all these but
Madeira is often added and the
macaroni sometimes left out
toulousaine cockscombs and
kidneys, mushrooms, truffles and
sweetbreads simmered with
Madeira and all covered with a
sauce allemande

French wine

Wine in French restaurants is frequently very expensive and
quite often not as good as it is in Britain. The French,
on the whole, do not make as much fuss about wine as we do
and, indeed, often know less about it. They are inclined
to drink it younger. Furthermore, many wines do not travel,
so that most French wine lists are full of names most of us
have never heard of.

For all these reasons, my usual practice is to drink
whatever the wine waiter tells me is the best local wine.
Wine waiters in general are out to help rather than merely
sell and they are usually proud of their region.

If you are determined to drink only the very best then
I would advise you to take the excellent companion volume
to this book—*Hugh Johnson's Pocket Encyclopedia of Wine*.
Listed in it is the finest wine of every district. In this case
you will be able to pick out the best of the Appellations
Contrôlées, which is a classification guaranteeing the source
of the wine, its method of manufacture and grape variety.

Drinking only these, you will miss the often excellent
value for money provided by the next class—V.D.Q.S.
(*Vins Délimités de Qualité Supérieure*). Even more you will
miss the adventure of the *vins du pays* which cost little, may
taste marvellous or rough but have just the same effect.

I merely exhort you to try something other than the
familiar clarets, Burgundies and Beaujolais you will find at
home. To this end I suggest a few names:

Apremont: light Savoie white
Arbois: unusual "yellow" Jura
wine (vin jaune)
Bandol: vigorous Provençal red
Beaumes de Venise: a sweet dark
white from the Rhône
Bellet: good Provençal
Bourgueil: rich Loire red
Cahors: the older, "blacker"
ones are terrific
Château Simone: pleasant
Provençal
Chinon: first class Loire red
Condrieu: gentle Rhône white
Corbières: rollicking Midi reds
Cornas: strong Rhône red
Côte Rôtie: wonderful Rhône red
Côtes de Duras: light Dordogne
Côtes du Roussillon: strong reds
and sharp whites from the south-
west
Fitou: strong Midi red

Gigondas: powerful Rhône red
Haut Comtat: vigorous Rhône red
Hermitage: used to be the most
famous wine— still tastes superb
Irouléguy: pleasant Basque white
Lirac: Rhône red and rosé
Metayer: a good cheap
champagne
Monbazillac: sweet Dordogne
white
Montlouis: Loire white
Pécharmant: Dordogne red
Quatourze: jolly Midi
Quincy: dry Loire white
Roussette de Savoie: merry white
Saint Chinian: Midi red
Saint-Péray: ponderous,
sparkling Rhône white
Saint Pourçain: drinkable from
near Vichy
Savennières: saucy Loire white
Seyssel: sparkling Savoie white

Useful words

For culinary terms not found here, see glossary (p. 239).

Addition bill

Aigre-doux sweet-sour

Ail garlic

Allumettes puff pastry strips, garnished or filled

Amandine garnished with almonds

Amer bitter

Anchoïade anchovy paste

Anchois anchovies

Arachide peanut

Assiette assortie a mixture of cold hors d'œuvre

Ballottine literally a "small bundle"; usually applied to meat or poultry, boned and stuffed and tied up or rolled into a bundle

Barquettes pastry boats

Basilique basil

Beurre butter

Bière beer

Bifteck beefsteak

Blanquette "white" stew, thick with egg yolks and cream

Boisson beverage

Bouchée tiny *vol-au-vent*

Bouilli boiled

Bouillon broth

Braisé braised

Brioche soft bread made from a rich yeast dough

à la Broche spit-roasted

en Brochette skewered and grilled

Café coffee

en Caisse see *en Papillote*

Câpres capers

Cassoulet haricot bean stew

Chaud hot

Charcuterie shop selling everything in the way of cold hors d'œuvre, particularly pork

à Choix the one of your choice

Chou light puff pastry. Also means cabbage

Choux à la crème cream puffs

(en) Cocotte (cooked in) a small ovenproof dish

Confit usually of goose, duck, turkey or pork, completely covered in its own fat, cooked and then preserved

Confiture jam

Contre-filet sirloin steak

Coquillages shellfish

Coquille de . . . served in a scallop shell

Coquilles scallops

Côte, côtelette chop, cutlet

Couvert cover charge

Crème cream

　frangipane almond-flavoured confectioner's custard

　pâtissière confectioner's custard

Crêpes thin pancakes

Crépinettes small, flattish sausages. Usually grilled

Croquettes small shaped moulds of cooked food, egg-and-breadcrumbed and fried

en Croûte cooked in a pastry case

Croustade small bread or pastry mould with a savoury filling

Cru raw

Cuisine minceur a way of cooking for slimmers

Cuit cooked

Darne thick slice of fish

Daube meat slowly braised in a rich stock with wine and herbs

Douce, doux sweet

Duxelles mushrooms cooked in butter with chopped shallots

Eau minérale mineral water, either *gazeuse* (sparkling) or *naturelle* (flat)

Entrecôte rib steak

Épices spices

Escabèche various fish, first fried then marinated in a *court-bouillon* and served cold

Estouffade dish where the meat is slowly braised, having been marinated and fried

Estragon tarragon

Étuvé stewed, braised

Farci stuffed

au Fenouil cooked over dry fennel stalks

Feuilletage puff pastry

Filet fillet

Foie-gras preserved liver of specially fattened goose or duck

au Four baked in the oven

Fraîche, frais fresh

Frappé surrounded by crushed ice

Fricadelle kind of meat ball

Frit fried

Fritots fritters

Froid cold

Fruits de mer seafood

Fumé smoked

Galette flaky pastry cake

Garni literally "garnished", with accompanying vegetables

Garnitures garnishes

Glacé iced, frozen, glazed

Gougère egg and cheese *chou* paste, usually baked in a round

au Gratin crispy browned topping of breadcrumbs or cheese

Grillade grilled meat

Grillé grilled

Haricot stew with vegetables (see *Vegetables*)

Hochepot thick soup-stew made with various fat meats and vegetables

Huile d'olive olive oil

Jambon ham

Lait milk

Macédoine diced fruit or vegetables

(de notre) Maison of the restaurant

Marjolaine sweet marjoram

Marmite earthenware or metal cooking pot with lid

Matelote properly speaking, a fish stew with wine, but also used of *matelote de veau*

Médaillon round or oval cut of meat, etc.

Mijoté simmered, stewed

Mirepoix mixture of chopped vegetables and ham

Moelle beef marrow

Mousse a light, fluffy and creamy dish usually made with ham, chicken livers or fish. It can also be a sweet concoction. The main ingredient is minced very finely and mixed with cream and egg whites. Served cold

Mousselines really baby *mousses* cooked in spoonfuls rather than in a large mould. See also *sauce mousseline*

Moutarde mustard

Navarin stew of lamb or mutton and young root vegetables

Noix nuts, usually walnuts

Nouilles noodles

Origan oregano

Oseille sorrel

Pain bread

Panade flour-based or bread paste, used for binding or thickening

Pané breadcrumbed

Pannequets like *crêpes* but slightly thicker and smaller when cooked

en Papillote cooked in oiled or buttered paper

Pâte pastry

   à chou cream puff pastry

Pâtisserie pastries

Paupiettes thin slices of meat or fish rolled up, probably with some stuffing

Persil parsley

Persillade mixture of chopped parsley and garlic

Pignons pine nuts

Piquant sharp or spicy

Poché poached

Pochouse fish stew

Poivre pepper

Pralin almond sugar

Prix price

Quenelles feathery oval dumplings, usually of fish

Raifort horseradish

Riz rice

Romarin rosemary

Rouille creamy garlic and chilli sauce, usually used with fish soups

Royale unsweetened custard cut into strips or decorative patterns. Used in soup

Sagou sago

Saucisse fresh, wet sausage

Saucisson large, dry sausage

Sauge sage

Sec dry

Sel salt

Selon grosseur *often just* **S.G.,** according to size

   quantité *often just* **S.Q.,** according to quantity

Semoule semolina

Service compris service included

Sucre sugar

Thé tea

Timbale dome-shaped mould or the pie cooked within it (often containing noodles or macaroni)

Tourte covered tart

Tranche slice

Varèche seaweed

Vin blanc, rouge white, red wine

Vinaigre vinegar

Vinaigrette oil and vinegar dressing

Vol-au-vent case of flaky pastry with a lid, which may contain a variety of light ingredients

---

Bon appétit!
Santé! cheers!

Germany and Austria

DENMARK

SCHLESWIG
HOLSTEIN

NORTH SEA

• Kiel

• Hambur

• Bremen

LOWER
SAXONY

HANNOVER
(HANOVER) •

NETHERLANDS

• Münster

Braunschweig
(Brunswick)

*Harz
Mountai*

NORTH RHINE-
WESTPHALIA

Ruhr

Düsseldorf • Dortmund

Essen

• Kassel

BELGIUM

BONN

Rhine

KÖLN (COLOGNE)

WEST
GERMANY

THURING

RHINE
LAND

HESSE

Koblenz •

LUXEMBOURG

Moselle

• Frankfurt

SAAR

Mainz •

Bamberg •

• Mannheim
• Heidelberg

NÜRNBERG
(NUREMBURG)

• Karlsruhe

FRANCE

*Black
Forest*
• Freiburg

• STUTTGART

BADEN-WÜRTTEMBER

Augsburg •

MÜNCHEN
(MUNICH)

• Innsbruck

SWITZERLAND

TYROL

ITAL

German food has no great reputation, unless it be for filling
you up. Almost the only things the average person could
name as being German would be sauerkraut and the frankfurter. This is hardly fair because the diversity of German
food is great, particularly as each region was, until comparatively recently, autonomous. Furthermore people who are so
interested in eating, many of them having five meals a day,
could scarcely help but produce some good food.

The problem lies in their completely different approach to
food. While most other European countries have gradually
refined their cuisines, Germany has largely been happy to
maintain the medieval patterns of cookery, the inheritance
of ancient Rome.

86

BALTIC SEA

• Rostock

chwerin

Elbe

BERLIN •

Magdeburg

**EAST
GERMANY**

POLAND

• **LEIPZIG**

• **DRESDEN**

CZECHOSLOVAKIA

Regensburg
(Ratisbon)
Danube

AVARIA

Linz

• **WIEN
(VIENNA)**

• **SALZBURG**

AUSTRIA   **STYRIA**   **HUNGARY**
                    • Graz

CARINTHIA

The Germans love contrasts. They have many sweet-and-sour dishes; mixing fruit with meat and fish, vinegar, sugar and apples with vegetables. They mix hot with cold; pouring hot fruit sauces over ice-cream. They like violent colours in food. All these are the hallmarks of Roman cooking which the rest of us have abandoned. Given this, and given that any peasant economy is inclined to rely on those foods which one man can raise (in Germany pork, potatoes and cabbages), there are, as counterweights, a great emphasis on quality of ingredients and a considerable ingenuity in varying the staples of the cuisine—the numbers of different kinds of noodles, dumplings, sausages and pancakes are incalculable. At the same time, variety is provided by the

German liking for whatever nature can provide, especially game and in particular venison which, if one can persuade them not to overcook it, is the best in the world. So it is possible to love German food, more especially south German food which has been more influenced by proximity to Austria.

Strictly speaking, there is no specific Austrian cuisine. The Austrians eat the food of their neighbours and former empire—to the south Yugoslavia, to the east Hungary, to the north Germany and Czechoslovakia. It is for this reason that I have included Austria with Germany, sharing as they do a common language.

The Hungarians have provided a little spice to the bland food of Germany. The Bohemians have provided a certain finesse (Austrian men always look out for Bohemian wives as they make the best cooks). It is only the Viennese who have contrived anything positively Austrian—the famous cakes and pastries. I have given these a section of their own.

Meals

Deciding where to eat in Germany requires an understanding of German mealtimes. First comes *Frühstück*, breakfast; usually bread with jam and coffee, but it can include meat or sausage and cheese. Then *Zweites Frühstück*, or second breakfast, in the middle of the morning. This is primarily a south German and Austrian agricultural custom, stemming from early rising but they can take it quite seriously, with cold cuts, smoked fish and sausages with plenty of beer. There is even a variation known as *Katerfrühstück*, or hangover breakfast, which involves herrings or goulash soup. A couple of hours later comes the real meal of the day *Mittagessen* with at least four courses. By four o'clock they are at it again with *Kaffee mit Kuchen*, which is a rich business of cakes and sweet pastries. Finally there is *Abendessen* or *Abendbrot*, which perhaps not surprisingly, is usually one course, although even that includes meat, sausage, fish, cheese and a salad.

Where to eat

The multiplicity of eating places caters for all these meals or variations on them. Roughly they work like this:

Gaststätte or **Restaurant:** full meals, with a varied universal menu

Ratskeller or **Rathauskeller:** taverns in the city hall cellar, serving traditional and local specialities. Originally for students but now a local centre, with good food at reasonable prices

Gasthof or **Gasthaus:** modest meals, catering for locals

Bierstube: properly a beer room, but providing elaborate bar snacks or even meals. Very often offering hangover breakfast

Weinstube: the wine equivalent of a *Bierstube*. The watershed (if that is the word for it) dividing the wine from the beer drinkers is the River Main. North of it they drink more wine, south more beer

Bierhalle: large beer hall, concentrating more on drink but providing some hot and cold food

Café: coffee and pastries

Konditorei: basically a pastry shop, but you can sit down and drink coffee or hot chocolate and try out the pastries

Schnellimbiss: a snack bar

Würstchenstand: a street kiosk selling sausages and bread

Once inside a German restaurant, the best thing is to find your own table. Even in quite smart restaurants this is regarded as normal. In smaller restaurants people may come and sit at your table if there is no other place.

The menu

The menu is likely to be in two parts—the *Speisekarte* which is the regular printed menu and the *Tageskarte* which is the typed list of dishes of the day. The *Tageskarte* is a simple list, but the *Speisekarte* is an object of national thoroughness, divided into anything up to 15 sections.

They go like this:

Vorspeisen: hors d'oeuvre
Suppe: soups
Eierspeisen und Mehlspeisen: egg dishes and farinaceous dishes
Hauptgerichte: main courses, subdivided thus:
  Fisch fish
  Wild und Geflügel game and poultry
  Fleischgerichte meat
  Pfannengerichte pan-fried dishes (omelettes or schnitzels)

Kaltespeisen cold dishes
  Belegte Brote open sandwiches
  Wurstgerichte sausage dishes
Spezialitäten des Hauses: specialities of the house
Gemüse: vegetables
Beilagen: extras (dumplings, salads, etc.)
Nachspeisen or **Süss-speisen:** desserts
Käse: cheese

Of course, you may come across a meticulous fellow who thinks all this is too vague. He will helpfully break down some of these loose categories into sections such as *Schnitten*—snacks, *Fertige Speisen*—ready cooked dishes, *Vom Kalb*—veal dishes, *Kompotte*—stewed fruits, and so on.

Once you have got to grips with all that, you must remember that the restaurant will be out to fool you with some of Germany's finest exercises in portmanteauism. A huge word full of irrelevancies will appear on the menu on these lines: tenderyoungcalfknucklestewedinthemannerofwesternbavaria. The trick is to spot the key word—*Kalb*, *Schwein*, *Geflügel* or whatever—and then to try to disentangle the rest of the word. The key words appear in their relevant sections below (Meat, Fish, Poultry, etc.), together with some of the more common combinations. The useful word list will also help with some of the components of long fancy words.

Vorspeisen— Hors d'oeuvre

Hors d'oeuvre did not play much part in traditional German cuisine but, as the Germans have started to rejoin the mainstream of European cooking, they are now commonplace even if not strikingly original.

Austern oysters
Bismarckhering pickled herring
Blätterteigpastete a pastry case filled with creamed veal or mushrooms
Brathering herring fillet baked then marinated and served cold
★**Bündnerfleisch** dried cured beef sliced paper thin. A Swiss dish

Fischmayonnaise cold fish salad
Gänseleberpastete goose liver pâté
Geflügelleberpastete chicken liver pâté
Geflügelsalat diced chicken in mayonnaise with apples and celery
Gemüsesalat vegetable salad
Geräucherter Aal smoked eel

89

Grüner Hering see *Matjeshering*
Handkäse mit Musik cheese with onion and vinegar garnish
Heringsalat pickled herrings, chopped with beets, apple, potatoes and onion in a sour cream dressing. A Polish dish
Holsteiner Katenschinken smoked raw ham
Kieler Sprotten smoked sprats
Königinpastete meat pies
Leberkäs a Bavarian meat loaf
Marinierter Hering pickled herring
Matjeshering salted fresh herring fillets
★ **Ochsenmaulsalat** slivers of tongue in a tart vinaigrette dressing
Ochsenzunge ox tongue
Quark mit Früchten cottage cheese with fruit
Ragout Fin chopped veal in a herb and cream sauce served in a pastry case
Räucherlachs smoked salmon

Rohkost raw vegetables, like *crudités*
Rollmops herring fillets spread with mustard and stuffed with sliced onion and pickled cucumber and marinated in vinegar, spices and herbs for several days
Rührei scrambled eggs
Rundstück warm an open sandwich of roast beef or pork served hot
Spargel asparagus
Spetzei, Spiegelei fried egg
Spickgans smoked goose
Strammer Max an open sandwich of ham and one or two fried eggs
Sülz, Sülze head cheese
★ **Westfälischer Schinken** Westphalian ham. Paper-thin slices of smoked cured ham, eaten raw
Wurst sausage of all kinds. See separate section
  -salat Bavarian sausage and onion salad

Suppe—Soups

Soups, particularly in the north, are very serious affairs. Many of the purées of slowly cooked dried beans, peas or lentils with meat or sausage, dumplings *and* potatoes would keep most of us going for two days. In the south the average soup is a bit lighter, usually clear, but still with dumplings. On the other hand, the fish soups are often delicate and fragrant—almost the equal of their equivalent in France or Italy. The cold fruit soups are interesting and a relic of the medieval habit of starting a meal with something sweet.

★ **Aalsuppe** eel soup, an elaborate dish of vegetables and fruit cooked in a meat stock with pieces of boiled, boned eel. Served with dumplings and beer. In Bremen the broth is eaten separately before the eel and dumplings
Bauernsuppe a peasant soup of vegetables and dried beans flavoured with herbs and bacon
Beetensuppe beet soup
★ **Biersuppe** beer soup. It can be hot (*heisse Biersuppe*), a Bavarian speciality in which the beer is spiced with cloves and cinnamon and beaten eggs are added, or cold (*Bierkaltschale*), in which spices, dried fruit and breadcrumbs are steeped in cold beer. *Leipziger Biersuppe* is a hot version with milk and cornstarch

Blumenkohlsuppe cauliflower soup
Bohnensuppe bean soup made with dried beans of all sorts
Brotsuppe a sweet-and-sour bread soup made with half black and half white bread soaked in apple juice, cooked with wine, raisins and spices
  von Metzelsuppe bread soup made with meat stock and garnished with fried onions
Erbsensuppe pea soup made with yellow split peas
  mit Speck with bacon trimmings
★ **Fischsuppe** this speciality of Germany's main sea port, Hamburg, is made from a mixture of fish and shellfish, freshly caught in the Baltic and North Seas
Flädlesuppe a Swabian clear soup with strips of pancake

Fleischbrühe, Fleischsuppe a clear meat broth served plain or with noodles, dumplings, strips of pancake or cubes of egg custard

Frittatensuppe soup with strips of pancake

Fruchtkaltschale cold fruit soup popular in north Germany. This could be made with pears, plums, apricots, strawberries or cherries

Frühlingssuppe young carrots, peas, cauliflower and asparagus cooked in a meat stock

Gaisburger Marsch Gaisburg broth, named after a suburb of Stuttgart. A rich beef soup served with diced potatoes and *Spätzle*

Graupensuppe mit Hühnerklein chicken giblet and barley soup

Griessnockerlsuppe clear soup with semolina dumplings

Grüne Bohnensuppe a thick cream soup made with string beans

Erbsensuppe green pea soup, usually served with cream and cubes of fried bread

Kartoffelsuppe potato and leek soup

Gulaschsuppe beef goulash thinned into a soup eaten at supper time and for second breakfast

Heisse Biersuppe see *Biersuppe*

Helgoländer Hummersuppe lobster soup with shrimps

★ **Hirnsuppe** Swabian brain soup

Huhnerbrühe mit Nudeln chicken noodle soup

Kaltschale cold fruit soup, see *Fruchtkaltschale*

Kartoffelsuppe potato soup, often served with cucumber or, in Swabia, with noodles or, in the Black Forest, with diced bacon and liver sausage

Kerbelsuppe a delicately flavoured chervil soup

Knödelsuppe bread dumplings or bacon and parsley dumplings (*Tiroler Knödeln*) served in meat broth

Königinsuppe chicken soup with rice

Kraftbrühe like *Fleischbrühe*, a clear meat broth

Krautsuppe cabbage soup flavoured with caraway seeds

★ **Leberknödelsuppe** dumplings made from ground liver, breadcrumbs, flour, egg yolks and herbs in a clear meat broth. Sometimes served as a main dish with cabbage and boiled potatoes. A Bavarian speciality

Leipziger Biersuppe see *Biersuppe*

Linsensuppe a thick soup made with brown lentils and served with the local sausage

Nockerlsuppe clear broth with semolina dumplings

Obstsuppe nach Hamburger Art a puréed mixture of soft fruits

Stoss-suppe a Styrian soup made with sour milk, potatoes and caraway seeds

Suppe hausgemacht home-made soup

Tagessuppe soup of the day

Wurstsuppe soup with sausage

Zwiebelsuppe onion soup

Wurst — Sausage

There are said to be several hundred different kinds of sausage in Germany and Austria; even small towns and villages have their own special variety. They may be made from bits and pieces of pork, veal or beef or a mixture of all three. Some are cooking sausages, meant to be boiled or fried; others are sliced and eaten cold like salami. They appear in meals from breakfast time onwards through the day. They can be in soups and main courses, in sandwiches and stand-up snacks in the street. The following are a selection of the main types of sausage but the best policy is probably to try the local sausage wherever you happen to be.

Aufschnitt a plate of various sliced sausages

Bierwurst a fat sausage with a dark reddish-brown skin, made from finely chopped pork, beef and pork fat

Blaue Zipfel a Franconian sausage dish made with *Bratwurst* stewed with onions and vinegar

Blockwurst beef and pork sausage similar to salami, eaten cold in the same way

Blutwurst the basic blood sausage with blackish-red skin, sold in circles. It is boiled or fried like black pudding. Eaten for breakfast in some areas

Blutzungenwurst a blood sausage containing chunks of tongue

Bratwurst a spiced pork frying sausage found everywhere in Germany with various regional variations. May be served fried or grilled with any of a number of sauces. Also grilled in special street kiosks called *Bratwurstgöckl*

Debrecziner an Austro-Hungarian sausage, similar to frankfurters but spicier and containing coarse pieces of pork

Extrawurst very fine veal sausage made with wine and nutmeg

Frankfurter Würstchen small boiling sausages served with bread and mustard, the ancestor of the hot dog

Frankfurterplatte a plate of sausage and sauerkraut

Gänseleberwurst goose liver sausage sometimes flavoured with truffles

★Himmel und Erde literally "heaven and earth", it is fried *Blutwurst* with potato and apple purée. In some areas the name refers only to the purée. This dish features prominently as part of the plot in children's open-air puppet shows which is rather reminiscent of Mr Punch and *his* sausages

Katenwurst a smoked sausage from Schleswig-Holstein

Knackwurst small cooking sausages not unlike frankfurters but much thicker and shorter, also eaten cold

Krakauer Polish ham sausage, one of the most popular in Germany

Landjäger literally "local policeman"—actually a Swabian smoked sausage

Leberwurst liver sausage

Lyonerwurst garlic-flavoured ham sausage

Mettwurst a red-skinned, smoked, coarse pork sausage

Milzwurst Bavarian veal sausage

Regensburgerwurst a stubby sausage of pork or pork and beef

Rindswurst beef sausage

★Rostbratwurst made from best ham seasoned with nutmeg and caraway seeds, traditionally roasted over a wood fire

Schinkenwurst ham sausage

Schlachtplatte a plate of sliced cold meats and sausages

Stadtwurst may be white or red, made from best pork and usually served with sauerkraut

Sülz, **Sülze** jellied meat loaf sometimes containing slices of hard-boiled eggs and vegetables, superior version of head cheese

Weisswurst a small pale sausage made with veal, wine and fresh parsley; special to Munich where it is often eaten for breakfast because it only stays fresh for a few hours; eaten with sweet mustard

Wellfleischsuppe a soup made with pork sausages and stock, traditionally eaten at pig-killings

Wienerwurst frankfurter sausages

Wurstbrötchen fresh roll with sliced sausages

Wurstsalat a Munich delicacy of sliced *Regensburgerwurst* with onions and dressing

Fisch — *Fish*

Germany's relatively short coastline traditionally limited salt-water fish to the northern areas, although smoked, pickled and salted fish are popular everywhere. In the north the herring predominates followed by eel, halibut and mackerel. In the south they rely more on freshwater fish, in particular the trout which is the principal fish of the Rhineland, Bavaria and Austria. Other freshwater fish like perch, tench, carp and pike appear frequently on menus.

Aal eel, very popular in north and East Germany where they are cooked and served in a wide variety of ways—in soups, stews, jellied, smoked and boiled

    Berliner Art eels cooked in beer and white wine with cloves, onion, black bread and lemon juice

in Gelee jellied eels

grün eels boiled in white wine and allowed to cool, served with a sauce made from masses of herbs, chopped onions and sour cream

Alse shad

Austern oysters

Barsch perch

Brachse, Brasse porgy

Brathering fried herring, served hot or cold

Dorsch cod. See also *Kabeljau*
-**rogen** cod's roe

Fischpastete Hamburger Art a pie of chopped halibut, sole, shrimps, asparagus and herbs in a cream sauce topped with a rich pastry crust

Fischragout fish stew

Fischrouladen flatfish fillets rolled, stuffed with bacon, onion and mushroom, and baked in butter and wine

Flunder flounder

Forelle trout

blau trout poached in vinegar and water and served with melted butter

in Gelee trout in aspic

nach Müllerin Art dusted with flour and baked in butter

Garnelen shrimp

Hecht pike

auf Badische Art pike baked with onion, bacon, sour cream, grated cheese and breadcrumbs

Heilbutt halibut

excesses of the morning blot out those of the night before

Hummer lobster

Hummerkrabben large shrimp

Jakobsmuscheln scallops

Kabeljau cod, served boiled or steamed, also poached in white wine with herbs or baked with mushrooms

nach Hamburger Art cod poached in white wine, served with oyster sauce

mit Schnittlauch und Zwiebel cod baked with onions and chives. A north German dish

★**Karpfen** carp, popular in Germany since the Middle Ages when carp ponds were a common feature of many monastic settlements. It is a traditional Christmas Eve dish in many parts of Germany, when it is cooked the Polish way, simmered in a beer-flavoured stock and served with a sauce including cake crumbs, spices, almonds and dried fruit. The fish is not descaled before cooking and it is customary for each diner to save a few scales from the carp as a good luck charm for the coming year. In Austria the Christmas Eve carp is sliced, dipped in egg and breadcrumbs, fried and served with potato salad and lemon

Krabbe crab

Krabben shrimps

Krebs crayfish

They [herrings] can be used fresh, salted, smoked, or marinated. They can be boiled, baked, fried, steamed, filleted, boned and stuffed, rolled around gherkins, or placed in oil, vinegar, white wine, and sour cream. Boiled with onions in salt water, they went well with Amanda Woyke's potatoes in their jackets. Sophie Rotzoll laid them on strips of bacon, sprinkled them with bread crumbs and popped them into the oven. Margarete Rusch, the cooking nun, liked to steam sauerkraut with juniper berries and throw in small, boned Baltic herrings toward the end. Agnes Kurbiella served tender fillets steamed in white wine as diet fare. Lena Stubbe rolled herrings in flour, fried them, and set them before her second husband.
Günter Grass *The Flounder*

Hering herring, generally available all over Germany. They are eaten as first or main courses, in salads, sandwiches and even as part of the apparently effective *Katerfrühstück*, the substantial hangover breakfast where the

Lachs salmon—the Rhine provides an excellent source of fresh salmon so the towns along its banks are the best places to eat it during the season between February and September

Lachs gebraten am Stück salmon

braised in butter and lemon juice, with a sour cream sauce

in Weisswein mit Champignons a Rhenish dish of salmon steaks poached in white wine, served with hollandaise sauce, mushrooms and asparagus

Makrele mackerel

Marinierter Hering pickled herring

Matjeshering salted herring fillets served cold either as a snack or main course with potatoes

Hausfrauen Art salted herrings with sliced onions, apples and tomatoes in a sour cream sauce

Muscheln mussels, in season from September to April, often cooked in white wine with chopped onions

Paprikakarpfen diced, fried carp in a paprika sauce

Räucheraal smoked eel, usually eaten with rye bread or with eggs,

either scrambled or in omelettes

Räucherlachs smoked salmon

Salat von Geräuchertem Aal smoked eel salad containing chopped apple, potatoes, lettuce and herbs

Salm salmon. See *Lachs*

Schellfish haddock

Schleie tench

Scholle plaice

Schwarzfisch poached carp in a rich sauce including almonds, prunes, white raisins and crumbled spiced honey cake

Seebutt brill

Seezunge sole

Steinbutt turbot

Stör sturgeon

Zander pike-perch, a large freshwater fish often served in elaborate wine sauces containing fruit and spices

---

. . . now I'm going to make that eel soup, don't be so squeamish . . . we're having eels and that's that, with milk, mustard, parsley and boiled potatoes, a bay leaf goes in and a clove . . . I didn't buy eels to throw them away, they'll be nicely cleaned and washed, we'll see when they're on the table, we'll see who eats and who don't eat.
Günter Grass *The Tin Drum*

Fleisch—Meat

Germany is generally thought to be a nation of great meat eaters and it is true that many of the classic dishes call for what sometimes seem like enormous quantities of meat. The Sunday joint, for example, is as typical of German domestic eating as it is of British, although the meat is more likely to be pork or veal than beef. Helpings are inclined to be dauntingly large and almost always smothered in thick, heavily seasoned gravy. Roast meat, in particular, tends to be vastly overdone for non-German tastes. However, there is another side to German meat cookery which may well stem from the fact that the history of Germany has been fraught with desperate economic upheavals when the mass of the population have been forced to live close to the breadline or even below it. This has spurred the invention of dishes which make the most out of very small amounts of meat and also out of those parts of the animal which, in more prosperous times, might be discarded.

★ **Bauernfrühstück** literally "peasant's breakfast", in north Germany, an omelette of bacon and potato; in Bavaria, black bread with butter and bacon

Bauernschmaus boiled pork with sauerkraut, sausages, dumplings and potatoes

Bauernspeck Tyrolean smoked bacon

Beefsteak Tartar steak Tartare, ground raw steak with spices, capers and a raw egg

Berliner Eintopf a Berlin "one-dish" stew of mixed meats, potatoes, beans and cabbage

Beuschel a stew of calf's liver, lungs and hearts with vegetables, anchovies, capers, mustard and sour cream, served with dumplings

Birnen, Bohnen und Speck pears, beans and bacon. This dish from Schleswig-Holstein has a typical combination of sweet and sour flavours. Very fatty

Bries, Bröschen sweetbreads

Debrecziner Gulasch a beef goulash with pieces of *Debrecziner* sausages

Deutsches Beefsteak the German version of a hamburger but more like a meat rissole as it is invariably made with breadcrumbs or flour and beaten egg and is usually served with a fried egg on top

Dicke Bohnen mit Rauchfleisch a Westphalian dish of fava beans with bacon and smoked belly of pork spiced with cloves

Edelgulasch a veal goulash with added cream popular in Austria

Eingemachtes Kalbfleisch cheap cuts of veal casseroled with vegetables in cream sauce

Eintopf a one-dish meal largely promoted during the last war, usually a stew containing meat, bacon and possibly fish, with vegetables

Eisbein pickled pork hocks or knuckles, a very fatty dish found all over Germany, usually served with mashed potatoes, and sauerkraut or a purée of split peas

Esterhazy Rostbraten an Austrian speciality consisting of fried steaks in a sauce made of shredded root vegetables, capers, lemon and sour cream

Faschierter Braten a meat loaf made from a mixture of ground beef, veal and pork. Eaten hot or cold

Fleischklösse meat dumplings

Frikadellen meat balls made from ground beef, breadcrumbs and beaten egg, often served cold

Gaisburger Marsch a rich beef stew from Stuttgart served with noodles

G'selchtes Bavarian smoked ham or bacon cooked with sauerkraut

Gulasch an Austrian speciality related to Hungarian *gulyás*. Usually made with beef but there are many variations. It can include potatoes, mushrooms, beans, even fish

Hackbraten meat loaf

Hämmchen mit Sauerkraut cured pork hock with sauerkraut, eaten with boiled potatoes

Hammel mutton
  -**braten** roast mutton
  -**brust** breast of mutton
  -**kotelett** mutton chop
  -**schulter** shoulder of mutton

Hammelkeule mit Senf roast leg of mutton marinated in mustard for three days, served with boiled potatoes and dumplings
  sauer eingelegt a Westphalian dish of pickled leg of mutton served with a cream sauce and cranberries

Hirn calves' brains, in Austria breaded and baked
  mit Rührei with scrambled eggs

★ **Holstein-Schnitzel, Holsteiner mit Spiegelei** a very popular dish named after Bismarck's foreign minister Count Holstein. A veal chop with a fried egg on top, garnished with smoked salmon strips and, if you're lucky, anchovies and mussels

Kaiserfleisch boiled rib of beef served in its broth with vegetables and horseradish, a favourite of Emperor Franz Josef of Austria

Kaiserschnitzel cutlet of veal in a cream sauce

Kalb(s) veal, the most popular meat in Germany after pork
  -**braten** roast veal
  -**bröschen** calf's sweetbreads
  -**brust** breast of veal, rolled and stuffed with bread soaked in milk and eggs

★ -**haxe** shin or knuckle of veal. The national dish of Bavaria, it is served roasted so that the skin is crisp, accompanied by a mixed salad or vegetables
  -**herz** calf's heart
  -**hirn** calf's brains
  -**kopf** calf's head
  -**kotelett** veal chop
  -**leber** calf's liver
  -**lunge** calf's lung
  -**milcher** calf's sweetbreads
  -**nieren** calf's kidneys, but *Kalbsnierenbraten* is roast veal stuffed with kidneys
  -**rollbraten, -rolle** rolled and roasted veal
  -**rouladen** fillet of veal rolled, stuffed with ground pork and casseroled

95

Kalbsschnitzel veal cutlet, surely the most ubiquitous cut of meat in Germany. *Kalbsschnitzel* indicates that the cutlet has been simply fried in butter with perhaps a sour cream sauce

Kaldaunen tripe

Kasnudeln a Carinthian speciality of noodles stuffed with meat, mushrooms and cheese for a main course or with fruit and poppy seeds for dessert

Kasseler Rippenspeer, Rippe, Rippenspeer, Ripperl the origins of this dish are hotly disputed between the people of Kassel and Berliners who argue that it was first created by their own master-chef Kassel. It consists of pickled, smoked pork chops on the bone, stewed with onions and traditionally eaten with mashed potatoes and sauerkraut cooked with apples or with red cabbage and dumplings

Kohlrouladen a Thuringian dish of cabbage leaves stuffed with ground beef and pork

Königinpastete meat and mushroom pie

Königsberger Klopse the favourite dish of the philosopher Kant. Poached dumplings, made from ground meats and anchovies, are served with a sour cream, lemon and caper sauce

Krenfleisch a Bavarian dish of boiled top round of beef, sliced and served with bread, gherkins and horseradish

-fleisch mit Rüben a Rhenish lamb stew with diced potatoes and turnips

-kotelett lamb chop

-schlegel leg of lamb

Leber liver

-käs a Bavarian meat loaf served hot with gravy or cold with salad

-knödeln dumplings made from minced pig's or ox liver. See *Leberknödelsuppe (Soups)*

Lungenragout stewed lung

Lüngerl und Semmelknödeln a Bavarian dish of meatballs made from ground lung and heart served with bread dumplings

Maultaschen a Swabian speciality consisting of envelopes of pasta-like dough filled with a mixture of ground veal, pork and spinach and seasoned with nutmeg. Often served in a rather salty gravy. Traditionally served on Maundy Thursday, which in Germany is known as *Gründonnerstag* (Green Thursday), hence the spinach. Sometimes small *Maultaschen* are cooked in broth

Ochsenschwanz oxtail

Ochsenmaul, Ochsenzunge ox tongue

Paprikaschnitzel veal escalope in a creamy paprika sauce

Pfefferpothast Westphalian "pepper-pot stew", beef ribs and onions in a thick gravy heavily laden with pepper and lemons

Pichelsteiner Bavarian picnic stew, a mixture of several different kinds of meat and vegetables

---

Who will join me in a dish of tripe? It soothes, appeases the anger of the outraged, stills the fear of death, and reminds us of tripe eaten in former days, when there was always a half-filled pot of it on the stove.
Günter Grass *The Flounder*

Kutteln tripe

Labskaus literally "seaman's hotpot". ground pickled pork or beef fried with onions and mixed with mashed potatoes and vinegar. May be garnished with a poached egg, pickled beets, gherkins and a rollmop herring. A speciality of Hamburg

Lamm lamb, not as popular as pork and veal and usually vastly over-cooked

-braten roast lamb

Pökelbrust pickled breast of beef

Pökelrippchen pickled pork ribs

Pökelzunge pickled tongue

Räucherspeck smoked bacon

Rind, Rindfleisch beef

Rinderbrust brisket of beef usually boiled with horseradish sauce

Rippchen small pork chops

Rostbraten in north Germany this means roast beef, which tends to be very well done. In Bavaria and Austria a *Rostbraten* is a minute steak with braised onions and gravy

Rouladen stuffed beef rolls

★ **Sauerbraten** dish of top round of beef marinated for several days then pot-roasted. In some areas the marinade is basically red wine and vinegar, in others, beer or even buttermilk is used. In the Rhineland it will contain wine, dried fruit and nuts, in Bavaria, lemon and sour cream. In north Germany spiced gingerbread is crumbled into the sauce. It is often served with cranberry sauce, dumplings and red cabbage or apple purée

Saure Leber liver stewed with wine or vinegar

Nieren pig's kidneys stewed with wine or vinegar and sour cream, served with mashed potatoes and apple sauce. Popular in the Köln area

Schinken ham

  in Brotteig a Silesian way of cooking ham *en croûte*, the ham being baked in a bread dough crust, usually eaten with asparagus

  -fleckerl an Austrian combination of baked pasta with ham and beaten egg

  -knödeln dumplings made with minced ham

  -pfanne potatoes and ham in a thick pancake

  -röllchen rolls of ham stuffed, often with asparagus

Schlachtplatte a plate of mixed cold meats

Schlesisches Himmelreich meaning "Silesian Heaven", is actually a rather simple dish consisting of sliced salted belly pork stewed with dried fruit and served with bread dumplings

Schwärtelbraten Silesian roast leg of pork cooked with sauerkraut, dumplings and sour cream

Schwein(s)(e) pork

  -bauch belly

  -braten roast pork, to Germany what roast beef is to England, served with appropriate regional accompaniments. In Silesia the meat will be seasoned with garlic and herbs and the gravy made from meat stock and tomato paste. In Swabia there will be noodles, and almost everywhere there will be spiced red cabbage, dumplings and apple sauce

  -brust belly pork, often served boned, rolled and stuffed

  -fleischkäse pork meat loaf

  -haxe pork hock. See *Eisbein*

  -kopf pig's head

  -kotelett pork chop

  -leber pig's liver

  -nackensteak sparerib pork

  -nieren pig's kidneys

  -ohren pig's ears, usually stewed with sauerkraut

Selchfleisch smoked loin of pork

Snuten und Poten a Hamburg dish of sauerkraut with pig's snout

Spanferkel suckling pig

Speck bacon smoked over wood

Sülzkoteletten pork chops in aspic

Szegedinergulasch a Viennese rich pork stew with paprika, garlic, sour cream and sauerkraut

Tafelspitz boiled top round of beef, traditionally accompanied by potatoes, root vegetables, freshly grated horseradish and any of a variety of hot or cold sauces. The eating of boiled beef became almost a cult during the time of Franz Joseph I and it is still the typical lunchtime dish of the Viennese. The famous Viennese restaurant of Meissl and Schaden served 24 varieties of this dish. Most of the variations stem from the particular cut of meat and no self-respecting Viennese would consider being anything other than absolutely specific about it

Tellersülze Swabian head cheese

Topfbraten a peasant stew using cheap cuts of pork spiced with gingerbread pieces and plum jam

Töttchen a Westphalian stew made with calf's head and offal

★ **Westfälischer Schinken** Westphalian lightly smoked raw ham, sliced very thinly and served with pumpernickel

★ **Wiener Schnitzel** escalopes of veal coated in flour, egg and breadcrumbs and fried in a mixture of lard and butter

Würzfleisch spiced beef stew

Zigeunerbraten smoked meat encased in a bread dough and baked over an open fire

Zigeunerspiess an Austrian dish-skewered cubes of meat with onions and peppers, roasted

Zwiebelfleisch pork or beef and onions

Geflügel und Wild—Poultry and game

Backhuhn chicken, rolled in breadcrumbs and fried, also called *Wiener Backhendl*
Brathuhn roast chicken
Ente duck
Fasan pheasant
  in Speck gebraten roast pheasant wrapped in bacon, served with red cabbage and potato purée
  im Topf pot-roasted pheasant
  mit weissen Bohnen stewed pheasant with haricot beans
Gans, Gänse goose, traditional Christmas Day dish in Germany when it is served with red cabbage and potato dumplings. The stuffing usually contains apples and onions and possibly raisins and nuts
  -braten roast goose
  -brust breast of goose, often smoked
  -fett goose dripping
  ★ **-hals** goose neck, stuffed with minced goose liver, pork, bacon, chopped truffles, almonds, and herbs with a dash of Madeira, fried in butter and eaten hot with cabbage or cold
  -klein goose giblets stewed with turnip and parsley
  -leberpastete goose liver pâté
  -schenkel in Schmorkohl goose legs braised with onions and shredded white cabbage, flavoured with sugar and vinegar. A north German dish
  -schmalz goose dripping
Geflügel means birds generally but usually refers to chickens
  -klein chicken giblets
  -leber chicken liver
  -leberpastete chicken liver pâté
Hahn, Hendl, Huhn chicken
  in Weinteig deep-fried chicken pieces in wine-flavoured pastry
Hähnchen small chicken
Hase hare
★**Hasenpfeffer** hare stew, heavily flavoured with pepper, spices and red wine
Hasenrücken saddle of hare
Kapaun capon
Königinpastetchen pastry cases filled with chopped chicken in a cream sauce
Küken baby chicken
Paprikahendl, Paprikahuhn chicken pieces cooked with chopped onions, tomatoes and paprika in a thick cream sauce. Very rich
Puter turkey
Rebhuhn partridge
Reh venison
  -braten roast venison
  ★**-rücken Schwarzwälder Art** marinated roast loin of venison served with a brandy-flavoured sauce, sour cream, noodles and cranberry sauce
  -schnitzel venison cutlets
  -schulter shoulder of venison
Schwarzsauer goose giblets stewed with pears, prunes and apples
Taube pigeon
Truthahn turkey
Vierlander Poularde chickens fried in butter. A speciality of Hamburg
Wild, Wildgeflügel game in general
Wildschwein wild boar

Gemüse—Vegetables

Apfel apple, often served in some form or other with meat and fish
  -mus apple sauce
  -rotkohl red cabbage stewed with apples, a favourite accompaniment to roast pork
Artischocken artichokes
  -herzen artichoke hearts
Auberginen eggplants, often served stuffed as a main course
★**Blind Huhn** nothing to do with chickens but a dish of string beans stewed with dried fruit, vegetables and perhaps some chopped bacon
Blumenkohl cauliflower
Bohnen beans
Bratkartoffeln fried potatoes
Champignons mushrooms
Chicoree chicory
  mit Schinken und Käse chicory baked with ham and cheese
Eierschwammerl chanterelle mushrooms often served with venison for a perfect combination of flavours

Erbsen usually means yellow split peas

  -brei a purée of dried green peas

  -püree puréed split peas

Erdapfel potato, see *Kartoffel*

Füllsel-Kartoffeln a Rhineland speciality of potatoes fried with onions, ground pork, the offal of a suckling pig and seasoned with nutmeg and marjoram

Austria it may be called *Erdapfel*

  -brei mashed potatoes

  -klösse potato dumplings

  -knödeln potato dumplings

  -puffer potato pancakes, a favourite especially in north and East Germany, accompanied by apple sauce or cranberry sauce

  -salat hot or cold potato salad dressed in sour cream or vinegar and oil

---

Today we eat mealy boiled potatoes, grated raw potatoes, parsley potatoes, or plain potatoes in their jackets with cottage cheese. We know steamed potatoes with onions or in mustard sauce, buttered potatoes, potatoes au gratin, mashed potatoes, potatoes boiled in milk, baked in aluminum foil, old potatoes, new potatoes. Or potatoes in green sauce; or mashed potatoes with poached eggs. Or Thuringia, Vogtland, or Henneberg potato dumplings in cream sauce, with bread crumbs. Or sprinkled with cheese in flameproof-glass pannikins, or, as the Nostiz brothers made them, dotted with crayfish butter and baked. Or (in wartime) potato marzipan, potato cake, potato pudding. Or potato schnapps. Or my Amanda's mutton with potatoes, when (on holidays) she browned flank of mutton in kidney fat, added quartered potatoes, filled the kettle with water, simmered until the broth was soaked up, and only then moistened with dark beer. Or her potato soup, which the domestics of the Royal Prussian State Farm at Zuckau spooned up evening after evening, as the sky poured forth its ink and the forest moved closer and closer.
Günter Grass *The Flounder*

Gebackener Schwammerl mushrooms prepared the Austrian way, breaded and baked

Gemischter Salat mixed salad

Gemischtes Gemüse mixed vegetables

Grüne Erbsen fresh peas

Grüner Salat green salad

Grünkohl curly kale, a winter vegetable often eaten baked with potatoes or fried *Bratwurst*

Gurke(n) cucumber

  -salat the most popular Austrian salad—finely sliced cucumber, dressed with vinegar, sour cream and paprika

Himmel und Erde "heaven and earth"—apple and potato purée. See *Sausages* section

Karfiol cauliflower

  auf Wiener Art cauliflower baked in a sauce of sweetbreads, anchovies and cream

Karotten carrots

Kartoffel potato. In some southern parts of Germany and in

Kohl white cabbage

  -rouladen stuffed cabbage

Kopfsalat lettuce salad

Kraut actually means "plant" but usually refers to cabbage

  -salat finely chopped cabbage with oil, vinegar, bacon and a little sugar

Kren horseradish

Kürbis pumpkin

Lauch leeks

Leipziger Allerlei a mixed vegetable dish containing carrots, peas, cauliflower, asparagus tips and mushrooms. A speciality of Leipzig

Linsen lentils

  auf Schwäbische Art lentils stewed with onions, bacon and any leftover meat, served with sausage and noodles. Very filling

Mais sweetcorn

Meerrettich horseradish

Möhren, Mohrrüben carrots

Pellkartoffeln potatoes boiled in their jackets

Pfifferlinge chanterelles, see *Eierschwammerl*

Pilze mushrooms

Radieschen, Rettich radish

Reibkuchen potato cake

Rohnen beets

Rosenkohl brussels sprouts, available fresh only during the winter months

Rösti Swiss roast potatoes, grated raw then fried like a pancake

Röstkartoffeln potatoes baked in the oven

Röstzwiebeln fried onions

Rohnen, Rote Beete beets

★Rotkohl red cabbage. There can be no better way of preparing red cabbage than as the Germans do. It is certainly one of the very best vegetable dishes in the world and displays perfectly their inventiveness when it comes to vegetables and their love of sweet-sour combinations. The cabbage is stewed with wine vinegar, sugar, onions, sliced apple and spices. This may well appear on the menu as *Apfelrotkohl* or *Rotkohl mit Apfeln* and is often served with roast pork and potato dumplings

   -rouladen stuffed red cabbage

   -salat shredded red cabbage with chopped fried bacon and sour cream

Rübe turnips

Sauerampfer, Sauersaufer sorrel

★Sauerkraut the most celebrated of German vegetables but to many minds not the most agreeable. Goethe is said to have loathed it. Nevertheless it is an ingredient of many classic German dishes and is eaten with practically everything, from oysters to sausages of all kinds. The making of sauerkraut—by salting shredded white cabbage

and leaving it to ferment—was known to the Romans but this knowledge was lost during the Dark Ages and not reintroduced into Europe until the thirteenth century, when the Mongols brought it from China to Austria. In Germany and Austria it is frequently cooked with a range of other ingredients including apples, potatoes, spices, pineapple and even champagne

Saure Gurke pickled cucumber

Schwammerl mushrooms

Schwemmkartoffeln boiled potatoes

Sellerie celery

Spargel asparagus, may appear on the menu as *Stangenspargel*, meaning "asparagus spears". The asparagus season from May to June is treated very seriously in Germany. Many restaurants make a great production of it and whole families embark on special excursions to such places to sample the new crop. Asparagus is usually served with hollandaise sauce, boiled, herbed potatoes and cooked or Westphalian ham

Speckkartoffeln fried potatoes with bits of bacon

Spinat spinach

Stampfkartoffeln mashed potatoes with diced bacon

Stangenspargel see *Spargel*

Steinpilz boletus mushroom

Tomaten tomatoes

Trüffeln truffles

Weinkraut sauerkraut cooked in wine

Wirsinggemüse savoy cabbage

Zwiebel onion

   grün scallion

   -kuchen an onion tart from Hesse made with yeast dough and filled with onions, chopped bacon, eggs, sour cream and caraway seeds

Potatoes

The potato is so popular and ubiquitous that it is hard to believe that it was not a staple of German life even in the days of the Tartar hordes. In fact, it arrived later in Germany than in the rest of Europe and when, in 1744, Frederick the Great distributed free seed potatoes as part of his programme of agricultural reform, the peasants were so resistant to it that the Emperor posted soldiers in the fields to ensure that they were properly planted. It now turns up on the table in countless different guises.

Süss-speisen— *Sweet dishes*, *Früchte*— *Fruit*, *Eis*— *Ice-cream*

The Germans like to eat sweet things in the afternoon, in the form of cakes and pastries, and do not bother much with sweets and desserts. So a restaurant menu may well limit desserts to fruit with cream and a few ice-creams. The ice-creams often come with a hot fruit sauce.

Ananas pineapple

Apfel apple

  -kuchen apple custard tart

  -pfannkuchen pancake stuffed with apples

  -reis rice pudding with apple

Apfelsinen oranges

Aprikosen apricots

Arme Ritter bread dipped in beaten egg or pancake batter and fried, sprinkled with cinnamon and sugar and served with apple sauce

Auflauf soufflé or pudding

Backobstkompott stewed dried fruit

Backpflaume prunes

Baiser meringues

Banane bananas

Berliner jam doughnut

Birnen pears

Blaubeeren blueberries

Böllebauschen balls of yeast dough deep fried and tossed in sugar

Bratapfel baked apple

Brombeeren blackberries

Dampfnudeln in the north these are steamed sweet dumplings served with stewed fruit. In Bavaria it is a dry yeast pastry served with custard sauce

Datteln dates

Dresdener Eierschecke yeast dough filled with cottage cheese, topped with chopped nuts and raisins

Eierschaum eggs beaten with sugar and cooked with wine

Erdbeeren strawberries

Feigen figs

Feingebäck pastry

Frankfurter Kranz an extravagant and very expensive layer cake flavoured with rum

Fruchtsalat fruit salad

Gebäck pastry

Griesstorte layer cake made with semolina, filled with apricot jam

Haselnusscreme hazelnut cream

Hefekranz coffee cake

Himbeeren raspberries

Kaiserschmarren an Austrian dessert, literally "Emperor's nonsense"—a shredded white raisin pancake dusted with sugar and sometimes served with fruit purée—the favourite pudding of Franz Josef I

Käsetorte cheesecake

Kasnudeln a Carinthian speciality —noodles stuffed with fruit and poppy seeds. Can also be stuffed with meat for a main course

Kirschen cherries

Kompott stewed fruit

Königskuchen rum-flavoured fruit loaf

Krapfen Bavarian fritters

Kronsbeeren like cranberries

Kuchen a cake or tart

★**Lebkuchen** these are the traditional spiced honey cakes which have been made in Germany for hundreds of years especially at Christmas time. Originally they were made by specialist bakers called *Lebkuchner* who vied with each other to produce the most ornate shapes which were then painted and even gilded. Nürnberg, then a centre for the spice trade, was reknowned for its *Lebkuchen*

Mandeltorte almond layer cake

Marillen apricots

Melonen melons

Mohnstriezel poppy-seed cake, like a swiss roll filled with a mixture of poppy seeds, raisins, almonds, eggs and cream

Mohr im Hemd Austrian steamed chocolate pudding

Mohrenkopf chocolate meringue with whipped cream

Obst fruit

  -torte a glazed tart filled with a mixture of fruits and topped with meringue or whipped cream

Omelette mit Konfitüre this can be an omelette filled with jam or, in Austria, a thick pancake

Orangen oranges

Palatschinken a favourite
Austrian dessert, sweet pancakes
stuffed with fruit or cottage
cheese, rolled and baked
Pampelmuse grapefruit
Pfannkuchen pancake
Pfefferkuchen gingerbread
Pfirsich peach
Pflaumen plums
Powidl a special Austrian
preserve made from plums and
used in the making of pastries
and puddings
Preisselbeeren cranberries
Quitte quince
Reineclauden greengages
Reisauflauf a cross between rice
pudding and a soufflé
Rosinen raisins
Rote Grütze literally "red
pennies" individual redcurrant
and raspberry creams
Rumtopf fruit marinated in rum
Salzburger Nockerl soufflé of
egg white baked on vanilla sauce
Schneenockerln sweet dumplings
with egg custard, served chilled
Schokolade chocolate

Schokoladenpudding steamed
chocolate pudding
★ **Schwarzwälder Kirschtorte**
Black Forest cherry cake—a
concoction of cherries, chocolate
cake and whipped cream
Stachelbeeren gooseberries
Streuselkuchen a yeast cake
covered with a spiced sugar
crumble. Served warm
Topfenknödeln cottage cheese
dumplings
Topfenpalatschinken pancakes
stuffed with cottage cheese
Torten cakes
Trauben grapes
Wassermelone watermelon
Weinchadeau like Italian
zabaglione but made with white
wine
Weingelee wine jelly with layers
of fruit
Zitrone lemon
Zwetschgen black plums
   -datscherl an Austro-Bohemian
pastry filled with *Powidl*
   -knödeln plum dumplings

Gebäck—(Viennese) pastries

Apfelstrudel this famous apple
pastry consists of sheets of paper-
thin strudel dough rolled with a
mixture of apples, sugar,
breadcrumbs browned in butter
and white raisins flavoured with
cinnamon and lemon
Bischofsbrot literally "bishop's
bread"; contains mixed dried
fruit and chocolate drops
Biskoten *or* **Biskuitschnitten**
sponge fingers
Biskuitroulade swiss roll
Buchteln square yeast buns served
hot with vanilla custard or filled
with jam
Busserl meaning "kiss", a small
pastry or biscuit (see
Kokosbusserl)
Cremeschnitten puff pastry slices
filled with vanilla custard or
whipped cream
Demeltorte pastry filled with
glazed fruit
Dobosschnitten layers of thin
sponge and chocolate butter
covered with a caramel crust
Dobostorte like *Dobosschnitten*
but baked in a round cake rather
than slices

Erdbeerschifferl short pastry
boats filled with strawberries and
whipped cream
Faschingskrapfen yeast dough
buns filled with apricot jam and
deep fried. These are made and
eaten during the Fasching—
the pre-Lenten carnival in
Vienna. They should be served
hot, dusted with vanilla sugar.
The Fasching is always a lavish
festival, but that of 1815—the
year of the Congress of Vienna
—was particularly glittering and
over 10 million *Faschingskrapfen*
were consumed
Gugelhupf a circular yeast cake
with a hole in the middle, dusted
liberally with vanilla sugar and
covered with chocolate or
blanched almonds
Ischlertörtchen biscuits
sandwiched with jam
Johannisbeerkuchen cake
containing red currants
Kanzlertorte chocolate gâteau
Kipferl crescent-shaped biscuits
Kokosbusserl small round cakes
made of coconut, egg white and
sugar flavoured with honey,

lemon peel and ground cinnamon
Linzertorte a round cake made of
grated hazelnuts, then covered
with a layer of thickened
raspberry jam and a lattice of
pastry strips
Mandelbögen very small
almond-flavoured croissants
Marmorgugelhupf *Gugelhupf* with
a marbled appearance from the
chocolate flavouring added
before baking
Mohnbeugel crescent-shaped
pastry filled with poppyseeds
Mohnkipferl *Kipferl* filled with
poppyseed
Mohnstrudel strudel with
poppyseed and white raisins
Mozartkugeln chocolate balls
filled with rum-flavoured sponge
Nussbeugel a crescent-shaped
pastry with walnuts and honey
Nusstorte walnut gâteau
Pischingertorte named after the
firm that used to supply the
special round wafers, *Oblaten*,
which are sandwiched together
with chocolate cream
Polsterzipfel a triangular puff
pastry filled with jam
Powidlkolatschen square pastry
filled with *Powidl*—a special plum
preserve—boiled in salt water,
then rolled in sugar and
poppyseed and served hot
Rehrücken an oblong chocolate
cake covered in chocolate icing

and decorated with blanched
almonds. The name derives from
its supposed resemblance to a
larded saddle of venison
Ribiselkuchen see
Johannisbeerkuchen
Sachertorte a rich chocolate cake
filled with apricot jam and
covered with chocolate icing. It
was invented by Prince
Metternich's chef Franz Sacher.
The original recipe specified 18
egg whites and 14 yolks. It is
probably the only cake ever to
have been the subject of a court
case. When Demel's, the famous
pastry shop, and the Hotel
Sacher went to law to decide
once and for all who had the
right to call their *Sachertorte*
"genuine", the whole of Vienna
was on tenterhooks for seven
years. The Hotel Sacher finally
won although many testified in
favour of Demel's. Demel's
version is not filled but simply
covered with a layer of apricot
jam and then the chocolate icing
Schaumrollen rolls of puff pastry
filled with whipped cream
Schokoladetorte chocolate gâteau
Spanische Windtorte a decorative
meringue case filled with cream
Stangerl small stick-shaped
biscuits or pastries
Vanillekipferl vanilla-flavoured
sweet croissants

Käse—*Cheese*

Allgäuer Allgäu in Bavaria is the
centre of the German cheese-
making industry. Apart from
authentic German cheeses, other
cheeses are made in Allgäu and
may appear on the menu as
Allgäuer Emmental, for example
Altenburger a mild-flavoured
goat's milk cheese
Bergkäse meaning "mountain
cheese", is made in the Bavarian
alps. It has a dark yellow rind
and is a hard cheese
Berliner Kuhkäse a small yellowy
low-fat cheese. See *Handkäse*
Bierkäse a low-fat cottage cheese.
See *Handkäse*
Frühlingskäse an Austrian
snack consisting of a mixture
of cream cheese, paprika and
caraway seeds on black bread

Graukäse a tough, sharp
mountain cheese
Handkäse small hand-moulded
sour cottage cheeses
Harzer also a *Handkäse*, from
the Harz mountains where they
like to eat it with bread and
goose dripping. In Hesse these
small cheeses are eaten *mit Musik*,
a garnish of sliced onions in a
vinegar and sugar dressing
Käseteller a plate of several
different cheeses
Limburger soft cheese with a
reddish skin covering a smooth
golden yellow inside. Should be
eaten fresh
Olmützer another *Handkäse*
Quark a low-fat rather runny
cottage cheese with a slightly
sour taste. Used in cooking

Räucherkäse smoked cheese
Romadur similar to *Limburger*
with a slightly milder flavour
Sahnekäse cream cheese
Schichtkäse "layer cheese", the
layers consisting of bands of
skimmed milk curds and fatty
milk curds. Very pretty
Schnittkäse meaning "sliceable
cheese", refers to cheeses which
are softer than *Emmental* and
harder than *Limburger*
Spitzkäse caraway seed cheese

Steinbuscherkäse a mild golden
Schnittkäse
Tilsiter one of the better German
cheeses, golden yellow with a
slightly darker skin, full of small
holes with an elastic very creamy
texture and mild in taste
Weisslackerkäse a Bavarian
Schnittkäse with a strong sharp
flavour
Wilstermarschkäse a sour-tasting
cheese with a smooth shiny
yellow skin

Wine

The trouble with German wine is that it takes the mind of a
mathematician or a crossword expert to understand the
cryptic news on a wine label. It is not going to matter much
which kind of wine you drink with your food because, unlike French wine, German wine, however subtle and beautiful, does not seem to have the same territorial connection
with the cuisine of the country.

The best thing is to ask the wine waiter to choose something and to show you the bottle before he opens it because
the wine list, however long the names on it, will not give
you the clues you need. If he brings one of those bottles
with a sentimental picture of a sweet old lady being pushed
through the streets of Pforzheim in a bath chair, send it
back.

If it has a normal label your detective work can begin. The
wine will almost certainly be white. The first name on the
label is of the town or village. Next comes the vineyard—
but this may mean a particular small vineyard, *Einzellage*,
or cover a group of adjoining or nearby vineyards which
produce similar wine, *Grosslage*. Which is which is hard to
tell, but an *Einzellage* name (there are some 3,000) is likely
to be better than a *Grosslage* which may mix good and bad
vineyards. Again there is a third possibility—a whole region,
Bereich, which allows a famous name, *Bernkastel*, for
example, to be applied to any wine from a large area, in this
case the Mittel-Mosel.

Then comes, possibly, the grape name (mostly *Riesling*)
and its degrees of ripeness—*Kabinett, Spätlese, Auslese,
Beerenauslese,* and *Trockenbeerenauslese,* the last being the
ripest, with the greatest natural sugar content. These defini-
tions apply only to wines with no added sugar. They will
also be marked *QmP—Qualitätswein mit Prädikat.* If it says
QbA—Qualitätswein bestimmter Anbaugebiete—you will
know that it has sugar added, but it will still be a good wine.
Are you still with me? After that comes a test number,
which will not tell you anything. The thing to look for then
is an *Einzellage, QmP.* As for taste, the *Kabinett* will be the
driest, the *Trockenbeerenauslese* the sweetest. Anything without a *QmP* or *QbA* will be a *Tafelwein*—an everyday table
wine—which will just have the village and regional name.
Aim for a *Deutscher Tafelwein.*

If the bottle is brown and the wine golden, it will be
Rhine, Nahe or Palatinate wine (what we call hock). If the
bottle is green and the wine pale yellowy-green, it will be
Mosel, including Saar and Ruwer. The other possibility is

that instead of a tall slender bottle, you will be brought a flagon or *Bocksbeutel*. This will be Franconian wine, also white and dry.

On the whole avoid names which seem familiar. Practically nobody in Germany or Austria drinks Liebfraumilch. Goldener Oktober is a mixture of hock and Mosel.

Perhaps more suitable with German food is beer.

Bier—Beer

Altbier dark copper-coloured aromatic beer of medium strength from the North Rhineland and Westphalia

Berliner Weisse a pale golden refreshing wheat beer

Bock a rich strong beer ranging in colour from pale to dark brown

Doppelbock extra-strong *Bock*. The strongest beer in the world is a *Doppelbock* brewed in Kulmbach near Bayreuth—the *Kulminator*

Dortmunder, Export a light golden lager-type beer

Dunkles Bier dark beer

Helles Bier light beer

Kölsch a speciality of the Köln area—a pale golden beer of medium strength

Kreusenbier a light beer available only in Bremen

Kupferbier a reddish-coloured malty beer brewed in the Nürnberg area

Lager the term in Austria for

their everyday light golden beer

Märzenbier an amber beer of above average strength. It was traditionally brewed in March and the extra strength kept it through the summer at the end of which any remaining was ritually consumed at festivals such as the *Oktoberfest* in Munich and the *Canstatt Wasen* in Stuttgart

Münchner traditional dark brown malty beers

Oktoberfestbier see *Märzenbier*

Pils, Pilsener pale golden lager-type beer

Rauchbier an aromatic smoky-flavoured beer produced in Bamberg

Spezial the term for *Märzenbier* in Austria

Weissbier a Bavarian light summer beer

Weizenbier a sparkling medium-strong wheat beer from Bavaria

Weizengold a wheat beer brewed in the Salzburg area

Useful words

Apfelwein apple wine

Art in the style of

Auflauf soufflé or pudding

Aufschnitt cold cuts

Bauernbrot dark coarse peasant bread

Bayrischer Bavarian

Beilagen supplementary dishes

Belegtes Brot open sandwiches

Berliner meaning "from Berlin", or a jam doughnut

Blau a favourite way of poaching fish in vinegar or wine and water so that the skin becomes blue and the flesh very white. Usually served with butter

Braten roast

Brot bread

Brötchen bread roll

Brust breast

Butter butter

Dicke thick or broad as in *dicke Bohnen*—broad beans

Ei egg

Eierspeisen egg dishes

Eierstich strips of egg custard added to soups

Eingelegte pickled

Eingemacht preserved or canned

Eintopf literally "one-dish", a casserole or stew

Essig vinegar

Farce stuffing

Flädle pancake

Frankfurter in the Frankfurt way, or refers to hotdogs

Fränkische from Franconia

Frisch fresh

Füllung stuffing

Gänsefett, Gänseschmalz goose dripping

Germany and Austria *Useful words*

Gebäck pastries
Gebacken baked
Gebraten roasted
Gebunden thickened
Gedämpft steamed
Gedeck cover charge, but also used for fixed-price meals
Gefüllt stuffed
Gekocht cooked
Gemischt mixed
Geräuchert smoked
Geschabt ground or grated
Geschmort pot-roasted
Griessklösse semolina dumplings
Grüne Sauce green sauce—a famous sauce from Frankfurt containing masses of herbs
Hamburger from Hamburg
Hartgekocht hard-boiled
Hauptgericht main course
Hausfrauen Art housewife's style—with sour cream and pickles
Hausgemacht home-made
Heiss hot
Herz hearts
Hirn brains
Jäger Art hunter's style—usually in a wine sauce with mushrooms
Kaffee coffee
Kakao cocoa
Kalt cold
Kapern capers
Kastanien chestnuts
Keule shoulder
Klare clear
Klein small or giblets
Klösse dumplings
Knoblauch garlic
Knödeln dumplings
Kopf head
Leber liver
Lunge lungs
Mandeln almonds
Mast grain-fed
Mehlspeisen flour-based dishes
Milch milk
Müllerin Art miller's wife style—dredged in flour and fried in butter
Münchner from Munich
Münsterländer from Munster
Natur plain
Nieren kidneys
Nockerln dumplings

Nudeln noodles
Nuss nut
Ohren ears
Öl oil
Paar pair
Pfannkuchen pancake
Pökel pickled
Rahm cream
Räucher smoked
Rechnung bill
Reis rice
Rippe ribs
Roh raw
Roséwein rosé wine
Rost grill
Rotwein red wine
Saft juice
Saftig juicy
Sahne cream
Sahnemeerrettich horseradish sauce
Salbei sage
Sauer sour
Scheibe slice
Schlagobers, Schlagsahne whipped cream
Schlegel leg
Schnitte slice
Schnittlauch chives
Schulter shoulder
Schwäbische Swabian
Schwarzwälder from the Black Forest
Schweizer Swiss
Semmelknödeln bread dumplings
Senf mustard
Sosse sauce
Spätzle Swabian noodles
Speckknödeln dumplings made with bacon
Spiess skewered
Stück portion
Tee tea
Tiroler Knödeln dumplings made with bacon
Topf stew or casserole
Tunke sauce
Wahl choice
Walnuss walnut
Wasser water
Weckklösse bread dumplings
Weisswein white wine
Zigeuner Art gipsy style
Zitrone lemon
Zucker sugar
Zunge tongue

Mahlzeit or **Guten Appetit!** bon appétit!
Prost! cheers!

Great Britain and Ireland

Industrial nations are inclined to have mediocre food. Good food comes from a close association with the land. Big cities demand mass food, easily transported and hastily cooked, and by their nature militate against freshness and improvisation.

Britain has suffered dreadfully in this way. Our once great tradition of cookery has been largely forgotten, to be replaced by either indifference in the form of watery vegetables, powdered custard and "fast food", or by poor imitations of French cooking or, almost worst of all, by an entirely fictitious John Bull cookery with roughly the subtlety of a Hollywood pageant.

Yet the British are obstinate, so that, almost like an undergound resistance, there has somehow been kept alive, in out-of-the-way pockets, the spirit of a really fine cuisine. There is a lot about real British cooking which is surprising. Perhaps the most striking thing to someone who thinks the British just eat beef and apple pie is the immense variety—the ingenious use of so many parts of an animal, the abundance of fish, the diversity of herbs, the unusual vegetables like samphire (from the shores of Norfolk and Wales).

In these listings, I have tried to give a notion of what British cuisine can be, but also tried to choose dishes that you will actually find on menus. Wherever appropriate I have given the geographical derivation of a dish, using abbreviations for England (Eng.), Scotland (Scot.) and Ireland (Irl.). I have not included dishes with names that are self-explanatory unless they are relevant for some other reason. These limitations have meant that one or two whole aspects of British cooking are not represented or appear unbalanced. In particular there is virtually nothing about preserved foods.

The British are tremendous preservers. They seem to have kept up this tradition more than other people who, as transport improved, abandoned it. Raised pies were a part of this tradition. In order to transport cooked meats, they were baked in "coffins" of thick hot-water pastry. (They still suit restaurant chains.) They were also easy to eat in your fingers. They survive today in the form of pork pies, especially Melton Mowbray pie, veal and ham pies and game pies.

The only trouble with all this is knowing where you are going to find these delights. There is, in fact, a revival of English food which I feel is going to burgeon. Already there are several new restaurants in London concentrating on interesting English food. Otherwise you will have to find it piecemeal. Large hotels usually have some good dishes. Pubs are good at maintaining the tradition of cold food (something the French have lost in the last fifty years) but you would do well to avoid most of the fashionable "Ploughman's lunches", which consist of a hunk of bread with a lump of cheese, a withered tomato and some soggy lettuce. Country pubs, small Scottish hotels and English market towns offer the best chance of finding the best British food.

As for what to drink with British food, the answer ought to be beer. The difficulty is that very little of the beer is worth drinking. It has got weaker and weaker and, since the invention of metal containers and gas pumps, it does not taste the same. The thing to ask for is *real* beer. You may not like it, but it is the genuine article and better than fizzy bottles of misnamed lager. In better establishments I should stick to wine. The British have always bought good wine.

Meals

The one aspect of the romantic picture of Olde Englande that was true was the size of their appetites. The Victorians thought nothing of five meals a day, of dinners with seven courses—that is to say the rich thought nothing of it. Modern times have reduced virtually everyone to a maximum of three meals and smaller meals at that.

The pattern of meal times in Britain is constantly changing and varies with the social strata. In Norman times the main meal of the day was at 9 a.m. Gradually it got later until Elizabethan times when dinner was at midday.

Jane Austen's characters ate their dinner at about four in the afternoon and, for the genteel the meal has got progressively later. The Emmas of today eat as late as 9 or 10 p.m.

Visitors to Britain should be prepared to eat at any time and for a midday meal to be called lunch or dinner and any meal after that to be called dinner, tea or supper and in the case of the last two to be anything from the lightest snack to a full-scale business with three courses or more.

Whatever became of breakfast? So much of British food was seemingly designed for it. A good breakfast spread, in a manor house before 1939, would include porridge, kippers, poached, boiled and scrambled eggs, bacon, kidneys, devilled pheasant, mushrooms, cutlets, snipe, potatoes, tomatoes, cold ham, and toast and marmalade (baps in Scotland). A few of the best London hotels might provide half that today.

Savouries

Savouries have virtually disappeared from British menus, which is to say they are nearly extinct, because they are a purely British course. Their purpose was to clean the mouth after the sweet course so that the port would not be spoilt. They were a "macho" Victorian dish, often missed out by women and gobbled up by men, who were inclined to miss out the sweet in a demonstration of masculinity. They were rather agreeable, I used to think; small, sharp little dishes, served very hot. As you will only find them in grand hotels or remote country establishments, I have listed those that are impossible to identify by name.

★Angels on horseback oysters, wrapped in bacon, on toast

Devilled ham toasts minced ham with Worcestershire sauce and mustard on toast

Devils on horseback chicken livers, wrapped in bacon, on toast

Loch Fyne toasts (Scot.) kippers and mushrooms on toast

Rarebit see *Eggs and cheese*

Scotch woodcock (Scot.) anchovies on toast, covered with creamy scrambled egg

Skuets tiny skewers of fried chicken liver and mushrooms served on fingers of toast

Soups

Soups, as one might expect in a more affluent world, are rather out of fashion; for soup was originally a poor man's dish, often his only meal of the day. It has largely been replaced by what is awkwardly known as a "starter". This is a pity, particularly in Britain where, until recently, a starter was someone who waved a flag at a racecourse, and soups were particularly good.

Almond soup (Eng.) a genuinely medieval dish. In the Middle Ages almonds were much used in cookery. It is wonderfully white

Apple soup (Eng.) chopped apples cooked in beef stock and sieved. Nowadays it often has barley or rice added

Bacon broth (Irl.) thick vegetable soup with barley and bacon

Bawd bree (Scot.) ham soup with vegetables

Brose (Scot.) what you get if you pour boiling water on oatmeal or oatcake. Implies that there is oatmeal in a soup

Brown Windsor soup (Eng.) a thick brown soup; usually nauseating, but when properly made with beef and mutton, carrots and onions, and perhaps some rice, and flavoured with Madeira, it is delicious

Cawl cennin (Wales) a rich peasant soup, with a basis of beef or ham stewed very slowly with root vegetables, all cooked together and served with chopped leeks and perhaps a marigold flower. "Cawl" is the Welsh word for soup

★**Cock-a-leekie** (Scot.) leeks simmered with prunes in stock in which a chicken has been boiled. Sometimes a little minced chicken is included

Cockle soup (Irl.) cockles in a cream soup with celery

Cullen skink (Scot.) "Finnan haddie" (smoked haddock) soup of milk and mashed potato

Gower oyster soup (Wales) oysters served in mutton stock

Hotch-potch (Scot.) mutton stewed for hours with young green vegetables, a few carrots and baby turnips. Before serving, the meat is taken out. The soup should be very thick

Kail (Scot.) Scottish for kale or any member of the same family, e.g. cabbage. As this was the staple vegetable of Scotland it came to mean soup or even dinner. Now implies there is cabbage in a soup, e.g. *Kilmeny kail* with rabbit and pickled pork; *muslin kail* vegetable soup with no animal ingredients at all

★**Laver soup** (Irl., Wales) a laver (seaweed) soup made with potatoes, onions and carrots, using a fish stock. The seaweed should be red rather than green

Mock turtle soup (Eng.) made with calf's head and vegetables, sometimes served with meat balls of brains and breadcrumbs

Mulligatawny soup (Eng.) a chicken curry soup, properly served with boiled rice and sometimes chopped apple. The word means "pepper water" (corrupted from the Tamil)

Mutton and leek broth (Wales) pretty well a meal in itself with pearl barley added to the meat and vegetables which include carrots, turnips and onions

Oxtail soup (Eng.) one of the most common soups restaurants put on to prove they are English. It should be clear, with a little of the meat in it. This is achieved by making it the day before and allowing it to cool, so that the fat rises and can be taken off

Palestine soup (Eng.) a thick soup of Jerusalem artichokes

Partan bree (Scot.) crab soup

Scotch broth (Scot.) much more than one might expect from a "broth". Made with neck or even shoulder of mutton (or, at a pinch, beef) with peas, onions, turnips, carrots, leeks, cabbage, parsley and a lot of barley

Skink (Scot.) vegetables stewed in beef stock, served with the sinewy part of a leg of beef chopped in it

Tartan purry (Scot.) another name for *kail brose*

Eggs and cheese

Anglesey eggs (Wales) hard-boiled eggs in a bed of mashed potatoes and leeks, covered with a cheese sauce and baked

★**Arnold Bennett omelette** (Eng.) an open omelette with a covering of mixed haddock, grated cheese and a little cream, put under the grill. It was invented for Arnold Bennett by the Savoy, which featured in many of his novels

Buck rabbit *or* **rarebit** (Eng.) like *Welsh rabbit* but with a poached egg on top

Curried eggs (Eng.) hard-boiled eggs in a sauce of onion and curry powder simmered in stock and mixed with cream

English rabbit *or* **rarebit** wine-soaked toast covered with sliced cheese and grilled

Glamorgan sausages (Wales) grated cheese, breadcrumbs, chopped leeks, parsley, thyme with a little mustard powder mixed and bound with egg yolk

Scotch eggs (Scot.) hard-boiled eggs, wrapped in sausage meat and fried

Welsh rabbit *or* **rarebit** (Wales) melted cheese and milk (or beer) poured on toast and grilled

Fish

★**Arbroath smokies** (Scot.) smoked haddock opened up and filled with butter, closed again and gently baked or grilled

Blawn fish (Scot.) the Scots have a way of salting fish and then hanging it up to dry in the wind. They do this with any white fish and then grill it over a slow fire

Bloaters (Eng.) herrings, very lightly cured and smoked

Cabbie claw (Scot.) salt cod in egg sauce

Crappit heids (Scot.) haddock heads stuffed with lobster or crab forcemeat and boiled in a fish soup. On the island of Lewis they stuff the heads with the fish liver and oatmeal

Cropaden (Scot.) haddock liver in an oatmeal dumpling

Cumberland shipped herrings (Eng.) herrings stuffed with their roes mixed with breadcrumbs, onion and anchovy, baked and served with a mustard sauce

Eel pie (Eng.) eel with sage baked in a pie. There are many variations; one famous one with shallots, nutmeg, egg and sherry

Elvers in the Gloucester style (Eng.) baby eels (caught in the spring) fried in bacon fat with beaten egg and served on bacon

Fillets of sole Tullamore (Scot.) sole simmered with mushrooms covered with a cream, egg and liqueur whisky sauce

Finnan haddie (Scot.) smoked finnan (Findon) haddock stewed in butter and boiled in milk.

Golden cod (Eng.) cod in oatmeal with parsnips and onions baked in a court-bouillon with saffron

Herring bake (Eng.) rolled fillets of herring, covered with a mustard, tomato and cream sauce. Baked.

★**Kedgeree** (Eng.) usually pieces of smoked haddock, but often salmon or kippers, mixed with rice and curry paste cooked in the haddock water. Served with sliced hard-boiled egg. One of the treasures of a real English breakfast, based on an Indian dish (*khichari*). People often leave out the curry paste which is a deadening mistake

Kiossed heids (Scot.) fish heads hidden for a while in a stone wall until they are rich, then roasted and eaten with potatoes

★**Kippers** (Eng.) herrings split open down the back, lightly cured and smoked over an open fire. Their violent red colour is a dye; they should be pale golden

Limpet stovies (Scot.) limpets and potatoes simmered with butter

Lowestoft herrings (Eng.) herrings poached in sea water

North Staffordshire swallows (Eng.) white fish sliced and put between two slices of potato dipped in batter and deep fried

Ormer (Eng.) ormers, known also as sea ears, are a species of mollusc found only in the Channel Islands. Their flesh is a mottled yellow and brown. They are inedible unless severely beaten and interminably cooked. On Guernsey they put them in a casserole with, one cannot help noticing, a lot of other strong-tasting ingredients

Oyster loaves (Eng.) fried oysters in hollowed out bread rolls with a cream and sour cream sauce made with the oyster liquor. (See *United States, la médiatrice*)

Partan pie (Scot.) not a pie but crabmeat with breadcrumbs, butter, seasoning and sometimes vinegar with mustard, put back in the shell and grilled

Pastai gocos (Wales) cockle pie made with scallions and chopped bacon

Sillocks (Scot.) baby coalfish, traditionally rolled in oatmeal and fried in butter and eaten in your fingers. They are cooked headless. When you squeeze them, their backbones conveniently pop out

Smoked herrings (Irl.) red herrings (smoked and salted) fried in butter and flamed in whiskey

Somerset casserole (Eng.) diced cod or haddock baked with cider, mushrooms and tomatoes; covered with its own sauce, bordered with mashed potatoes and sprinkled with cheese

Stargazey pie (Eng.) pilchards stuffed with onions and breadcrumbs and arranged in a pie dish with bacon, hard-boiled eggs and onion so that their heads stick up. Before the dish is covered

with pastry, cider is poured in. The fish heads protrude above the pastry, so that when the pie is baked the oil from the inedible heads trickles down

Super scadan (Wales) rolled herring fillets embedded in layers of thinly sliced potatoes, onions and apples, flavoured with sage and baked

Trout in a blanket (Eng.) trout with herbs, wrapped in a pancake and baked with green butter

Trout Rob Roy (Scot.) trout coated with oatmeal and breadcrumbs and fried

Tweed kettle (Scot.) pounded salmon simmered with shallots and vinegar

Twice laid (Eng.) cod mixed with mashed potato, rolled into balls, covered in breadcrumbs and fried

Meat

Balmoral tripe (Scot.) tripe rolled up with bacon and onions and fried. Served in onion sauce

Bangers and mash (Eng.) large fried sausages with mashed potatoes

★**Baron of hare** (Eng.) the hind legs and back of a hare all in one piece, roasted

Beef cecils (Eng.) beef rissoles made with onions, breadcrumbs, lemon rind and spices

Beef olives (Eng.) thin slices of beef stuffed with forcemeat, rolled up and simmered in beef stock. Olives can be small rolls of any meat stuffed with forcemeat

Beef royal (Eng.) an elaborate Elizabethan dish of rump beef cut in half and made into a sandwich with spices and gammon rashers, tied together and stewed. Served cool with a port, anchovy and pickled walnut sauce

Black pudding (Eng.) large sausages made with pork fat, blood and barley or oatmeal

Brawn (Eng.) meat from a pig's head and feet set in the jelly from the reduced cooking stock

Bubble and squeak (Eng.) finely sliced beef sautéed in butter and covered with fried cabbage. Mrs Beeton added onion to the cabbage; nowadays potato is often mixed with the cabbage

China chilo (Eng.) boned, diced lamb cutlets stewed with lettuce, peas and onions, served on rice

Collar and cabbage (Irl.) boiled collar (or forehock) of bacon, coated in breadcrumbs and brown sugar and baked. Served with mashed cabbage, boiled in the bacon stock

Collared beef (Eng.) spiced, rolled beef, boiled, pressed and served cold

Collops (Eng.) a thin slice of any meat. Originally it applied only to bacon. Can also be ground meat

Cornish pasty (Eng.) beef, potatoes, onions and sometimes turnip, chopped, mixed and enclosed in shortcrust pastry and baked. Served hot or cold.
In Cornwall, individual pasties had the eater's initials in one corner. Thus the ingredients could be varied for personal idiosyncrasies of taste and if you put it down, you could recognize your own

Cottage pie see *Shepherd's pie*

Crown of lamb (Eng.) a row of cutlets turned inside out, while still joined by their skin, to form a crown. They are roasted and served with mashed potatoes in the middle of the crown

Crubins *or* **crubeens** (Irl.) pig's feet boiled with bay leaves, thyme and parsley. The meat is then cut off, dipped in egg and mustard, coated with breadcrumbs and fried

Culloden collops (Scot.) fried ground beef, onions and mushrooms, stewed in stock with whisky and oatmeal

Cumberland sausage (Eng.) long pork sausage with plenty of fat, flavoured with herbs

Devilled chicken (Eng.) chicken pieces coated with a paste of butter, mustard, flour, chutney, Worcestershire sauce and grilled

★ **Devilled cutlets** (Eng.) grilled lamb cutlets coated with butter, Worcestershire sauce, mushroom ketchup, mustard and cayenne

Devonshire squab pie (Eng.) expect no squab. It is a pie of lamb, apples, prunes and spices, baked and served hot with clotted cream

Dublin coddle (Irl.) layers of forehock of bacon, pork sausages, potatoes and onions, stewed very gently

★ **Duke of Wellington's fillet of beef** (Eng.) fillet with mushrooms and liver pâté encased in puff pastry and said to look like a well-polished brown leather boot. All too often more like Wellingtons in taste

Faggots (Eng.) pork, pig's liver and any other bits of a pig that may be around, ground and mixed with onions, herbs and spices, made into balls, wrapped in caul fat and baked

Fidget pie (Eng.) layers of bacon, onion and apples in a pie

Forfar bridies (Scot.) narrow, short strips of beaten steak, sprinkled with suet wrapped in pastry and baked

Grampian grouse pudding (Scot.) chopped steak and grouse baked in a suet crust with port

Guard of honour (Eng.) two rows of lamb chops still joined together, arranged so that the thin ends of their bones criss-cross alternately and then roasted

★ **Haggis** (Scot.) the stomach of a sheep, stuffed with minced sheep's heart, lights and liver, suet, onions and oatmeal, boiled and served with mixed mashed potatoes and turnips. A spoonful of whisky makes it even better

Haricot of mutton (Eng.) mutton, onions, carrots, turnips and potatoes stewed slowly. Now dried navy beans are used instead of potatoes

Hindle wakes (Eng.) a chicken stuffed with prunes, herbs and suet cooked in a vinegar stock and served cold, covered with a butter, cream and lemon coating with prunes and lemons and chives embedded in it

Inky pinky (Scot.) left-over roast beef hash with carrots, onions and a bit of vinegar

Irish stew (Irl.) the original consists only of neck of mutton, almost as much potato as meat, sliced onions and herbs arranged in layers and stewed. Pearl barley and root vegetables are a later (probably British) refinement

Jugged hare (Eng.) hare cooked in stock with herbs, served with a rich gravy made of its blood, red-currant jelly and port

★ **Lancashire hotpot** (Eng.) layers of hind end of loin, kidneys, mushrooms, ham, onions and potatoes, cooked slowly in stock, browned on the top and served in the pot, accompanied by pickled red cabbage. Bolton hotpot used to have oysters in it as well

Love in disguise (Eng.) calf's heart coated with vermicelli and breadcrumbs and roasted

Mixed grill (Eng.) chops, sausages, eggs, kidneys, bacon or whatever, grilled

Monckton-Milnes mutton pie (Eng.) mutton and oysters in a suet crust; named after my great-grandfather who knew how to brighten things up, the usual mutton pie of this kind being made with onions, not oysters

Mutton dormers (Eng.) chopped mutton, onions, suet and rice fashioned into sausage shapes, breadcrumbed and fried

Pigeons in Pimlico (Eng.) stuffed squab rolled in a slice each of veal and bacon and roasted, served with small pastry puffs filled with the same squab's liver, ham, mushroom and parsley stuffing as the squabs

Pig's head (Irl.) pig's head boiled and grilled, served with boiled cabbage

Planked steak (Wales) steaks sealed under the grill then cooked with herbs on an oak plank. The wood chars slightly, giving the meat a smoky taste

Spiced beef (Eng.) beef salted for several days, rolled up after being rubbed with spices and herbs, boiled with vegetables. Pressed, served cold with a stock glaze

---

Great eaters of meat are in general more cruel and ferocious than other men. The cruelty of the English is known.
Jean-Jacques Rousseau

Pork olives (Eng.) pork fillet rolled up with sage and onion stuffing, simmered with onions

Rabbit in the dairy (Eng.) rabbit, bacon and onions, cooked in the oven in milk

★ **Reform Club cutlets** (Eng.) a crown of lamb cutlets, coated with a mixture of chopped ham, tongue and breadcrumbs and fried. Served with Reform Club sauce—a brown sauce flavoured with mushroom, sherry-soaked ham, beets, gherkin and red-currant jelly

Rissoles (Eng.) any ground meat mixed with herbs and spices, rolled into sausage shapes, breadcrumbed and fried

★ **Roast beef and Yorkshire pudding** (Eng.) traditionally the piece of beef to be roasted should be large, so that there is great variety in the result—crisp on the outside and very pink in the middle. The best Yorkshire pudding was always made by putting the batter in the pan under the roasting beef so that the drippings fell into it

Salmi (Eng.) usually game, but can be fish. The principal ingredient is roasted, chopped and reheated in a wine sauce with lots of spices and herbs

Scotch collops (Eng.) veal escalopes simmered in a thick brown sauce with forcemeat balls and mushrooms, served with fried ham steak rashers

★ **Shepherd's pie** (Eng.) ground lamb or mutton, usually with onions, stewed in stock, then put in a pie dish, covered with a layer of mashed potatoes and baked

Skuets (Eng.) sweetbreads, bacon and mushrooms skewered and grilled, sprinkled with browned breadcrumbs and served with bread sauce

Spiced mutton ham (Wales) leg of mutton or lamb cured in salt, sugar and spices and then smoked

Steak and kidney pie (Eng.) with steak and kidney pie greater latitude is allowable than with steak and kidney pudding. Onions, mushrooms and oysters, baked under pastry

★ **Steak and kidney pudding** (Eng.) the charm of a steak and kidney pudding lies in its absolute simplicity. Just steak, kidney and stock steamed in a crust of suet. It is heresy to put in onions or to try to enhance the taste in any way, except possibly to add oysters

Steak MacFarlane (Scot.) steaks dipped in oatmeal and fried

Stoved chicken (Scot.) cut up chicken baked with sliced onions and potatoes

Stoved howtowdie with drappit eggs (Scot.) chicken simmered with onions and herbs, served on spinach with poached eggs

Tattie pot (Eng.) like Lancashire hotpot with black pudding

Tatws a cig yn y popty (Wales) rolled up breasts of lamb on a bed of sliced potatoes and onions baked in a brown sauce

Tatws reost (Wales) a hotpot of bacon, onion and potatoes

Toad in the hole (Eng.) fried sausages set in batter and baked

Tripe and onions see *Balmoral tripe*

Veal flory (Scot.) veal, bacon, forcemeat balls and mushrooms, baked in a pie

Veal rolls (Eng.) escalopes of veal rolled up with a stuffing of herbs, skewered and spit roasted

Venison collops (Scot.) slices of venison fried and served in a red wine sauce

White pudding (Eng.) large sausages of ground pork, cereal and chopped parsley

113

Vegetables

Bashed neeps (Scot.) mashed turnips

Clapshot (Scot.) potatoes and turnips

Colcannon (Irl.) a mushy stew of chopped cabbage and mashed potatoes, carrots and turnips

Comfrey leaf fritters (Eng.) comfrey leaves (*Symphitum officinale*) fried in batter

Kail and knockit corn (Scot.) barley and kale boiled with a little pork or smoked mutton

Kailkenny (Scot.) mashed cabbage and potatoes with cream

Lang kail (Scot.) kale in butter

Laverbread with bacon (Wales) laver (seaweed) made into cakes with oatmeal and fried in bacon fat

Leeky stew with a nackerjack (Eng.) stewed leeks and diced potatoes served with a suet dumpling

Lenten pie (Eng.) potatoes, onions and apples in a pie

Pan Haggerty (Eng.) finely sliced potatoes, onions and cheese in layers, fried in dripping

Pease pudding (Eng.) dried peas cooked and puréed, then mixed with butter and egg

Rumbledethumps (Scot.) another mush of potatoes, cabbage and kale, sometimes sprinkled with cheese and browned in the oven

Salamagundy (Eng.) raw and cooked vegetables, fruit and diced meat or fish all mixed with a salad dressing

Stovies (Scot.) potatoes simmered in very little water, sometimes with onion

Stuffed cabbage (Eng.) forcemeat wrapped in cabbage leaves and baked

Teisen nionod (Wales) finely sliced potatoes and onions, baked

Puddings and desserts

Almond flory (Scot.) a puff pastry pie filled with custard, flavoured with ground almonds and brandy, mixed with currants, butter, sugar, cinnamon and nutmeg and baked

Apple amber pudding apple tart covered with meringue

Apple charlotte apples and breadcrumbs baked in a tin lined with slices of bread and covered with more bread

Bakewell pudding (Eng.) a flaky pastry case with a filling of raspberry or strawberry jam, covered with a custard of beaten eggs, butter, sugar and ground almonds and baked

★Bread and butter pudding bread with currants and raisins, covered with egg and milk custard and baked. Sounds revolting, but the British, who have had it in their nurseries for three hundred years, think it wonderful

Burnt cream the richest cream custard, with a layer of caramelized sugar covering it

Cabinet pudding a mixture of diced sponge cake, ratafia biscuits, glacé cherries, angelica, white raisins and currants, covered with a vanilla custard and baked

Castle pudding individual moulded cakes served with a lemon sauce

Christmas pudding *or* **plum pudding** can be traced back to a frumenty taken at the winter solstice by our animist ancestors. By the Middle Ages the milk frumenty had become beef broth, acquiring dried plums and ginger and in Scotland became plum porridge, still a soup. The Elizabethans added suet and wine or beer, but it did not lose its meat or become dry until a hundred years later

Cloutie dumpling (Scot.) a steamed suet pudding mixed with dried fruit, apples, raisins, white raisins, currants and molasses

College pudding individual baked suet pudding with candied peel, currants and brandy

Cranachan *or* **cream crowdie** (Scot.) toasted oatmeal mixed with whipped cream, flavoured with vanilla and rum

Crumble any fruit covered with a crumbly mixture of butter and flour and baked

Diplomatic pudding alternate layers of a stiff cream custard and brandy-soaked sponge biscuits, glacé cherries, angelica, white raisins and currants

Edinburgh fog (Scot.) whipped cream mixed with ratafia biscuits and chopped almonds

Eve's pudding sliced apples with cloves, covered with sponge

Flummery a mould made with wine, sugar, egg yolk, lemon juice and brandy, set with gelatine

Fool any fruit, stewed or raw, crushed and mixed with cream

Fritters apples or other fruit deep fried in batter

Frumenty boiled wheat with spices, milk and sugar

Glister pudding (Scot.) a steamed marmalade pudding

★ **Hedgehog pudding** a delicious steamed meringue mixture covered with caramel, stuck all over with roasted almonds and with a thin frothy custard

Her Majesty's pudding a thick, creamy, vanilla custard, decorated with crystallized fruit

Holyrood pudding (Scot.) a pudding mixture of milk, semolina, ratafia biscuits, egg yolk and marmalade, folded with stiff white of egg, steamed and served hot with almond sauce

Jam roly poly steamed suet pastry rolled up with jam

Junket basically sweetened milk set with rennet. It may be flavoured with lemon, wine etc.

Lemon posset cream beaten with lemon juice, grated lemon rind and white wine, stiffened with beaten egg white

Madeira pudding tart with a filling of raspberry jam covered with a sponge mixture and baked

Marquis pudding rice pudding arranged in layers with jam and stewed apples, covered with ground almonds and baked

★ **Mince pie** Mrs Beeton put ground rump steak in her mince pies, together with raisins, currants, dark brown sugar, candied lemon and orange peel,

nutmeg, apples, lemon rind, lemon juice and brandy. Today few people put in meat

Oxford and Cambridge pudding (Eng.) apricot tart covered with meringue

Pippin tart a pie of apples and tomato mashed together and baked with cream

Plum duff (Eng.) a boiled suet pudding with raisins

★ **Poor Knights of Windsor** (Eng.) slices of bread soaked in sherry, dipped in milk and egg yolk and fried. Served with a butter, sherry and sugar sauce

Queen of puddings a breadcrumb and custard base, baked, spread with jam and covered with a meringue mixture, then re-baked until meringue is brown

Rice pudding rice baked with milk, sugar and butter in a low oven, until a golden crust appears. A noted nursery dish

Spotted dick *or* **dog** a steamed suet pudding with raisins

★ **Summer pudding** lightly stewed berry fruits and black- or red-currants put in a basin lined with slices of bread, covered with more bread and allowed to stand overnight. Comes out as a beautiful purple juicy pudding which tastes wonderfully fresh

Syllabub basically some kind of drink whipped up with cream and sugar. The commonest is made with sherry and lemon

Treacle roll a steamed suet pudding rolled up with molasses and breadcrumbs

★ **Treacle tart** golden syrup and breadcrumbs baked in a tart

Trifle slices of sponge cake soaked in brandy and sherry, covered with custard and decorated with cream and candied fruit

Turnovers any fruit put into a puff pastry envelope and baked

Welsh border tart raisin and white raisin tart covered with meringue

Custard

There must be a moral for theologians to draw from custard. That a concoction of such simple ingredients as butter, flour, milk, sugar and egg yolks can be either the embodiment of horror and evil or the most felicitous accompaniment to so many things, even a delight on its own, is surely a paradox worthy of close attention.

Ambrose Bierce called custard "a detestable substance produced by a malevolent conspiracy of the hen, the cow and the cook." Plainly, he had in mind the sickly sweet slop or gunge which schools, vicars' wives and indolent producers of mass food pour over any sweet dish or fruit, thereby eliminating whatever natural merit it might have had.

Biscuits, breads and cakes

The prodigious number of breads, biscuits and cakes which England, Wales, Scotland and Ireland produce would be impossible to encompass. So, if the opportunity arises, any visitor to Britain should try to visit one old-fashioned tea-shop and indulge in an orgy of baps, shortbread and drop scones in Scotland or crumpets, muffins, and scones in England. In Devon and Cornwall, cream teas are the thing, with thick layers of clotted cream spread on warm bread and covered with home-made jam. Ah yes, it was a happier world before some fool discovered the calorie.

Cheese

Blue vinney a Dorset cheese, round and fat, with blue veins in a loose, white body. It tastes strong and sharp

Caerphilly the one Welsh cheese, cream coloured and gently crumbly, with a milky taste

Cheddar the best hard cheese for cooking. Can be huge, weighing as much as a 10-year-old child. The farmhouse ones from Somerset are quite sharp and nutty and very solid

Cheshire an excellent crumbly, white or orange pressed cheese. The blue or green version used to be a chance happening; now one family produces it commercially having found out how to turn the cheese automatically. Someone has copied them with a blue Shropshire, but it is inferior

Double Gloucester a large, flat round cheese, deep yellow and piercingly sharp in taste

Dunlop the best Scottish cheese, somewhat like Cheddar but, properly, moister and softer

Lancashire very like Cheshire but always white

Leicester large, round, browny-red cheese; flaky and mild

Red Windsor a white cheese marbled with red smudges of red wine which is added during the manufacturing process. I am always a little suspicious of this cheese. It looks spurious and unappetizing

Sage Derby large, round, flat cheese, compact and white, marbled with green smudges of sage, mild and herby

Stilton the finest blue cheese in the world

Wensleydale round, flat, double-cream cheese but quite firm, with a delicate almost salty taste. Goes beautifully with fruit. There is also a blue version

Useful words

Aubergine eggplant
Bill check
Biscuits cookies
Chicory endive
Chips french fries
Courgettes zucchini
Crisps potato chips
Grill broil
Maize corn

Minced ground
Offal variety meats
Prawns shrimp
Sautéed pan fried
Scones biscuits
Spring onions scallions
Swede yellow turnip
Sweets candy, dessert
Treacle molasses

Greece

People are always saying that Greek food is all taken from the Turks and the Venetians and the Magyars. It is an absurd proposition really, because the origins of all western cuisines must lie in ancient Greece. The Romans certainly employed Greek chefs and the Turks learned their cooking from the Byzantine empire—the descendant of Rome.

What distinguishes Greek cooking today is the freshness of the ingredients and the simplicity of their preparation. Egg and lemon soup, taramosalata, stuffed vine leaves, spit-roasted meat, roast chicken with herbs, stuffed eggplants, tomatoes and peppers, cheese wrapped in flaky pastry. These dishes are all very simple and, when well-cooked by a light hand, quite excellent. The small appetizers or *mezes* are perfect accompaniments to an *ouzo* in Greece, and in many Greek restaurants all over the world a selection from the best of them is often enough to constitute a whole meal in itself.

The Greeks are exuberant eaters-out and, particularly in Athens, there is a huge range of eating establishments, starting with the grandest hotels and restaurants, which provide universal food, down to the far jollier tavernas.

On the islands you may have a less extensive choice and possibly no menu, or one translated rather erratically into strange English. The fish will be excellent, particularly red mullet and squid, and most dishes can be personally selected from bubbling cauldrons in taverna kitchens, which augur well. Be prepared, however, for most food to be lukewarm by the time the journey from kitchen to table is completed.

The Greeks are dedicated drinkers, but for outsiders the taste for what they drink takes some acquiring. I happen to like anis so *ouzo*, despite its sweetness, quite appeals to me. I would not expect anyone else to care for it. The same goes for *retsina*, the resinated white wine, tasting of high quality floor polish, which is made in the area round Athens. If you don't want to acquire such tastes, there are a very few ordinary wines which you may find reasonable. The names to remember are *Demestica, Hymettus, Mavroudi, Mavro Romeiko* (from Crete), *Naoussa* and, at a pinch, *Nemea*.

Greek alphabetical order is: *A, B, Γ, Δ, E, Z, H, Θ, I, K, Λ, M, N, Ξ, O, Π, P, Σ, T, Υ, Φ, X, Ψ, Ω*
α, β, γ, δ, ε, ζ, η, θ, ι, κ, λ, μ, ν, ξ, o, π, ρ, σ/ς, τ, υ, φ, χ, ψ, ω

'Ορεκτικά καί μεζεδάκια (orektika ke mezedhakia)—Hors d'oeuvre and canapés

κεφτεδάκια (keftedhakia) tiny meat balls

κρεατόπιττα (kreatopitta) triangular flaky pastry pies filled with ground meat

μελιτζανοσαλάτα (melidzanosalata) creamy purée of baked eggplants mixed with grated onion, chopped tomato, crushed garlic, olive oil and vinegar. Served cold

μπουρεκάκια (burekakia) generic term for all the tiny stuffed pies made with thin *filo* pastry

ντολμαδάκια (dolmadhakia) tiny rolls of ground meat and rice or rice on its own wrapped in vine leaves

σπανακόπιττα (spanakopitta) triangular flaky pastry pies filled with spinach and *feta* cheese

συκωτάκια τηγανιτά (sikotakia tiganita) cubes of lamb's liver sautéed in oil with lemon juice and oregano

★ ταραμοσαλάτα **(taramosalata)** creamy pink cod's roe paste made by crushing the roes with olive oil, lemon and soaked breadcrumbs

τυρόπιττα **(tiropitta)** triangular flaky pastry puffs filled with a mixture of *feta* cheese, eggs and parsley

Οἱ σουπες (I supes) — Soups

κακαβιά **(kakavia)** Greek fish soup-stew

κοτόσουπα **(kotosupa)** chicken soup

μαγειρίτσα **(mayiritsa)** Easter soup made with lamb's liver, lungs, heart and intestines, finely chopped with scallions, dill and rice. Egg and lemon sauce is added at the end

ρεβυθόσουπα **(revithosupa)** chick pea and onion soup with added oil and lemon

★ σούπα αὐγολέμονο **(supa avgholemono)** rice cooked in chicken stock with added egg and lemon sauce

φακή **(faki)** lentil soup with onion, garlic, bay leaves, olive oil, and vinegar

φασόλια **(fasolia)** white bean soup with vegetables

φάβα **(fava)** a purée of yellow split peas with onions, olive oil and lemon. Served hot or cold

ψαρόσουπα **(psarosupa)** fish soup

Ψάρια καί θαλασσινά (psaria ke thalasina) — Fish and seafood

ἀστακός μαγιονέζα **(astakos mayioneza)** spiny lobster served with mayonnaise

ἀχινός **(akhinos)** sea urchin

γαρίδες **(gharidhes)** shrimp

καλαμαράκια **(kalamarakia)** baby squid

★ κρασάτα **(krasata)** squid sautéed in oil and then simmered in wine with tomatoes and parsley. Served cold

κέφαλος **(kefalos)** mullet

μαρίδες **(maridhes)** small fish like whitebait

μπακαλιάρος μὲ σκορδαλιά **(bakaliaros me skordhalia)** salt cod fried in batter and served with a thick garlic sauce

μπαρμπούνια **(barbunia)** red mullet

μύδια **(midhia)** mussels

σαρδέλλες **(sardheles)** (fresh) sardines

χταπόδι **(khtapodhi)** octopus

μὲ σάλτσα **(me saltsa)** octopus sautéed with oil, garlic and onions and then simmered in red wine and tomatoes

ψάρι πλακί **(psari plaki)** fish baked with a thick sauce of onions, garlic, tomato, parsley and wine

σπετσιώτικο **(spetsiotiko)** fish baked with tomatoes, oil, white wine, garlic and parsley, covered with a layer of breadcrumbs

Ἐντράδες (entradhes) — Main dishes

ἀρνί **(arni)** lamb

★ γιουβέτσι μὲ μανέστρα **(yiouvetsi me manestra)** cubes of lamb casseroled with onion and tomatoes, to which small grains of pasta are added. Grated cheese is sprinkled liberally over the dish

ἐξοχικό **(exohiko)** literally "country style"; small parcels of flaky *filo* pastry filled with a lamb chop, some peas, potatoes, tomatoes, *kaseri* cheese and parsley. Baked in the oven

κapamάς **(kapamas)** cubes of lamb stewed with onions, tomatoes, parsley and garlic. Potatoes are often added

σούβλας **(suvlas)** spit-roasted lamb

φρικασέ **(frikase)** sautéed cubes of lamb, simmered with chopped scallions, cos lettuce and dill, to which an egg and lemon sauce is added at the end

ψητό μὲ πατάτες **(psito me patates)** roast leg of lamb, stuck with garlic, and roast potatoes

γαλοπούλα **(ghalopula)** turkey
γουρουνόπουλο τοῦ γάλακτος
(ghurunopulo tu ghalaktos)
suckling pig
κεφτέδες **(keftedhes)** meat balls
made with ground veal or beef,
egg, breadcrumbs, chopped
onions, oregano, mint and
parsley mixed with a little olive
oil and vinegar and fried
κοκορέτσι **(kokoretsi)** kidneys,
tripe and liver, rolled in braided
intestines and grilled on a spit
κολοκύθια γεμιστά **(kolokithia
yemista)** scooped zucchini
stuffed with ground meat, onions
and rice. Baked in the oven with
a tomato sauce
κοτόπουλο **(kotopulo)** chicken
  στιφάδο **(stifadho)** braised
chicken with tomatoes, lots of
baby onions, garlic, oil and red
wine
κουνέλι **(kuneli)** rabbit
μακαρόνια μὲ κιμα **(makaronia me
kima)** spaghetti with a ground
meat sauce
  μὲ σάλτσα ντομάτα **(me saltsa
domata)** pasta, usually spaghetti,
served with a tomato sauce
★μελιτζάνες παπουτσάκια
(melidzanes paputsakia) literally
"little shoes"; eggplant halves
stuffed with a ground meat,
onion, tomato, egg, cheese and
breadcrumb mixture, covered
with béchamel sauce and baked
μοσχάρι **(moskhari)** beef
ψητὸ στὸ φούρνο **(psito sto
furno)** veal pot-roasted with
tomatoes, onion, garlic and wine
★μουσακᾶς **(musakas)** what we
know as "moussaka"; layers of
cooked, sliced eggplant
alternating with a mixture of
ground meat, grated onions,
tomatoes, parsley and spices,

each layer sprinkled with cheese.
A thick béchamel sauce covers
the dish, liberally sprinkled with
cheese
μπριζόλα **(brizola)** chop or cutlet
μυαλα **(miala)** brains
νεφρὰ **(nefra)** kidneys
ντολμάδες **(dolmadhes)** rolls of
ground veal, chopped scallions,
rice, dill and mint wrapped in
fresh vine leaves, cooked in
water
ντομάτεμιστὲς **(domates
yemistes)** tomatoes stuffed with
ground veal, onions, mint,
parsley and rice, sprinkled with
breadcrumbs and baked
παϊδάκια ἀρνίσια **(paidhakia
arnisia)** lamb chops
πάπια **(papia)** duck
παστίτσιο **(pastitsio)** macaroni
baked in the oven with grated
cheese and a ground meat, onion
and tomato sauce
πιτσούνια **(pitsunia)** young squab
σουβλάκι **(suvlaki)** tender meat
grilled on skewers, first
marinated in lemon juice and
olive oil with bay leaves and
oregano
σουτζουκάκια **(sudzukakia)**
small fat sausages from
Smyrna, made from ground
meat, breadcrumbs, onion,
cummin and garlic
★σοφρίτο **(sofrito)** a delicious
dish from Corfu. Slices of steak
are stewed in vinegar and water
with garlic until a thick sauce
results
στιφάδο **(stifadho)** a rich
casserole of stewing steak or veal
with small onions, tomatoes, bay
leaves, rosemary, vinegar and wine
συκωτάκια **(sikotakia)** liver
χοιρινή μπριζόλα **(khirini brizola)**
pork chop

Λαχανικά καί σαλάτες *(lakhanika ke salates)*—Vegetables and salads

κολοκύθια **(kolokithia)** zucchini
μελιτζάνες **(melidzanes)**
eggplants
μπάμιες **(bamies)** okra
ντομάτες **(domates)** tomatoes
πατάτες **(patates)** potatoes
πιπεριά **(piperia)** green pepper
ραδίκια **(radhikia)** dandelion
leaves

σατζίκι **(sadziki)** chopped
cucumber, garlic and dill mixed
with a little olive oil, vinegar and
yoghurt. Served chilled as a dip
χωριάτικη **(khoriatiki)** mixed
country salad of tomatoes, onion,
cucumber, sweet peppers, olives,
feta cheese, oregano and olive oil
σκορδαλιά **(skordhalia)** a garlic

119

dip—made from pounded cloves of garlic and soft breadcrumbs or potato, mixed with plenty of olive oil and a little lemon

σπανάκι **(spanaki)** spinach

φασόλια **(fasolia)** beans

Γλυκά καί φρούτα *(glika ke fruta)*— *Desserts and fruit*

ἀμυγδαλωτό **(amighdhaloto)** a mixture of ground almonds, sugar, semolina and orange-flower water baked and coated with icing sugar

ἀχλάδι **(akhladhi)** pear

βερύκοκα **(verikoka)** apricots

★ γαλακτομπούρεκο **(ghalaktobureko)** a delicious custard pie filling enclosed in thin sheets of flaky pastry, doused in syrup. Actually made with milk, eggs, semolina and butter

καρπούζι **(karpuzi)** water-melon

καταΐφι **(kataifi)** rolls of shredded wheat pastry stuffed with nuts, breadcrumbs and sugar and soaked in syrup

κρέμα καραμελέ **(krema karamele)** cream caramel

λουκουμάδες **(lukumadhes)** fluffy honey puffs made with yeast dough. Sprinkled with cinnamon and served dripping with honey

λουκούμι **(lukumi)** Turkish delight

μπακλαβᾶς **(baklavas)** sticky pastry made from thin layers of paper-thin *filo* pastry stuffed with almonds, walnuts, breadcrumbs, sugar and cinnamon, baked in the oven and doused in hot syrup. Served cold

παγωτό **(paghoto)** ice-cream

πεπόνι **(peponi)** melon

ρυζόγαλο **(rizoghalo)** cold rice pudding sprinkled with cinnamon

ροδάκινο **(rodhakino)** peach

σταφύλι **(stafili)** grapes

σῦκα **(sika)** figs

τηγανίτες **(tighanites)** fritters

Useful words

αὐγό **(avgho)** egg

βούτυρο **(vutiro)** butter

γάλα **(ghala)** milk

γιαούρτι **(yiaurti)** yoghurt

γλυκό **(ghliko)** sweet

ἐλαιόλαδο **(eleoladho)** olive oil

ἐλιές **(elies)** olives

ζάχαρη **(zakhari)** sugar

ζεστό **(zesto)** hot, warm

κασέρι **(kaseri)** soft yellow cheese

κατάλογος **(kataloghos)** menu

καφές **(kafes)** coffee

  φραπέ **(frape)** iced

κεφαλοτύρι **(kefalotiri)** hard, crumbly, salty cheese

κρασί **(krasi)** wine

  ἄσπρο **(aspro)** white

  γλυκό **(ghliko)** dessert

  κόκκινο **(kokkino)** red

κρέας **(kreas)** meat

κρύο **(krio)** cold

λογαριασμός **(loghariazmos)** bill

λουκάνικο **(lukaniko)** sausage

μαυροδάφνη **(mavrodhafni)** a red dessert wine

Μεταξά **(metaxa)** a famous brand of Greek brandy

μπύρα **(bira)** beer

νερό **(nero)** water

οὖζο **(ouzo)** aniseed liqueur

πίττα **(pitta)** flat bread

ρετσίνα **(retsina)** dry white resinated wine. Sometimes rosé

ρίγανη **(righani)** Greek oregano

ρύζι **(rizi)** rice

τσάϊ **(tsai)** tea

τυρί **(tiri)** cheese

φέτα **(feta)** crumbly, white and salty goat or ewe's milk cheese

ψωμί **(psomi)** bread

στήν ὑγειά σας! **(stin iyia sas)** cheers!
καλή σας ὄρεξη! **(kali sas orexi)** bon appétit!

Hong Kong— *See* China
Hungary— *See* Eastern Europe
Iceland— *See* Scandinavia

The Indian sub-continent

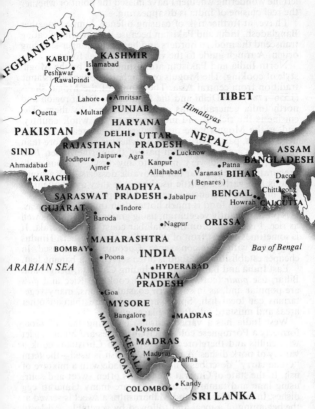

Indian food is as complicated a subject as any other in India, which is to say that there are almost as many opinions about each dish as there are Indians. It is further confused by the huge number of languages so that the same dish may have ten different names. I have used Hindi names for the most part, together with Tamil for dishes more common in the south. Indian cooking is governed also by the various religions of the countries which make up the sub-continent, not to mention the superstitions. There are cooks who would not dream of working without a string tied round their big toes, others who would refuse to cook in a kitchen which was wrongly situated.

Despite all these refinements, it always seems to me that there is a dull sameness about Indian food. Unlike many cuisines, (e.g. Spanish or Balkan) which seem all the same to start with but gradually reveal themselves, Indian cooking, which at first sight seems so varied, has an inexcusably repetitive basis. It is all brown and yellow. The main ingredient of any stewed dish, albeit tender, is hardly important, being cooked to non-existence and shrouded in a sauce which conceals any thin character it may have left. I realize that this is a subjective judgement, likely to offend many sensibilities and, indeed, I have occasionally had in private houses dishes which left me wondering whether I have missed the point or whether the real cuisine of India is disappearing.

I have, at further risk of causing offence, lumped together Bangladesh, India and Pakistan because the patterns of eating transcend the modern borders and have a far longer-standing origin. A rough guide to the variations goes as follows:

North India and Pakistan are distinguished by the Mogul style of cooking. The Moguls or Mughals brought an Islamic tradition from central Asia. The capital of the Mogul shahs (1556–1784) was Delhi and the food of the Delhi region and north India generally was greatly influenced by them. The cuisine is the richest and most lavish of the whole country, and as the Moguls were meat eaters, has a great variety of meat dishes, particularly lamb. As wheat is grown more than rice, breads are an important part of the northern diet. *Dals* are important and very much to my taste. Various milk preparations are popular but unlovable desserts. In Kashmir, onions and garlic are little used because they are thought to heat the blood and encourage unbridled passions.

South Indian food is much hotter than that of other areas. It is predominantly vegetarian, using grains and lentils as well as rice. Fish is good on the Malabar coast and in Kerala. It is sometimes called "fruit of the sea" so that southern Hindus may eat it with clear conscience. Coconut is much used. In cheaper establishments, food is often served on a banana leaf.

East India and Bangladesh, including Calcutta, Bengal and Bihar, use *panir* (cottage cheese) in cooking. Rice and *dals* are popular and, as in southern coastal regions, many vegetarians eat local fish. Spices are used more than in other areas and mustard oil often replaces *ghee*.

West India has a varied cuisine, including that of Goa, formerly a Portuguese colony. Goan curries are often scarlet with chillis and therefore *very* hot. Goan Christians cook a variety of pork dishes. A great deal of fish is used—the term "Goan curry" describes a liquid dish made with a mixture of fish. In the state of Gujarat the food is often sweet and sour, using lime and tamarind, and there are many Gujarati egg dishes. In both Gujarat and Maharashtra a sweet is served at the beginning of a meal and followed by vegetable and lentil dishes. In Maharashtra it is common to eat vegetable dishes and *puris* with *shrikand*, a sweetened curd dish. In Bombay and Gujarat the Parsis have their own style of rich cooking.

In most grand hotels there are Chinese restaurants. I would avoid these as combining the worst characteristics of both cuisines. On the other hand I would not hesitate to eat the lovely *samosas* and little snacks sold in wayside stalls. I even like the tea they sell—tea leaves, milk and sugar all brewed up together and strained through an old sock. But of course, tourists are warned against this sort of thing and are expected to eat jam roly-poly in their echoing hotel dining-room.

Anda, baida, unda(h)—Eggs

Akoori see *Ekuri*

Anda ki kari egg curry

Baida vindalu Goan egg *vindalu*

Ekuri a Parsi dish of scrambled eggs with coriander and ginger

Khagina spiced omelette, turned over twice, first to make a half-moon and then a wedge

Nargis(i) preparations using halved hard-boiled eggs, so-called because they look like narcissi

Undah khitcherie scrambled eggs with onions, tomato, chilli and coriander

Chat—Snacks

Alu chat boiled potato slices mixed with chillis, tamarind, fresh coriander and salt

Appam, appum south Indian pancake, made with rice flour and coconut milk

Bhaji(y)as spicy fritters made with flour, vegetables and even bananas. Served with fresh mint and chutney

★ **Bhelpuri** small deep-fried *puris* (see *Bread*) served with finely chopped onion, puffed rice, *chiura*, cubed boiled potatoes, lemon juice, coriander leaves and chutney. A speciality of Bombay

Chiura a mixture of deep-fried *phoa* (flattened rice flakes), *dal*, chick pea noodles and peanuts seasoned with salt, sugar and chilli powder

Dhokla batter made with *dal*, rice and chillis, steamed, then fried

Golgappas small deep-fried wafers served cold with cooked *channa*, potatoes and a sweet-sour sauce

Kachoris pastry balls stuffed with a spicy lentil or potato filling

Oothappam spicy pancake made with lentil and rice flour. South Indian

Pakoras, pecoras savoury fritters. North Indian version of *bhajias*

Pappadam, poppadom, puppadum crispy, spicy wafer biscuit, like a potato chip. Baked or fried. Often crushed and sprinkled over main dishes. Called *papar* in the north

Pustholes wheat-flour puffs, usually stuffed with curried meat, vegetables, etc.

★ **Samosa** deep-fried triangular pie stuffed with ground meat or peas and potatoes

Shinghara vegetable pie from Bengal

Vad(d)a, vadi *or* **wada** small, savoury fried snacks made from lentil or chick pea flour. Grated vegetables, ground nuts and spices may be mixed with the flour. Served dry with chutney or soaked in yoghurt

Chav(w)al—Rice

Bath, buth west coast and south Indian word for rice

Biri(y)ani elaborate rice dish flavoured and coloured with saffron or turmeric. It is richer than a *pilau*, having more *ghee*, or butter. The amount of meat or fish included is double that of the rice

Copra kana rice cooked in coconut milk, either plain or spicy. May be coloured with turmeric

Dahi bath rice with yoghurt

Dal bath rice served with lentils

Gili *or* **geeli khichhari** moist *khichhari* made without butter and seasoned with bay and peppercorns. Often given to children or invalids

Hazur pasand *pilau* with meat, fruit and nuts

Kesar chav(w)al rice flavoured with saffron

Kitcheri(ee), khichhari rice and lentils cooked together, highly spiced. The word means "hodge-podge" and is the origin of the English word kedgeree.

Sometimes refers to scrambled eggs

Makhani chav(w)al buttered rice

Mattar pilau rice with peas

Memna pilau fairly hot *pilau* with lamb, almonds, carrots and cucumber

Murgh pilau rice with chicken

Narial ka chav(w)al coconut-flavoured rice

Nimbu ka chav(w)al lime-flavoured rice

Pi(u)lau rice that is first cooked in *ghee* and then in water or stock. There are many variations on the basic dish

Sabzi pilau rice with mixed vegetables

Shahi pilau *pilau* using almonds, cream, yoghurt, light spices and plenty of butter and stock

Shahjahani biriani literally "in the style of the Shah Jahan" (builder of the Taj Mahal). Spiced saffron rice with lamb; a spicy festive dish, often garnished with silver leaf

Vengi bath eggplant and rice

Machchi, machli, meen, min, muchlee, myhee—Fish

Ballachong balchao pickled shrimp, very hot

Bombay duck, bommaloe machee a fish similar in size to a herring, caught in quantity off the west coast of India, especially in the neighbourhood of Bombay. The name probably derives from the fact that the fish skim the surface of the water. It is cut open, cleaned, plentifully salted and so thoroughly dried in the sun that it often resembles wood. It is fried before being served as a snack, a side dish or in a curry

Chingri jhoal spicy shrimp curry with coconut. Very popular in Bengal

Chorchuri Bengali dish made with vegetables and fish heads

Ginga or **jhinga** shrimp

  kari shrimp curry

  ki tikka fried shrimp patties

  patia Parsi dish of spicy shrimp with lemon and tomatoes

Kabab tikkah machchi marinated fish grilled on skewers

Kekra crab

Kofta shami machchi fish croquettes

Kurlleachi kari crab curry

Machchi bhurta spiced fish purée, served cold

  dumphokat fish steamed with spices

  hazur pasand whole fish spiced and baked with tomatoes, cream and yoghurt

imlidarh fried fish with tamarind

jhal frazi fish with sautéed spices

khasa fish that is first poached then coated with spices and crisply fried

turrcarri sadah simple, mild fish curry

Machli aur tamatar spiced fish with tomatoes

  ki tikki rolled fish fillets, stuffed and baked

Meen molee south Indian spicy fish curry where the fish is cooked in a thick coconut milk sauce

Min mappas carp cooked with fruit and coconut milk

  pulicha baked whole fish

  tulika whitebait with coconut milk

  vela fish curry from Kerala. A mixture of fish cooked with chilli and tamarind

Myhee mahali fish marinated with yoghurt and onion, fried and served with a spiced cream and almond sauce

Pakki hui machli baked fish with coriander *masala*

Patrani machli pomfret (a common Indian fish) stuffed with green chutney, wrapped in a banana leaf and steamed. From Bombay

Tali machchi fried fish in batter

Teesri clams

Gosh(t), mha(a)ns—Meat

Aab ghosh meat, usually lamb, boiled in milk. A Moslem dish

Ahtoo koottee lamb (Tamil)

Baffat Goan pork or beef curry with radishes

Bakra goat

Barra kabab massalam spiced skewered meat on the bone

Bathak duck

Bhuna gosht a dry, spicy dish of lamb or beef

Boti kabab small pieces of very tender meat, marinated, skewered and basted with butter

Chirga whole roasted chicken. The chicken is rubbed with cayenne, paprika, lime juice,

vinegar and salt. It is then rubbed with a paste of yoghurt, green ginger, onion, salt and pepper, and roasted on a spit

Chourisam spicy pork and liver sausage from Goa

Degh bhurta mhaans meat, usually lamb, with chick peas, lentils and dumplings that have been poached in yoghurt. Fairly hot and spicy

★**Dhansak** a Parsi casserole of meats and fresh and dried vegetables

  fasli meat cooked with a variety of dried beans. Aromatic, but not hot

Ghai ka gosht beef

Gobi mhaans braised meat with cauliflower

Gosht do pyaza meat cooked with onions

   ka salun a Deccan meat curry

Goshtaba a Kashmiri dish of lamb and curd meatballs

Gurda kidney

Hurran ka gosht kabab grilled venison steaks

Indad a Goan sweet-and-sour pork curry

Jungli budhuk ka salun wild duck curry

Kabab usually describes small pieces of meat, fish or vegetables packed on skewers and grilled or roasted. Also describes larger pieces of meat cooked in their own juice, or ground meat formed into patties and fried. They originated in the Steppes, but became a Mogul speciality. The word comes from *kum aab,* "a little water"

   darayhee *or* **husainee** skewered meat and vegetables grilled and then simmered in a sauce

   dehin *kabab* using yoghurt

   kaishgee glazed pork chops with a fruity aromatic sauce

   moghlai ground spiced lamb grilled on skewers Mogul style

   puksand two pieces of meat, or meat and cheese, tied together with string and skewered

   pursindah seekhi skewered lamb

   seek long rolls of finely ground meat

   shami meat ground with lentils, spices and onions

   shikhampuri ground mutton or lamb *kabab*

   tikia, tikka(h) cubed meat cooked in a *tandoor,* or on charcoal

Kaleja, kaleji liver

   sheesh spiced liver with onions

Khargosh, kurghosh hare or rabbit

Kheema ground meat

   aur bhaji ground meat with greens

   mattar ground meat with peas

Khubab hans roast goose

Kofta, kooftah balls of ground meat or vegetables cooked in *korma* style, and sometimes curried or spitted

kabab sheer-mal meat balls in a spicy sauce made with milk

nargesi ground meat balls stuffed with whole hard-boiled eggs, served cut in half in a curry sauce

Kohlee chicken (Tamil)

   molee south Indian dish made with coconut milk

Kookarh, kookurh chicken

Korma a dish that is braised with yoghurt and/or cream. Usually rich and spicy, though rarely very hot

   badam malai khatai piquant lamb *korma* with cream and almonds

   Bahadhar shahi braised lamb in a mild but rich *korma* dish of almonds, yoghurt, heavy cream and egg yolks

   dil-pasand braised meat and vegetables in a mellow garlic sauce. One of the few Indian dishes that feature garlic

   ★**hazur pasand** a special braised lamb dish finished with egg white and a mixture of nuts, raisins and saffron

   jogurath meat braised in spices and yoghurt and finished with heavy cream

   kasa casseroled meat balls with vegetables

   lowabdarh a *korma* braised in milk and finished off with yoghurt

   ★**roghan josh** lamb *korma,* sometimes reddened with beet juice

   sadah plain meat *korma* in yoghurt

Madoo beef (Tamil)

Magazh brains

Masaledar raan spiced roast beef

Matan lamb

Mhaans dumphoktai an aromatic pot roast, garlicky and moderately hot

   kabab machchi finely ground and spiced meat, made into fish shapes, strongly garlic flavoured, fried and served cold

   phali cooked with beans

   turrcarri sadah simple, mild meat curry

Moorgee, murg, murgh, murghi *or* **murgo** chicken

   badam sheer-jogurath with almonds in a sauce made with milk, yoghurt and cream

dehin spiced chicken in yoghurt, hot and very garlicky

do pyaza cooked with onions

dumphokat a mild spicy chicken casserole

kabab seekhi whole stuffed chicken cooked on a spit

khara massaledarh casseroled with whole spices

khasa mild aromatic chicken curry

korma cooked with yoghurt and spices

makhani cooked with butter and tomatoes

★ **massalam** one of the best-known chicken dishes, of Mogul origin. The chicken is marinated in yoghurt, cummin, onion and chillis, then casseroled with spices and served sprinkled with nuts

masthana spiced chicken casseroled with rice and chick pea dumplings

★ **moghlai** rich, elaborate saffron-flavoured chicken, Mogul style

sabz with green herbs, such as chives and coriander leaves, and yoghurt

sadah plain mild chicken curry

talawa kasta fried in batter made with *besan*, spices and yoghurt

tandoori marinated in spicy yoghurt and cooked in a *tandoor*

tikka spicy chicken *kabab*

Murghabi duck

Kashmiri with walnuts

pistadarh with pistachio nuts

Muzbi a special first course at Mogul feasts—marinated lamb cooked on hot stones

Parcha kabab yakhni rolled mutton with spices and egg

seekhi leg of lamb on the spit

Pursindah seekhi skewered lamb

Pyazwala khare masale ka gosht meat with spices and onions

Qabargah dry lamb dish cooked by Kashmiri Brahmans

Raan (ka kabab) marinated leg of lamb cooked in its spicy yoghurt marinade. The Nawab of Rampur, whose father had 27 cooks, once produced a leg of lamb that had been reshaped after grinding the meat

Rarrah saddle of lamb

★ **Roghan josh** traditional north Indian Moslem dish of spiced lamb. Rich and dark red

Sadah mutton

Sag mhaans mild garlicky meat with spinach and yoghurt

Serpathala spicy dish made with pig's blood, liver and other pork

Shami kabab Noor-Mahali an elaborate meat, lentil and onion *kabab* flavoured with aniseed and *kalonji*, and mixed with yoghurt

Suvar mas pork. Forbidden to Moslems

mas ka salun pork curry

mas korma pork braised with yoghurt and sometimes honey

mas vindalu hot south Indian vinegar curry

Shythani kabab ka salun a devilled *kabab* curry

Sindhi gosht meat dish from Sind. The meat, usually lamb, is first marinated in a spicy paste

Sorpotel pickled pork casserole. A Goan Christian dish

★ **Subh degh** a dish traditionally made on feast days. The meat, usually lamb, is partly made into *kofta* and partly cubed and cooked with spices. It contains both cooked and brined vegetables mixed with yoghurt and steamed

Teetur, tithar partridge (or any game)

Vath, vathoo duck (Tamil)

ka salun duck curry

Vindalu, vindaloo sour vinegared curry from Goa and west India. Usually hot and made with rich meat, such as pork, fat duck or goose

Sabzi, dals — *Vegetables and pulses*

Aloo, alu potato

badam dum smothered with almonds

dam, dum steamed spiced potatoes smothered in a paste of yoghurt and spices

gobi cooked with cauliflower

ki tikya patties

raita potato salad with yoghurt

Arbi, arvi a variety of yam

ki kari yam curry

Arhar dal pigeon pea or Tuvar pea from Madras, Usually served with chillis as a very hot dish

Avi(y)al a south Indian vegetable curry containing bananas, green jackfruit seeds, green mango and coconut as well as traditional western vegetables. Served particularly during the Onam festival—the celebration of the rice harvest

Baigan see *Brinjal*

Band(h)gobi cabbage

Behndi, bendikai, bhindi okra, ladies' fingers

Bhaji, bhugia, bhuji(y)a vegetables cooked in *tarka* style. Often very hot and dry. *Bhujiya* also means deep-fried vegetable fritters. Popular in Maharashtra and similar to the *pakora* of north India

Bharela kheera stuffed cucumber

Brinjal, byngun eggplant

  (ka) bharta spiced eggplant purée. A north Indian dish

  ka tikka baked eggplant with vegetable stuffing

Cachumbar, kachumbar spiced onion salad, usually with fresh hot chillis. The name is also given to salads in general

Chan(n)a dal, chenna, kab(u)li channa chick peas

  masaledar a Punjabi dish of chick peas cooked with onion, garlic, ginger and hot spices

Chukunda beet

Dahi bara, dahi boora lentil cakes in yoghurt

  vada deep-fried lentil purée balls in yoghurt

Da(h)l, dhall Hindi name for all members of the pulse or legume family. The word actually means "split". There are many varieties, which are listed separately. The word also describes dishes made from lentils. In north India a *dal* is usually quite thick in consistency. In Maharashtra, Gujarat and south India, it is often smooth and liquid

Dal moong see *Moong dal*

Foogath, fugath savoury dish of vegetables fried with *masala*, onions and coconut

Gagar, gagur, gajjar carrot

Gob(h)i overall word for cabbage or cauliflower

Gooda, guda squash

Guchhi black mushrooms

Guranthor alu a sweet red yam

Kabuli channa see *Channa dal*

Kadoo, kaddu pumpkin

Kakadi cucumber

Kala chana a small black chick pea

  aur alu a sharp and spicy dish of *kala chana* and potatoes

Karhi north Indian dish made from buttermilk and *besan*

Kela banana or plantain

Kheera, khira cucumber

  raita cucumber and yoghurt relish

Khumb(i) mushrooms

Lobia dal, lombia black-eyed peas or beans

Manh see *Urd*

Masoor, masur a red lentil. Also means "of Mysore"

  rasam a *very* hot lentil consommé

Mat(t)ar, mutter peas

  panir a dish of peas cooked with cubes of curd cheese and spices

  sukhe a dry dish of peas cooked in butter and flavoured with turmeric and coriander

Molee, muli radish

Moong dal, mung dal mung bean. The split mung is said to be very nourishing and was at one time used as a restorative for the aged

Motth round brown lentil

Mutchakotay spiced dried beans

Navrattan sabzi dum steamed mixed vegetables

Ooduth see *Urd*

Pachadi a vegetable (such as potato, onion, cauliflower or okra) and curd dish with chillis, from Gujarat and south India. Usually served cold

Palak spinach

  paneer a spinach and cheese dish from north India

  shalgam a north Indian dish of spinach and turnips

Patiya potatoes with green bananas

Peaz, piaz, pyaz onion

Phali word used to describe peanuts, green beans or other unspecified vegetables

Philouri semolina or lentil flour fritter

Phulgobi cauliflower

  bharta cauliflower purée

Phul-varhia small dried rice puffs

Puli ingi hot ginger curry served in Kerala during the festival of Onam

Pyazwale sookhe alu a dry potato dish with onions

Raita, rayta a salad of vegetables in curd or yoghurt. There are also sweet raitas

Rajma whole red kidney beans

dal curried kidney beans

Sabzi mughlai mixed vegetables with almonds, pistachio nuts and spices, cooked in *ghee* and yoghurt, Mogul style

Sag(h) usually means spinach, but sometimes green vegetables in general

Sambar south Indian dish made with *arhar dal* and vegetables. Often served with *idlis* (see *Bread*)

Same green beans

ki bhaji spiced green beans

Sarson ki sag mustard and cress

Savia, sev vermicelli made from *besan*

Shalgam turnip. Used a great deal in the Punjab

bharta turnip purée

Simla mirch green pepper

Tam(m)at(t)ar tomato

Thuckaley tomato (Tamil)

Toor, toovar dal *or* **tur dal** see *Arhar dal*

Uppama, upuma spicy dish from south India. Vegetables, nuts, vermicelli, etc., are fried with herbs and spices and then simmered until the mixture is thick. Served hot

Urd, urhad a small black pea or bean

ki dal curried black beans

Roti — Bread†

Bajre ki roti bread made with millet flour

Bakarknani crisp thin bread

Bhatura deep-fried leavened bread usually made with plain white flour and served with spiced chick peas as a snack in the Punjab

★**Chap(p)ati** wholewheat unleavened griddle bread. Elephants are commonly fed with chapatis the size of a car wheel

Diliya dosa oat pancake

Dosa ground lentil and rice pancake bread. Sometimes served with a spicy potato filling, in which case it is called *masala dosa*

Double roti Western-style leavened loaf

Idli a steamed round whitish bread or cake made from rice, usually served with *sambal* and eaten for breakfast in south India. It may have various flavourings, such as coconut or lentils, and be sweet or spicy

Luchchi a variety of fried bread from Bengal, similar to a *puri*, made with plain white flour

Makki ki roti corn griddle bread. Traditionally eaten in the Punjab with mustard and cress

★**Na(a)n** tear-drop shaped, flat leavened bread, baked in a *tandoor*

Paratha, paratta flaky wholewheat griddle-fried bread. Made with *ghee* or butter. Sometimes stuffed with spiced meat or vegetables

Phoolkay *or* **phulka** a small puffed-up *chapati*. After the bread is cooked on the griddle, it is held over or dropped onto the open flame

Puri deep-fried wholewheat puffed bread

Roghni nan, shirmal flat leavened bread, baked in the oven

Tandoori roti wholewheat flat bread cooked in a *tandoor*

† See also *Snacks*

Ach(ch)ar, chatni — Pickle and chutney

Achar tandal pickled cauliflower stalks

Avakkai mangai south Indian mango chutney

Chatni brabarr tamattar ripe and green tomato chutney

Kashmiri green ginger chutney

khasa very hot, exotic chutney

with mango or quince paste

purpoo *dal* chutney

Chunda hot Gujarat mango chutney

Garam nimboo achar spiced lime pickle in oil

Kanji carrot pickle

Min pada very hot fish pickle

Shirnee—Sweets

A(a)m mango, the most common fruit in all parts of India

Alebele Goan pancakes with coconut filling

Aliathrum sweet fritters made with rice flour and eggs

Amphulia baked mango and rice

Annanas pineapple

Aru peach

Balushahi sugar-coated doughnuts

★ **Barfi, barphi** milk sweetmeat made with *khoya* and often decorated with silver leaf

Beebeek baked coconut cake

Beveca coconut-flavoured rice pudding, from Goa and south India

Bundi similar to *jalebis*, but batter is poured through a sieve to form very small drops

Chirupayaru payasam a sweet lentil dish served during the Onam festival in Kerala

Chuckolee dumplings cooked in sweetened cinnamon-flavoured milk

Dudh pera *barfi* formed into balls

★ **Firni, phirni** ground rice pudding. It sometimes contains nuts and is flavoured with cardamom or nutmeg

Gajjar halwa carrot *halwa*, eaten as a dessert

★ **Gulab jamun** small balls made from flour, butter and yoghurt, sometimes with ground almonds, fried and soaked in syrup

Halva, halwa heavy confection made by reducing cereal, fruit or vegetables with sugar

  Bombai with semolina and white raisins

  Karachi jellied confection with almonds and pistachio nuts, flavoured with cardamom

  Madras coconut and semolina *halwa*

  sohan semolina *halwa*

★ **Jalebi, jellabies** deep-fried batter twirls soaked in syrup

Kalkals see *Kulkuls*

Karanjia *puris* stuffed with a sweet coconut, nut and white raisin mixture

Karrah mahli semolina and almond *halwa*

Kathal jackfruit, particularly popular in Bengal

Kela banana

Kervai stuffed banana balls

Kesar pilau sweet rice with saffron

★ **Kheer, khir** creamed rice cooked in thickened milk, sometimes decorated with gold or silver leaf

Koykotay (Tamil) steamed dumplings made with rice flour, sugar and coconut

★ **Kulfi** Indian ice-cream, made with *khoya* and nuts

Kulkuls semolina and coconut milk cake

★ **Laddoo** small balls made from chick pea flour, fried and soaked in syrup. Literally means "sweet". They are offered to the god of plenty at the festival of Ganesh—a very spectacular event in the Bombay area

Mall-pura, malpu(r)a sweet pancakes

Masur pak a spongy confection from Mysore, made from chick pea flour, sugar and *ghee*, with almonds and cardamom

Meeta, mitha pilau sweet rice dish with nuts and white raisins. A festive dish from Kashmir

Modak sweet, steamed coconut dumplings, flavoured with cardamom. Usually made during the Ganesh festival

Nar(e)al, nari(y)al coconut

Panyarums banana fritters

Payasam semi-liquid sweet rice dessert

Peras confection made with *khoya* and pistachios. Flavoured with cardamom or nutmeg

Petha confection made from white pumpkin

Phirni see *Firni*

Qulfi see *Kulfi*

Rabarhi, rabri sweet made with *khoya*

Ras malai, roshmalai cream cheese balls in cream or thickened milk

★ **Rasgollahs, rasgullas, roshgullas** sourmilk and flour balls in syrup

Sandesh, sondesh cheese fudge flavoured with cardamom and pistachio nuts

Savia sweet vermicelli with white raisins, pistachio nuts and almonds

★**Shahi tukra** "royal" bread: a bread pudding made with *khoya* and cream. Served cold with pistachio nuts and *kewra* flower essence sprinkled on top. Garnished with silver leaf
Shakar puri sugar puffs. Made from pastry glazed with syrup and eaten during Diwali, the Hindu New Year festival

Shrikand saffron-flavoured curd sweet, usually served with hot *puris*. Popular in Maharashtra
Susiam sweet potato balls
Tho-thole similar to *halwa*
Zarda pilau sweet rice flavoured with saffron, cloves and cardamom. Garnished with almonds, pistachios, white raisins and silver leaf

Sharbats—Drinks

Falsa, phalsa blackberry juice
Faluda, phaluda tapioca milk
Gajar kanji cold carrot drink with mustard seed and chilli
Gudumba mango drink with cummin and cardamom flavouring
Jal jeera, jeera pani cold drink made with tamarind, cummin and mint, served as an appetizer

Kahwa sweet tea
★**Lassi** curd or yoghurt drink, sweetened or salted
Nimbu pani fresh lime juice, sweetened and diluted with water
Piyush see *Lassi*
Rasam pepper water
Sharbat badam almond drink flavoured with cardamom and *kewra* flowers

Useful words

Aata, at(t)a wholewheat flour
Adrak green ginger
Badam almonds
Baghar, chamak technique where spices and flavourings are cooked separately and then added to the main dish to complete cooking. Mainly used in Bengal
Besan chick pea flour
Bhart(h)a, bhurta, boortha purée or hash
Bhuna, bhuni fried
Bombay duck see *Fish*
Boondi ka dahi yoghurt relish with tiny *besan* dumplings
Chai tea
Chasnidarh sweet and sour. The food is flavoured with lime juice or vinegar and sugar
Dahi, dhai, dhye curd or yoghurt
Dal-chini, dhall cheene cinnamon or cassia sticks. Once used as an aphrodisiac
Dam, dhum see *Dum*
Degh means "pot", hence a casseroled dish
Dhan(y)ia dried, powdered coriander
Doh peeazah, do pyaza a variation of *korma* using two lots of onions often equal in weight to the meat. One half is browned and braised with the meat, and the other half is usually grated or

pulverized and added when the meat is almost cooked
Dum a technique where a dish is gently steamed between two low fires, one above and one below
Ela(i)chi cardamom
Garam masala a blend of ground mixed spices usually added to food at a late stage in the cooking, or just before serving. *Garam* means "hot". Typically consists of cinnamon, cardamom, cloves, cummin, coriander and black peppercorns
Ghee a kind of clarified butter. For daily cooking most Indians use vegetable *ghee*, hydrogenated vegetable cooking fat
Gram see *Besan*
Haldi turmeric
Hara dhania fresh coriander leaves
Hari mirchi green chillis
Hing asafoetida. Dried gum resin from the roots of an east Indian plant
Hisa(a)b bill
Im(a)li tamarind
Jaiphal nutmeg
Jal water
Jeera, jira cummin
Ka(a)fi(i), kehwa coffee
Kali mirchi black peppercorns
Kari (Tamil) seasoned sauce, probably the origin of the

English word curry
   patta, katmin curry leaves
which are used for flavouring.
Nothing to do with curry powder
Kasta crusty, crisp
Kesar, kesram, khesa saffron
Khara technique where meat is
prepared with whole spices,
either bruised or slightly crushed.
The advantage of this is that the
spices can be picked out
Khoia, khoya very thick
condensed milk
Khus khus poppy seed

mixture of five spices, often hot
Paneer, panir curd cheese
Parcha meat or vegetables, rolled
and often stuffed before being
roasted
Pasendah, pasinda see *Pursindah*
Phal fruit
Pista pistachio nut
Pudina mint
Pura pancake
Pursindah meat which is filleted
or sliced before and after it is
cooked
Rai mustard seed

Nose, nose, jolly red nose,
And who gave thee this jolly red nose? . . .
Nutmegs and ginger, cinnamon and cloves,
And they gave me this jolly red nose.
Beaumont and Fletcher *Knight of the Burning Pestle*

Ko(o)ftas meat balls
Kulmie darchini see *Dal-chini*
Lal mirchi red chillis
Lao(o)ng, laung, lavang, *or* long
cloves
Lassan, lusson garlic
Makhan butter
Malai cream
Massalam, massaledarh a spiced
or savoury dish
Mawa see *Khoya*
Methe(e), methi fenugreek
Milee see *Imali*
Mirchi chilli peppers
Mitha nim see *Kari patta*
Mog(h)lai *or* **mughlai** of Mogul
tradition
Molee a south Indian white curry
made with coconut milk, green
chillis and fresh ginger
Mulligatawny a corruption of the
Tamil words *milagu-tannir*, which
mean "pepper water". Soup is
not generally eaten in India, but
mulligatawny soup is a popular
Anglo-Indian dish. It is a spicy
soup with meat stock as a base.
In south India, pepper water of
some kind is often served with
dry dishes
Nimboo, nimbu lemon or lime
Paan betel leaf stuffed with lime
paste, spices, nuts or tobacco and
chewed after meals as a digestive
aid and breath freshener. It is
also a polite indication that
guests should be leaving
Pa(a)ni(i) water
Panch puran, panch phoran

Sambals, sambols, sumbols similar
to our hors d'oeuvre, but often
served as side dishes or
accompaniments to a main dish
Saunf aniseed, eaten as a
digestive after meals
Seek(h) an iron skewer—thus
meaning that the food is
skewered
Sharbat chilled drink made from
fruits, flower petals or nuts
Shoorva soup
Soojee, suji semolina
Soondth dried ground ginger
Talawa deep fried
Tandoor, tandur a clay oven,
usually sunk neck deep in the
ground. The meats in *tandoori*
cooking are usually marinated in
yoghurt and spices before being
cooked
Tandoori, tanduri food cooked in
a *tandoor* or in a way which
simulates this technique
Tarka (Hindi) see *Baghar*
Tarkari, turrcarri curry. Used
mainly in Bengal
Tikki, tikia, ki-tikiya cutlet or
cake
Til sesame seeds
Udruk green ginger
Var(a)k very fine, edible, real
gold or silver leaf—a traditional
garnish for certain dishes.
Sometimes regarded as an exotic
way of getting one's daily ration
of roughage and minerals
Zeera cummin
Zuffron saffron

131

Sri Lanka

While their cooking is very similar to South Indian, the Sinhalese have accepted more readily than the Indians influences from Europe, which give their food an extra variety. This applies particularly to the sweet things based on Portuguese ideas, and to cakes using eggs and butter, brought by the Dutch.

As in South India, the diet of the people is largely vegetarian and the curries are inclined to be very hot. A useful guide is the colour of a curry. "White" curries are based on coconut milk and are comparatively mild—the key word is *kiri*. Black curries are the commonest and are made with roasted spices; pretty hot—the key word is *badun*. Red curries are ferociously hot, using an inordinate amount of chilli—the key word is *rathu*.

If you cannot find something in the Sri Lanka section, it is worth looking under India, particularly in the list of words.

Abba mustard made with black mustard seed and added to curries or served with them

Albassara stuffed savoury pancakes

Alla potato

Alu kehel green bananas

Aluwa see *Halva*

Ambu thiyal sour fish curry

Amu miris green chillis

Appam, appé see *Hopper*

Arak spirit made from the distilled sap of coconut palm

Babath tripe

Badhapu lunis sambola a fried onion side-dish

Badun a fried, dry, dark curry

Bandakka okra

Bath *or* **buth** rice

Bith(th)ara *or* **bittara** egg

  roloung spiced, scrambled egg

Blachan(g) hot shrimp side-dish

Bolo folhado many-layered cake, like a Danish pastry with a cashew nut filling

Breudher Dutch yeast cake served at Christmas and New Year

Brinjal pahie *or* **pohie** very hot, spicy eggplant pickle

Cadju cashew or cadjun nut

Cu cu lu chicken

Dehi limes

  achcharu temperado lime oil pickle, very hot

  lunu sambola a *sambol* of salted limes with onions and chillis

  rata indi lime and date chutney, very hot

Dhallo badun fried-squid curry

Elolu kiri hodhi "white" mixed vegetable curry

Enasal cardamom

Foguete a Portuguese deep-fried pastry with sweet filling

Frikkadels very small meat balls flavoured with dill, egg-and-breadcrumbed and deep fried

Gova, gowa cabbage

Hakuru palm sugar or *gur*

Harak mas meat curry

★Hopper bowl-shaped pancake made with rice flour, yeast and coconut milk. Served with curry or *sambols*. Often with a fried egg in the middle

  miti kiri coconut cream *hopper*

Iddi yappam "string" *hopper*. Dough is forced through a perforated mould to form lacy circles, which are then steamed. Served at breakfast or supper with curries and *kiri hodhi*

Idi appung dodol moulded rice with coconut milk and cinnamon

Ismoru see *Smoore*

Isso shrimp

  thel dhala dry-fried shrimp

Kaha turmeric

★Kaha bath *or* **buth** yellow rice, an important festive dish consisting of spiced rice, tinted with saffron and cooked in coconut milk

Kakuluwo crab

Kalupol roasted coconut

Karavadu vambotu salt fish and eggplant curry

Karavila bitter gourd

Karrapincha curry leaves

Kiri bath simple preparation of rice in coconut milk. Traditionally eaten on New Year's Day and for breakfast on the first day of each month.

Often served with coconut *sambol* and sometimes with grated sugar
Kiri hodhi coconut milk gravy
Kiri malu white fish curry
Koonee tiny dried shrimps
Koppé bath *kaha bath* moulded in a cup with coconut *sambol* and hard-boiled eggs
Kos ambul jackfruit—a huge, spiky fruit with large, fleshy, very sweet pods
Kukul chicken
Kurundu cinnamon, native to Sri Lanka
★**Lamprais** or **lampries** *the* "special occasion" meal. Individual portions of rice cooked in meat stock, mixed meat curry, *frikkadels* and *sambols* (usually *seeni* and *blachan*) packed in banana leaves and baked
Lunu onion
Malu fish
Mas meat
Mas paan yeast buns with a curried meat filling
★**Mellung** dish of shredded boiled green vegetables, flavoured with cummin and grated coconut. Served with most meals
★**Molee** meat or fish in a spiced coconut milk sauce
Mologothannie *Mulligatawny*
Moong ata sambola bean sprouts as a *sambol*
Muss meat
Ogu roloung flavoured scrambled eggs
Ooroomas pork
Paccai payaru mung bean
Paripoo a spiced lentil dish
Peegodu liver
Phla sweet egg custard
Pipinge or **pipinja** cucumber
 hodi cucumber curry
Pishpash savoury meat soup
Pittu a combination of flour and freshly grated coconut steamed in a bamboo cylinder. Like a very light suet pudding, served with fresh coconut milk, hot *sambols*

and curries. Sometimes served as a sweet with sugar
Pol coconut
Pukkai Tamil Hindu name for *kiri bath*
Rabu kollé radish leaves
Rampé Pandanus leaf. It has an aromatic flavour and is used in curries
Rathu miris red chillis
Sambol(a) a side dish
Sapattu mal red hibiscus flowers used in *sambols*, curries and drinks. Said to purify the blood
★**Satay** or **sathe curry** skewered meat in a spicy sauce
 jaggery skewered meat with sugar. A hot and salty sweet-sour dish
Seeni sambola very hot, rich, fried onion sauce
Seer a fish sometimes described as the "salmon of Sri Lanka"
Simore or **smoore** meat or fish cooked in a spicy coconut mixture
Sudu bath plain rice
Tamil arnung fish in a hot sauce
 sothie as above
Thakkali or **thuckaley** tomato
 malu fish curry with tomato
 miris sweet peppers
Thala sesame seeds
★**guli** sesame seed and palm sugar balls
Thambung hodhi sour soup, spiced and soured with tamarind
Thara padre duck curry with *arak*
Thora malu siyambala achcharu fish pickle with tamarind
Umbalakada Sinhalese for Maldive fish, which, dried and powdered, is a common ingredient
Val-ooru-muss wild boar curry
Vambotu eggplant
Vatakka yellow pumpkin
Vatakolu ridged gourd with a sweet and delicate flavour
★**Wattalappam** rich, spicy, steamed egg custard

Rasawath aharak! bon appétit!
Jayawewa! cheers!

Indonesia—*See* Southeast Asia
Iran—*See* Arab food
Israel—*See* Jewish food

Italy

Italian food is largely about nourishment. The Italians, almost
alone among Europeans, seem always to be conscious of the
connection between eating and survival. In other countries
this link has been forgotten and eating has become either
an art, as in France, or a habit, as in Britain. The Italians
eat for the joy of being alive—their food is simple, filling
and immediately appealing. They love to press food upon
you, which is why Italian waiters are the best in the world.
Nobody could ever be frightened of an Italian waiter, as
one might be of a French one who was practising some
snobbery on his customer. An Italian waiter's purpose is the
same as yours—to see that you eat to be well and happy, to
give you life.

The cuisine of Italy reflects this attitude. It is not based on
complicated *roux* and *fonds*, is not concerned with *mousses*
and *quenelles*, is not doctrinal or rigid. It is more interested
in making the best of available ingredients. It is colourful,
as anyone who has looked at a stuffed olive must realize. It
is straightforward, taking an ingredient, perhaps marinating
it, and cooking it—then adding to it some other ingredient
which has been equally simply prepared.

Such simplicity is, nevertheless, deceptive. While Italian
food is peasant food, in that it is markedly regional and, to
a greater extent than more sophisticated cuisines, essentially
seasonal, it is based in a tradition of many centuries and
informed by a huge variety of influences.

The Greeks and Romans had elaborate cuisines and the
simpler forms survived even through the Dark Ages in such
things as *polenta* (albeit now made with corn instead of

134

wheat) and *agrodolce*, the sweet-sour sauce which echoes the Roman use of honey to soften the salty preservatives which were essential in those times. There was a strong Arab influence, particularly on sweet dishes. The explorers brought tomatoes, the string bean, corn and turkeys from the Americas. Italian food in the 16th century was infinitely more varied than that of any other European country.

At the same time the separate states of Italy were inevitably not as rich as larger countries and in consequence the everyday food of Italy concentrated on cheap ingredients, vegetables, flour, fish, little birds and odd bits of meat which few other people eat, such as brains or even lung, and of course there was always the multiplicity of sausages.

Piedmont is a region of truffles, game, cheeses and milk dishes. Lombardy has saffron, cured beef, *panettone* and frogs. In these two regions, cooking is done largely in butter, as it is in the Veneto and Emilia-Romagna. In Calabria nobody would cook in anything but olive oil, their pasta is tubular, not flat, they like peppers and eggplants. In the Veneto they love *polenta*, in Lombardy they prefer rice; in Sicily they like round pasta, in Sardinia flat.

The variations are limitless and largely dictated by the land. It is for this reason that the best food in Italy is to be found in the simpler establishments, where the local food is inclined to survive, while in grander eating places sophistication may have brought inappropriate importations. So don't judge Italian eating places by the same standards as you would your local café and don't be put off by a rough exterior—the food will probably be far more genuine and representative than in a place dressed up for tourists.

Where to eat

It used to be easy to tell where to eat, but Italians, who must be the world's most insouciant etymologists, play fast and loose with the titles of restaurants. As a rough guide the plethora of names goes like this:

Ristorante: a sophisticated place (the word is pinched from the French). There is unlikely to be much adherence to local dishes. It will also be relatively expensive

Trattoria: the town version of an *osteria*, more for passing trade. Serves quite modest meals of a local character and is likely to be far more interesting than a *ristorante*—certainly cheaper

Buco: a Tuscan word meaning "hole". It usually applies to a cellar *trattoria*

Locanda: originally a staging post. A country place to eat and lodge. Slightly more sophisticated than an *osteria*

Osteria: a village meeting place, primarily for locals to drink wine. The peasants of Italy don't usually eat out, but will manage to find here a simple *minestra*, an omelette or a salad with salami

Pizzeria: a post-war innovation (pizzas used just to be eaten in the streets). Serves pizzas and often other things as well

Tavola calda: another new invention. A snack bar, where you usually sit at the counter and have a hot dish

Rosticceria: a snack bar serving hot and cold food and providing take-away

Gelateria: ice-cream parlour, serving all types of home-made ice-cream and variations on ice-cream sweets

Latteria: basically a dairy, but provides sweet things and pastries

---

Meals

Meals in Italy fall into the following categories:
Prima colazione (breakfast): for an Italian this usually consists of coffee with a *brioche* or *cornetto* (the French *croissant*).
Colazione or **pranzo** (lunch): a fairly important meal for Italians.
Cena (dinner): the full works.

The menu

The Italian menu, if there is one, can be quite easily decoded. There are basically three courses, with the possibility of having some appetizers to start with. These appetizers are called *antipasti*. The next course (*primo piatto*) is either soup (*minestra*), or *pasta asciutta* (spaghetti, tagliatelle, macaroni, etc.), or *pasta in brodo*, which is a broth with some type of pasta in it (particularly recommended for dinner). One never has two of these, so they may all be listed under *minestre*, or they may be listed separately, when the spaghettis are lumped together with the rice dishes and headed *farinacei*. Or, of course, they may be given some singular heading that the owner has thought up to confuse the unwary.

Egg dishes, which are rarely very superior, may wander about in this area of the menu, with *farinacei* or in a block on their own, called *uova*.

Fish may be put in with the main dishes or, particularly in coastal areas, have their own section, headed *pesce*. There may also be a heading *crostacei* (shellfish).

The main course of an Italian meal is, to my mind, seldom the best dish, though I have to admit that this is partly because I find *pasta asciutta* irresistible and always eat too much of it. In a grander establishment, the main course (*secondo piatto*) is usually divided in two. First, particular dishes of the day, *piatti del giorno*, which are, as in any country, the ones to go for because they will be made of whatever has looked good in the market that morning (leftovers are seldom used in Italy except in pasta sauces or perhaps to liven up a *minestra*). These are *piatti pronti* (ready to serve).

The second category of main course is made up of dishes which have to be specially made, *piatti da farsi*. It is worth remembering that menus in Italy are not as rigid as elsewhere and restaurateurs will not bother to list many dishes which they will be quite happy to make on request. As one goes down the scale of grandeur, the main courses will all be *del giorno*—indeed more often than not there is quite likely to be no menu at all.

After the main course, things get a bit erratic. Vegetables (which can be called *contorni*, *ortaggi* or *verdura* on the menu) are served separately. Or you can just have a salad (*insalata*). Italians do not usually eat cheese *and* a sweet dish, but cheese often comes with fruit such as pears, melon or figs. So there may well be a cheese heading (*formaggi*). Finally the sweet things may be divided into *gelati* (ices) and *dolci* (pastries, cream caramel, etc.).

Rules, however, are not the point in Italy. I once asked a carpenter to make me a round table. He made me a hexagonal one. Why? "*Credo di far meglio*," he said. "I think it's better." So it may be with what you order to eat. If the waiter or the chef feels that he can improve on what you have chosen, he will—to make you happy.

Antipasti—Hors d'oeuvre

Italian *antipasti* can be hot or cold. They may be simply slices of salami, covered in oil with an occasional radish or they may be elaborate concoctions with such delicacies as lobster involved in them. Often the best consist of some simple but unexpected combination—slivers of raw carrot in a cocktail sauce or little rounds of eggplant baked with mozzarella cheese and anchovies. An *antipasto misto* will give you a selection of the restaurant's best.

Agoni freshwater shad often cooked with thyme and served cold

Anguilla marinata marinated eel

Antipasto alla genovese a Genoese hors d'oeuvre of fava beans, salami and sardo cheese

★**Bagna cauda** a Piedmontese hot sauce made with garlic, anchovies and, with luck, truffles, into which you dip your raw vegetables—celery, artichokes, peppers, etc.

★**Bresaola** dried salt beef with a waxy look, usually eaten with oil and lemon

Bruschetta bread toasted in the oven, rubbed with garlic and served dripping with olive oil

Buttàriga (*also* **Bottarga**) dried grey mullet roe served sliced with oil and lemon

Capocollo cured neck of pork

★**Caponata** a mushy mixture based on fried eggplants to which are added fried celery, capers, olives, onions and anchovies, plus some tomato paste, nuts and sugar

marinara a rough dish made of ship's biscuits soused in oil and mixed with olives, anchovies and herbs

★**Cappon magro** an elaborate fish salad using bass, crayfish, tuna and shrimps and a variety of vegetables, served with a garlic, caper and pickle sauce. Often served as a main course

Coppa cooked, pressed neck of pork

Cozze in salsa piccante mussels in a sharp sauce of anchovies, vinegar and white wine

Crostini di fegatini chicken liver paste often with capers and anchovies on fried bread or polenta

di fegato di maiale pork livers, anchovies, peppers and herbs mixed and spread on fried bread

col "merollo" a Roman speciality of bone marrow on toast

di mozzarella e acciughe a fried sandwich of anchovies and mozzarella

piccanti an anchovy paste with capers and parsley on fried bread

alla provatura skewers of bread and cheese, cooked over wood ash and served with an anchovy sauce

Culatello di Zibello pork cured like Parma ham

Fagiolini in padella string beans sautéed with onions and tomatoes

col tonno string beans and scallions with chunks of tuna fish, seasoned with oil, lemon and black pepper

★**Fagioli toscani col tonno** as above but with white beans

Fettunta see *Bruschetta*

Fitascetta bread rings baked with onions

Focaccia a dimpled savoury bread

alla salvia as above but flavoured with sage

Fricco del Friuli a sharpish cheese fried with fat salt pork, butter and eggs

★**Fritto di fiori di zucca** squash flowers, sometimes stuffed with anchovies and cheese, fried in batter

Insalata di carciofi raw artichoke hearts in oil and lemon

di finocchi e cetrioli fennel and cucumber salad mixed with tomatoes, onions and hard-boiled eggs

di frutti di mare a salad of mussels, shrimp and tiny boneless fish

di funghi e frutti di mare a salad of raw mushrooms, shrimp and baby squid (*fragoline di mare*). This dish can be varied with scampi and a tomato mayonnaise

di lingua di bue tongue salad with eggplants and peppers

di riso e gamberetti a rice and shrimp salad

Lumache alla milanese snails with a sauce of oil, butter, garlic, anchovies, fennel, parsley, onion and wine

Melanzane ripiene eggplants, served stuffed in different ways

al forno halved eggplants stuffed with tomatoes, meat, rice, herbs, and so on, baked in the oven with a crispy topping

alla parmigiana halved eggplants baked with mozzarella and Parmesan in a tomato sauce

Mortadella large pork sausage with hideous blobs of white fat, flavoured with coriander and whole peppercorns, from Bologna

★ **Mozzarella in carrozza** a sandwich of bread and mozzarella dipped in milk and egg and fried

Olive ripiene green olives stuffed with forcemeat, egg-and-breadcrumbed and fried

Ostriche alla veneziana oysters on their shells with caviar

Pandorato bread dipped in milk and egg, then deep fried. Can be stuffed with cheese and ham or anchovies

Panzarotti half-moons of pastry filled with three cheeses and deep fried

Peperonata sweet peppers, onions and tomatoes cooked in oil and garlic and served cold

Peperoni imbottiti alla napoletana baked sweet peppers stuffed with pasta, tomatoes, anchovies, garlic, etc.

alla piemontese baked sweet peppers stuffed with tomatoes, anchovies and garlic

sott'olio sweet peppers preserved in oil, cut in strips and served with fresh olive oil and garlic

Polpettone di tonno a sort of tuna fish sausage bound with eggs and capers

Pomodori farciti (*or* **ripieni**) stuffed tomatoes—often with tuna fish

★ **Prosciutto di Parma e melone** the best cured ham from Parma, with melon. Often also served with figs (*fichi*) or pears (*pere*)

al miele bread and honey with a slice of smoked ham

Rane in guazzetto frogs' legs in butter and white wine

Salami, Salumi may be made of pork, beef or even donkey meat, but you may prefer not to know. All Italian salami is worth trying

Taralli pastry rings much as for a pizza, sprinkled with fennel seeds, rolled up and baked

Uova di tonno tuna fish roe, dried and salted

Uova tonnate hard-boiled eggs with a tuna fish sauce

★ **Vitello tonnato** cold veal with a tuna fish sauce

Uova—Eggs

Canapè di uova fritte con polenta fried eggs on rounds of fried polenta, covered with tomato sauce

Crocchette di uova egg croquettes

Frittata omelette. Italian omelettes are usually heavy things with any ingredients thrown in and fried until gruesomely solid. Worse still, they are often served cold

genovese spinach omelette

alla Trentina fluffy omelette with a sweet or savoury filling

Occhio di bue fried egg, literally

"ox eye"

Uova affogate poached eggs, literally "drowned eggs"

affogate con burro alla parmigiana poached eggs covered with Parmesan and baked until the cheese melts

affogate in gratin eggs baked under a crust of Parmesan and breadcrumbs

affrittellate fried eggs

bazzotte lightly-boiled, three minute eggs

da bere fresh eggs that can be eaten raw

al burro baked eggs with butter

in camicia poached eggs, literally "in their shirts"

alla coque soft-boiled eggs

fritte fried eggs

al guscio soft-boiled eggs

mollette soft-boiled eggs

mollette con funghi e formaggio soft-boiled eggs put with fried mushrooms in an egg dish and covered with Parmesan

in padella fried eggs

al piatto con patate sliced boiled eggs, mozzarella and sliced potatoes, covered with carefully broken raw eggs, baked in the oven with a thick sprinkling of Parmesan

al piatto con pomodoro chopped tomatoes, fried in oil with onion.

Eggs are added on top and either fried or baked

con puré di patate poached eggs on a bed of creamed potato purée, sprinkled with Parmesan

sode hard-boiled eggs

sode alla francese hard-boiled eggs simmered in milk with nutmeg and onion

stracciate scrambled eggs

stracciate al formaggio eggs scrambled with a little cream and sprinkled with Parmesan

strapazzate scrambled eggs

al tegame eggs individually fried or baked with butter or oil

al tegame al formaggio eggs on mozzarella and sometimes with a slice of ham, all fried in an individual dish or baked in the oven

Minestre — Soups

This heading, as I have said before, can include *pasta*, but I have limited it to soups. I use the term "limited" rather rashly, because the thick Italian soups are often more than enough for a meal. Certainly *minestrone*, which means "the big soup", is as final as Humphrey Bogart's Big Sleep, and any *zuppa di pesce* (fish soup) is more of a stew. Most soups, even consommé, are thickened with lavish additions of Parmesan. In Italy there is no such thing as a little soup.

Acquacotta sweet pepper and tomato soup

Brodetto usually means a fish soup, particularly on the Adriatic coast. The fish used are mainly white fish with clams, eel and a lot of squid. The broth is made with the fish heads, while the fish are cooked in oil and tomato purée. The broth and fish are served separately but simultaneously. Well-known local versions are: *alla anconetana, alla ravennate, alla riminese*

pasquale an extravagant Roman broth of beef and lamb, served at Easter

Brodo, in brodo *brodo* is the basic stock used for all *pasta in brodo* dishes. It comes from boiling chicken, beef, and vegetables together

Brodo di manzo beef consommé

con reale alla bolognese lamb broth with toast and cheese

Budino di pollo in brodo chicken broth with a fine mousse of chicken breast in it

Burrida either a Genoese or a Sardinian fish stew

Busecca a thick soup of tripe and vegetables

Cacciucco alla livornese a justly famous fish stew with squid, shrimps, cod, scallops and halibut, flavoured with sage, garlic and tomatoes. Usually a main course

Cappelletti in brodo dunce-cap-shaped pasta stuffed with pork, veal, prosciutto and brains in chicken broth

Cavolata Sardinian pig's trotter and cauliflower soup

Celestina clear soup with star-shaped pasta in it

Consommé alla Benso chicken consommé with pieces of a kind of custard mould, made of eggs and puréed chicken breast, in it

Iota friulana a spicy bean soup with cabbage or, often, turnips mashed with their leaves and soaked for weeks in the dregs of wine pressings

Malfattini in brodo egg pasta shaped like grains of rice in broth

Minestra di bavette alla genovese a broth with fine noodles, oregano and cheese

di lenticchie e pasta lentil soup with tomatoes, garlic, herbs, a little ham and pasta

di ortaggi e salsiccie vegetable, sausage and bacon soup—a rough, peasant minestrone

di passatelli di Urbino consommé with meat dumplings, made of beef, spinach and bone marrow. The *passatelli* are forced through a kind of pastry tube and actually look like little worms

Minestrone a plain minestrone usually contains white beans, celery, onion, peas, ham, tomato paste, garlic, herbs, a little wine and some form of pasta, but pretty well anything can go in, depending on the region

alla genovese a soup of green and dried beans, cabbage, celery, peas, zucchini, eggplants and a garlic paste but no meat

alla milanese with many vegetables, salt pork and macaroni

di pasta e broccoli macaroni and broccoli-based minestrone

di pasta e ceci macaroni and chick-pea based minestrone

Panata bread, eggs, cheese and nutmeg mixed to form a kind of pancake and served whole, in broth

Pancotto bread and tomato soup

Passatelli in brodo little worms of a home-made mixture of breadcrumbs, cheese, egg, nutmeg and lemon in a chicken or beef stock. Particularly recommended for invalids

Passato di verdura a thin soup of sieved green vegetables

Pasta in brodo any type of pasta served in a chicken or beef broth

Pasta e fagioli a soup of white beans, half of which are puréed to make the soup thick, pieces of salt pork and pasta

Ribollita a Florentine soup of white beans, olive oil, vegetables, bread and cheese. This soup tastes even better when reheated, with the addition of more oil, bread and cheese

★**Sopa coada** a squab soup from the Veneto, in which there are squab breasts and fried bread. Very rich

Stracciatella a light soup of beef or chicken stock with egg, semolina and cheese paste worked in

Zuppa di baccalà all'italiana a salt cod soup

✦**di castagne** chestnut soup

✦**di cozze** mussel soup

di fontina bread and cheese soup

di gamberi shrimp soup flavoured with bay leaf, cayenne and white wine

alla pavese said to have been invented by a cottager for François I after he had lost the battle of Pavia. Boiling broth is poured over fried bread, raw eggs and Parmesan already in the soup plate

di pesce alla romana a fish soup rich in shellfish

di vercolore a green soup based on string beans, squash, and watercress

di verdura a vegetable soup

di vongole clam soup

Pasta e farinacei

In this section I have included the gnocchis, polentas, rice dishes and the stuffed pastas such as ravioli. Trying to sort out the names of all the pastas is a bit like trying to remember who is who in *The Brothers Karamazov*. You master the first names and the patronymics and the diminutives. Then you have to get to grips with the pet names and the nicknames. What are called *tortiglioni* in one place are called *fusilli* ten miles away. *Maniche* are ribbed one day, but are still *maniche* the next day when they are smooth. *Gnocchi verdi* are not really *gnocchi*, but even less are they *ravioli*—so that is what the Tuscans call them. It doesn't matter, of course, for one pasta is much like another—which is probably why there is such confusion. The only important distinction is that *tagliatelle/fettuccine*, *maccheroni alla chitarra*, *pappardelle* and *lasagne* are all made with egg, as are the stuffed pastas. Often they are home-made. Everyday pasta sauces such as *ragù* or *salsa bolognese* and *salsa verde* appear in the word list. Others such as *salsa di pomodoro* or *salsa di gamberi* are easily identified also from the word list. Some sauces, such as *arrabbiata* or *pesto*, are almost always attached to one pasta, e.g. *penne all'arrabbiata*, *trenette al pesto*. (S) indicates a sauce.

Agnolotti see *Ravioli*
Amatriciana see *Spaghetti all'amatriciana* (S)
Anolini small ravioli, usually served in stock
Arrabbiata see *Penne* (S)
Bavette a small ribbon-shaped pasta, commercially made
   con cipolle with a purée of onions
   con fave fresche with a sauce of peeled fava beans, scallions and Parmesan
   in salsa d'uovo with egg-yolk, anchovy and mozzarella sauce
   alla trasteverina mixed with a sauce of tomatoes, tuna fish and anchovies, with another mushroom sauce poured over the mixture. Add no cheese
Bigoli coll'anatra a buckwheat pasta like spaghetti but without holes, cooked in duck stock with a sage and duck giblet sauce and Parmesan. (The duck itself is served as a second course)
Bolognese see *Spaghetti alla bolognese* (S)
Boscaiola see *Bucatini* (S)
Bucatini very small tube pasta, commercially made
   con acciughe with a peppery anchovy sauce. Add no cheese
   alla boscaiola with a tomato sauce, covered with slices of fried eggplants and mushrooms
Campagnola typical country sauce of tomatoes, onions, etc.
Cannelloni very large tubes or rolled sheets of pasta, home-made with eggs and filled with various mixtures. They are also commercially made without eggs. The term can also include a pancake. They are generally stuffed with a ragù, perhaps also with spinach mixed with Parmesan, cream, eggs and oregano, baked in a tomato sauce

and covered with a topping of béchamel sauce
   alla partenopea stuffed with ricotta, mozzarella and ham, covered with a sauce of tomatoes, basil and Parmesan and baked in the oven
Cannolicchi very short tube pasta, sometimes ribbed. Commercially made
Cappellacci yet another pet name for a type of ravioli
Cappelletti egg pasta shaped like little cocked hats and stuffed
   con salsa bolognese stuffed with cold roast meat and mortadella sausage, served in alternating layers with Bolognese ragù and grated Parmesan
Carbonara see *Spaghetti alla carbonara* (S)
Casalinga with a homely, simple sauce
Chitarra see *Macaroni alla chitarra*
Crespolini small pancakes stuffed with spinach, cream cheese, egg, chicken livers and Parmesan, covered with a béchamel sauce and baked in the oven
Fagottini pancakes, also used of cannelloni
Fatto in casa home-made
Fettuccine flat, long strips of pasta made with egg. This is the name used in Rome and the south for what in Florence and the north are usually called *tagliatelle*. Technically, fettucine might be fractionally larger, though in practice they are indistinguishable. As they are so easy to make, they are the most common home-made pasta, often served just with melted butter and grated cheese (*al burro*)
   con carne e pomodoro alla veneta this used to be made with *bigoli*, which have virtually

disappeared. The sauce is made of tomatoes, ground veal and pork with fried vegetables and basil

★ **al doppio burro** cooked with lots of butter, cream and cheese. A famous dish from Alfredo's in Rome

alla marinara with a fresh tomato sauce and basil. This is the most common way of serving fettuccine, originating in Naples, and one of the best

verdi con funghi green fettuccine (made with the addition of spinach), are often served with simple sauces, as for instance with tomatoes and mushrooms, or with a Bolognese sauce

Genovese see *Gnocchi alla genovese*, *Ravioli alla genovese*, *Tagliatelle verdi* (S)

Gnocchi small dumplings made with potato and flour, semolina, or corn flour

alla genovese potato gnocchi served with a *pesto* sauce of basil, garlic, bacon and pine nuts and pecorino

alla parmigiana potato gnocchi served with tomato sauce and Parmesan

di patate potato dumplings served with grated cheese and butter

di polenta dumplings made with corn flour, served with butter and grated cheese

di ricotta dumplings made with ricotta, butter, Parmesan, eggs and flour. Served with butter and grated cheese

alla romana potato dumplings served with tomato sauce and cheese. Some authorities argue wrongly that these are made of semolina

di semolino semolina dumplings served with butter and cheese

★ **verdi** these dumplings are known as *ravioli* in Tuscany. They are made with spinach, ricotta, eggs and Parmesan and served with butter and cheese

Gramigna small ribbed tubes of pasta, slightly curved, from Emilia-Romagna, usually served with a pork sausage, cream and tomato sauce

Lasagne the largest of the flat pastas, generally made with egg, often with the addition of spinach and therefore green, and always baked in layers with a filling between each sheet

pasticciate (verdi al forno) green lasagne baked with layers of ragù and béchamel sauce

Lasagnette a wide flat pasta with a rippled edge

del lucchese with a sauce made of spinach, ricotta, chicken livers and mushrooms, flavoured with cinnamon and nutmeg

Lingue di passero the narrowest commercially made pasta without egg; it means "sparrows' tongues"

Linguine a narrow, flat pasta without egg

alle vongole linguine are most commonly served with a sauce of baby clams, tomato and parsley

Macaroni *or* maccheroni the real Italian spelling of this familiar commercially made tube pasta is maccheroni, but it originated in Naples, where they spelt it as we have done. It is often broken in short pieces and baked in pies. See *Pasticcio* and *Timballo*

★ **alla chitarra** this isn't macaroni as we think of it but an egg pasta, which is home-made in the Abruzzi using an instrument with steel wires somewhat like a musical instrument. It comes out in a flat ribbon, not a tube, rather thicker than fettuccine. It can be served just with olive oil and hot chilli peppers or with more elaborate pork or lamb sauces. It will always have the hot peppers

"cu a siccia" a southern dish, with a sauce of cuttlefish (including the ink sac), celery, tomato and wine. Add no cheese

★ **dolci con ricotta** with ricotta to which cinnamon and sugar have been added. Macaroni is also served merely with ricotta, perhaps with a little chilli powder. Either way, add no cheese

in salsa verde with a sauce of spinach, onions and anchovies. Add no cheese

con le sarde a pie of alternating layers of cooked macaroni, fennel, anchovy and tomato sauce and fried sardines, baked in the oven

Maccheroncini a small version of macaroni, often with shellfish

143

Maniche a short tube pasta, commercially made, either smooth or ribbed

all'ortolana with peas and artichoke hearts

Marinara see *Fettuccine alla marinara* (S)

Napoletana see *Spaghetti alla napoletana* (S)

Orecchiette commercially made pasta in the shape of ears

ai broccoli with flowering broccoli. The Sicilian version of this includes tomatoes, anchovies, chilli, white raisins and pine nuts

Paesana rustic sauce of mushrooms, tomatoes, bacon, etc.

★ **Paglia e fieno** a mixture of green and white tagliatelle, looking like "straw and hay", served with a sauce of pork sausage meat and mushrooms with a little cream. Sometimes peas are added

Pappardelle a large, flat, long pasta made with egg

★ **con la lepre** depending on the restaurant, this comes with either the meat of a whole hare, cooked in herbs and wine, or with a less filling sauce made from the hare's legs. One of Tuscany's particularly good dishes

Parmigiana with Parmesan

Pasticcio di anolini a sweet pastry pie, filled with *anolini* and baked in the oven

di lasagne alla napoletana layers of lasagne, ricotta, eggs and Parmesan, fried sausages and mozzarella, baked in the oven

di maccheroni a sweet pastry pie filled with macaroni and a variety of savoury extras

di maccheroni coi piccioni a sweet pastry pie of macaroni and squab in a béchamel sauce, baked in the oven

Penne (*also called* **Maltagliati**) short, commercially made tubes. Can be smooth or ribbed

★ **all'arrabbiata** with a sauce of tomatoes, bacon and hot red peppers

Pesto see *Trenette al pesto* (S)

Pizzaiola fresh tomato sauce with garlic and herbs

Primavera raw spring vegetables with garlic and olive oil (S)

Puttanesca see *Spaghetti alla puttanesca* (S)

Ragù Bolognese meat sauce

Ravioli a small, square, filled pasta envelope. Purists would say that ravioli should be filled with spinach, ricotta and herbs. The term also covers meat-filled pasta of this type which should strictly be called *agnolotti*. The two words are now used indifferently

alla genovese classically made with a stuffing of lamb's brain and liver, capon or boiling fowl, ham, spinach, cheese and egg yolks, now more usually veal, calf's udder, calf and lamb's brain, sweetbreads and escaroles (special endives). Usually served in stock, but can be eaten with a cream sauce or a tomato and beef sauce. A very rich dish

alla piemontese the stuffing is made with beef and vegetables. It is served with a brown sauce and lots of Parmesan sprinkled on top

Rigatoni fat, shortish tubes of ribbed pasta, commercially made, feeling a little bit like the roof of one's mouth

Romana see *Gnocchi alla romana* (S)

Rustica see *Spaghetti alla rustica* (S)

Spaghetti I wonder whether there is anyone who does not know what spaghetti is. You can, of course, ask for it to be served any way you like. I often have it with cream and masses of grated nutmeg (*noce moscata*)

★ **con aglio e olio** with olive oil in which a lot of garlic has been fried. Add no cheese

all'amatriciana with bacon (or originally pig's cheek), tomatoes, onion, chilli pepper and cheese

alla bolognese with a sauce that is properly made with ground beef and pork, prosciutto, mushrooms, onion, vegetables, herbs and a touch of garlic

con cacio e pepe with pecorino (or strong Parmesan), and masses of coarsely ground black pepper

alla carbonara with strips of fried bacon, eggs, lots of Parmesan and sometimes cream. Add black pepper liberally

★ **alla cavalleggera** with eggs and walnuts, cream and Parmesan

alla napoletana a non-meat

sauce with tomatoes, garlic, onion and olive oil

alla puttanesca a rough sauce of garlic, tomatoes, capers, black olives, chilli peppers, anchovies, oregano and parsley. "Puttana" is a rather low word for a prostitute, so you can give the dish your own interpretation

alla rustica a sauce of garlic, anchovies and oregano served with pecorino

alle vongole with baby clams

Strascinati/e where pasta is coated in sauce before serving

Tagliarini smaller version of tagliatelle, not made with egg

Tagliatelle flat strips of pasta, made with egg. They can be green (spinach) or white, and are served with most of the usual sauces

  con salsa di noci with a walnut sauce

★ **verdi alla genovese** these tagliatelle are made from a special dough enlivened with spinach, borage, sausage meat and sweetbreads served with a mushroom and tomato sauce

Tagliolini smaller version of tagliatelle, not made with egg

  bebé with chicken, truffles and mushrooms, all mixed with the pasta and some béchamel and finished under the grill

  San Bernardo with tomato, pea and tuna fish sauce. Add no cheese

Timballo pasta with a variety of savoury mixtures, some sort of sauce and cheese baked as a pie in the oven

  di lasagne layers of lasagne, béchamel sauce, Bolognese sauce and Parmesan, baked in the oven

  di maccheroni e melanzane layers of macaroni and eggplants baked as a pie with pecorino, basil and tomato sauce

Tortelli di erbette ravioli stuffed with spinach, ricotta, Parmesan, eggs and nutmeg. Eaten with butter and Parmesan

  di zucca ravioli with a pumpkin stuffing

Tortellini a small stuffed pasta, shaped like an ear, usually served in stock, with cream, or with a Bolognese sauce. They are stuffed with a mixture of ham, mortadella sausage, chopped chicken, pork and veal, eggs, nutmeg and Parmesan. Well worth eating in Bologna

  alla crema, alla panna served with thick cream and Parmesan

  gratinati cooked tortellini baked with butter and Parmesan

  pasticciati alla bolognese cooked tortellini baked with Bolognese sauce, cream, butter and Parmesan in the oven

Toscana with ham, chicken livers, mushrooms, tomatoes and red wine (S)

Trenette flat pasta, commercially made, slightly smaller than tagliatelle

★ **al pesto** with a very strong-tasting sauce of basil, pine nuts, garlic and lots of grated pecorino

Vermicelli spaghetti-shaped pasta, usually smaller, but in Naples an alternative name for spaghetti

Vincisgrassi rather like *lasagne al forno*. A thick egg pasta alternates with layers of a rich sauce made with such things as chicken livers, sausages and mushrooms. It is baked in the oven

Zite largest of the tube pasta

Pizza

The pizza scarcely needs an introduction. Originating in the south of Italy, it is now a common quick and cheap meal in the north as well. Whole families of Italians go to the pizzeria, particularly on Sundays or after the cinema, to drink lager and eat this dish of bread dough—properly made with durum flour—covered with a wide variety of fillings.

Calzone pizza dough is used for this Neapolitan speciality. It is a half-moon shaped pizza stuffed with ham and mozzarella—a stuffed "trouser leg"

Pizza aglio, olio e pomodoro a pizza with garlic, oil, oregano and tomatoes

  capricciosa a pizza with whatever filling the chef fancies, such as ham, sausages, artichokes, eggs, tomatoes, etc.

ai funghi pizza with mushrooms, garlic and parsley or with mushrooms and tomato sauce

margherita like a *napoletana*, but with tomatoes, mozzarella, basil and Parmesan

napoletana the classic pizza. Made with tomatoes, mozzarella, anchovy fillets and oregano. Sometimes with capers

quattro stagioni a pizza with four filled compartments, for the four seasons. They are generally a seafood section, one of tomato

and anchovies, one of mozzarella and Parmesan with tomato and oregano, and one of tomato, anchovy, capers and oregano. A fried egg is usually put in the middle

alla romana pizza with mozzarella, Parmesan and basil

rustica more of a pie than a pizza. Onions and tomatoes are covered with anchovies and olives

alla siciliana pizza with tomatoes, capers, anchovies and black olives

alle vongole pizza with clams, tomatoes, garlic and parsley

Polenta

America, where corn originated, makes little use of the stuff—except for making bourbon, which is probably the best thing to do with it. Unfortunately the countries to which the Americans exported, decided that as grain it was fit for humans rather than pigs. Italy ground it into polenta (which the Romans used to make of millet or primitive wheat). Northern Italians love polenta and ruin perfectly good dishes with it. It is made by boiling cornstarch in water until it becomes thick and stodgy. Then it may be left to get cool, when it can be cut into layers for frying, baking or grilling. It can also be eaten plain.

Migliaccio napoletano slices of polenta alternating with mozzarella, sausage meat and pecorino, baked in the oven

Polenta e fontina in torta alternate layers of cooked polenta and fontina cheese baked in the oven

fritta cold polenta cut up in various shapes and fried golden brown. They may be sandwiched with a piece of cheese, egg-and-breadcrumbed and fried

pasticciata slices of polenta

alternate with a cheese sauce and mushrooms, sausages, meat or any other kind of savoury filling. Baked in the oven. Extremely heavy on the stomach

stufata alternate slices of polenta, tomato and sausage sauce, and grated cheeses, sprinkled with cheese and butter and baked in the oven

e uccelletti small birds served on a bed of polenta

alla valdostana see *Polenta e fontina in torta*

Riso—Rice

The Italian rice for risotto and other dishes comes from the Po valley in northern Italy. The most common polished large white grain is called *Arborio*—it is also the best—and the unpolished grain is called *Vialone*. This rice cooks quite differently from oriental rice, ending up soft outside and *al dente* (still firm) inside. Northerners are particularly fond of rice and often prefer it to pasta. The names *riso* and *risotto* are interchangeable in many dishes.

Arancini tomato-flavoured rice balls, usually stuffed with a cheese, meat and vegetable filling

Bomba di riso onion, squab and

chicken are first simmered in tomato paste and white wine and then baked in the oven with alternating layers of risotto

Frittelle di riso rice fritters, either sweet or savoury

★**Risi e bisi** a thick Venetian soup of bacon, onion, fresh peas and rice, served with Parmesan

Riso in bianco boiled rice

★ **giallo** plain saffron rice served with butter and Parmesan

al limone rice with lemon juice

ai quattro formaggi rice alternating with layers of mixed cheeses—four different varieties—baked in the oven

Risotto rice cooked in butter or oil with a small chopped onion, then in stock or wine with additional meat, vegetables, etc., until the liquid is absorbed. Usually served with additional butter and grated cheese

bianco this is a plain risotto. The rice is mixed with a chopped onion in butter and then cooked in water until it absorbs the water and becomes thick and creamy

alla bolognese rice cooked in white wine and stock with bacon and ham and served with a *ragù bolognese*

alla certosina a seafood—usually crayfish—risotto with tomatoes, peas and mushrooms

alla finanziera rice cooked in beef stock with chicken livers, onions, wine and cheese

di frutti di mare rice cooked in fish stock with seafood

★**ai funghi** mushroom risotto

alla genovese rice cooked in wine with vegetables, herbs and meat

di magro rice cooked with a variety of different things but never with meat

alla marinara rice cooked with any variety of seafood

★**alla milanese** the most famous risotto. Rice cooked in beef marrow and wine, with onions, saffron and Parmesan. Often served as an accompaniment to *osso buco* (see *Meat*)

nero alla fiorentina a black risotto of cuttlefish—and its ink sac—with Swiss chard

alla parmigiana rice cooked in beef stock with chicken livers, sausage, mushrooms, bacon, vegetables and herbs

alla piemontese rice cooked in meat stock with butter, cheese and sliced truffles on top

alla pilota a Mantuan rice dish with sausages, nutmeg and cinnamon

al salto cooked rice fried with mozzarella

alla toscana rice cooked with ground beef, veal kidney and liver, tomatoes and cheese

alla valdostana rice cooked with Parmesan and fontina cheese

alla veronese rice cooked with ham and mushrooms

di vongole rice cooked in a fish stock with garlic, parsley, white wine and clams

con la zucca rice cooked with pumpkin

Sartù di riso alla napoletana a famous Neapolitan dish like a timbale. A rice mould is filled with such rich ingredients as beef meatballs, bacon, chicken livers, sausages, mushrooms, mozzarella, ham and sliced hard-boiled eggs. A further layer of rice seals the dish, which is then covered in tomato sauce, cheese and breadcrumbs and baked in the oven

Supplì al telefono rice balls with a filling of mozzarella and sometimes chicken livers or ground meat. They are so called because the long threads of hot cheese look rather like telephone wires

Timballo di riso see *Sartu' di riso*

Pesce —Fish

In the matter of fish one sees most clearly the Italian ability to eat anything. I remember having a whole sea-urchin stuck into the bottom of my foot and thinking how solicitous it was of a small boy to come and pull it out. Having got it off, he scooped its innards out, gobbled them down and wandered off with a grin, leaving me to a couple of painful hours to get the spines out of my flesh. (He did in fact eat it in quite the proper way.)

There are beautiful fish in the seas of Italy (and in the lakes) but, as the Mediterranean gets more polluted, it seems as if it is the monsters which survive. The hairy mussel, the angler (or frog fish) and the whole family of squid. The names, I need hardly tell you, are massively confusing, varying from place to place, seldom having fewer than three names per fish, often having two different fish with the same name. No matter what they are, the Italians eat them all and, unless you belong to the school which thinks that squid tastes like rubber bands and that all fish should be as boneless as deep freezers can make them, then the fish dishes of Italy are some of the best.

Acciughe anchovies
Agoni freshwater shad
Aguglia garfish
Alici anchovies
Alosa shad
Anguilla eel
Aragosta langouste, popularly lobster
Aringhe herrings
Arselle baby clams
Astaco river crayfish, popularly lobster
Baccalà dried salt cod
Bianchetti small fish, whitebait
Bisato eel (Venetian dialect)
Boldrò angler fish
Bonito small tunny
Branzino sea bass
Buttàriga dried grey mullet roe

Coda di rospo angler fish tail
Corvi black umber
Cozze mussels
Cozze pelose mussels with hairy shells
Cozzolo star-gazer
Datteri di mare date mussels
Dentice species of gilt-head which looks like a sea bream
Dorata gilt-head
Folpi octopus (Venetian dialect)
Fragoline di mare sea strawberries, actually a tiny form of squid
Gallinella sea-hen, gurnard
Gamberetti shrimps
Gamberi big shrimp
Gamberi di fiume freshwater crayfish
Gamberoni giant shrimp

The fish appeared. And what was it? Fried inkpots. A *calamaio* is an inkpot: also it is a polyp, a little octopus which, alas, frequents the Mediterranean and squirts ink if offended. This polyp with its tentacles is cut up and fried, and reduced to the consistency of boiled celluloid.
D. H. Lawrence *Sea and Sardinia*

Calamaretti baby squid
Calamari squid
Canestrelli di mare small clams
Canocchie kind of shrimp
Capitone large conger eel
Cappe various shellfish in the cockle and mussel line
Cappe sante scallops
Cappone scorpion fish
Cardi cockles (also cardoons, see *Vegetables*)
Carpa carp
Carpione lake fish of the trout family, from Lake Garda
Cavedano chub
Ceca young eel
Cèfalo grey mullet
Cernia grouper
Cicala di mare squilla, kind of shrimp
Ciriole little eels

Grance(v)ole spiny spider crabs from the Adriatic
Granchio crab
Grongo conger eel
Lampreda lamprey
Leccia leer-fish
Luccio pike
Lucerna moon-gazer
Lumache snails
Mazzancolle very large shrimp
Merlano whiting (or near enough)
Merluzzo cod
Molecche soft-shell crabs (Venetian dialect)
Morena lamprey
Muggine grey mullet
Muscoli mussels
Nasello hake
Ombrina black umber
Orata gilt-head
Ostriche oysters

Palombo type of dogfish
Passerino plaice
Peoci mussels (Venetian dialect)
Pescatrice frog fish, angler
Pesce persico perch
Pesce prete moon-gazer
Pesce San Pietro John Dory
Pesce spada swordfish
Pesciolini small fry, like whitebait
Polipetto, polipo, polpo squid or octopus
Poveracci clams (in the Marches)
Rana pescatrice frog fish, angler
Rane frogs
Razza skate
★ **Ricci** sea-urchins
Rombo liscio brill
  maggiore turbot
Rospo angler
Salmone salmon (but I shouldn't eat it)
Sarde, sardelle, sardelline sardines of varying ages

Scampi large shrimp
Seppie cuttlefish
Sgombro mackerel
★ **Sogliola** sole. The English are inclined to despise Italian sole, quite wrongly
Spannocchi large shrimp
Spigola sea bass
Squadro monk fish, angel-fish
Stoccafisso stockfish
Storione sturgeon
Tartufo di mare Venus clam
Telline cockles (in Tuscany)
Temoli grayling
Tinca tench
Tonno tuna
Totani squids
Triglie red mullet
Trota trout
Trota salmonata salmon trout
Ventresca di tonno tuna stomach —the best part
Vongole clams

Fish dishes

Agoni seccati in graticola (Missoltitt) Lake Como shad, dried and pressed with bay leaves, grilled and marinated in vinegar
Anguilla alla fiorentina eel marinated in oil, then baked in oil, garlic and sage
  coi piselli eel cooked with garlic, onion, peas, tomato sauce and white wine
  in umido eel browned in oil and butter and simmered in white wine, garlic, lemon and tomato paste
Baccalà alla livornese dried salt cod braised in olive oil and white wine with vegetables and cooked slices of tripe
  alla milanese dried salt cod boiled, then fried in batter
  con le olive verdi dried salt cod baked with onions, tomatoes, gherkins, capers and olives
  alla vicentina dried salt cod braised in wine, oil and milk, with anchovies, onion, garlic and herbs
Calamaretti ripieni baby squid stuffed with squid tentacles, garlic, anchovies, parsley, eggs and breadcrumbs, and grilled
Calamari in umido rings of squid stewed with onion, tomatoes, herbs, garlic, red wine and tomato paste

Capitone marinato conger eel simmered in garlic, olive oil and wine vinegar and served cold
★ **Cappon magro** Genoese fish salad
★ **Cozze al vino bianco** cooked mussels served with a white wine, garlic and parsley sauce
★ **Fritto misto di mare** seafood— squid, shrimp, etc.—first boiled, then deep fried. Served with lemon
Insalata di frutti di mare shellfish salad, seasoned with oil, lemon and parsley
Luccio alla marinara pike marinated in oil and wine and then simmered with onions, celery and carrots in the marinade
Palombo arrosto dogfish roasted whole on the spit, basted with oil, or baked in the oven
Pesce spada ripieno sliced swordfish stuffed with a mixture of cooked swordfish, onion, breadcrumbs, brandy, mozzarella and herbs, grilled
Polipo alla luciana boiled octopus
Sarde a beccafico sardines stuffed with breadcrumbs, white raisins, pine nuts, anchovies, onion, and parsley, baked in the oven and sprinkled with lemon or orange juice
  in tortiera baked sardines

alternating with layers of breadcrumbs, garlic and parsley

al vino bianco sardines sandwiched together with anchovy butter and baked in white wine

Sogliola al marsala sole cooked in butter with Marsala

alla parmigiana sole simmered with butter and Parmesan

Tonno alla livornese fried slices of tuna stewed in a tomato and garlic sauce

Vongole alla marinara clams served with chopped parsley and garlic

Carne—Meat

Beef in the north of Italy can be excellent. Florence, particularly, specializes in huge T-bone steaks. In Emilia-Romagna there is a great deal of pork, which apart from going into sausages and being smoked for ham, is cooked in unexpected ways. The most common form of meat is veal, the best of which is found in Lombardy.

In the south any beef is likely to be an old ox too worn to work any longer in the fields. Instead, the lamb and the kid are, almost without exception, a delight of simplicity. Kid is often eaten at Eastertide. The Italians like lemon to flavour plainly cooked meat.

★**Abbacchio** baby lamb. This is the word usually used in Rome and the south. Lambs in the south feed on scrubby hillsides, full of herbs, which gives the meat a special flavour

   brodettato alla romana braised lamb in egg, lemon and white wine sauce

   alla casalinga pot-roasted lamb with egg and lemon sauce

   al forno roast lamb

Agnello lamb, the more usual northern word

   allo spiedo all'aretina marinated lamb on the spit

Animelle di vitello veal sweetbreads fried in butter and Marsala

   alla ciociara veal sweetbreads cooked in a white wine sauce with chopped ham and mushrooms

Arista loin or saddle of pork

   alla fiorentina pork roasted in water or a little oil in the oven with garlic, rosemary and cloves

   alla perugina pork roasted with garlic and fennel

Arrosti misti roasted meats

Arrosto di vitello ubriacato "drunken roast veal"—a pot roast with vegetables, herbs and white wine

Bistecca a large rib steak. Ask for it *al sangue* (rare), *cotta a puntino* (medium) or *ben cotta* (well done)

   alla Bismarck fried steak topped with a fried egg

★**alla fiorentina** huge T-bone steak grilled over a charcoal fire, needing no accompaniment

   alla pizzaiola steak served in a tomato and garlic sauce, often to disguise the toughness of the meat

Bocconcini literally, delicious little morsels of veal rolled up with ham and cheese, cooked in butter

★**Bollito misto** mixed boiled meats—tongue, sausage, beef, veal and chicken—usually served with a *salsa verde* (green sauce)

Braciola di maiale pork chop

Braciolette di abbacchio a scottadito see *Scottadito*

Braciolette ripiene small veal rolls stuffed with white raisins, cheese, pine nuts and ham, cooked in oil and white wine

Bracioline cutlets

Brasato di manzo alla bresciana beef braised in oil with garlic, onion, bacon and red wine

   alla certosina beef braised in red wine with anchovies and parsley

   alla genovese beef braised in red wine with onions, mushrooms, carrots and tomatoes

   alla lombarda beef braised in red wine, preferably Barolo or Barbera, with vegetables

Bue another word for beef

Capretto al forno roast kid (except in Milan, where it means "roast lamb")

alla pasqualina an Italian Easter dish of kid roasted with olive oil, carrots, onion, celery, rosemary and black olives in white wine and stock

al vino bianco kid cooked with vegetables in white wine

Carne suina pork

★ **Carpaccio** very thin slices of raw, lean, fillet beef, with a mustard sauce or dressed with olive oil and lemon juice, often topped with shavings of Parmesan

Casoeula a Milanese dish of stewed pork and cabbage

Castrato mutton

Cervella al burro nero calf's (or lamb's) brains with black butter sauce

fritte alla fiorentina calf's (or lamb's) brains marinated in oil and vinegar, egg-and-breadcrumbed and fried, decorated with anchovies and served on spinach

panate calf's (or lamb's) brains, egg-and-breadcrumbed and fried

★ **Cima di vitello alla genovese** breast of veal, stuffed with vegetables, sweetbreads, hard-boiled eggs and pistachio nuts, poached and served cold. A pretty dish with a marbled effect when cut

Coda di bue alla vaccinara braised oxtail with celery hearts

Controfiletto sirloin steak

Coratella di abbacchio lamb's lung and intestines

Cosciotto di agnello allo spiedo leg of lamb roasted on the spit

Costa di maiale pork chop

Costata (di bue) entrecôte steak

Costolette di abbacchio lamb cutlets

Costolette di agnello alla Villeroy con carciofi lamb cutlets, breadcrumbed and fried, in a Villeroy sauce (white sauce thickened with egg yolks, plus ham, tongue and black truffles) served with artichokes

Costolette di maiale alla modenese pork chops braised with herbs in white wine

Costolette di vitello alla castellana (*or* **duchessa**) veal escalopes stuffed with ham, cheese and white truffles, egg-and-breadcrumbed and fried in butter

alla milanese veal cutlets coated with beaten egg and breadcrumbs and fried in butter

alla valdostana very thin veal cutlets stuffed with fontina cheese and white truffles and fried

Cotechino con lenticchie a speciality of Modena—a large rich pork sausage, boiled and served hot with lentils

Cuore (di bue) (ox) heart

Cuscinetti di vitello braised escalopes of veal, stuffed with ham and cheese

Farsu magru (alla siciliana) a beef roll stuffed with hard-boiled eggs, grated cheese, salami and spices

Fegatelli di maiale alla toscana chunks of pork liver with garlic, sage, breadcrumbs and fennel, wrapped in caul fat, threaded on skewers, alternating with pieces of fried bread and bay leaves

Fegato di vitello alla milanese calf's liver first marinated in oil, then egg-and-breadcrumbed and fried

★ **alla salvia** calf's liver fried with fresh sage leaves in butter

alla toscana slices of calf's liver fried in oil with sage

alla veneziana thinly sliced calf's liver cooked with onions

Fesa di vitello leg of veal

Fettine di manzo alla pizzaiola slices of beef covered with a thick tomato and oregano sauce

Filetto fillet steak

Foccaccia di vitello veal rissoles

Foiolo tripe

Fracosta di bue rib of beef

Fritto misto mixed fry, usually of veal, brains and a variety of sliced vegetables, deep fried in batter. Also refers to fish

alla fiorentina mixed fry of chicken breasts, brains, sweetbreads and artichoke hearts

alla milanese mixed fry with thin slices of veal, calf's liver, cockscombs, brains and vegetables, egg-and-breadcrumbed and fried in butter

Girello in umido pot-roasted topside of beef with tomato sauce

Granatina ground beef mixed with bread and egg, shaped into a cutlet, egg-and-breadcrumbed and fried

Involtini thin slices of veal and ham with sage leaves, rolled and cooked on a skewer

   alla cacciatora thin escalopes of veal with a chicken liver stuffing, rolled up and skewered and cooked in butter

Lesso boiled meat

   rifatto cold boiled meat, warmed up in an onion and tomato sauce

Lingua di bue ox tongue

   in gelatina tongue in aspic

   salmistrata cold pickled tongue

Lombata (*or* lombo) di maiale loin of pork

Lombatine in intingolo veal chops braised in white wine with vegetables

Lonza cured fillet of pork

Luganega pork sausage, fried or grilled, or dried and eaten raw

Magro alla mormora veal escalope cooked in butter with parsley and lemon

Maiale al latte pork cooked in milk with herbs

Manzo carpionato beef—already boiled to make *brodo*—marinated in onions, vinegar, sugar, garlic, herbs and white wine and eaten cold

Medaglioni alla primavera rounds of veal fried and served with a sauce of onion, mushrooms and parsley, garnished with cooked vegetables

   screziati di vitello top round of veal ground with bread, egg yolks and Parmesan, stuffed with chicken livers, mushrooms, ham, peas and hard-boiled eggs, fashioned into a roll, cooked in the oven with some stock and served hot in slices

Messicani alla milanese veal rolls stuffed with ham, pork, garlic, Parmesan and nutmeg, braised in white wine and served with rice

Montone ram, mutton

Muscolo alla fiorentina beef casserole with wine, vegetables and herbs, generally accompanied by white beans

Noce di vitello arrosto roast top round of veal

   in bella vista roast top round of veal with a béchamel sauce

Nodino di vitello alla milanese veal loin chop dipped in flour and fried in butter with white wine and sage

Olivette di vitello alla pesarese small rolls of veal stuffed with ham, anchovies and capers and fried

★**Osso buco alla milanese** knuckle of veal sawn to make thick pieces, with bone and marrow surrounded by meat, braised in white wine and tomatoes

Pagliata di vitello veal intestines made into small circles, basted with butter and grilled over an open fire

Paillard di manzo originally thinly beaten grilled steak named after a French chef-restaurateur, now the same way of doing a veal steak. It comes with attractive burnt stripes from the open fire

Piccata al Marsala thin escalope of veal cooked in butter and Marsala

Piccatina small thinly beaten escalope of veal

   partenopea escalope of veal with mozzarella

Piedini di maiale pig's feet

Polpette meat balls

Polpettone alla casalinga a meat loaf, a rough affair

Porceddu Sardinian suckling pig flavoured with myrtle, roasted whole on the spit

Porchetta suckling pig flavoured with garlic and rosemary, roasted whole on the spit

Prosciutto fresco al Marsala fresh ham braised with vegetables in Marsala

Punta di vitello al forno roast boned shoulder of veal

Quagliette di vitello veal rolls with ham on skewers, alternating with onion, sage leaves and pieces of bread, cooked on the spit

Rognoncini di vitello trifolati finely sliced veal kidneys sautéed in butter and oil with lemon juice or Marsala

Rognoni trifolati calf's kidneys sliced, cooked in butter with lemon juice and parsley

Rolé di manzo beef roll stuffed with Parma ham, hard-boiled eggs and flavoured with sage, simmered in white wine

di vitello veal roll stuffed with an omelette of eggs, cheese, parsley and mortadella sausage, simmered in milk

Salsicce con fagioli pork sausages fried and served with beans in a tomato sauce

alla romagnola pork sausages fried with sage leaves and then simmered in a tomato sauce

Saltimbocca alla romana slice of veal covered with sage leaves and ham, either rolled up or left flat, cooked in butter and Marsala

Sanguinaccio black pudding

Scaloppine thin escalopes of veal sautéed in butter and served in various ways—*ai funghi* (with mushrooms), *al limone* (in lemon juice), *al Marsala* (in Marsala), *alla crema con funghi* (in a white cream and mushroom sauce), *alla perugina* (served with chopped chicken livers), *al vino bianco* (in white wine), *alla zingara* (fried in breadcrumbs and finished with Marsala wine, sliced ham and mushrooms)

Scottadito grilled lamb cutlets, to be eaten with the fingers

Spezzatino di vitello veal stew with wine, tomatoes and sweet peppers (or almost anything)

Spiedini skewered meat and vegetables

Spuntatura di maiale pork ribs or breast

Stecchini alla bolognese (or alla petroniana) equal squares of veal, Gruyère, mortadella and bread, skewered, egg-and-breadcrumbed and then fried

Stracotto beef stewed with sausage and vegetables in white wine

Stufatino veal stewed in white wine

alla romana beef stewed in red wine and tomatoes

Stufato beef stewed with

vegetables and herbs in red wine

di manzo alla genovese beef stewed with vegetables and herbs in white wine

Testa di maiale pig's head

Testarelle di abbacchio/agnello lamb's head roasted in the oven with rosemary

Testina di vitello calf's head

in frittura boned calf's head, boiled, pressed and reshaped, then fried in oil and lemon

alla gratella boned boiled calf's head stuffed with ham and mushrooms, wrapped in caul fat, rolled in breadcrumbs and grilled

alla toscana calf's head, boiled then sautéed

Trippa alla fiorentina braised tripe in tomato sauce flavoured with marjoram, topped with Parmesan

alla romana braised tripe in tomato sauce flavoured with mint, topped with pecorino

Uccelletti di campagna Roman name—"country birds"—for thin slices of beef rolled and grilled on skewers over charcoal

Uccelli scappati thin pieces of veal, bacon and sage leaves, skewered and grilled or fried

Vitello alla genovese slices of veal cooked in butter and white wine with artichoke hearts

alla petroniana thick veal escalopes cooked in butter with Marsala, truffles and Parmesan

all'uccelletto veal escalopes cooked in butter, oil and garlic with a bay leaf and served with lemon

alla Villeroy veal dipped in a béchamel sauce with egg yolks, grated cheese, chopped ham and tongue, fried in breadcrumbs

★**Vitello tonnato** cold braised veal with a tuna fish sauce

★**Zampone** a speciality of Modena. Pork meat stuffed into the skin of a pig's foot and boiled (see *Cotechino*)

Pollame e cacciagione—Poultry and game

As with fish, so with birds. Anything from a lark to a turkey may appear on the menu. Italy is not a country in which to have moral scruples. Most little birds are really not worth eating, being bitter and bony, but the thrush and fig-pecker are exceptions. Squab, rabbit and duck are nearly always bred for eating, unless they are called respectively *palombaccio*, *coniglio selvatico* and *anitra selvatica*. Chicken may be referred to as *pollo, gallina, pollastrella, pollastrino*. As they are more often than not free-range to the point of being sprinters, the best kinds of chicken are the hundreds of different *petti di pollo* (chicken breasts). *Uccelli* and particularly *uccelletti* may be little birds, but more frequently turn out to be little rolls of veal.

Allodole larks

Anitra duck

  in agrodolce in sweet-sour sauce

  all'arancia duck in orange sauce

  arrosto roast duck

  alla nizzarda duck cooked with tomatoes, mushrooms, olives, herbs and brandy

  in salmì duck marinated in red wine with onion, garlic, herbs and anchovies, fried and then simmered in the marinade

  selvatica wild duck

Beccaccia woodcock

Beccaccino snipe

  allo spiedo snipe roasted on the spit and served on squares of fried bread spread with a purée of snipe giblets

Beccafichi fig-pecker, warbler

  al nido fig-peckers on large mushrooms covered with olive oil and baked in the oven (literally "on their nests")

Camoscio chamois

Cappone capon

Capriolo roe-deer

Cervo venison of all kinds, large deer

  alla Mario venison marinated and then roasted in a wine sauce

  con salsa di ciliege venison marinated and then cooked in a casserole with mushrooms, bacon, herbs and spices, served with a cherry sauce

Cinghiale wild boar

  ★ **in agrodolce** wild boar marinated in wine, herbs and spices and roasted in a sweet-sour sauce

Coniglio rabbit bred for the table

  all'agostino rabbit pieces in oil and red wine with white raisins, pine nuts and lemon

  alla borghese rabbit sautéed in white wine, herbs, onions and mushrooms

  del buongustaio rabbit cooked with vegetables, herbs and Marsala

  alla cacciatora rabbit cooked in oil with vegetables, herbs, wine and garlic

  fritto alla lombarda pieces of rabbit dipped into an egg and herb mixture before being breadcrumbed and fried

  in padella rabbit sautéed in oil with bacon, tomatoes, garlic, white wine and parsley

  selvatico wild rabbit

Crocchette di pollo chicken croquettes

Daino fallow deer

Fagiano pheasant

  in casseruola pheasant cooked in butter and cognac

  alla norcese pheasant stuffed with truffles, herbs and chopped onion, soaked with grappa and roasted in the oven or on a spit

Faraona guinea-hen

  al cartoccio guinea-hen stuffed with juniper berries, thyme and garlic, covered in sage and bacon, wrapped in caul fat, parcelled up in paper and roasted in the oven

  alla piemontese guinea-hen stuffed with herbs, juniper berries, breadcrumbs and its liver, cooked in the oven with white wine and vegetables

Fegatini di pollo alla salvia chicken livers fried in butter with fresh sage leaves, strips of ham and Marsala. Often served on pieces of fried bread

Filetti di tacchino alla bolognese turkey breasts fried with ham, cheese and white truffles

  alla cardinale turkey breasts fried with slices of tongue or ham, white truffles and Parmesan

★ **Finanziera di pollo** chicken giblet stew with sweetbreads, mushrooms and truffles in a rich sauce

Gallina fowl

Germano mallard

Lepre hare

  alla montanara hare stewed with pine nuts and white raisins

  in salmi jugged hare— marinated in wine and herbs, cooked in the marinade and served with it and additional garlic, wine and anchovies

Merli blackbirds
Oca goose
  arrosto roast goose, stuffed with sage, rosemary and thyme, traditionally eaten in Florence on All Saints' Day
Palombacci alla perugina an Umbrian dish of roast squab in a sauce of red wine, olives, juniper berries, sage and sometimes with their intestines
Pernice partridge
  in brodo cooked in stock
★**Petti di pollo alla bolognese** boned chicken breasts browned, then baked with a slice of ham and fontina cheese, possibly also with sliced white truffles
  alla Cavour boned chicken breasts sautéed in butter, with a slice of ham and cheese, served in a truffle sauce
  alla fiorentina boned chicken breasts fried in butter
  alla principessa fried boned chicken breasts topped with a fried egg
  sorpresa boned breasts stuffed with some kind of filling, rolled up and deep fried
  sovrana boned chicken breasts cooked with artichokes in cream
  alla valdostana boned chicken breasts cooked with a slice of cheese and white truffles in white wine and brandy
Piccioni squab bred for the table
  coi piselli squab stewed with tongue, ham, onion, peas and basil in white wine
  selvatici wild squab
Pollastrino spring chicken
Pollo arrostito roast or grilled chicken
  arrosto plain roast chicken
  alla cacciatora chicken cooked with mushrooms, tomatoes and herbs in white wine *or* braised chicken in a black olive and anchovy sauce
  alla castellana a slice of Gruyère, ham and white truffles sandwiched between two chicken breasts, egg-and-breadcrumbed, then fried
  alla contadina braised chicken with ham, tomatoes, rosemary and garlic
  alla diavola grilled chicken
  alla duchessa same as *alla castellana* but with Parmesan

  in fricassea alla fiorentina pieces of chicken, poached, and served in a thick egg and lemon sauce
  fritto fried chicken
  imbottito roast stuffed chicken
  al latte chicken cooked in milk
  alla livornese casserole-cooked chicken with lemon
  alla Marengo chicken fried in oil with tomatoes, garlic and white wine. The Italians leave out the crayfish of the French original
  alla montagnola pieces of chicken rolled in egg and breadcrumbs and baked
  alla Nerone half a chicken sautéed in oil and flambéed in cognac
  in porchetta roast chicken stuffed with ham, garlic and fennel
  alla romana pieces of chicken braised with onion, ham, sweet peppers, tomatoes, rosemary, oil and butter
  alla tetrazzini chicken in a mushroom sauce, alternating with layers of pasta, topped with grated cheese and baked
  tonnato cold chicken in a tuna fish sauce
  in umido pieces of chicken stewed with herbs and vegetables
Quaglie quails
  arrosto con polenta roast quails served on fried polenta
  alla fiorentina quails cooked in butter, oil and white wine with parsley, thyme and a bay leaf
  alla piemontese roast quails served in a cream sauce with chopped truffles and Marsala
Rotolo di tacchino boned, rolled turkey breast
Selvaggina venison (on a menu), otherwise game
Starna grey partridge
Tacchino arrosto ripieno (con castagne) roast turkey, stuffed (with chestnuts)
  in carpione turkey, first cooked and then marinated in wine, oil, vinegar and herbs
Tordi thrushes
  in salmì whole thrushes served with a sauce of puréed thrush meat, juniper berries, oil, Marsala and olives
Uccelletti small birds, skewered and roasted

Contorni, legumi, verdure, ortaggi— Vegetables

It was from Italy, in the 16th century, that so many interesting vegetables spread to France and the rest of Europe. On the whole, vegetables are lightly cooked in Italy—a practice which the French have recently adopted, imagining that it is a Japanese innovation. They are also often eaten cold when cooked, like a salad, with oil and lemon. Were I to become a vegetarian, which God forbid, Italy would be the country where I would choose to indulge my folly.

Asparagi asparagus
  alla fiorentina boiled and served with melted butter, with fried eggs on the top
Barbabietola beet
Bietola Swiss chard
Broccoli broccoli
  alla romana braised in white wine

★ **all'uccelletto** a Tuscan dish. The beans are boiled, then cooked in oil, garlic, sage and tomato sauce
Fagiolini string beans
Fave fava beans
  al guanciale fava beans simmered with onion and bacon in water

---

. . . the artichoke is not a suitable meal for the businessman or the salesgirl. It is by nature inaccessible to him who is used to cutting up his greens, shovelling them on to the fork together with meat and potatoes and swallowing in haste.
Edith Templeton *The Surprise of Cremona*

Carciofi artichokes
  alla contadina stuffed with various things like garlic, breadcrumbs, parsley, etc., and stewed in oil
  alla giudia artichokes deep-fried in oil, called after a Jewish restaurateur in Rome specializing entirely in artichokes. These look like open flowers when cooked
Carciofini, cuori di young artichoke hearts
Cardi cardoons
Carote carrots
Cavoletti, cavolini di Bruxelles brussels sprouts
Cavolfiore cauliflower
Cavolo cabbage
  rosso red cabbage
Ceci chick-peas
Cetriolini gherkins
Cetriolo cucumber
Cicoria chicory
Cima di rape turnip tops
Cipolla onion
Cipolline small white onions
Crescione watercress
Fagioli white haricot beans
  con le cotiche white beans cooked slowly with pork rind and tomato sauce

Finocchio fennel
  al forno boiled fennel baked in the oven with butter and grated cheese
★ **Fiori di zucca** (*or* **zucchini**) squash flowers, usually fried in batter
Funghi mushrooms
  affogati mushrooms cooked in olive oil and garlic
  alla parmigiana mushrooms stuffed with breadcrumbs, Parmesan, garlic, parsley and oregano and baked in the oven
  porcini boletus mushrooms
  trifolati mushrooms sliced and fried in oil and garlic. Served with chopped anchovies, parsley, butter and lemon
Giardiniera mixed chopped vegetables
Indivia del Belgio Belgian endive
Insalata salad. *Condita* means that it has already been dressed, while *non condita* is the opposite. The most common salads are *mista* (mixed), *di pomodori* (with sliced tomatoes) and *verde* (green). These are all side dishes
Lattuga lettuce
Lenticchie lentils

Melanzane eggplants (see *Hors d'oeuvre*)

Navoni another name for turnips

Olive (nere, verdi) olives (black, green)

Patate potatoes. Mashed potatoes can be delicious in Italy, and are often mixed with cheese. Look for *purea* or *puré*

Patatine novelle new potatoes

Peperonata see *Hors d'oeuvre*

Peperoncini small hot chilli peppers

Peperoni sweet peppers (see *Hors d'oeuvre*)

Piselli peas

   alla romana peas cooked with a little onion, ham and butter

Pomodori tomatoes

Porri leeks

Radicchio di Treviso red-leafed bitter lettuce, chicory or endive

Radici, rapanelli, ravanelli radishes (both red and white)

Rape turnips

Scarola Batavian endive, curly lettuce, escarole

Sedano celery

Sottoaceti pickled vegetables

Spinaci spinach

   alla parmigiana spinach served with butter and grated cheese

   alla piemontese spinach with garlic, butter and chopped anchovies, served with fried bread

★**Tartufi** truffles. A great delicacy, especially the white ones (*tartufi bianchi*). The season in Piedmont lasts from October to December. Also black truffles (*tartufi neri*)

Verdure cotte cooked vegetables

Verza savoy cabbage

Zucca pumpkin, vegetable squash

Zucchini baby squash, zucchini

   fritti zucchini cut into various shapes, egg-and-breadcrumbed and fried, or fried in batter

   alla napoletana baked in the oven with mozzarella in a tomato sauce

Dolci— Desserts, *Gelati*— Ice-cream, *Frutta*— Fruit

The Italians have had an infinitely sweet tooth ever since the Venetians started to import cane sugar from the East. At one time meals used to start and end with a sweet course. It was Italy, also, which pioneered the ice. Any home-made ice in Italy is worth eating. The rest are now as chemically glutinous as anyone else's. There is a superabundance of all sorts of cakes. Everyone on Sundays goes to the *pasticceria* (cake shop) to stock up with innumerable pastries against the inevitable arrival of grandmothers and aunts and uncles and cousins and armfuls of children.

Albicocche apricots

Amaretti macaroons

Ananas pineapple

Arance oranges

   caramellate whole peeled oranges in caramel syrup and kirsch

Banane bananas

Biscotti biscuits

Bongo-bongo Florentine name for *profiteroles*

Budino pudding

Cannoli Sicilian pastry horns filled with sweetened ricotta, candied peel and cocoa

Cassata alla siciliana sponge cake, ricotta, candied fruits and chocolate flavoured with Marsala *or* Strega *or* ice-cream

in coloured layers flavoured with candied fruits and nuts

Castagnaccio a chestnut flour paste mixed to a cake with pine nuts, almonds, raisins and candied fruits

Castagne chestnuts

Cenci alla fiorentina fried pastry twists sprinkled with icing sugar

Cialde wafers

Ciambellone a fruit and nut bread ring

Ciliege cherries

Cocomero watermelon

Colomba Easter cake in the shape of a dove

Composta di frutta stewed fruit

Coppa gelato ice-cream of different flavours and colours

Crema custard
  caramella baked custard with a caramelized topping
Crostata an open fruit or jam flan usually criss-crossed with pastry strips
  di amarene flan with a wild black cherry filling
  di ricotta Roman cheesecake with egg, Marsala, lemon and ricotta filling
Dattero date
Dolce Torinese chilled chocolate loaf with biscuits, almonds and rum
Fichi figs
Fragole strawberries
Fragoline di bosco small wild strawberries
Frutta cotta stewed fruit
  fresca di stagione fresh fruit in season
Gelato ice-cream
  di tartufo ice-cream with chocolate sauce
Granita water ice, generally flavoured with lemon, orange, coffee, strawberry, etc.
Kaki persimmon. Be wary of eating too close to the skin of the fruit as it irritates or sears your lips
Lamponi raspberries
Limone lemon
Macedonia di frutta fruit salad
Mandarino tangerine
Mandorle almonds
Mantecato type of soft ice-cream
Marrone large chestnut
Melacotogna quince
Melagrana pomegranate
Mele apples
  renette type of cooking apple
Melone melon
Menta mint
Meringa meringue
Mirtilli blueberries
★**Monte bianco** sieved chestnut or chestnut purée with whipped cream
More mulberries, blackberries
Nespola medlar
Nocciole hazelnuts
Noce walnut
Noce di cocco coconut
Pan di Spagna sponge cake, used as a basis for many sweets
Pandoro (di Verona) sweet sponge cake sprinkled with icing sugar, very popular at Christmas
Panettone light raisin and candied peel sponge cake, a speciality for Christmas
Panforte di Siena hard rich cake of nuts, cocoa, candied peel and spices
Pere pears
Pesca noce nectarine
Pesche peaches
  ripiene baked peaches stuffed with macaroons
Pinoli pine nuts
Pistacchi pistachio nuts
Pompelmo grapefruit
Profiteroles small cream puffs, covered with chocolate sauce. See *Bongo-bongo*
Prugne plums
Rabarbaro rhubarb
Ribes nero black currants
  rosso red currants
Ricciarelli Sienese almond biscuits
Salame dolce see *Dolce Torinese*
Semifreddi frozen desserts with cream, sponge, ice-cream, fruit, etc.
Sfogliatelle flaky pastry cases filled with sweetened ricotta and candied fruit
Sorbetto water ice, sherbet, soft ice-cream
Spuma mousse
Spumone kind of soft ice-cream, mousse
Susine plums
Tarocco type of Sicilian orange
Tartufi di cioccolata chocolate truffles
Torrone nougat
Torta flan, tart
  millefoglie countless thin layers of pastry alternating with a custard filling and sprinkled with icing sugar
  di riso a sweet rice pudding cake
Uva grapes
  passa raisins
  spina gooseberry
Visciola sour cherry
Zabaglione whipped egg yolks, sugar and Marsala (supposedly an aphrodisiac)
Zuccotto a dome-shaped ice-cream cake with whipped cream and chocolate, soaked in liqueur
Zuppa inglese kind of trifle, with sponge cake (often suspiciously bright red), cream and liqueur

Formaggi—*Cheese*

Bel Paese a soft, smooth, bland cheese made from cow's milk

Caciocavallo a firm, sharp cheese made from buffalo or cow's milk

Caciotta a soft cheese made from the milk of various animals

Dolcelatte a mild, veined cheese

Fontina a fat, bland cheese made from cow's milk

Gorgonzola a veined blue cheese. It can be either *dolce* (sweet) or *piccante* (strong)

Mascarpone unsalted cream cheese from Lombardy

Mozzarella a rubbery white cheese technically made of buffalo's milk, now more often of cow's

Parmigiano reggiano (grana) the most famous Italian cheese—Parmesan. It is salty and

sharp and used mainly for seasoning and cooking. It will have been matured for 2–4 years and is grated just before use. Fresh Parmesan can be eaten as a table cheese

Pecorino romano a hard, sharp cheese made with fresh ewe's milk, curdled with lamb's rennet

Provolone a spicy sharp cheese, often fashioned into amusing shapes

Ricotta a fresh, moist cottage cheese made from ewe's milk

Sardo a sharp, strong cheese made from ewe's milk

Stracchino a soft, white cheese from the milk of "tired" cows wintering on the plains

Taleggio a mild, creamy cheese made from dry, salted curds

Coffee punctuates an Italian day. I list only a few of the possible variations:

Caffè alto, corretto, doppio, Hag, lungo, ristretto weak coffee, coffee with liqueur, two *espresso* coffees in one cup, decaffeinated coffee, weak coffee, strong coffee

Caffelatte milky coffee

Cappuccino strong, frothy

espresso coffee with milk, often sprinkled with cocoa

Espresso tiny cups of strong black coffee from the machine

Latte macchiato milk with a spot of coffee

Moka Mocha coffee

Italian wine

As with eating, it is sensible in Italy to try the local wine. There are hazards. A friend of mine has a farmhouse in Tuscany. Filling our glasses as we sat on his terrace, he said grandiloquently, "This is our own wine. It comes from just over there, not two hundred yards away." An American lady sipped it and said ruminatively "It doesn't travel."

I have made a short list of the best wines of various regions and the type of dish with which they go well. Some are expensive. On the whole in Italy it is best to follow Hugh Johnson's advice: ". . . aim for the youngest available white wine and experiment with the oldest available red . . . within reason."

The best Italian wine is now classified as DOC (Denominazione di Origine Controllata), which guarantees its authenticity. All except those marked † belong in this category.

un bicchiere a glass

una caraffa a carafe

una bottiglia a bottle

una mezza bottiglia a half-bottle

un fiasco a flask

un litro a litre

un mezzo litro a half-litre

un quartino a quarter-litre

vino bianco white wine

vino rosso, nero red wine

vino rosato rosé wine

vino abboccato, dolce, frizzante, secco, spumante semi-sweet, sweet, fizzy, dry, sparkling wine

Regional wines

Abruzzi

Montepulciano d'Abruzzo
(dry red, sometimes rosé)—
chicken

Trebbiano d'Abruzzo (dry
white)—fish

Basilicata

Aglianico del Vulture (dry red)–
minestrone, lamb

Calabria

Cirò di Calabria (dry red)—
lamb and heavy pasta

Lazio

Colli albani (dry white)—shellfish

Est! Est!! Est!!! (dry white)—
fish pasta

Frascati (dry and sweet white)—
chicken, veal, fish. The sweet goes
well with strawberries

†Velletri (dry red)—lamb, kid

Liguria

Cinque Terre (dry white and
sweet, called *Sciacchetra*)—
dry: shellfish, sweet: pastries

Come the morning and you get up and taking the greatest
delight in your delectable skill you wait till a couple of chops
or an omelette or a cutlet call you to table; and after you've
lifted up your mug and shaken the napkin and put it back on
a table which is always laid and always presided over by the
jug of wine, standing in front of it with constant lovingness,
you eat to live rather than live to eat.

You go out for a walk whenever it suits you, providing
yourself out of your own money with some liver or tasty
sheeps' heads for a stew. You buy a little fish or some eggs all
fresh from the country, honouring Easter with a fat capon
and solemn feast-days with a chicken or two, not forgetting
the goose for All Saints and never returning to your lodgings
without a radish in your hand and a salad in your
handkerchief, singing as you go.

Come the summer and it brings you your plums, with a
handful of figs, two flasks of Moscatello and a bunch of
grapes, and having ventured to buy a nicely ripened melon,
small but very heavy, you take it along home. Enjoying fresh
water on the dinner-table, you fill your jug full from the tub,
and plunging your nose and your knife together into that
melon, finding it sweet and succulent, you are as pleased as
Punch, and after you've eaten two slices, you guzzle the lot
and the flavour penetrates your very bones; and, despising
what's eaten in all the courts of the world, you finish your
meal with a scrap of meat or some cheese, and you're
convinced that to live any other way would be folly; for it's a
vile thing to make one's gullet a Paradise of food or one's
body a packing-case for provisions.

Pietro Aretino *Selected Letters*

Campania

†Lacrima Christi (dry red and
white)—pizza and pasta

Emilia-Romagna

Albana (dry white)—fish

Lambrusco (sparkling dry red)—
heavy pasta, guinea-hen

Sangiovese di Romagna (dry
red)—pork

Friuli-Trentino

Grave del Friuli (dry red and
white)—almost anything

Picolit (sweet white)—desserts

Lombardy

†Frecciarossa (dry white)—
light risottos, *osso buco*

Grumello (dry red)—veal,
chicken

Lugana (dry white)—trout

Sassella (dry red)—salami, meat
risotto

Sforzato (dry red)—game,
guinea-hen

Valtellina (dry red)—beef

Piedmont

Asti spumante (sparkling sweet

white)—cakes
Barbaresco (dry red)—liver, kidneys
Barbera (dry red)—salami, meat pasta
Barbera d'Asti (dry red with a slight fizz)—heavy pasta, guinea-hen
Barolo (dry red)—game
Dolcetto (dry red)—spicy food and cheese
Gattinara (dry red)—beef, rich meat dishes
Nebbiolo (dry red)—veal, chicken, liver
Puglia
San Severo (dry red and white)—a general light wine, red with meats, white with fish
Sardinia
Cannonau di Sardegna (dry red)—kid, lamb
†Nuraghe majore (dry white)—bigger fish, fish pasta
Vernaccia di Oristano (fortified sherry-type, dryish)—*antipasti*
Sicily
†Corvo (dry red)—tomato pasta, veal, lamb
Marsala (fortified wine like sherry)—sweets
Malvasia delle Lipari (white and sweet white)—desserts
Moscato di Pantelleria (white dessert)—desserts and cooked fruit
Moscato di Siracusa (white

dessert)—desserts
Tuscany
Brunello di Montalcino (dry red)—game and rich dishes
Carmignano (dry red)—veal and chicken
Chianti (dry red)—meat, heavy pasta
Chianti classico (dry red from the central district)—beefsteak
Vino nobile di Montepulciano (dry red)—guinea-hen
Vernaccia di San Gimignano (dry white)—*antipasti*
†Vinsanto (strong sweet dessert wine)—at the end of a meal (often with biscuits)
Umbria—The Marches
Orvieto secco (dry white)—creamy pasta
Rubesco di Torgiano (dry red)—steaks and game
Verdicchio dei Castelli di Jesi (dry white)—fish pasta
Veneto
Bardolino (dry red)—veal and light meat
Prosecco di Conegliano (dry white and sweet)—with cakes
Recioto Amarone della Valpolicella (dry red)—guinea-hen, liver and rich veal dishes
Soave (dry white)—fish pasta
Tocai (dry white)—chicken
Valpolicella (dry red)—ham, veal

There are two Italies—the one is the most sublime and lovely contemplation that can be conceived by the imagination of man; the other is the most degraded, disgusting and odious. What do you think? Young women of rank actually eat—you will never guess what—garlick!
Percy Bysshe Shelley

Useful words

Acciughe anchovies
Aceto vinegar
Acqua minerale mineral water, either *gassata* (sparkling) or *naturale* (flat)
Affettato sliced (cold meats)
Affumicato smoked
all'Agliata with a pressed garlic, bread and wine vinegar sauce
Aglio garlic
Agnello lamb
Agro, agrodolce sour, sweet-sour

Albergo hotel
Amaro bitter
Aperitivo apéritif
Arachide peanut
Arrosto, -ti roast, roast meats
Assortito, -ti assorted
Basilico basil
Besciamella béchamel
in Bianco boiled, plain
Birra beer
Biscottini small biscuits
Bollito boiled

Bovoloni species of large snail, eaten in the Veneto on Christmas Eve

alla Brace grilled over a charcoal or open fire

Braciola, braciolette, braciolini large chop, chops, cutlets

Brasato braised

Budella intestines

al Burro cooked in butter

Caldo warm, hot

Calzone see *Pizza*

Candito candied

Carciofi, carciofini artichokes, artichoke hearts

al Carrello from the trolley

in Cartoccio cooked in the oven in a paper casing

della Casa of the restaurant

Casalinga home-made

Cestino di frutta basket of fruit

Ciccioli pork fat after rendering

Cioccolata, -to drinking chocolate, chocolate

Cipolle onions

Conto bill

Coperto cover charge

Cosce legs (of chicken, etc.)

Costata, costolette chop, cutlets

Cotto cooked

Cozze mussels

Crostacei shellfish

Crostini small slices of white toasted or fried bread with a savoury topping

Crudo raw

Digestivo an after-dinner drink, said to soothe the generally ailing Italian liver. Usually tastes like medicine

Dolce sweet

Dorato literally "golden", i.e. dipped in egg and fried

Fagioli, fagiolini white beans, string beans

Farcito stuffed

Farfalle butterfly-shaped pasta

Fave fava beans

Fegatini, fegato chicken livers, liver. The Italians are the best liver cooks. It is usually pretty pink and tender. Italian restaurants outside Italy often cheat by giving one liver other than calf. So insist on it

ai Ferri grilled "on iron" over an open fire

Fichi figs. A dangerous word about which to get muddled over genders. The fruit is decidedly masculine

Finocchio fennel. An ambiguous colloquial term when applied to a male

al Forno baked or roasted in the oven

Freddo cold

Fresco fresh

Frittelle fritters, either sweet or savoury

Fritto fried

Frullato whipped; milkshake

Frutti di mare seafood

al Funghetto sautéed in very hot oil

Funghi mushrooms, but including many varieties of what we call toadstools

Gallina fowl

Gelato ice-cream

Ghiaccio ice

del Giorno of the day

al Girarrosto spit-roasted

Glassato glazed

Grana generic name in Emilia for Parmesan

Granita water ice

alla Graticola grilled over charcoal

Gremolata mixture of lemon peel, garlic and parsley sprinkled over *osso buco*

alla Griglia grilled

Grissini breadsticks

Guarnito garnished

Insalata salad

Latte milk

Lenticchie lentils

Lesso boiled

al Liquore with brandy or another liqueur

Maionese mayonnaise

Manzo beef

Maritozzi buns with raisins, candied peel and pine nuts

Melanzane eggplants

Merenda tea-time snack

Misto mixed

Mortadella large pork sausage

Mostarda di Cremona Lombardy sweet-sour pickle

Mozzarella rubbery white cheese

Noci nuts, often walnuts, as in *salsa di noci*

Nostrale, nostrano locally or home-grown

Olio di oliva olive oil, *con olio* always means with olive oil

Origano oregano

Pane bread

Panna cream
  montata whipped cream

Passato, puré, purea purée (or mashed, for potatoes)

Pasta frolla, sfoglia short pastry, flaky pastry

Pasticceria cake or pastry shop

Pasticcini teacakes, pastries

Pasticcio literally means a pie, but is usually layers of pasta baked with a savoury filling

Pecora ewe (sheep)

Pepe pepper

Peperata a sauce of beef marrow, breadcrumbs, Parmesan and ground black pepper served with boiled meat or poultry

Peperoncini chilli peppers

Peperoni sweet peppers, *rossi* (red), *verdi* (green) and *gialli* (yellow)

Pesto Genoese green sauce made of fresh basil with garlic and pine nuts and *sardo* or Parmesan

Pezzo piece

a Piacere according to taste, in the way you like it

Piccante sharp or spicy

Pinzimonio an oil, salt and pepper dressing into which raw vegetables are dipped

Piselli peas

Pizzaiola fresh tomato sauce with oregano or basil and garlic. From Naples

Pollo chicken

ruspante free-range chicken

Polmone lung

Polpo octopus

Pomodoro tomato

Prezzemolo parsley

Prezzo fisso fixed-price menu

Prosciutto ham. The word on its own usually means smoked ham, but also includes raw ham. Distinctions are made by *prosciutto crudo* which is raw or cured ham. *Prosciutto cotto* is a cooked ham, *prosciutto di Parma* is the best ham

Radicchio type of red lettuce

Radici red or white radishes

Rafano horseradish

Ragù Bolognese meat sauce of pork and beef, finely chopped vegetables, wine and tomato paste

Ravanelli radishes

Ricotta properly a soft cheese of ewe's milk, now often a cottage cheese of cow's milk

Rigaglie di pollo chicken giblets

Ripieno stuffed

Riso rice

Salsa sauce

verde green sauce of lemon, oil, capers, parsley and anchovy

Saltato sautéed

Salvia sage

a Scelta the one of your choice

Sciroppo syrup

Secco dry

Selvaggina game, particularly venison

Semifreddo frozen cream dessert

Senape mustard

Servizio compreso (non compreso) service included (not included)

Spiedino cooked on a skewer

allo Spiedo on the spit

Spuntino a snack

Stagionato well-aged, hung

Stufato braised, stewed

Sugo sauce

Supplì fried balls of rice often called "al telefono" when filled with cheese which pulls out like telephone wires when hot

Tartufi truffles. The white ones (*bianchi*) are especially prized (and priced). They smell so strongly that Mussolini banned them from being carried on trains, but their taste is a miracle. Often scattered on rice (Milan), mixed with anchovy (Piedmont)

Tortiglione almond cake

Tost Italian toasted sandwich with ham and cheese

Trancia slice

Trippa tripe

in Umido stewed

Uova eggs

Vaniglia vanilla

Vari assorted

Vellutata a soup of whatever, thickened with egg yolk

Verdure green vegetables

Vino bianco, rosso white, red wine

Vitello veal

Vongole baby clams

Zucchini baby squash

Zuppa soup (except *zuppa inglese* which is trifle)

Buon appetito! bon appétit!
Cin-cin! Salute! cheers!

Japan and Korea

Japan

While Chinese food is instantly likeable, Japanese food is something of a shock to foreign palates. Until fairly recently, Japan's was a primarily vegetarian cuisine, relieved by fish. The 19th century saw the encouragement of meat, but dairy products have never caught on. Cheese is regarded as mouldy stuff, butter is not used in cooking and milk is rarely used. The Portuguese introduced frying in the 16th century, but most food is boiled. The taste of Japanese food is either of extreme freshness or of things to which we are not accustomed such as bean curd and a rather bitter pickle. Part of its pleasure is visual; no other people devotes so much attention to the appearance of food, even in southeast Asia. As the majority of people over the centuries were extremely poor, subsisting largely on rice, most dishes are small and simple, depending for their effect on prettiness and a strong sharp taste. Once you have learned to like it, Japanese food is full of surprises and excitement.

There is a multiplicity of eating places ranging from the grand *restoran* to the *ba*, which is a bar possibly serving snacks, certainly providing thirsty hostesses. While a *restoran* may serve Western food, a proper Japanese restaurant is a *ryoriya*. Many of these specialize in producing only a few or even only one dish—for example *tempura*, *sushi* or noodles.

The menu, therefore, may be quite unimportant. On the other hand, it may be very confusing. The Japanese language is a misty affair. While they have, for instance, a three letter word (*iai*) for "the art of drawing a sword while sitting down", they have no positive word for "blue". Words change in a most complicated way in different circumstances and are often omitted when we would feel them to be essential. There is no singular or plural, yet adjectives have tenses (though, of course, there is no future, for who can say what it might be?).

I have divided the dishes into conventional sections—soup, fish, meat, etc.—for convenience of identification. A Japanese meal has no particular pattern, many dishes coming at once. Soup often comes second, but it may come at any time. Food is often cold which the Japanese do not mind, because it was once very fashionable since the Emperor's kitchens were so far from his banqueting rooms that the food could not be anything but tepid when it got there. There is virtually never a dessert. The Japanese eat cakes at other times and, anyhow, the food is inclined to be sweet. Fruit is the most you will get. Every meal ends with plain boiled rice. The Japanese always eat at least two bowls—one is for the dead.

I have listed a great number of words rather than dishes in the hope that you can either fasten onto one in a long name, or ask for what you want. The Japanese love food—using it in many metaphors: *gabei* means "a failure", but literally is "a painted rice-cake, which cannot appease hunger". So rely on the guidance they will give you, particularly when staying in a real Japanese inn (*ryokan*), which is one of the delights of the country.

The main Japanese alcoholic drink is *sake*, quite a mild rice wine which is drunk warm. They produce extremely good beer and very passable whisky, of which *Suntory* is the most famous brand. The wine made from grapes is not yet a success but may very well be in the future.

Shiru—Soups

Hamaguri ushiojiru clam broth, simply boiled with a little *sake*

Kakitama jiru beaten eggs poured in a thin stream into *dashi* so that they form threads, garnished with snow peas

Kenchin jiru chicken and bean curd broth

Kuzuhiki jiru broth with bean curd and soy sauce, flavoured with ginger

★ **Miso shiru** *aka-miso* is the red bean paste added to all manner of soups to thicken them. The Japanese eat a plain form of this soup for breakfast. It has a faint taste of manure, to which, after a year or so, you can get quite attached

Noppei-jiru vegetable broth with bean curd

Ozōni New Year soup. Nobody is very particular about what goes into this, provided it has some rice-cake of a gluey type called *mochi*

Sakana ushiojiru fish broth, simply boiled with a little *sake* and chopped scallions, flavoured with soy sauce

Satsuma jiru *miso shiru* with chicken and mushrooms

Sumashi jiru *udon* in chicken soup with noodles

Gohan—Rice

Donburi the name of a bowl which has come to mean a bowl of rice, covered with left-overs, sometimes mixed with a kind of scrambled egg, all moistened with *dashi* (see *Soups*)

Gohan rice—the *go* part of the word is an honorific so that the whole means honourable food

Gomoku meshi rice boiled with bean curd, *konnyaku*, burdock root, chicken and carrots, with *sake* and soy sauce

Gomoku soba rice noodles served in a broth with pork cubes and vegetables

   udon wheat noodles, as above

Hiyashi somen cold, very fine noodles served with shrimp and scallions on top and a soy and *mirin* sauce

Inarizushi bags of fried bean curd, filled with *sushi* rice and sometimes vegetables

Katsudon breaded fried pork pieces stewed in *dashi* with onions, on the top of boiled rice

Kitsune soba rice noodles served in a broth with bean curd and scallions, flavoured with soy sauce and *mirin*

   udon rice noodles served as above

Kurigohan rice with chestnuts

★ **Maze gohan** rice boiled with peas, carrots and shrimps, flavoured with ginger, gingko nuts, soy sauce and *sake*

Mi-iro gohan "three-coloured rice"; actually it is not coloured rice but white rice, green peas and brown ground beef

Nori chazuke boiled rice, sprinkled with toasted *nori* seaweed, over which tea is poured

Norimaki much like *sushi* but rolled into cylinders, wrapped in seaweed with a core of fish, omelette or vegetable and sliced

Oboro chicken, peas, mushrooms and omelette strips on top of boiled rice, moistened with the chicken cooking liquid of soy sauce, *mirin* and sugar

Onigiri rice balls, containing any of the things you might find in *sushi*, sprinkled with roasted sesame seeds

Raisu rice—curiously this word, deriving from English, is now almost more commonly used on menus than the Japanese word *gohan*, perhaps in reaction against honorifics which could be truly absurd, the loo even being called *o-tearai*, (the *o-* part is the honorific)

Sekihan rice steamed with red beans

★ **Sushi** small thin circles or rectangles of rice cooked with seaweed, bound together by a mixture of vinegar, salt, sugar and *aji-no-moto*, and covered with a variety of things—fish, omelette, mushrooms. They are like an elaborate canapé

165

Takenoko meshi boiled rice with bamboo shoots
Tendon *tempura* shrimp and vegetables stewed in *dashi* with soy sauce, *mirin* and scallions, served on top of boiled rice
Zaru soba cold buckwheat noodles, served with a soy and *mirin* sauce

Sakana—Fish

Aji scad or horse mackerel
Aji-no-nitsuke scad simmered in soy sauce with sliced ginger, served with snow peas
Anago conger eel
Ayu river fish, a bit like trout
Awabi abalone
Bora mullet
★**Chirinabe** eaten in the same way as *sukiyaki*. Fish and vegetables are simmered in stock and dipped in a soy and *mirin* sauce, flavoured with ginger
Dotenabe eaten in the same way as *sukiyaki*. Oysters, bean curd, *konnyaku* noodles and chrysanthemum leaves are simmered with bean-paste in *dashi* flavoured with *sake*
Ebi shrimp or lobster
  onigara grilled shrimp basted with a soy, *mirin* and *shichimi* sauce
★**Fugu** blowfish. See *Sashimi*
Hamaguri clams
Hirame flat fish, often halibut
Hōbō gurnard, gurnet
★**Hōraku-yaki** fish, salted for half-an-hour, baked on a bed of pine-needles with shrimp, mushrooms and chestnuts
Hotategai scallop
Ika cuttlefish, squid
  no mirinyaki cuttlefish boiled, marinated in a soy, *mirin* and *sake* sauce, then grilled while being basted with the marinade
Ise-ebi lobster
Ishikari nabe a northern stew of salmon with mushrooms, spinach, cabbage, chrysanthemum leaves and bean curd
Iwashi sardine
Kabayaki grilled eel basted with soy, *mirin* and *sake* sauce
Kaibashira scallops
Kaki oysters
Kani crab
Kamaboko fish sausage or cake, often dyed red
Kamasu pike
Karei flatfish, often plaice

Kimini shrimp simmered in *dashi*, soy sauce and *sake* covered with beaten egg yolk
Kisu smelts
Ko-ebi shrimp
Koi carp
Kuruma-ebi shrimp
Maguro tuna fish
Masu trout
Negima nabe leek and tuna fish stew
Nishin herring
Nizakana fish simmered in soy sauce, *dashi* and *sake* flavoured with ginger
Nuta fish salad
Saba mackerel
  no tataki salted for several hours, marinated in vinegar and sugar, served with a *julienne* of raw radishes, carrots and ginger
Sakana uniyaki fish, salted for half-an-hour, coated with an egg yolk and water chestnut paste and grilled
Sake salmon
★**Sashimi** raw fish. I cannot imagine why other nations, which eat one raw fish—oysters in Europe, clams in America, herrings in Holland, etc.—have never realised how excellent so many other raw fish are. The Japanese eat a great variety. The best are *tai* (porgy), *sake* (salmon), *ika* (cuttlefish) and, if you dare, *fugu* (blowfish). This last must be cleaned by someone licensed to do so, otherwise it can poison you. Some two hundred people a year die of it. You will not be kept in suspense as it kills in five minutes. On the whole I would avoid raw river fish; *koi* (carp) has a nasty liver fluke which quite likes human beings. *Sashimi* is served with soy sauce and very hot horseradish sauce
Sawara mackerel-like fish
Shitabirame sole
Shirano whitebait
Suzuki perch
Tai porgy

Tara cod
★Tarako to tasai no niawase
shirataki noodles, cod's roe, leeks
and carrots, simmered in *dashi*,
soy sauce and *mirin*
★Tempura pieces of fish, shrimps
and vegetables, dipped in batter
and deep fried. There are many
tempura bars in towns. They have
the advantage that the food is
extremely hot and crisp, since
you sit at the bar while the cook

cooks behind it and pops pieces
on your plate straight from the
pan. In restaurants the batter is
often soggy. Although this is one
of Japan's most famous dishes, it
was actually introduced by the
Portuguese in the 16th century
Unagi eel
Uo suki a fish version of *sukiyaki*,
using a variety of fish instead of
beef
Zarigani crayfish

Iwashi no atama mo shinjin kara.
Faith makes even the head of a sardine the object of worship.

Niku—Meat, **Tori**—Poultry, *Ahiru* — Duck

Asuka nabe a stew usually of
chicken with *shirataki* and
vegetables, in stock and milk
Butanabe eaten in the same way
as *sukiyaki*. Pork slices are
simmered in a seaweed stock
with bean curd, cabbage and
chrysanthemum. The diners dip
the meat and vegetables in a soy,
mirin and vinegar sauce
Butaniku pork
Chanko nabe a chicken stew
with mushrooms, bean curd,
shirataki, bamboo shoot, carrot,
cabbage and leeks. This is said to
be what *sumo* wrestlers eat and
so appears on boastful menus
Gacho goose
Goma yaki marinated chicken
fried in sesame oil and sprinkled
with sesame seed
Gyniku beef
Hato squab
Iridori chicken stewed with
vegetables
★Jingisukan nabe there is a
special convex pan for cooking
"Ghengis Khan pot". Mutton or
beef are grilled on it with
mushrooms, onions and leeks.
Diners help themselves from the
pan and there is usually a
selection of about five spices and
a sauce to dip bits in
Kawari yanagawa nabe a pork
stew with beansprouts, *konnyaku*,
string beans, ginger and eggs
Kiji pheasant
Kimo liver
Kohitsuji lamb
Koushi veal

Matsumae nabe chicken, shrimp,
oysters, leeks and seaweed, stewed
Mizutaki cubed chicken, bean
curd, mushrooms and vegetables
are simmered in water with root
ginger and dipped in a soy,
vinegar and lemon sauce
Niwatori chicken
Nōmiso brains
★Shabu-shabu the principle of
shabu-shabu is much the same as
for *sukiyaki* except that the
ingredients are simmered in stock
rather than fried. The meat is the
same, possibly a little thicker, the
vegetables may include cabbage.
The guests dip the food in a
sauce made with sesame seeds,
sesame oil, two kinds of soy
sauce, chillis, *dashi* and vinegar
Shita tongue
Suizō sweetbreads
★Sukiyaki the dish always given
to Westerners, and unknown in
Japan until the last century when
it was devised as a way of
persuading the Japanese to eat
more meat. It is primarily beef
(preferably Kobe beef—the cattle
are massaged, so that the fat
disperses through the flesh to give
it a speckled look) cut very thin.
A large pan is put over a flame in
the middle of the table and some
fat melted in it. The host keeps
filling the pan with slices of beef,
scallions, bamboo shoots,
mushrooms, onions, *konnyaku*
(or *shirataki*) noodles and bean
curd. He also adds soy sauce, *sake*
and perhaps sugar. As the things

167

cook he will help the guests to each morsel. Everyone has a bowl with a raw egg broken in it, into which he dips the food

★**Tonkatsu** pork marinated in soy sauce and *mirin* with garlic and *shichimi-togarashi* (seven spice pepper) dipped in egg and breadcrumbs and fried

Toriniku no dango chicken dumplings made with minced chicken, mushrooms, scallions, carrots and breadcrumbs and fried

 no nanbanyaki chicken pieces marinated in *mirin*, *sake* and soy sauce, then grilled while being basted with the marinade with added chopped scallions, egg yolk and cayenne pepper

Tsumiire nabe very finely minced chicken mixed with red bean paste stewed with cabbage rolls,

bean curd and leeks in *dashi*, *mirin* and soy sauce

★**Yakitori** pieces of chicken and vegetables skewered in a soy sauce, *mirin*, *sake*, sugar and cayenne pepper marinade — grilled, dipped in the marinade and grilled again, repeatedly

Yosenabe eaten in the same way as *sukiyaki*; chicken, pork, shrimp, bean curd and vegetables are simmered in stock with mixed rice and wheat noodles

Yudebuta pork boiled with ginger and scallions, served cold

Yudōfu eaten in the same way as *sukiyaki*. Bean curd is simmered in seaweed stock with chrysanthemum leaves and mushrooms and dipped in a soy, *mirin*, dried bonito, scallion and ginger sauce. I can't say that I recommend this for beginners

Yasai—Vegetables

Aburage deep-fried bean curd
Aemono salad
Daikon huge white radish
★**Dobin mushi** "teapot-stewed"; shrimp, chicken and mushrooms cooked in a teapot with *dashi*, soy sauce, chrysanthemum leaves and lemon juice. The broth is poured from the pot into bowls
Endō pea
Gobō burdock root
Hakusai Chinese cabbage
 nabe cabbage and vegetable stew with shrimps and ham
Harusame soy bean noodles
Hōrensō spinach
Ingenmame string bean, kidney bean
Jagaimo potato
Kabocha pumpkin, squash
Kikujisha chicory
Kimpira burdock root braised in soy sauce and *mirin* with sugar, oil and cayenne pepper. Can also be made with other roots
Kinoko mushroom
Kinome prickly ash leaf
Kinome-ae salad with *kinome*, cuttlefish, spinach, bamboo shoots, with a bean paste and *dashi* dressing
Kombu seaweed-kelp
Konnyaku devil's tongue, arum root (*Amorphophallus*) from which is made a kind of translucent rice

cake and noodle (see *Shirataki*). Not to be confused with *konyaku*, a promise of marriage
Kyūri cucumber
Matsutake "pine" mushrooms — much-prized forest mushrooms
Menrui noodles
Moyashi beansprouts
Naganegi leeks
Namasu fish salad: raw fish and/or vegetables in vinegar
Nasu eggplant
Ninjin carrot
Nori black, thin seaweed — purple laver
Oden a stew of bean curd, cabbage, cuttlefish, fish, sausage, radish, eggs and *konnyaku*, made with *dashi*, *mirin*, *sake* and soy sauce. Often made with meat balls rather than fish
Renkon lotus root
Sayaingen string bean
Shiitake a dark, strong, dried mushroom
Shirataki noodle made from *konnyaku*
Shira-ae a salad of carrot, *konnyaku*, sesame seed and bean curd
Shungiku chrysanthemum leaves
Soramame fava bean
Takenoko bamboo shoot
Takiawase bamboo shoots mixed with chicken dumplings

Tamanegi onion
Tōfu bean curd
Tomorokoshi corn
Tonasu see *Kabocha*
Udon wheat noodles
    suki a version of *sukiyaki* with

noodles, clams and chicken
Wakame seaweed—lobe-leaf
Warabi edible fern
Yakidōfu grilled bean curd
Yasai moriawase mixed
vegetables

Kudamono—Fruit

Anzu apricots
Ichigo strawberries
Ichijiku figs
Kaki persimmons (not to be
confused with oysters, flowers, or
summer, all called *kaki*)
Kiichigo raspberries

Mikan tangerine
Momo peach
Nashi pear
Remon lemon
Ringo apple
Suika watermelon
Tachibana clementines

Useful words

Ageta fried
Dango dumpling
Fōku fork
Ginnan gingko nut
Ginshi-yaki cooked in foil
Goma sesame seed
Gyūnyū milk
Hashi chopsticks
Karashi mustard
Kohi coffee
Kushi-yaki cooked on a skewer or
spit
Mirin rice wine for cooking
Misozuke pickled in bean paste
Mizu water
Mushi-yaki cooked in a casserole
Naifu knife
Nama raw, fresh, unripe
Ninniku garlic
Nita boiled
Ocha tea, honourable green tea
O-kanjo bill (note the *o-*:
honourable for whom, one
wonders?)
Pan bread
Ponzu sauce made of sour orange
juice, soy sauce and *dashi*
Sake rice wine, drunk warm in
tiny cups. The Japanese are often
amazed at westerners' capacity
for this stuff. Their fat-free diet
makes them more susceptible
Shichimi-tōgarashi a mixed spice
(of variable burning power) made
with poppy seed, rape, hemp and
sesame seeds, dried tangerine peel
and pepper leaf

Shio salt
Shio-yaki method of cooking fish,
first covering it thickly with salt
and leaving it for half an hour,
then grilling it over charcoal
Shōga ginger
Shōyu soy sauce
Su vinegar
Suimono clear soup
Supūn spoon
Takidashi boiling rice (for the
sufferers in an emergency?)
Tamago egg
Tempiyaki shita baked
Teppan-yaki method of grilling
on a hot iron plate, often done
at the table
Teriyaki method of cooking
birds, fish and meat—marinating
the flesh in soy sauce, *mirin* and
sake for half an hour, then
grilling it over charcoal
Tōgarashi chilli or cayenne
pepper
Tsukemono pickles
Tsukeyaki method of cooking—
marinating in soy sauce, *mirin*,
sake, ginger and garlic and then
grilling while basting with the
marinade
Waribashi chopsticks
Wasabi horseradish, very strong
in Japan and soothingly green in
appearance when powdered, so
beware
Yaita grilled
Yaki baking or roasting

Hadakaimasu! bon appétit!
Kanpai! cheers!

Korea

Korean food has a certain amount in common with both Chinese and Japanese, but lacks the variety of the former and the delicacy of the latter.

There are excellent restaurants (*schick dahng*) in the grander hotels of big towns like Seoul, but in smaller towns and particularly in *kisaeng* (the equivalent of the Japanese geisha house) you will find more traditional food.

Bindae tok, bina tok pancakes made from dried green beans, ground and mixed to a batter with eggs and flour

★ **Bulgogi, bul-ko-kee, pul gogi, pul-ko-kee** slices of steak, marinated in a spicy sauce and barbecued at the table over a charcoal fire

Dak jim, tak chim chicken meat with green peppers, mushrooms and gingko nuts, simmered in a stock flavoured with sesame, soy sauce and chilli

★ **Doyaji bulgogi** thin slices of pork marinated in soy sauce, fresh ginger, sesame seed, garlic and sugar, then fried or grilled

Jeotkal a variety of fish—herring, squid, anchovy, etc.—pickled in salt and vinegar. Served cold

Joni gol, juhn kol thinly sliced raw beef steeped in soy sauce, sesame seed and garlic, accompanied by sliced onions, mushrooms and carrots all cooked in broth at the table

Kalbee beef spare ribs, marinated then grilled and served with a sesame seed sauce

Keem chee, kimchee, kim chi pickled vegetables, served with almost every Korean meal. Vegetables (usually Chinese cabbage, white radishes, cucumber or greens) are shredded and seasoned with salt, pepper, garlic, anchovy and chilli

Kong na-mool kuk soup of beansprouts, beef, garlic, sesame seeds and spring onions

Mandoo kuk, man-tu kuk clear beef broth flavoured with soy sauce and sesame seeds served with dumplings stuffed with spiced ground beef and vegetables

Na mool bland vegetable side dishes to counteract spicy food

Saengson-cheem, sansuhn jim fish steamed with vegetables, soy sauce and garlic

Sanki san jok, songi sahn juk strips of beef marinated in soy sauce with scallions, carrot and sesame oil, skewered, dipped in beaten egg and flour and fried

See-kum-chee kuk soup of spinach, cubed beef, garlic, soy sauce and sesame seed

★ **Shinsonro, shinsulro, sin sollo** the Korean "royal casserole"; a meat broth, with seaweed, seafood, boiled eggs and vegetables all cooked at the table

Song Pyun small sweet steamed rice cakes stuffed with a purée of chestnuts and beans

Yachae tweegim spoonfuls of finely sliced potatoes, onion, carrot, sweet peppers and zucchini, mixed into a batter and fried in hot oil

Yookehjang kuk, yukkai jang kuk a soup-stew of beef slices and scallions in a very hot broth flavoured with chilli, garlic and sesame seeds

Useful words

Gaesan bill
Jungjang rice wine
Kook, kuk soup
Mool water

Pahb rice
Pang bread
Saewoo shrimp
Soju spirit similar to vodka

Dubsida! cheers!
Mani duseyo! bon appétit!

Jewish and Israeli food

When Bernard Levin first went to Israel, he let out a wail of despair about the food—"Has no-one in this country got a Jewish mother?"

Jewish food is in fact a tremendous jumble, held together by two themes—the dietary laws and the customs associated with particular ceremonials. In each country where they have settled, the Jews have adapted the native cuisine to conform with the Kosher laws. At the same time, dishes such as *haroset*, *hamantaschen* and *kreplach* are associated with events in Jewish history and are, roughly speaking, universal. The numerous stuffed vegetable dishes, like *holishkes*, celebrate the harvest at *Succot*. An unusual aspect of Jewish cookery is the quantity of slow-cooking dishes, set to cook overnight so as to avoid any work on the Sabbath.

There are two further strands of tradition—the Ashkenazi style, which is more familiar in Britain and America, based mostly on Polish and German cuisine, and Sephardi, based on Spanish and Portuguese.

In the listings I have noted those dishes which have a particular connection with festivals and holy days, naming these in brackets, though nearly all the dishes are eaten throughout the year. I have given the Hebrew names. The English translation or equivalent meanings are: **Chanuka:** The feast of lights; **Pesach:** Passover; **Purim:** The feast of lots; **Rosh Hashanah:** The new year; **Shabbat:** The Sabbath; **Shavuot:** The feast of weeks (Pentecost); **Succot:** Tabernacles (harvest festival).

Basically Israeli dishes are marked thus: (I)

Hors d'oeuvre

Carmel purée (I) avocado puréed with oil, lemon juice and garlic

Felafel (I) deep-fried balls of minced chick peas and spices

Gehakte ayehr hard-boiled eggs chopped and mixed with onions and chicken fat

Gehakte leber pâté of grilled chicken livers minced with hard-boiled eggs and fried onions

Haroset a mixture of grated apples, ground almonds, red wine and spices (Pesach)

Helzel chicken neck stuffed with *matzo meal*, chopped onion and chicken fat, served with gravy

Hirring herring

    gehakte salt herring minced with soaked bread, hard-boiled eggs, onions, apples and spices

gepikilti pickled herrings

    schmaltz sliced herrings sprinkled with lemon juice, chopped scallions and pepper, served on black bread or *challa*

Hummus cooked chick peas puréed with garlic, oil and lemon juice. Served with *pitta*

Salat chatzilim (I) purée of baked eggplant, raw onion, oil, lemon juice and tomato

Tahina (I) sesame seeds blended with oil, lemon juice and garlic to a mayonnaise-like consistency

Toureto (I) purée of cucumber, soaked bread, oil and lemon juice, served chilled with *pitta*

Tsibilis mit ayehr *gehakte ayehr* but with more onions

Soups

Borscht beet soup flavoured with lemon juice and sugar. Sometimes thickened with eggs, served hot with a boiled potato or cold with sour cream

Gilderneh yoich the legendary chicken soup traditionally served every Shabbat

Krupnik mushroom and barley soup

Marak avocado (I) avocado soup
Marak peyrot (I) almost any
variety of chopped fruit cooked
in an orange and lemon juice

stock, thickened with cornstarch
Schav iced sorrel soup garnished
with sliced hard-boiled eggs and
sour cream

Accompaniments

Farfel egg-based dough grated,
dried and cooked in the soup
Knaidlach dumplings of *matzo
meal*, ground almonds, chicken
fat and beaten egg
Kreplach tiny three-cornered
pasties, filled with ground beef.
Said to symbolize the three
Patriarchs, Abraham, Isaac and

Jacob (Rosh Hashanah)
Lokshen egg noodles
Mandeln egg-based dough
enriched with oil and fried or
baked to a crispness before being
dropped into the soup
Triflach similar to *farfel* only
lighter and fluffier due to a higher
proportion of egg

Main dishes

Charshofay natseret (I) artichokes
stuffed with ground lamb, pine
nuts and spices
Cholent slow-cooked brisket with
butter beans, pearl barley and
potatoes (Shabbat)
Gedempfteh fleisch heavily spiced
slow-cooked beef stew
Gefillte fish balls of minced fish,
chopped onion, *matzo meal*, egg
and flavourings simmered in a
fish stock, fried or baked
Gikochteh hindel chicken stewed
with onions and paprika
Holishkes ground beef wrapped

in cabbage leaves and braised in
a sweet and sour sauce (Succot)
Of sum-sum (I) chicken coated
in sesame seeds and fried in oil
Perogen ground beef pies
Petcha jellied calf's foot
Sweet and sour halibut poached
halibut in an egg and lemon sauce
Tzimmes slow-cooked casserole
of brisket sweetened with carrots
and golden syrup, prunes or
dried fruit and topped with
potatoes and dumplings (Rosh
Hashanah)
Würst lightly spiced lean salami

Vegetables and salads

Chatzilim be'agvaniot (I) slices of
eggplant dipped in batter, fried
till crisp and served in a spicy,
garlic-flavoured tomato sauce
Kartoffel kugel mashed potatoes
mixed with chopped onion,
chicken fat and eggs, baked
Latkes pancakes of grated raw
potato fried until crisp and
golden and garnished in a variety
of ways. They can also be made
with *matzo meal* fried in a light
egg batter (Chanucah)
Levivot halamit (I) chopped wild
mallow (or spinach) mixed with
flour and eggs and fried
Mayeren Kugel pudding of grated
carrots, *matzo meal*, raisins,

dates, sugar and spices (Pesach)
Salat hadarim ve'avocado (I)
segments of *pomela*, grapefruit
and orange mixed with slices of
avocado pear, topped with a ball
of cottage cheese and sprinkled
with lemon juice and sugar
Salat hakibbutznikim (I) salad
composed of finely chopped raw
vegetables, hard-boiled eggs,
yoghurt, cottage cheese, sour
cream, herbs and a variety of
dressings. This salad originated
on the *kibbutzim*, where it was
eaten for breakfast
Tfihat kishuim (I) vegetable
squash soufflé

Desserts and sweets

Apfelshalet deep-spiced apple
pudding
Blintzes pancakes filled with a

rich cottage cheese mixture
(Shavuot)
Cheesecake rich sweetened cream

cheese filling on a pastry, sponge or biscuit-crumb base (Shavuot)
Gugelhupf yeast cake
Hafta'aht solet (I) semolina and citrus juice whip
Haman's ears deep-fried ear-shaped pastries (Purim)
Hamantaschen meaning "Haman's purses"; little three-cornered cakes symbolizing the downfall of Haman, who planned the massacre of the Jews in Persia in the fourth century. The cakes are stuffed with a wine and walnut, poppy seed, apple, apricot or prune mix (Purim)
Ingberlach confection of carrots cooked to a pulp with sugar, ginger, almonds and lemon juice (Pesach)
Kos-anavim vemilon (I) fruit cup of green and black grapes and water-melon and honeydew melon balls dressed with honey, lemon and pomegranate seeds
Lekach honey and spice cake (Rosh Hashanah)

Lokshen Kugel egg noodles baked in a custard base (Shavuot)
Mandelbrot spongy almond cake
Miktzefet limon (I) lemon snow
Mohnlach honey, almond and poppy seed candies (Purim)
Mohn Torte poppy seed cake
Plava fatless sponge (Pesach)
Pletzlach squares of heavily sweetened, cooked, pulped apricots (or plums) (Pesach)
Prelato sponge finger made with potato flour—eaten at Passover
Rafrefet hadagan (I) pudding of cornstarch, orange juice and eggs
Shabbas-kugel a kind of bread and butter pudding with chicken fat instead of the butter, and diced fresh fruit and spices
Strudel crisp buttery pastry rolled around a variety of fillings such as spiced apple, cherry, dried fruit and chopped nuts or sweetened cream cheese (Succot)
Tayglach plaited dough pieces cooked in syrup or honey

Useful words (Jewish)

Bagel crusty bread ring
Bulkes fruit and nut buns
Challa traditional Shabbat plaited loaf
Charain horseradish mixed with chopped, cooked beet

Kichel crisp, slightly sweet biscuit
Matzo flat unleavened bread
Matzo meal *matzo* ground to a powder, used as flour
Pampalik flat onion bread
Schmaltz chicken fat (rendered)

Useful words (Israeli)

Basar meat
Beitzim eggs
Chatzilim eggplants
Dagim fish
Gvina cheese
Heshbon bill
Leben yoghurt
Lechem bread
Mayim water

Ofot poultry
Pitta flat, hollow bread
Pomela cross-bred citrus fruit
Salatim salad
Tafrit menu
Tahina sesame paste
Yayin wine
Yerakot vegetables
Zeitim olives

Lehitraot! cheers!
Bete-avon! bon appétit!

Jordan—*See* Arab food
Korea—*See* Japan and Korea
Lebanon—*See* Arab food
Luxembourg—*See* Belgium
Malaysia—*See* Southeast Asia

Mexico

Mexican cuisine is, at its finest, one of the most interesting in the world. When the Spanish arrived, there was already a thriving Aztec and Mayan cuisine, based on the abundant and immensely varied produce of the country. A contemporary account says: "For Montezuma were daily cooked hens, cocks, pheasants, partridges, quails, ducks, deer, porcupines, small birds, doves, hares, rabbits and many kinds of fowl and things that grow on this land, so many that I would never end mentioning them." So many things which we now take for granted were unknown to the Spaniards but normal in Amerindian cooking: vanilla, turkey, potatoes, tomatoes, chocolate and above all, corn.

I have an entirely unsubstantiated theory that there may have been some ancient connection between Oriental cooking and that of the Aztecs. The two have so many ingredients in common. The tortilla in which the Mexican wraps food is identical (apart from the grain used) with the pancakes used to roll up Peking duck. The Mexican hairless dog, being vegetarian, would be perfectly edible (though I have to admit they do not eat it now). The Mexicans eat raw fish, like the Japanese, and custard cubes in soup (though the Japanese make their *tofu* with beans).

However that may be, Aztec cuisine was sufficiently sophisticated for it to have joined Spanish cuisine as an equal partner and for many of its constituents to have survived unchanged until today. The famous *moles*, sauces made with hot peppers and chocolate, are purely Aztec, the word deriving from the Aztec for chilli sauce — *molli*. The tortilla (the object, not the name, of course) was Indian, the *pibil* or baking pit, a myriad of corn dishes—all these survive. In many ways Mexico retained what it took from Spain (so many dishes, if not here, may be in the Spanish section). Then with the Emperor Maximilian in 1865 came a strong, new French influence, contributing to the variety of Mexican food.

The only trouble with traditional Mexican cooking is that it is labour intensive. A proper *mole poblano*, with everything ground by hand and prepared according to the old rules, takes three days to make. I have had quails which have been lightly steamed for fourteen hours. True Mexican cuisine is much concerned with texture and this is a manual demand. The heavy handed can ruin Mexican dishes by overdoing the chillis, which is why they have a reputation for being hot.

The Mexican love of food is evidenced by the number of times they eat every day. They have breakfast (*desayuno*) early, often not at home but in a hotel or club or, in the case of poets, in the market where you can buy gruel (*atoles*), *tacos*, *enchiladas* and fruit. At 11 a.m. they have a snack (*el antojo*), a kind of sandwich (*tortas*) and *tacos*. At noon another snack and a drink (*la botana y la copa*). Coffee with more *tortas* and *tacos*. Lunch (*el almuerzo*) can be at any time from 1 p.m. till 4 p.m. when it will turn into supper. Most people, however, eat at about 2 or 3 p.m. What kind of lunch will, in Mexico City, depend on the type of restaurant you choose, ranging from a *tacos* stall to a high-class, largely French restaurant. If you are lucky, at about 5 p.m. there is chocolate time (*el chocolate* or *merienda*), now rather out of fashion, but it is the time to try sweet *tamales* and all those sticky cakes as well as drinking chocolate. Dinner (*la cena*) is at any time after 8 p.m.

Entremeses—Hors d'oeuvre

Aguacates encamaronados avocado with shrimps

Apios rellenos celery sticks, stuffed with a mixture of cream cheese, blue cheese and ground almonds

Cacahuetes peanuts roasted or simmered with chilli, garlic, coarse salt and oil

★ **Ceviche acapulqueño** raw fish or shellfish (often scallops) marinated in lime juice, mixed with chilli, onion, tomato, salt, oregano and olive oil, served with slices of avocado or peppers

Guacamole a thick sauce made with mashed avocados, lime juice, chilli and herbs. Used as a sauce for meat, a filling for tortillas or in the United States as a dip for snacks

Huevos moldrados poached eggs served cold in custard made with beef stock, egg and *poblano* chillis

Jitomates rellenos stuffed tomatoes

Mariscos scallop or shrimp cocktail

Panuchos see *Corn*

Pico de gallo sliced *jicamas*, cucumbers, oranges, limes and alligator pears with *piquín* chillis

Semillas tostadas de calabaza roasted pumpkin seeds

Sopas—Soups

Soups in Mexico can be either what you would expect from a soup, or a *sopa seca*, dry soup, which really means a rice, pasta or corn dish.

Arroz blanco a la mexicana plain white risotto

  con pollo chicken risotto with saffron and peppers

  con puerco pork risotto with vegetables and *poblano* chilli

  verde see *Sopa seca de arroz*

Caldo espinazo pork chine consommé

  largo tomato and green pepper soup with diced cheese

  xochitl beef broth with *ancho* chilli, rice and chick peas, flavoured with tomato and coriander

Frituras de árroz rice and ham rissoles

Menudo tripe and corn kernel (hominy) soup, with onion and coriander

Pozole see *Corn*

Sopa de aguacate cream of avocado soup, flavoured with sherry, served hot or cold

  de albóndigas meat balls in broth, with *ancho* chilli, vegetables and rice, flavoured with lime

  de Apatzingán melon, potato and egg soup

  de elote molido see *Corn*

  de flor de calabaza con flan de elote creamy pumpkin flower soup with diced baked custard made with corn

  de frijoles negros black bean soup, with chopped vegetables and diced ham

  de Guadalajara a huge soup of pork, red beans, carrots and whole corn on the cob, with garlic, herbs and powdered chilli

  de huitlacoche see *Corn*

  de Jericalla cubes of baked custard in a beef broth

  de lechuga broth thickened with tomato and onion sauce, served with a diced lettuce tortilla in it

  ★ **de lima** lime soup, but in Yucatán, a chicken liver soup flavoured with sour limes

  de poro y papa leek and potato soup

  de tallarines verdes strips of a pasta made with spinach and lettuce in meat broth

  estilo Puebla a pleasant vegetable soup, served with grated cheese and diced avocado

  seca de arroz a risotto with onions, tomatoes, medium hot green peppers and olives

  seca de tortillas see *Corn*

  seca de tortuga layers of toast and thickened turtle stew, baked in the oven

  sonorense see *Corn*

  tabasqueña tapioca and bean soup

Elote—Corn

Corn or Indian corn or sweetcorn is the staple grain of Mexico. It is used to make *tortillas, enchiladas, tacos,* hominy and *pozole* and has many other uses in the kitchen. I have therefore gathered most dishes made with corn into a separate section here.

Budín de elote a creamy corn pudding served with meat

Burritos a soft tortilla, folded to enclose a filling—usually cheese and bean or eggs scrambled with chilli

★**Chalupas** "narrow boats"; tortillas, curled up at the edges, with a ground pork filling covered in a green tomato and chilli sauce

Chilaquiles layers of fried tortillas, beans, ham, chicken and tomato sauce and cheese, baked. Reputedly good as a cure for hangovers

Chimichangas a large tortilla folded with a filling and deep fried

Dedos de charro special tortillas rolled up with pork, *pasilla, ancho* and *mulato* chillis, fried and then baked in cream

★**Enchiladas** fried tortillas, rolled round any of a hundred different fillings, of which I list a few of the better varieties. Enchiladas should not be crisp as they are rolled after frying, not fried already filled

    de Acapulco turkey, olives and almonds

    de jocoque cheese, sour cream and scallion

    de pollo de Uruapán cheese with chicken legs on top

    de puerco dobladas pork and chillis, folded rather than rolled

    rojas *ancho* chillis, cinnamon and chocolate

    verdes *poblano* chillis and green tomatoes

Enrollados much the same as *enchiladas*

Flautas a sandwich of tortilla with a filling, rolled up and deep fried

Gorditas potato and cornmeal dough mixed with cheese and fried in sausage shapes, served with ground pork and guacamole

Panuchos fried tortillas, with a mixture of black-bean paste and ground pork with chilli, in a hot sauce

Pastel de pobre see *Sopa seca de tortillas*

Pozole skimmed corn kernels (hominy) and pork soup

Quesadillas tube or crescent-shaped tortillas made with chillis, filled with cheese (and often chillis) and deep fried

    de huitlacoche a folded tortilla with a filling of fungus which grows on green corn cobs—sounds grim but is wonderful

Sopa de elote molido corn soup

    ★**de huitlacoche** a black soup made with the fungus grown on green corn cobs

    seca de tortillas layers of tortillas with a mixture of chillis, cream, onions, tomato paste and grated cheese in between, baked in the oven

    sonorense corn soup (from Sonora), with diced peppers and chilli

Sopes a tortilla sandwich of beans and cheese, served with sausage

★**Tacos** properly means a snack, and is applied to almost any filling in a folded tortilla. In the United States it means a crisply fried tortilla filled with meat and spices

★**Tamales** small parcels of corn dough and a filling, wrapped in corn husks and steamed. The filling may be of turkey, chicken or meat with *mole poblano* or other sauce. There are also sweet *tamales* made with almonds and raisins

Tortillas flat pancakes made only with cornmeal flour, water and salt. They were a major ingredient of the original Aztec cuisine. Sometimes *ancho* chillis are ground in with the flour, as for *quesadillas* and *sopes*. They have no connection with the omelettes of Spain, which are known as *tortillas de huevos* (egg pancakes)

Platos principales—Main dishes

Adobo de pescado a casserole of red snapper with tomatoes, *ancho* chillis and spices

★**Amarillito** a yellow stew from Oaxaca—chicken or pork stewed with green tomatoes, green pumpkins and very hot chillis

Bandera de frijoles layers of mashed beans and stewed pork, garnished with strips of avocado, cheese and red peppers, to represent the Mexican flag (red, white and green)

Bistec de Jalisco beef steak flavoured with orange juice

Buñuelos de Tabasco nothing to do with tabasco sauce. Rice and egg fritters, served with honey

Calabacitas a la mexicana diced pork and baby squash with corn and chillis

Caldo miche catfish stewed with tomatoes, chillis, herbs and sliced greengages

Camarones en frío fried shrimps in a vinegar, oil and chilli dressing, served cold with sliced onions, tomatoes and hot *jalapeño* chillis

Cangrejos horneados baked crab

Carne asada this will appear on many menus and may just mean roast meat or thin strips of loin of pork or beef, marinated in vinegar, oil and oregano, grilled and served with a chunky tomato, onion and green pepper sauce (*salsa fresca*)

most famous versions of stuffed peppers—with ground pork, onions and almonds, covered with a walnut, cheese and spice sauce, garnished with pomegranate seeds

rellenos sweet peppers or mildly hot chillis may be stuffed with almost anything. The most common form is with a meat *picadillo*. Other usual ones are *de elote*, with corn; *de frijoles* with beans; *estilo arriero*, with peas, tomatoes and cheese

★**Cochinita pibil** a pig stuffed with oranges, chillis and annato, wrapped in banana leaves, traditionally baked in a hole in the ground (*pibil*). Served with Ixnipec sauce—a Mayan sauce of fiery *habanero* chillis, tomatoes and sour orange juice

★**Coloradito** a red stew from Oaxaca—chicken or pork and *ancho* chillis stewed with tomatoes and red peppers

Conejo alcaparrado rabbit stew with tomatoes, potatoes, peas and a lot of capers

almendrado rabbit stew with tomatoes, potatoes, peas and a lot of ground almonds

Estofado de res beef stew, with potatoes and *poblano* chillis

Frijoles refritos boiled beans mashed and fried with *piquín* chillis; a standard filling for *tortas, tacos*, etc.; also served rolled with cheese on top

---

Abstain from beans.
Pythagoras

---

picada con rajas ground beef with sliced *poblano* chillis and potatoes

Chilaquiles see *Corn*

Chile con carne an American dish but, like chop suey in Hong Kong, it is slowly creeping into Mexico. The Mexicans improve the basic mixture of ground beef, red beans, tomatoes and chillis with spices and serve it with avocado and coriander

verde sweet peppers and other green chillis in a meat stew

★**Chiles en nogada** one of the

★**Guajolote relleno de gala** a turkey smeared with a herb and vinegar paste, stuffed with ham, dried fruit, almonds, nuts, candied peel, olives and chillis, and stewed in wine and stock

Guisado de huesitos stew of "small bones", involving calf's foot, pigs' feet, oxtail, chicken wings, beans, avocados, and *chilacas* (long yellow chillis)

Huevos rancheros tortillas, with fried, poached or scrambled eggs, covered with any of a dozen sauces, usually quite hot

Jaibas en chilpachole fried crabmeat in tomato sauce with *cuaresmeño* chillis and saltwort

Lengua de res con salsa de chipotle boiled ox tongue simmered with tomatoes and *chipotle* chillis

nitrada rellena tongue pickled with saltpetre, cleaned, stuffed with ham, pork and much else, boiled with herbs, pressed and served cold with orange aspic

Lomo de cerdo adobado pork loin stewed with chilli, spices and herbs

prepared sauce which at the end is thick and dark brown. Turkey is the traditional meat for *mole poblano (de Guajolote)* but the same sauce is used with chicken or pork. *Mole* is one of the world's greatest gastronomic creations. It is the chocolate that makes it so magical though one would be hard put to isolate its taste. In the days before blenders, a good cook would require three days' notice to make a *mole*. Now it comes in packets

---

. . . a milk shop under its sign *Lecheria* (brothel, someone insisted it meant, and she hadn't seen the joke), dark interiors with strings of tiny sausages, chorizos, hanging over the counters where you could also buy goat cheese or sweet quince wine or cacao . . .
Malcolm Lowry *Under the Volcano*

---

de puerco mechado pork cut with deep gashes filled with herbs, spices and chopped ham, stewed with mashed tomatoes

★**Mancha manteles de cerdo** literally "pork which stains the tablecloth"; pork stewed with herbs, covered with a mixture of fruits and green vegetables and simmered in a sauce of walnuts, green tomatoes and *ancho*, *mulato* and *pasilla* chillis

Maneas tabasqueñas *tamales* of pork, cornmeal flour and *serrano* chillis, wrapped in banana leaves and steamed

Mitos *frijoles refritos*, rolled up with sardines and fried

★**Mole** strictly speaking means a sauce, coming from the Aztec word *molli* (a chilli sauce), but it is also used in the names of dishes, in particular *mole poblano*, which is virtually Mexico's national dish. The *mole* for this is extremely elaborate. It requires three kinds of chilli—*ancho*, *mulato* and *pasilla*—almonds, onions, green tomatoes, raisins, sesame seeds, pumpkin seeds, garlic, cinnamon, cloves, coriander seeds, aniseed, black peppercorns, shredded tortilla and chocolate. All the hard ingredients are pounded until they are finely powdered, so that the sauce is infinitely smooth. The already cooked turkey is simmered in the

verde as with *mole poblano*, this is usually made with turkey, but chicken or pork can be used. The sauce is made with green tomatoes, onions, pumpkin seeds, walnuts, almonds and *poblano* chillis, so it is quite mild

Ostiones en escabeche cooked oysters, pickled in vinegar with slices of *jalapeño* chillis served on their shells on green-coloured ice

Pastel de Montezuma layers of turkey in a green tomato sauce, of shredded tortilla and of roughly grated cheese, baked

Pavo con fruta pieces of turkey, simmered with sausage, *ancho* and *pasilla* chillis, almonds, cinnamon and fruit

Pescado a la jarocha baked fish with mayonnaise, cream, parsley and olives

a la poblana baked fish with peas, scallions and mayonnaise

a la veracruzana red snapper simmered with tomatoes, olives, capers and *jalapeño* chillis

Yucateco red snapper baked with olives, red peppers, coriander and fruit juice

Pez espada al horno a la manzanilla swordfish baked with masses of scallions

★**Pichones a la antigua** squab stew with tomatoes, peas, almonds and ham, flavoured with sherry

encebollados squab stew, with onions, carrots and turnips flavoured with white wine

en tres pozuelos squab stewed with bacon, onions, chocolate and sherry

Pierna de cordero estilo Yucateco leg of lamb stuffed with orange and corn breadcrumbs, smeared with *achiote*, and roasted

★**Pipián** chicken, with a sesame seed and pumpkin seed sauce

de camarones shrimp with a pumpkin seed, coriander seed, tomato and *piquín* chilli sauce

Pollo borracho cut up chicken stewed with onion, tomato, *chipotle* chilli, herbs and *pulque*

bravo chicken stewed with red and green tomatoes, peas and *piquín* chilli. Ferociously hot

con gabardina chicken fried in batter

con naranjas chicken braised with oranges, onion, garlic, cinnamon, cloves, capers and saffron

elegante not so elegant; chicken on lettuce covered in white sauce, sprinkled with peas, surrounded with mashed potatoes

encebollado chicken stewed with onions, green peppers, *serrano* chillis and olives

en salsa chicken stewed with red peppers, *ancho* chillis and spices. Fairly hot

mariscala chicken stewed in a chicken liver and garlic sauce

verde chicken in a thick green pea sauce

★**Puchero** a Yucatán hot pot, rather like a Spanish soup-stew.

Into the pot go beef, pork, a chicken, chick peas, potatoes, sundry vegetables, fruit and corn cobs. When cooked, the solid ingredients are taken out and served as a main course, preceded by the soup

Puerco perdigado con salsa de chile rojo braised pork with red chilli sauce

Rollo de carne a roll of ground beef, stuffed with vegetables, chopped ham and spices, and boiled

Tamal de cazuela pork chops baked between two layers of cornmeal dough with an *ancho* and *mulato* chilli sauce, flavoured with *acuyo* leaves

Tapado de pollo cut up chicken and bits of pork in a casserole with raisins, almonds, olives, cinnamon and cloves

Tinga de cerdo y ternera diced pork and veal stewed with green tomatoes and *chipotle* chillis

Tortilla de huevos Spanish omelette

Tortillas de huevo Maya scrambled eggs, rolled in tortillas with pumpkin seed sauce, grilled

Tortitas de bacalao salt cod in batter

Venado en pipián venison stewed with pumpkin seeds, tomatoes, annatto, green plums, chillis and saltwort leaves

★**Zik de venado** a cold Yucatán dish of venison cooked in a hole in the ground, shredded and served with chopped coriander, onions, sour oranges and *serrano* chillis

Postres—Puddings

Mexican puddings are no great shakes—mostly custards, sponges and syrupy cakes. Usually the Mexicans eat fruit, of which there is an amazing variety, much being unfamiliar and exciting. From this range of fruit they make wonderful fruit salads and exquisite sorbets.

Arroz con leche rice pudding flavoured with cinnamon

Buñuelos de plátano banana fritters

Calabaza enmielada pumpkin cooked in a syrup of dark brown Mexican sugar (*piloncillo*)

Capirotada baked bread pudding with cinnamon and nuts

Cocada coconut custard

Chayote relleno tropical squash stuffed with a sweet mixture of cake, its own flesh, raisins, eggs and sherry

Chongos lemon and cinnamon custard squares set quite hard. They taste slightly sour, so may sometimes be served in a sweet syrup

Churros pastry spirals, fried
Dulce de elote green corn stewed
with milk and sugar
Flan cream caramel
Huevos reales baked custard
squares in a sherry syrup
Leche quemada see *Arroz con leche*
Panetelas en leche de coco
pancakes with coconut milk
Pioquinto yet another almond,
sherry and cinnamon dessert
Postre de yema entera sponge

cake with a thick, spiced custard
especial trifle
Queso de almendra soft almond
biscuits
Torta reyna a very sticky
pudding of biscuits soaked in
syrup and sherry in layers with
prunes and dates
Yemitas de mi bisabuela egg yolks
cooked with sherry in a thick
syrup, made into small balls and
rolled in sugar and cinnamon

Useful words

Achiote annatto; Yucatec
bright orange spice and colouring
Atole a gruel made with cornmeal
Café coffee: *café de olla* is sweet
brewed coffee in a clay pot often
sold at stalls
Caguama sea-turtle
Camote sweet potato
Cerveza beer, not bad
Chile there are about 150 kinds of
peppers grown in Mexico, ranging
from the tame pimiento (sweet
pepper, bell pepper, red pepper,
green pepper or whatever you
happen to call it) to the ferociously
hot chilli called *serrano*, a tiny
green one which turns red as it
ripens. Some names of chillis you
may come across in Mexico or
the United States are: *ancho,*
brown, largish, heart-shaped, mild
pepper; *fresno*, pretty hot;
jalapeño, green, fairly hot;
güero (or Californian) greeny-
yellow medium; *pasilla*, brown,
pretty hot; *chipotle*, dark red,
very hot; *hontaka*, small, red
wizened, very hot; *poblano*, large
dark green, mild; *malagueta*,
small, green or red, very hot;
mulato, brown, large, hot; *piquín*,
dark green, very small, very hot
Codornices quails
Criadillas bull's testicles, often
served with turkey; sometimes
coyly translated as "mountain
oysters"
Gusanos de maguey grubs which
feed off the *maguey* cactus, said

to be delicious to eat
Horchata sweet, melon-seed drink
Huachinango red snapper
Jicama a root vegetable looking
somewhat like a turnip but crisp
Jitomates what we call tomatoes.
See *Tomates*
Licuados fruit squashes
Limas limes
Masa harina corn flour from
which tortillas are made
Mescal spirit distilled from the
maguey cactus
en Nogada in a walnut sauce
Nopalitos cactus leaves, often in
salads
Pibil a hole in the ground for
cooking meat; the method half
cooks and half smokes the meat
Picadillo a beef, almond, tomato
and spice stuffing
Piña pineapple
Plátanos bananas, often served as
a vegetable
Pulque a weak alcoholic drink
made from the fermented sap of
maguey cactus, tastes rotten; an
original Aztec drink
Té tea
   de manzanilla camomile tea
Tequila distilled from the root of a
plant similar to the *maguey*,
usually about 80° proof. Tequila
is a town in Jalisco where the
drink is made
Tomates, tomatillos a small kind of
tomato, green and sharp in taste
Tunas prickly pears
   xoconoxtles alligator pears

¡**Salud!** cheers!
¡**Buen provecho!** bon appétit!

Morocco — *See* **Arab food**

The Netherlands

I have long believed that one can get along perfectly well in Holland simply by speaking broad Yorkshire. Koop o' tay, you say, and sure enough you get a cup of tea. Nevertheless, I have included a short list of Dutch dishes just in case.

The Dutch are tremendous eaters but Dutch cuisine is not particularly interesting or full of unexpected tastes. It is generous and wholesome. Dutch dairy products are superb, their herrings are a delight and in better restaurants one can find things that have virtually disappeared from other European tables, such as snipe and woodcock.

Apart from traditional Dutch food, there is now a powerful Indonesian influence, with restaurants all over the country. For these it would be better to refer to the Indonesian section.

The Dutch maintain that they eat only one meal a day. Breakfast, of course, does not count and will consist only of cheese, ham, salami, eggs, possibly a steak, rolls and jam, chocolate vermicelli and other such fripperies. You can have a full lunch, but many restaurants serve what is called *koffietafel* (coffee table) with nothing more than soup, a few shrimp, meat croquettes, a bit of cold ham, beef, chicken or pork, a pâté, some pumpernickel and a little currant bread, rounded off with some cheese and fruit. Besides the restaurants, you may lunch at a *broodjeswinkel* or sandwich shop, where you can get sandwiches with a cup of coffee.

The real meal of the day is dinner, which they eat early compared with other European nations. (Well, they are hungry, poor things, with only little snacks all day.)

The most sensible thing to drink with Dutch food is beer, with the exception of raw herrings, which need *jenever* (the aromatic original of gin). There are various "ladies'" versions, flavoured with fruits, which are interesting to try. Advocaat, served in Holland in glasses and eaten with a spoon, is as nasty in its homeland as it is in bottles here. The fruit brandies, though sweet, are first class.

Aal gestoofd eel stewed with herbs and wine

Aardappelsoep potato soup

Appeltaart tart with apples, white raisins, cinnamon and grated lemon rind with a lattice of pastry on top

Arnhemse meisjes small puff pastry cakes. A speciality of Arnhem

Bami goreng an Indonesian (qv) dish of fried noodles with chicken, garlic, vegetables and chilli

Beschuit hard rusk very popular for breakfast and at lunch as part of the *koffietafel*

Biefstuk beef steak, usually eaten very rare

Bitterballen a mixture of jellied stock, béchamel sauce, chopped chicken and ham, formed into small balls, coated with egg and breadcrumbs and deep fried. Served as a snack with *jenever*

Bleufort a creamy blue-veined cheese

★**Bocrenkool met worst** casserole of curly kale and potatoes with smoked sausage

Bokking salted smoked herring

Botermoppen vanilla-flavoured butter biscuits

Broodje sandwich

half om a combination of liver and salt meat served in a sandwich

tartare raw hamburger on a soft bun

warm vlees hot meat sandwich covered with heavy brown gravy and eaten with a knife and fork

Chocolade hagelslag very thin strands of chocolate eaten on bread and butter or cake, traditionally at breakfast or lunch

Drie in de pan literally "three in the pan". Pancakes with dried fruit, fried and sugared

Edammer kaas Edam semi-hard cheese (its familiar red wax coating is used only for export, so do not be surprised if it comes naked)

Eierpannekoeken large pancakes

★**Erwtensoep** thick pea soup made from dried peas, rich pork stock, onions and thyme. Often served with pieces of smoked sausage, cubes of pork fat, pig's hock and slices of brown and white bread

Filosoof 'philosopher's dish''; ground meat, onion and mashed potato casserole, baked

Flensjes a stack of pancakes layered with jam or apple or rhubarb purée

Fricandel croquette of ground meat with onions and herbs

Friese kaas cheese spiced with cloves. Rather horrid

Gebakken zeetong fried sole

Gehaktballetjes small meat balls

Gerookte paling smoked eel

Gestoofde bieten stewed beets

Goudse kaas Gouda cheese made from whole milk. Usually with a yellow wax coating

Groentensoep a consommé with vegetables and small meat balls

Haagse bluf a fluffy dessert of red-currant juice, sugar and egg white

Hachee meat stew (usually beef or veal) with potatoes, numerous onions and red cabbage

Ham rauwe raw ham. May be smoked. Served in very thin slices

★**Haring** herring. Raw herring is served from street stalls and is traditionally held up by the tail and eaten "head first" (although the head is removed). Often dipped in a bowl of sliced onion before eating

   groene or **nieuwe** the first (or green) herring of the season. Available from late May to July

Haringsla mixed herring salad

Hutspot met klapstuk casserole of potatoes, carrots and onions with beef

Jachtschotel a "hunter's dish" of cubed meats, fried apples and onions, casseroled. Served with mashed potatoes

Jan in de zak "John in the sack"; steamed pudding with molasses. It used to be made in a pillow-case

Kaasfondue cheese fondue made with kirsch

Kaassouffle a cheese croquette. Fried quickly so that the inside remains as a liquid egg and cheese mix. Eaten as an hors d'oeuvre

Kapucijners marrowfat peas with boiled potatoes, chunks of stewed beef, fried bacon cubes, fried onion, raw onion, dill pickles and mustard pickles

Kernhemsekaas a round, flat cheese

Kerstkransjes Christmas butter biscuits flavoured with vanilla

Kippensoep a thick soup of chicken and vegetables

Korstjes spiced bread sticks

Koude schotel literally "cold cuts". Describes the variety of meats served at breakfast or at lunch for the *koffietafel*

Kruidkoek spiced bread

Lamsvlees Texel lamb from the Friesland Islands. Considered the best home-reared lamb

★**Leidse kaas** Leiden cheese flavoured with cummin or caraway seeds

Lekkerbekjes fried whiting

Limburgse vlaai pastry flan filled with fruit, such as black cherries soaked in cherry brandy

Maatje same as *Haring*

★**Nasi goreng** an Indonesian (qv) dish of beef and fried rice spiced with soya sauce and shrimp paste and often garnished with a chopped omelette. Accompanied by beer and shrimp chips

Oliebollen yeast-based dough with currants, candied peel and apple, deep fried and served hot with a dusting of icing sugar. Traditional at New Year's Eve and on fairground stalls

Palingbrood roll stuffed with eel

Pannekoek pancake

Peperkoek gingerbread

Poffertjes kind of doughnut

Rodekool spiced red cabbage

Roereiren scrambled eggs

Rolpens met rodekool thin slices of spiced, pickled beef and tripe sautéed in butter, topped with sliced apple and served with red cabbage

Russisch ei Russian egg. Hard-boiled egg dressed with mayonnaise, shrimps, anchovies and cold vegetables

Speculaas biscuits spiced with cinnamon, nutmeg, ginger and cardamon, often fashioned into windmill shapes

Spekkoek alternate layers of butter sponge and spices. The name means "bacon cake" and comes from its streaky bacon-like appearance

Spekpannekoek a large pancake filled with grilled streaky bacon and drenched with apple syrup or molasses

Stamppot potatoes, turnips, kale, etc., puréed and served with smoked sausage

Stokvis dried cod cooked in milk,

drained and served with potatoes, rice, fried and raw onion, dill pickles and mustard sauce

Stroopwafels waffles fried in butter and smothered with syrup

Suikerbrood sweet bread

Uitsmijter a slice of bread topped with ham and fried eggs

Vlaai pastry tart filled with fresh fruit in season and cream

Vleeswaren cold meats. Part of the lunch *koffietafel*

Zuurkool sauerkraut. Often served with streaky bacon, ham steak and sausage

Useful words

Appelmoes apple sauce
Azijn vinegar
Bief beef
Bier beer
Borrel a shot of *jenever*
Boter butter
Brood bread
Eend duck
Eethuisje eating place
Ei (Eieren) egg(s)
Gebakken fried
Gebraden roast
Gekookt boiled
Gerookt smoked
Geroosterd grilled
Gevuld stuffed
Groenten vegetables
Havermout pap oatmeal porridge
Hersenen brains
Houtsnip woodcock
Ijs ice-cream
Kaas cheese
Kabeljauw cod
Kalfsvlees veal
Kalkoen turkey
Kersen cherries
Kip chicken

Koffie coffee
Konijn rabbit
Kool cabbage
Kopstoot glass of beer with a glass of *jenever*
Koud cold
Kreeft lobster
Lever liver
Melk milk
Niertjes kidneys
Rekening bill
Room cream
Rijst rice
Rijsttafel "rice table" with various dishes
Sla salad or lettuce
Snip snipe
Spek bacon
Suiker sugar
Thee tea
Tong sole
Uien onions
Varkensvlees pork
Vis fish
Vruchtensap fruit juice
Wijn wine
Wild game

Gezondheid! cheers!
Smakelijk eten! bon appétit!

New Zealand—*See* Australia
Norway—*See* Scandinavia
Oman—*See* Arab food
Pakistan—*See* India
Peru—*See* South America
The Philippines—*See* Southeast Asia
Poland—*See* Eastern Europe

Portugal

Asked to name half a dozen Portuguese dishes, most people would get stuck after *bacalhau* (salt cod) and *feijão* (bean stew). The fact is that it is rather dull stuff. Portuguese cookery, with its dismal quality, is not helped by generations of poverty. One imagines that all those exiled kings must have eaten something more interesting than the strictly peasant cuisine of their country of refuge. Doubtless, they imported their own customs.

That said, peasant cuisines have always, of course, the great advantages of honesty and simplicity. They make what they can of local produce and do not muck about with a lot of ingredients which they do not understand. Much of Portugal is poor land—scrubby in the north-east, scorched in the south. The answer to both problems is pigs. Suckling pig in Portugal is quite excellent. Portugal's other great asset is the sea. In the north-west, fish is abundant and there are several interesting dishes of lamprey. In Estremadura, the most prosperous region of Portugal, the lobsters are superb. There is also a certain amount of beef here, but it is inclined to be tough, which may account for the excessive number of stews which feature in Portuguese cooking.

The things to look for, then, are the simply cooked plain things: the roast pig, the grilled fish, the fresh vegetables, the partridges and the rest of the game.

While few people know anything about Portuguese cooking, everyone knows about Portuguese wine. Port is one of the world's great wines. The British, however, may be surprised to find that in Portugal itself they pay less attention to vintage port than they do to tawny port. As one maker put it to me, "Vintage port is an act of God, but tawny is the product of our skill and knowledge spread over forty years." Tawny port is made by judicious blending and maturing of port in the wood over many years and I would recommend any visitor to Portugal to try it—the older the better. The table wines of Portugal are not great travellers, with the exception of *Mateus Rosé,* which travels altogether too far. When Sacheverell Sitwell discovered this innocent little vineyard some 30 years ago I imagine it produced a charming wine and 5,000 bottles a year. Today a million bottles a week of rather sickly, carbonated pink stuff are sold all over the world under this name. But in Portugal you will find some wonderful wine—notably the very dry *vinho verde* (green wine) from Minho. Despite its name, which refers to age rather than colour, 70 per cent of it is red. The best of the "green wines" comes from Monção. If you spot that name on a label, try it.

Next in size as a wine-producing area comes Dão, which again produces red and white wine. The reds are the more interesting as they have a velvety quality due to their especially slow fermentation.

There are many other interesting wines to try—the strong, sweet apéritif wine of *Carcavelos,* if you can find any, the almost equally rare *Ramisco* from Colares, made from pre-phylloxera vines, the sweet fortified *Moscatel* from Setúbal, and *Bucelas,* a delicate scented wine of a lovely gold colour.

Açorda bread soup
alentejana bread soup based on fish stock, with olive oil and coriander, flavoured with garlic

Almôndegas meat balls made from a mixture of veal and pork
★**Amêijoas à Bulhão Pato** clams cooked with garlic and coriander

Arroz açafrão saffron-flavoured rice served with fish and chicken

de manteiga rice cooked with butter and onions

doce cold egg and rice pudding sprinkled with cinnamon

Atum com arroz a mould of rice with tuna, lettuce, tomatoes and olives

★**Bacalhau** the famous Portuguese salt cod. There are said to be 365 ways of cooking it—one for each day of the year

à Brás fried with onions, potatoes and olives with added beaten eggs

dourado baked with tomatoes, parsley, garlic and white wine

à moda de Minho wrapped in cabbage leaves and baked. Served with fried onions and boiled potatoes but without the cabbage leaves

à transmontana braised with bacon, parsley, garlic, tomatoes and white wine

Beringelas fritas sliced eggplants dredged in flour and fried in oil

Bolo de carne yeast bread dough stuffed with vegetables, ham, chicken and *chouriço* and baked

Caldeirada de peixe fish stew— most regions have their own variations but it usually includes a mixture of white fish and shell- fish. In the Algarve it will have lots of garlic

Caldo verde this cabbage soup is eaten throughout Portugal for both lunch and dinner, usually with *pão de broa*, dark corn bread

Camarões com vinho do Porto shrimp fried with onions and port, covered with beaten eggs and cream and baked

Cebolada à portuguesa onions fried in butter with tomato paste, garlic and parsley. Often used as a sauce for eggs or fish or as an omelette filling

Chouriço very popular sausage flavoured with paprika and garlic

Coelho à caçadora rabbit marinated in wine, oil, garlic and bay, then casseroled with onions, bacon and mushrooms

Conchas de camarão shrimp in béchamel sauce sprinkled with breadcrumbs and cheese and baked in scallop shells

★**Cozido à portuguesa** a stew of various meats usually including beef, chicken and sausage, with rice cooked in stock with vegetables

Creme pastor "shepherd's soup"; chopped vegetables, pork or bacon, eggs and cream in a chicken stock base

Dobrada à portuguesa tripe with navy beans and sausage

Ervilhas guisadas green peas are a favourite Portuguese vegetable. Often served stewed with onions and herbs

Escabeche de sável shad marinated for three days in olive oil, onions, garlic, herbs and wine then fried. Served cold

Farófias meringues cooked in hot milk with sugar and lemon. Served with a custard made from the milk and egg yolks. Chilled and sprinkled with cinnamon

Favas frescas em salada a salad of cooked fava beans dressed with olive oil, garlic, parsley and seasoning

★**Feijão guisado** kidney beans stewed with bacon, covered with tomato sauce

verde à provincia string beans stewed with onion, garlic, tomatoes and *chouriço*. Served with poached eggs

★**Frango no espeto à moda de Minho** chicken brushed with olive oil and chilli sauce and spit- roasted

Gaspacho à alentejana a chilled vegetable soup with Alentejo bread, also containing chunks of sausage flavoured with cummin

Grão com espinafres chick peas stewed with onion and spinach. Often served with *bacalhau*

com tomates chick peas in a purée of tomatoes, oil and garlic

★**Iscas à portuguesa** liver marinated in wine, vinegar and spices and cooked with *presunto* and potatoes

Lagosta à moda de Peniche layers of crayfish or lobster meat and a mixture of onions, tomatoes, chillis, herbs, spices and wine, covered in port and baked

★**Lampreia à moda de Minho** lampreys stewed in red wine, onions and their own blood

★**Leitão assado** spit-roasted

suckling pig. A speciality of the Bairrada area

Linguiça fine garlic sausage sometimes burnt with brandy and eaten with bread

Lombo de porco à camponesa loin of pork marinated in wine, herbs and spices and roasted with potatoes and onions

Lula de caldeirada squid stewed with onion, parsley, tomatoes and potatoes

  em sua tinta squid cooked in its own ink

Morcela spiced pork blood sausage

Ovos especiais Quinta das Torres fried eggs coated in béchamel sauce, egg-and-breadcrumbed and deep fried

  moles a mixture of egg yolk, sugar and water used as a sauce or filling! In Aveiro it is served on its own, sprinkled with cinnamon

Pescada à Viriato fried white fish served with potato salad

Pudim flan a very popular dessert similar to cream caramel

Rissóis balls of dough filled with thick white sauce containing shrimps, flaked *bacalhau* or veal, egg-and-breadcrumbed and fried

Salmonetes grelhados à Setúbalense grilled red mullet, a speciality of Setúbal

Salpicão smoked spiced pork sausage

Sardinhas no forno fresh sardines sprinkled with oil and seasoning and baked in the oven

Sonhos "dreams"; fritters, sometimes with fruit, served hot in cinnamon flavoured syrup

Torta de Viana cake similar to a swiss roll, with an *ovos moles* filling

Useful words

Açúcar sugar
Água water
Alho garlic
Amêndoas almonds
Assado roasted
Azeite olive oil
Azeitonas olives
Batatas potatoes
Batida a rum cocktail
Cabrito kid
Caça game
Café coffee
Cardápio, ementa menu
Carne meat
Cerveja beer
Chá tea
Conta bill
Cordeiro lamb
Cozido boiled or poached
Fígado, iscas liver
Frito fried
Fruta fruit
Frango, galinha chicken
Gambas shrimp
Garrafeira "a bottling", meaning a better than ordinary wine
Gelado ice-cream

Guisado stewed
Hortaliça, legumes vegetables
Leite milk
Manteiga butter
Mariscos shellfish
Melão melon
Nata cream
Pão bread
Peixe fish
Polvo octopus
Porco pork
Presunto smoked ham
Queijo cheese
Sopa soup
Toucinho bacon
Uvas grapes
Vaca beef
Vinho wine
  branco, doce, do consumo,
  espumante, generoso white, sweet, ordinary, sparkling, strong
  do Porto port, fortified dessert wine from the Douro
  rosado, seco rosé, dry
  tinto red
  verde "green", i.e. young, wine
Vitela veal

Saúde! cheers!
Bom apetite! bon appétit!

Romania — *See* Eastern Europe
Saudi Arabia — *See* Arab food

Scandinavia

ARCTIC OCEAN

ICELAND
• REYKJAVIK

ATLANTIC OCEAN

USSR

LAPPLAND

SWEDEN

Gulf of Bothnia

FINLAND

• Trondheim

NORWAY

**HELSINGFORS
(HELSINKI)**

• Bergen

Gulf of Finland

OSLO •

LAKE VÄNERN

STOCKHOLM
• Örebro

• Stavanger

LAKE VÄTTERN

BALTIC SEA

• Göteborg
(Gothenburg)

**DENMARK
JUTLAND**

NORTH SEA

KØBENHAVN
(COPENHAGEN) • Malmö

The Scandinavians, with justifiable pride and a certain self-knowledge, do not care for being lumped together. They are indeed very different peoples with marked characteristics but, since food is dictated to a large extent by geography, there are bound to be great similarities in the cuisines of neighbouring countries. It is the nature of the climate and the produce that makes these countries concentrate in summer on the cold buffet, which is common to all of them, and in winter on stews of pork and mutton or even reindeer and elk, with cabbage and kale or root vegetables.

The charm of Scandinavian food is that it is essentially the food of the fisherman and the hunter, as opposed to the agricultural cuisines of the rest of Europe.

Denmark

Of all the countries in this group, Denmark is the one that owes most to the rest of Europe in its cuisine. Danish food, being considerably influenced by Germany, is richer and heavier than that of her northern neighbours. The Danes

187

themselves prefer to emphasize the post-Napoleonic French influence, but this is not dreadfully obvious to foreigners, who notice more the pork and dumplings, the beer-and-bread soup, the sugar in the potatoes and the creamed kale.

At the same time, the fish dishes, especially the smoked fish, are extremely fresh and good, and a Danish *smørrebrød* is every bit as good as the Swedish equivalent.

Denmark is the one country which has easy-going drinking laws. *Snaps (akvavit)* and beer are permitted at all hours. Perhaps the most useful word in Danish is *tak*—thank you. If you have been somewhere before, you start right off with *tak for sidst* (thanks for the last time), as soon as the meal is over you say *tak for mad* (thanks for the meal) and you can say that when you leave as well. Next day you ring up to say *tak for igår* (thanks for yesterday). The Danes also go in for the embarrassing *skål* ritual (only with *akvavit*, never with beer), where every diner (except the hostess, who is expected to be getting on with her job) toasts another, looking deeply into the victim's eyes with heavy significance. It gets easier as time and *akvavit* go on.

Danish alphabetical order is: a–z, æ, ø, å

Agurkesalat thinly sliced cucumber in a dressing of vinegar, sugar, salt, pepper and parsley or dill

Bankekød beef stew

Brunede kartofler a favourite Danish way with potatoes, which involves boiling them and then browning them in butter and sugar. Carrots, onions and white cabbage are also prepared in a similar way

Bøf med løg ground beef served with brown sauce and fried onions

Danablu Danish blue cheese

Esrom a mild buttery cheese

Fiskefars a mixture of ground fish with flour and cream, either fried in cakes or baked in moulds. Served with various sauces and boiled potatoes

Flæskesteg roast pork, usually served with spiced red cabbage and *brunede kartofler*

Flæskeæggekage resembles a thick bacon omelette

Flæsk i kål meat, usually pork, and cabbage

Fløderand a rather superior blancmange moulded in a ring and filled with stewed fruit

Forloren skildpadde an elaborate dish prepared from very simple ingredients. The meat from a calf's head is combined with *fiskefars, frikadeller* and vegetables in a thick cream sauce. Traditionally the brain of the calf

is also made into balls and added to the stew. The labour involved in preparing this dish is so considerable that if you do find it in a restaurant it is quite likely to be tinned

Frikadeller the most typical of all Danish meat dishes, made from finely ground mixtures of veal or beef and pork formed into balls and fried in butter. They can be eaten hot or cold

Frugtsuppe fruit soup made from dried apricots, prunes and apples. Served hot or cold as a first course or dessert

★ **Gravlaks** raw salmon fillets marinated for several days in spices, a few drops of cognac and lots of dill

Gule ærter an elaborate yellow split pea soup with bacon, vegetables and chunks of sausage. The meats and broth are usually served separately

Gåsesteg roast goose

Hachis a hash of leftover meat and onions served with fried eggs and potatoes

Hakkebøf hamburgers or rissoles made from ground beef and usually served with onions and fried eggs

Havarti a smooth, pale yellow cheese with a sprinkling of large and small holes, said to be Denmark's finest

Helleflynder halibut

Hellig Tre Konger kage Twelfth Night cake, eaten on 6 January. It contains one whole almond. Whoever finds it is crowned with a paper crown and becomes "king" for the evening. There is also a traditional feast served at 11 p.m., beginning with onion soup and including *pølsegifler* (crescent-shaped sausage rolls), *tarteletter* (vol-au-vents stuffed with liver pâté and mushrooms), biscuits covered with *rygeost* (smoked cottage cheese flavoured with caraway seeds), and *flodeost* (cream cheese) as well as the cake, of course

Jule risengrød rice pudding with almonds traditionally served on Christmas Day *before* the roast

Klejner rich Christmas biscuits

Kogt torsk boiled cod, often served with lots of dill or parsley and "fish mustard" (*fiskesennep*)

Kransekager small finger-shaped iced marzipan cakes

Krydret and pickled duck

Kråsesuppe soup of goose giblets with apples and prunes. Served with dumplings

Kyllingesalat salad of diced chicken, noodles, tomatoes, green peppers, lettuce and mushrooms

Kærnemælkskoldskål sweet buttermilk soup served cold with oatcakes *after* a meal

Kødboller meat dumplings

Kørvelsuppe chervil soup served with poached eggs

Labskovs a stew of beef, potatoes carrots and onions

Lagkage wafer-thin layers of sponge cake sandwiched together with various fillings. Served with whipped cream

Leverpostej liver pâté

Linser small covered pies filled with vanilla custard

Makrel mackerel—both fresh and smoked

Medisterpølser spiced meaty pork sausages usually boiled, then fried and served with brown sauce (*brun sovs*), potatoes and salad. Also a street snack served with bread and mustard from a *pølsevogn*

Melboller flour dumplings served in soups

Mycella a mild blue cheese

Pandekager pancakes filled with fruit or strawberry jam, dusted with sugar and served with whipped cream or ice-cream

Plukfisk fish with chopped hard-boiled eggs in a cream sauce

Rejer shrimps

Rullepølse spiced breast of lamb, veal or fresh beef

Rødbedesalat diced beets and apples in horseradish dressing

Rødgrød a pudding consisting of a mixture of red berries—red currants, raspberries, strawberries and sometimes even rhubarb—stewed and thickened with cornstarch. Eaten with cream (*fløde*). A favourite Danish joke is to ask visitors to their country to say *rødgrød med fløde*, a task which is well-nigh impossible for non-Danes

Rødkål red cabbage, usually stewed with apples, vinegar and sometimes red-currant jelly

Rødspætte plaice

Røget gåsebryst smoked breast of goose

Samsø the everyday Danish cheese; mild with small holes

Sandkage a popular brandy-flavoured sponge cake

Sildesalat diced salted herring, potatoes, beets, apples and onion in a thick sauce. Served cold

Skidne æg hard-boiled eggs and chopped bacon in a cream sauce

Skæbnekage "destiny cake", eaten on New Year's Eve. A silver coin, thimble and ring are hidden in the cake. Whoever finds the first will become rich during the coming year, the second will not marry, the third will fall in love

★ Smørrebrød literally "buttered bread", an unassuming term for one of the main distinguishing characteristics of Danish food—open sandwiches. The variety is extraordinary. One restaurant in Copenhagen offers 200 different kinds of *smørrebrød*. The fillings usually comprise an infinite variety of fish: eel, salmon, always shrimps, herrings—soused, salted and pickled—as well as vegetables, meats and meat pastes, with lots of mayonnaise and sauces of all kinds. There are also several different kinds of bread to choose from and sweet or salted butter. All is beautifully presented, very colourful with a variety of decorative garnishes. The traditional drink with *smørrebrød* is lager. *Akvavit* is sometimes drunk

Stegt and roast duck, usually stuffed with apples and prunes

Stegt flæsk crisp fried slices of fresh bacon often served with parsley sauce (*persillesovs*)

Stegte hjerter calves' or pigs' hearts stuffed with butter and parsley and baked

Syltesild pickled herring

Tybo a firm waxy cheese that is sometimes flavoured with caraway seeds

Wienerbrød "Vienna bread", the Danish term for what everyone else knows as Danish pastry

Æbleflæsk bacon with fried apple rings and onion

Æblekage a pudding consisting of layers of sugary crumble, cream and apples

Æbleskiver doughnuts deep fried in hot oil and dusted with sugar

Æggekage "egg cake", scrambled eggs with chopped onions or chives, potatoes and bacon

Øllebrød a sweet hot soup made from bread and beer. A meal in itself and very fattening. In the old days it was often eaten for breakfast and every housewife had her own special way of preparing it

Ålesuppe eel soup, usually including dried fruit and served with dark bread

Useful words

Akvavit, snaps the Danish national drink, a spirit distilled from potatoes or rye. It is taken in small glasses, very cold. The first one should be tossed straight back and is sometimes followed by a beer chaser. It is never drunk with hot food

Brød bread

Bøf beef

Dild dill, an ingredient of many Danish special dishes

Dyreryg venison

Fisk fish

Fløde cream

   skum whipped cream, served with almost all sweet dishes and pastries

Frugt fruit

   saft fruit juice

Grønlangkål kale, a very popular vegetable, usually cooked in a thick cream sauce with a pinch of sugar

Grønsager vegetables

Gulerødder carrots

Hvidvin white wine

Is ice-cream

Kaffe coffee

Kage cake

Kalv veal

Kartofler potatoes

Kaviar caviar

Krydder thick soft rusks eaten for breakfast, usually with butter and jam

Kylling chicken

Kød meat

Lam lamb

Linse lentils

Lys øl light beer

Mælk milk

Mørkt øl dark beer

Okse beef

Ost cheese

Porrer leeks

Regningen bill

Rødvin red wine

Røget smoked

Skinke ham

Smør butter

Småkager small cakes or biscuits

Snaps see *Akvavit*

Stegt roasted

Sukker sugar

Svin pork

Te tea

Vand water

Vildt game

Æg egg

Øl beer

Østers oysters

Ål eel

Skål! cheers!
Velbekomme! bon appétit!

Finland

My grandmother once had a Finnish cook. She seemed quite
unable to prepare any dish. Asked what she could do, she
replied succinctly. "Milk elk." Of course, the blueberries and
forest mushrooms, the cloudberries and reindeer tongue, to
which she was accustomed, were not freely available in
Cheshire.

In fact the wild produce of the lakes and forests of Finland
makes their food most attractive, except that, with little
agriculture, almost the only vegetable seems to be the potato.
It is tempting to speculate whether the cold fruit soups came
to Finland via Hungary, with whose language Finnish has a
common root. Whatever the case, they are marvellous. The
sad part is that restaurants are inclined to serve international food, which is thought grander than home cooking.

The drinking laws are fairly savage, though you can now
buy beer before noon and spirits after midday, but schnapps
is never sold without food. Most Finns, in public, seem to
drink buttermilk with meals and quantities of weakish coffee
at other times. At home, in the long winter nights, things are
very different. Should you be offered them, the liqueurs made
from the forest berries are superb, especially *Mesimarja*,
made from the Arctic raspberry.

Finnish alphabetical order is: a–z, ä, ö

Hampurilainen hamburger
Hiilillä paistettua silakkaa Baltic
sprats grilled over charcoal
Jauhelihapihvi beefburger
Kaalikeitto milk-based cabbage
soup with onions and potatoes
Kalakeitto fish soup; fish, onions
and potatoes in milk, seasoned
with allspice and dill
★ **Kalakukko** literally "fish
rooster"; *muikku* or other small
fish baked with pork in a rye-flour
crust. A Karelian speciality
Kaalikääryleet cabbage rolls
filled with rice and ground meat
Karjalanpaisti Karelian meat stew
Karjalanpiirakka Karelian pies
made with rye flour and filled
with rice. Served with chopped
hard-boiled eggs and butter
Kesäkeitto summer soup of young
vegetables simmered in milk and
water, flavoured with dill and
parsley
★ **Kiisseli** clear fruit soup for
dessert, made with berries and
sugar, thickened with potato
flour. Served warm or cold
Kyljys (pork) chop
Lammaskaali cabbage and lamb
casserole
Lammin voileipä hot open
sandwich
Lanttulaatikko boiled, puréed

turnips slowly baked in the oven
until golden brown. Traditional
for Christmas
Lasimestarinsilli raw slightly
salted herring pickled in spirit
vinegar with onion and carrots,
spiced with peppercorns, mustard
seed and bay leaves
Lihakeitto a soup of beef,
potatoes, carrots, turnips and
onions, flavoured with allspice
Lihamureke ground beef loaf,
baked and served in slices
Lihapiirakka deep-fried savoury
doughnut filled with ground beef
and rice
Lihapullat, lihapyörykät small
meat balls fried and served in a
brown sauce or on their own
Lindströminpihvi ground beef and
beet beefburger
★ **Makkara** generic name for a
whole range of cooked and
uncooked sausages, salami,
luncheon meats, etc. Often eaten
hot in a brown sauce
(*makkarakastike*). Very much a
Finnish institution, more often
found in private houses
Maksalaatikko minced liver, rice,
onions, eggs and milk, baked
until set and served with
cranberries
Muikku very small fish from east

Finland, regarded as a delicacy
Munakas omelette
★**Mustikkapiirakka** open blueberry tart, often made with *pulla* dough
Ohukaiset small pancakes
Oopperavoileipä hot open sandwich with ham and fried eggs
Perunalaatiko mashed potatoes baked in the oven
Pinaattilaatikko rice and spinach in milk and egg custard, baked till set
Poronkieli reindeer tongue, often served with lemon sauce
Poronkäristys chopped reindeer meat, fried in bacon fat
Puolukkapuuro cowberry or cranberry juice with semolina, whisked until light and fluffy
Puuro general name for puddings using cereals combined with any sort of liquid, usually hot

★**Rapu** crayfish, in season from July to September, when it is served boiled, flavoured with dill, at special parties
Rosolli salad of chopped cooked vegetables, onion, apple, pickled cucumber and salted herring garnished with chopped hard-boiled eggs. Served with a separate cream, vinegar and beet juice dressing
Silakka Baltic sprat
  -laatikko gratin of potatoes, Baltic sprats and onions topped with milk and egg custard
Silli herring
Taimen trout
Tilliliha veal stew with cream
Uunijuustoa cream cheese baked in the oven. Served sliced
Viili jelly-like sour milk eaten with sugar and cinnamon

Useful words

Alkupalat hors d'oeuvre
Grillattu grilled
Hauki pike
Hedelmä fruit
Häränliha beef
Jugurtti yoghurt
Juusto cheese
Jäätelo ice-cream
Kahvi coffee
Kakku cake
Kala fish
Kalja non-alcoholic malted drink which tastes like beer
Kana chicken
Kefiiri soured milk, like yoghurt
Keitetty boiled
Keitto soup
Kerma cream
Kinkku ham
Lakka cloudberry
Lampaanliha mutton, lamb
Lasku bill
Leipä bread
Liha meat
Lohi salmon
Maito milk
Maksa liver
Mansikka strawberry
Marja berry
Muna egg
Munkki doughnut

Mustikka blueberry
Naudanliha beef
Näkkileipä crispbread
Olut beer
Paistettu fried
Pihvi steak
Piimä buttermilk
Piirakka filled pie
Pulla sweet yeast dough, plaited or in other shapes, flavoured with cardamom
Punaviini red wine
Puolukka cowberry, cranberry
Riisi rice
Ruokalista menu
Salaatti salad
Sianliha pork
Sieni mushroom
Sitruuna lemon
Sokeri sugar
Tee tea
Tuoremehu fruit juice
Uunissa paistettu baked
Vadelma raspberry
Valkoviini white wine
Vasikanliha veal
Vesi water
Viini wine
Voi butter
Voileipä open sandwich
  -pöytä Finnish cold table

Kippis! Terveydeksi! cheers! to your health!
Hyvää ruokahalua! bon appétit!

Iceland

It is an austere land, dependent almost entirely on fish, especially cod and herring. Otherwise a little lamb (exquisite smoked), some beef and an occasional reindeer are the order of the day. (How the British can have had the nerve to conduct a co[l]d war with this handful of hungry people is unimaginable.) So you will find a heavy emphasis on vegetables and rather little general interest in cuisine.

Icelandic alphabetical order is: a, á, b, c, d, ð, e, é, f, g, h, i, í, j, k, l, m, n, o, ó, p, q, r, s, t, u, ú, v, w, x, y, ý, z, þ, æ, ö

Bjór beer (difficult to find)
Brauð bread
Fiskur fish
Flatbrauð flat bread made with rye flour. Served with lamb, etc.
Glóðaður sjávarréttur grilled mixed seafood, actually baked in the oven in béchamel sauce with a golden cheese topping
★ **Hangikjöt** smoked lamb
Harðfiskur dried fish
Hörpudiskur scallops
★ **Hreindýr** wild reindeer, considered a delicacy
★ **Humar** small "virgin-lobster". Only the tail is eaten
Kaffi coffee
Kjöt meat
Kjötsúpa traditional lamb soup with vegetables and rice

Lax fresh salmon
Matseðill menu
Mjólk milk
Nautakjöt beef; usually eaten dried or salted
Reikningur bill
Rjúpa ptarmigan
Rækjur shrimp
Saltfiskur salt cod, often plain boiled
Síld herring, served in a variety of ways, often marinated
Skyr an original Viking dish; yoghurt-like dessert served with sugar and cream
Sykur sugar
Te tea
Vatn water
Vín wine
Þorskur cod

> **Skál!** cheers!
> **Verði per að góðu!** (singular) bon appétit!
> **Verði ykkur að góðu!** (plural) bon appétit!

Norway

Norway is, if anything, fishier than Sweden. The Norwegians are very keen on cod. Apart from serving it plainly with boiled potatoes, they have many dishes involving the head, the liver (boiled and then fried in slices), the roe and even the tongue. The commonest meat is pork, often made into sausages. Their version of *smörgåsbord* is called *koldtbord*.

The Norwegians are very harsh about drink. Spirits are not sold before 3 p.m. in towns, or before 1 p.m. in resorts, and there are severe restrictions at weekends and on holidays.

Norwegian alphabetical order is: a–z æ, ø, å

Betasuppe farmhouse mutton soup
★ **Bløtkake** sponge filled with cream and fresh fruit or jam, covered with thick cream
Blåbær blueberries
Bringebær raspberries
Dravle a concoction of curds and whey, sweetened with syrup

★ **Dyrestek** roast venison, often served with a sauce of goat's cheese and red-currant jelly
Eggedosis a rich, sweet, egg sauce to which brandy or rum may be added. Eaten alone or often with tart fruit such as blueberries
Elg elk

Ertesuppe thick pea soup
Fenalår dried, salted smoked mutton
Fiskeboller fish balls, made with same ingredients as *fiskepudding*
Fiskepudding flaked fish, butter, breadcrumbs, cream and seasoning cooked in a mould
Fisksuppe fish soup. Fish boiled in stock with carrots, parsnips, leeks, potato, onion, bay leaf and celery. Thickened with cream and egg yolks
Flatbrød flat bread rather like a large biscuit
Fløtevaffle waffles made with a sour cream, ginger or cardamom batter
Fårerull spiced, pressed mutton roll
★**Får i kål** stew of mutton and crisp cabbage or kale seasoned with salt and black pepper
Gammelost brown mould-splotched cheese with a strong aroma and sharp flavour
Gjetost sweetish goat's cheese
★**Gravlaks** salt-cured salmon
Hellefisk halibut
Himmelsk lapskaus fresh fruit and nuts served with *eggedosis*. The name means "heavenly pot-pourri"
Hummer lobster
Hvalkjøtt whalemeat
Kalvefilet veal steak or chop
Kjøttkaker med surkål meat balls with sauerkraut
Klippfisk dried, salted cod
Kongesuppe thick soup with tiny meat balls, peas, onions and carrots
Kransekake cake for festive occasions, made of layered marzipan rings
Kylling chicken
Laks salmon
Lammekjøtt lamb
★**Lapskaus** thick soup-stew of chopped pork and vegetables
Lumpe thin pancakes made of mashed potato, cream and flour. Grilled and served with sugar and jam

Lutefisk cod steeped in a lye of potash. May be served with butter and cream sauce
Makrell mackerel, often marinated and grilled
Multer cloudberry preserve served as a dessert
Nøkkelost semi-hard cheese with cloves and caraway seeds
Oksekjøtt beef
Pinnekjøtt salt-cured mutton or pork traditionally steamed on a bed of birch twigs. Each piece of meat has the entire rib attached, to be used as a handle for eating with the fingers
Puss pass stew of mutton and kale or cabbage with carrots and potatoes
Pultost soft mountain cheese, usually with caraway seeds
Pølser sausages
Rabarbragrøt rhubarb compote
Rakørret fermented trout
Rekesaus shrimps in a cream, milk, butter and lemon juice sauce, flavoured with dill. Served with fish dishes
Ribbe pork chops usually roasted and served with sauerkraut
★**Rype i fløtesaus** ptarmigan in cream sauce
Røket fisk smoked fish
Rømmegrøt thick, sour porridge
Rädyr venison
Sild herring
Skalldyr shellfish
Spekemat salt-cured meat
Spekesild salt herring
Spekeskinke smoked ham
Stekte hjortekoteletter venison cutlets, marinated in oil and lemon juice. Sautéed and served with red-currant or cranberry jam
Svinekjøtt pork
Torsk cod
  med eggsaus cod poached and served in a sauce of chopped hard-boiled egg, tomato, parsley and chives
Tyttebær cranberries
Tørrfisk dried fish
Ørret trout, particularly brown
Ål eel

Useful words

Akevitt potent spirit of distilled potatoes or barley. True *akevitt* should pass the Equator twice and is often shipped in barrels to

Australia and back to achieve the right degree of maturity
Brigg almost non-alcoholic beer
Brød bread

Fisk fish	**Poteter** potatoes
Fjærkre poultry	**Regningen** bill
Fløte cream	**Ris** rice
Forretter hors d'oeuvre	**Ristet** fried, grilled, roasted
Grønnsaker vegetables	**Smør** butter
Kaffe coffee	**Spisekartet** menu
Kjøtt meat	**Sukker** sugar
Krem sour cream	**Te** tea
Kål cabbage	**Vann** water
Melk milk	**Vin** wine
Ost cheese	**Øl** beer

Skål! cheers!
Velbekomme! bon appétit!

Sweden

Once you have got to Sweden, you are in the true realm of
what one might call the sumptuous canapé. As in the sur-
rounding countries, the Swedes eat little and often. *Frukost*
is breakfast with cold meat and cheese. Lunch is at 11.30,
usually as *smörgås*. *Middag* is the largest meal, at about 5
p.m., despite its name. Then *kvällsmat* (supper) at 9 p.m.

Smörgåsbord is probably Sweden's most famous affair and
it can run to about five courses eaten in a traditional order.
First, herring, often pickled, served with boiled potatoes.
Then more fish—salmon, sprats, eels, sardines. Next a hot
course of boiled beef, smoked reindeer, beef or just liver
paste. Then salads, fruit or vegetables and finally cheese.

The Swedes are comparatively strict about drink. None is
served before noon.

Swedish alphabetical order is: a–z, å, ä, ö

Ansjovis marinated spiced sprats
Bakelser pastries, fancy cakes
Biff beefsteak or ground meat
  à la Lindström ground steak,
  onions, beets, capers and egg
  mixed and fried
Björnbär blackberries
Blodkorv black pudding
Blåbär blueberries
Bruna bönor brown beans, usually
  with pork in a very thick sweet-
  sour sauce'
Bräckkorv smoked pork sausage
Bräckt lax salmon steaks egg-
  and-breadcrumbed and fried
Böckling buckling
Dillkött lamb or veal boiled with
  dill, in a thick egg sauce
Dopp-i-gryta ham and sausage
  stock served on Christmas Eve,
  when everybody dips bread into a
  large pot of it
Falukorv lightly smoked pork
  sausage, sliced and fried
Fasan pheasant

Femöring med ägg small steak with
  fried eggs and onions on top
Fiskbullar smooth fish balls,
  served in a white sauce
Fisksoppa fish soup
Fläsk pork
  korv large pork sausage
Forell trout
Frikadeller boiled meat balls
Får mutton
Getost soft goat's cheese
★**Glasmästarsill** literally
  "glassblower's herring"; herring
  in vinegar with carrots, onions
  and horseradish
★**Gravad lax** salmon marinated
  with dill, salt, sugar and pepper.
  Served with a mustard, dill and
  sour cream sauce
Gröt porridge
Hackad jägarbiff veal hamburger
  with mushroom sauce
Hallon raspberries
Hasselbackspotatis peeled
  potatoes, scored and roasted

Havskräftor saltwater crayfish
generally boiled with dill
Helgeflundra halibut
Herrgårdsstek "manor steak";
pot-roasted joint of beef
Hjortron cloudberries
Hovdessert meringue and cream
mould with melted chocolate
Hummer lobster
Höns fowl
Inlagd sill salt, pickled herring
★ Janssons frestelse "Jansson's
temptation"; layers of ansjovis,
onions and potatoes with cream,
baked in the oven
Jordgubbar strawberries
Jägarschnitzel ground veal
escalope with mushroom sauce
Järpe grouse
Kabeljo salt, slightly dried cod
Kaffebröd sweet yeast-based
bread and buns
Kalops beef stewed with bay
leaves, onions and allspice
Kalvdans literally "calf dance"; a
dessert made from fresh cow's
milk, resembling egg custard
Kalvfrikassé boiled veal with a
dill, lemon or caper sauce,
thickened with egg yolks
Kalvsylta veal head cheese
Kanelbullar cinnamon buns
Kasseler smoked pork fillet, baked
whole or fried in slices
Kolja fresh haddock
Kroppkakor egg, flour and potato
dumplings, filled with chopped
bacon and onion and boiled.
Served with cream, melted butter
and wild cranberries
Kryddsill spiced, pickled herring
Kräftor crayfish. Special parties
(kräftkalas) are held in August
during the crayfish season
Kycklinggryta chicken casserole
ugnstekt chicken roasted with
spices or mushrooms
Kåldolmar cabbage rolls, stuffed
with ground meat and fried
Kålsoppa cabbage soup-stew with
chunks of boiled lamb
Köttbullar fried meat balls served
with boiled potatoes and lingon
Köttfärsgrotta ground meat loaf,
sometimes with stuffing, baked
Köttfärsröra ground meat fried
with onions and other vegetables
Köttsoppa med klimp meat soup
with dumplings
Lammkotletter lamb chops
Lapplandslåda smoked reindeer

meat with mushrooms, onions
and potatoes, first fried then
baked with béchamel sauce
Lax salmon
Laxöring trout
Lingon type of wild cranberry
sylt cranberry jelly. Often used
in place of less plentiful vegetables
Lutfisk ling or cod
Lövbiff thin slices of steak
Makrill inkokt mackerel poached
with dill or bay leaves
Matjessill pickled salt herring,
eaten in summer with new
potatoes, chives and sour cream
Mimosasallad pineapple, tomato,
apples, pears and grapes in
mayonnaise
Norrlandspudding casserole of
fried onions and boiled potatoes
with a top layer of smoked sausage
and béchamel sauce, baked
Nyponsoppa cold rosehip soup
served with whipped cream and
almonds for dessert
Nässelsoppa spring nettle soup
with halved hard-boiled eggs
Orre black grouse
Ostfromage rich cheese mousse
Ostlåda baked cheese custard
Oxjärpar beef rolls stuffed with
parsley and bacon
Oxsvanssopa oxtail soup
Pannbiff ground beef rissoles
Pannkakor pancakes
Parisersmörgås ground meat
mixture on fried bread, garnished
with a fried egg
Pariservåfflor crisp pastry slices
sandwiched together with a
liqueur-flavoured buttercream
Pastej pie, patty
Pepparkaka spiced ginger cake
Pepparrotskött boiled beef with
horseradish sauce
Piggvar turbot
Plankstek steak fried on a wooden
board of hickory or oak
Plättar small pancakes
Pressylta veal and pork head
cheese
Purjolökslåda med skinka och ost
cooked leeks rolled in ham,
covered with cheese and grilled
Pytt i panna diced cooked meat,
onions and potatoes fried together
Raggmunkar grated raw potatoes
mixed with egg and milk and fried
Rapphöns partridge
Renklämma thin slices of smoked
reindeer meat in unleavened bread

Revbensspjäll spare ribs

Ripa ptarmigan

Ris à la Malta cooked rice mixed with cream and sugar. Served with fruit

Risgrynsgröt rice porridge served with cinnamon and sugar

Rotmos mashed potato and turnip

Rulader slices of meat rolled up with various stuffings

Rullsylta fresh bacon or veal, spiced, rolled and boiled. Served cold in slices

Rådjur venison

Råkosttallrik raw vegetable salad

Räkor shrimp

Rödspätta plaice

Rökt lax smoked salmon

Saftsoppa thin fruit soup

Sill herring, usually salt

sallad chopped salt herring, beets, apples, potatoes, cooked meat and onions, garnished with hard-boiled eggs and cream

Sjömansbiff "sailor's beef"; beef, onion and potato casserole

Sjötunga sole

Skaldjur shellfish

Skarpsås a sharp sauce of egg yolks mixed with mustard, oil, vinegar and cream

Slottsstek pot-roasted joint of beef with onions, *ansjovis*, vinegar, syrup and cream

Slätvar brill

Smultron wild strawberries

Smörgås open sandwich with combinations of salads, meat, fish, egg and pickles, generally cold. Eaten with a knife and fork for lunch as part of the *smörgåsbord*

Sölöga chopped *ansjovis*, onion, beets and capers served around a raw egg yolk; also part of *smörgåsbord*

Spettekaka orginally a wedding cake from Skåne. A smooth egg and sugar mixture is poured slowly over a metal cone turning in front of an open fire. When the cone is removed, the pyramid cake may be several feet high

Strömming Baltic herring

Torsk cod

Ugnsomelett egg and milk mixture baked and served with a savoury sauce

Våfflor waffles, bought in the streets. Served with cream

Varm korv hot dogs, sold from street kiosks

Västkustsallad seafood salad

Ädelost dessert cheeses

Ål eel

Älgstek roast elk

Äppelkaka med vaniljsås alternate layers of fried breadcrumbs and apple sauce, served with custard

Ärter med fläsk yellow pea soup with diced pork, traditional Thursday supper followed by *plättar*

Ättiksgurka pickled gherkins

Useful words

Akvavit spirit distilled from potatoes or rye

Brännvin same as *akvavit*

Bröd bread

Frukt fruit

Grönsaker vegetables

Gås goose

Kaffe coffee

Kakor cakes or biscuits

Kall cold

Knäckebröd crispbread

Korv sausage

Kött meat

Lever liver

Matsedel, meny menu

Mjölk milk

Njurar kidneys

Nota bill

Rött vin red wine

Skinka ham

Smör butter

Socker sugar

Te tea

Vatten water

Vin wine

Vitt vin white wine

Ägg eggs

Öl beer

Skål! cheers!
Smaklig måltid! bon appétit!

South Africa — *See* Africa

South and Central America

With the exception of Mexico (q.v.), no Central or South American country has developed a great cuisine—perhaps because the Indians farther south had no cuisine comparable to that of the Aztecs to build upon. I have therefore gathered them all together.

The influences are predominantly Spanish and Portuguese and there is therefore a great similarity between the cookery of each country, though each has adapted the base according to the wide variation in the climate and terrain of the continent.

Brazil had the additional influence of the large number of African slaves. Their style is centred around Salvador and is known as Bahian food, hence the Brazilian saying, "the blacker the cook, the better the food". The Peruvians work wonders with the potato. In Argentina, beef is naturally the most important ingredient. In Surinam there is a strong Dutch and Indonesian influence.

As the food of Argentina, Paraguay and Uruguay is so similar, I have combined them into an area which I have labelled Pampas.

For extra dishes and for useful words you should refer either to Spain and Mexico or Portugal.

Soups

Ajiaco con pollo, ajiaco bogotano (Colombia) potato and chicken soup

Chupe de camarones (Peru) soup of potatoes, milk, dried shrimps, chillis and eggs

Hervido (Venezuela) soup with a mixture of chicken, meat and fish

Mondongo (Venezuela) soup of tripe and vegetables

Peto (Colombia) soup of sweet-corn and milk

★San cocho (Venezuela) a thick soup-stew of fish, pumpkin, sweetcorn, tomatoes, lemons, potatoes, cassava and several other native roots

Sopa criolla (Peru) soup with shredded beef, noodles and chilli

Tacaca thick soup flavoured with dried shrimps and garlic. From the Amazon delta

Hors d'oeuvre and snacks

Almojábanos (Colombia) muffins made from corn meal and stuffed with white cheese

Anticuchos (Peru) skewered cubes of beef heart with green peppers, charcoal grilled and brushed with a piquant sauce. Served as an hors d'oeuvre or bought from street vendors. Can also be made with chicken livers or fish

Arepas (Colombia, Venezuela) cornmeal buns usually crisp on the outside with a soft centre. Sometimes a piece of cheese is pushed into the dough before it is cooked. When the centre is removed and replaced with mixtures of meat, chicken and cheese or salad they are known as *tostadas*. Sold at *areperías*

Bollos pelones (Venezuela) *arepa* dough stuffed with spiced minced meat and fried or poached like dumplings

Buñuelos (Colombia) fried balls of corn flour mixed with cheese. Usually eaten for breakfast

Carimanolas (Panama) similar to *empanadas*

Chupe de mariscos (Chile) scallops with a cream and cheese sauce

Empanadas (Colombia, Venezuela, Chile) pies stuffed with chopped meat, onions, eggs, dried fruit and olives. Served as a first course with red wine or as a snack

Garullas one of the many varieties of bread in Colombia, these are simple rolls made with flour and eggs

Hallacas (Colombia, Venezuela) cornmeal mixed with beef, pork, vegetables and spices, wrapped in pieces of banana leaf and boiled. Similar to Mexican *tamales* and the *humitas* of Ecuador and Peru

Humitas (Chile, Ecuador, Peru) corn dough flavoured with chopped onion, sweet peppers, spices and possibly cheese,

wrapped in corn husks and cooked slowly in milk or water

Pan de horno (Chile) coarse country bread

Roti (Surinam) an Indian dough pancake stuffed with curried chicken and potatoes

Tequeños (Venezuela) pieces of cheese wrapped in dough and deep fried until crisp

Tostones (Venezuela) slices of plantain fried until crisp

Fish and shellfish

Bobópara Ibeiji (Brazil) an African dish originally prepared during religious ceremonies as an offering to the gods. It is a bland purée of dried shrimps, beans, sweet potatoes and bananas. Contemporary tastes being more demanding than those of the ancient gods, the modern version will also contain tomatoes, sweet peppers, cassava, coconut and a variety of spices

★**Caldillo de congrio** conger eel (the Chileans' favourite fish) stewed with onions, potatoes and tomatoes

Carurú a Bahian stew of shrimps, okra, onions, red peppers,

tomato, manioc meal, coconut milk and *dendê* (palm oil)

Centollas (Chile) marine crabs

Chipi chipi (Venezuela) tiny clams

Cholgas (Pampas) giant clams—a speciality of Tierra del Fuego

Cornalitos (Pampas) fried whitebait

Muelas de cangelo (Colombia) large crab claws, a speciality of Cartagena

Vatapa Bahian stew of dried shrimps, fish, peanuts, coconut milk and palm oil

Vindo de pescado (Colombia) fish stew traditionally cooked in a hole dug in the ground, lined with hot rocks

Meat

Bife beef is the favourite and ubiquitous meat in the Pampas Lands and is eaten in enormous quantities mostly in the form of large succulent steaks

  a caballo steak with two fried eggs on top

  a lo pobre (Chile) steak with potatoes, onions and two fried eggs on top

Carbonada criolla (Pampas) pumpkin stuffed with diced beef and baked

Carne con cuero (Pampas) beef roasted in its hide

Cazuela de ave (Chile) a soup-stew of rice, sweetcorn, chicken, beans, pumpkin and herbs

Churrasco (Brazil) skewered cubes of beef grilled over charcoal and served with a tomato and onion sauce

Curanto (Chile) a mixture of pork, seafood and vegetables baked in pits dug in the ground

Cuscuz paulista a speciality of São Paulo, related to the north African *couscous*; steamed cornmeal and manioc meal with a mixture of meat and vegetables and possibly fish or shellfish

★**Cuy** guinea pig, roasted or baked, the Ecuadorian national dish. Eaten also in Peru

★**Empanada saltena** the national dish of Bolivia: a mixture of ground meat, chicken, olives, raisins and diced potatoes in hot pepper sauce, stuffed into a large bread roll

★**Feijoada** an elaborate dish from Rio de Janeiro—a thick soup-stew made from black beans and containing pieces of beef, pork, sausage, pigs' tails and ears. Served with rice, *faròfa* and a pepper sauce. Garnished with sliced oranges

Galleto al primo canto (Brazil) young chicken, cut up, basted

with wine and oil and spit-
roasted

Lechón al horno (Bolivia) roast
suckling pig

Matambre (Pampas) meaning
"hunger killer"; a mammoth
steak, split, stuffed with spinach,
hard-boiled eggs, carrots and
onions, rolled up and roasted or
pot-roasted. Served hot or cold

Moksie metie (Surinam) several
kinds of meat with rice

Muchacho (Colombia) literally
"boy", a piece of beef stuffed
with whole carrots, onions,
bacon, hard-boiled eggs, and
flavoured with garlic and herbs
then roasted or pot-roasted.
Sometimes lamb is prepared in
the same way

Pabellón criollo (Venezuela) hash
of beef in tomato sauce served
with black beans, plantains and
rice

Pachamanca (Peru) a mixture of
meats and vegetables cooked in a
pit dug in the ground and lined
with hot stones and a layer of
aromatic leaves and grasses

Parilla criolla (Venezuela)
marinated pieces of beef grilled
over charcoal in the streets

Parillada (Chile, Pampas) a
mixture of meat and offal grilled
over charcoal and served with
potatoes and salad

Pastel de cambraye (Pampas)
ground meat, spiced, sweetened
and decorated with meringue and
sliced peaches

de choclo (Chile) a mixture of
beef and chicken with raisins,
eggs and onion covered in
cornmeal and a sprinkling of
sugar and baked

Pato no tucupi pieces of duck in a
rich spicy sauce. From the
Amazon delta

Picante de pollo (Bolivia) chicken
fried with potatoes and rice and
served with salad and plenty of
aji (chillis)

Rijsttafel (Surinam) see *The
Netherlands*

Sarapatel Bahian casserole of
sheep's or pig's liver and hearts,
fresh blood, tomatoes, sweet
peppers and onions

Side dishes

Acara, acaraje small fritters
consisting of spoonfuls of
mashed black-eyed beans with
minced dried shrimp, onions and
sweet peppers fried in palm oil. A
Bahian dish

Angú (Brazil) a thick "porridge"
of coconut milk and rice flour,
served with meat

Cambuquira (Brazil) pumpkin
flowers, usually fried or frittered

Caraotas negras (Venezuela)
black beans

★**Causa a la limeña** an Andean
dish of mashed potatoes mixed
with lemon juice, oil, onion and
chillis and decorated with fresh
vegetables

★**Culonas** (Colómbia) a delicacy
of fried ants from the
Bucaramanga area of Santander

Farófa a preparation of manioc
meal, mixed with a variety of
ingredients and browned in oil or
butter, used for stuffing meats
and vegetables or as a side dish

Guasacaca (Venezuela) a peppery
sauce made from avocados,
tomatoes, lime juice, hard-boiled

eggs, chillis and spices. Served
with grilled meats

Llapingachos (Ecuador) dish of
baked mashed potato and
cheese

Metemgee (Guyana) a mixture of
yams, cassava and plantains
cooked in coconut milk

Palacones de plátano (Panama)
fried plantains

Palmitos (Brazil) palm hearts,
used in salads, soups and a
variety of baked dishes

Papas indigenous Andean
potatoes have been a staple for
centuries. The poorest Indians
eat them boiled and flavoured
with a little chilli (*aji*) or possibly
covered in a thick cheese sauce
(a recent addition, the Indians
having learnt the art of cheese-
making from their Spanish
conquerors)

chorriadas (Colombia) boiled
potatoes covered with cheese,
onions and tomatoes and
flavoured with coriander, a
favourite South American herb.
From Bogotá

★ **a la huancaina** (Peru) a more
sophisticated version of the
traditional Peruvian dish—
boiled potatoes with a cheese and
chilli sauce, decorated with
olives, onions, the mild Peruvian
chilli (*mirasol*), hard-boiled eggs
or whatever else is available
Pirao (Brazil) cornmeal or rice
flour and coconut milk porridge,
moulded and chilled

Porotos granados (Chile) a
mixture of cooked beans, sweetcorn and chopped pumpkin or
squash, with garlic and onions.
An Indian dish
Purée de apio (Venezuela) a
chestnut-like flavoured purée of
local roots (*apio*) with added
butter and seasoning
Sopaipillas (Chile) fried pumpkin
rissoles

Manioc

Manioc (*Manihot utilissima*) has been a staple food of the
Amerindians for centuries. It is very easily cultivated and its
thick tuberous roots produce quantities of a starchy, rather
bland, but nutritious food which is still widely used throughout South and Central America and parts of the Caribbean.
Known also as cassava, *mandioca* or *yuca* in Spanish areas and
aipím or *macaxeira* in Brazil, there are two varieties, bitter and
sweet. The roots of bitter cassava contain a deadly poison
which is laboriously extracted by peeling and grating the roots
and pressing out the juice, leaving the dry crumbly manioc
meal behind. Manioc juice was one of the substances used by
some of the more ferocious Amerindians to poison the tips of
their arrows and darts. The poison may also be expelled during
the long hours of cooking needed to make cassava roots
edible. Manioc meal is used in a multitude of different dishes,
in soups, stews and purées, and it can be boiled or fried and
mixed with spices to form an accompaniment to main dishes.
It is also used in cakes and bread in the form of a flour known
simply as *farine* in French Guiana and as *farinha de mandioca*
in Brazil where it often appears on the table in a shaker and
is sprinkled over everything and anything to mop up the juices.
John Hemming says in *Red Gold*, his book about the
Brazilian Indians, "Europeans ate Indian dishes made from
manioc: mingau porridge, beiju cakes like unleavened bread,
tapioca, and the sawdust-like roast flour or farinha. The
first governors of Brazil all ate bread made from manioc."
Manioc is best known outside Latin America as tapioca.

Desserts and fruit

Chirimoya a tropical fruit
particularly associated with
Ecuador and Peru. Has a rather
lumpy greenish skin, pure white
flesh and black seeds. Very sweet
with a slight tang. Sometimes
called "strawberry of heaven"
Crema de abacate (Brazil) sieved
avocado flesh flavoured with lime
juice and sugar. Served chilled
Cujado con melado (Colombia) a
dessert consisting of milk curds
in a syrup of cane juice
Dulce de leche (Pampas) a
concoction of milk and
caramelized sugar
Foo foo (Guyana) African

influenced plantain cakes
Guanabana (Venezuela) see *The
Caribbean*
Lechosa (Venezuela) papaya
Mamão (Brazil) papaya
Maracuja (Brazil) passion-fruit
Mazamorra morada (Peru)
dessert made with cornstarch and
dried fruit
Pan de Pascua (Chile) fruit cake
eaten at Easter
Pepinos (Ecuador) fruit similar to
cucumber but sweet
Picarones (Peru) a kind of
doughnut made with cassava
flour, fried in oil and soaked in
syrup

The pattern of eating throughout southeast Asia is so similar that I have grouped all the countries together. The diet everywhere is based on rice, usually plainly boiled or steamed, often rather sticky and undercooked, in the hope that it will swell in the stomach and give hungry people the illusion of having eaten more. The second common denominator is the extensive use of spices, most of them obvious, even familiar, such as chilli and coriander. Some are more obscure such as *laos*, a powdered root that looks like ginger but tastes more medicinal; lemon grass, an aromatic grass; citrus leaves; tamarind, a pod used to give an acid taste to sweet-and-sour sauce; and

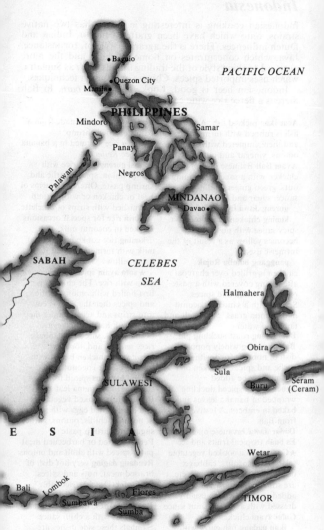

a fish paste made of salted, dried shrimps (incidentally rather what *garum*, which the ancient Romans put on everything, must have been like). Finally, they all share an interest in the presentation of food, which is often served in hollowed-out fruit or vegetables or surrounded with flowers.

In general, you will find that all the food comes at the same time, soup included. Desserts other than fruit are rare, except in Thailand. The only other thing to remember is that manners are infinitely important. Service may be slow, but it will be exquisitely courteous. Rather the same behaviour is expected of the guests.

Indonesia

Indonesian cooking is interesting in that it has two native strains, onto which have been grafted Chinese, Indian and Dutch influences. There is the agrarian style of, for instance, Java, which concentrates on home produce, and the more outward-looking style of the trading islands, such as Sumatra, which uses imported spices, Chinese and Indian techniques.

Indonesian beer is good. Look for *bintang baru*. In Bali there is a fierce rice wine called *bremu*.

Acar ikan pickled fish. A whole fish is rubbed with turmeric, fried and then simmered with chillis, onions, vinegar and nuts

Ayam Bali Balinese dish of fried chicken with a sauce containing nuts, green ginger, chillis, soy sauce, sugar and vinegar

  goreng Jawa fried chicken

  kuning chicken simmered in a spicy sauce with no chillis. It becomes yellow as a result of the turmeric used

  panggang bumbu Rujak chicken is grilled over charcoal after being covered with a paste of coconut milk and spices. Served with a sauce of coconut milk, lemon grass, sugar, salt and tamarind water

Babi guling roast suckling pig

Bakmi goreng widely popular dish of noodles fried with onions, garlic and spices. Chicken or shrimp may be added

Bebek betutu spiced duckling wrapped in banana leaves and baked in embers. A festive dish from Bali

Dadar Jawa Javanese omelette

És buah tropical fruits and ice

★**Gado-gado** a cooked vegetable salad. Beansprouts, cabbage, beans, potatoes, cucumber, etc., are stir fried, a hard-boiled egg is added, and the dish is usually dressed with a spicy peanut sauce

Gulai ayam chicken curry

  ikan padang fish curry with tamarind, *laos*, turmeric, chillis, lemon grass and coconut milk

Ikan asam manis sweet-sour fish with sugar, vinegar and spices

  masak Bali fish with shrimp paste and green ginger

Kalio ayam chicken curry. The sauce is thickened with coconut milk and ground nuts

Ketupat boiled glutinous rice wrapped in a coconut leaf

Krupuk crispy puff made from a batter of dried shrimp

Lontong rice steamed in a banana leaf. See *Ketupat*

★**Nasi goreng** fried rice with chillis, onion, spices, garlic and shrimp paste. Often with strips of beef or chicken or with shrimp. Garnished with strips of omelette

  gurih rice for special occasions cooked in coconut milk

  kuning rice cooked in coconut milk with turmeric so that it turns yellow

★**soto ayam** spiced chicken soup with rice. The chicken is first boiled with onions, garlic and spices then the flesh is cut into strips and accompanies the soup, with hard-boiled eggs, beansprouts, shredded cabbage, rice, *sambal*, and noodles

Opor ayam chicken baked with spices in thick coconut milk

Pangai bungkus spiced fish steamed in a banana leaf

Pecel lightly cooked vegetables and hard-boiled eggs with a sauce of peanuts, chillis, onions, garlic, sugar and shrimp paste

Perkedel fried or barbecued meat patty spiced with chilli and onions

Rendang daging very hot dish of braised meat, nuts and spices

Rijsttafel (Dutch) "rice table" with a vast array of dishes

Rujak Javanese dish of fruit and vegetables with a chilli sauce

Sambals these side dishes are mostly very fiery sauces, eaten in small quantities to complement the main dish

  goreng hati liver fried in a hot chilli sauce

  goreng telur hard-boiled eggs in a chilli and coconut sauce

  kacang spicy peanut *sambal*

  kelapa grated coconut mixed with chilli and shrimp paste

  trasi steamed shrimp paste

mixed with chilli, onion, sugar, oil and lime juice. From Java
★ **Saté** the national dish of Indonesia, served for every festive occasion and sold at street stalls. Cubes of meat or seafood are coated with spices and barbecued on bamboo skewers. Served with a hot peanut sauce
  ayam boned chicken marinated in garlic and soy sauce and barbecued
  daging strips of meat marinated and barbecued
  kambing bumbu kecap goat or mutton cubes marinated in garlic, onion, soy sauce and shrimp paste
  padang cubes of heart, liver or tripe marinated and skewered
  udang skewered shrimp coated in chilli, shrimp paste and ground nuts, then barbecued

Sayur asam sweet-sour vegetable soup
  lodeh mixed vegetables in coconut milk spiced with ginger, tamarind and coriander
Semur daging meat fried in soy sauce with ginger and sugar
Serundeng peanut and coconut *sambal* with ginger and sugar
Singgang ayam chicken flattened and spread with a spicy paste, simmered in coconut milk, then roasted
Soto ayam spicy chicken soup
Tahu goreng kecap deep-fried soya bean curd served with beansprouts, cabbage and cucumber and a spicy sauce
Tumis stir-fried vegetables with chillis, onions and garlic
Urap green vegetables served in a spicy coconut sauce

Useful words

Air water
Blakhan shrimp paste
Bon bill
Buah fruit
Gula sugar
Gulai curry
Jeruk citrus fruits
Keju cheese
Kelapa coconut
Kopi coffee

Mah mee, mee hoon noodles
Mentega butter
Nasi cooked rice
Roti bread
Sayur vegetables (in broth)
Sop, soto soup
Susu milk
Teh tea
Telur egg
T(e)rasi shrimp paste (Java)

Selamat makan! bon appétit!
Selamat! cheers!

Malaysia

Traditional Malay food is very like Indonesian and many of the dishes have similar names, so consult the Indonesian section for dishes not listed here.

Ayam golek whole chicken simmered in a spicy sauce with tomatoes, onions, vinegar and coconut milk
  kecap feast-day dish of spiced chicken with green ginger, soy sauce, garlic, onion and lemon grass
  kelantan chicken spread with a mixture of coconut milk, onions, chillis and shrimp paste, barbecued
Gulai daging lembu beef curry with carefully combined spices,

simmered in coconut milk and tamarind water
Hai yup yue cubes of fish deep-fried and served with a coconut milk and crab sauce
Jarp we mun yue whole fish stewed in a chilli, onion, soy and sugar sauce with shredded pork, salt cabbage and mushrooms
Jarp yun yuk cubes of beef marinated in sugar and tamarind, then rolled in a spicy nut, shrimp and ginger paste and simmered in coconut milk and the marinade

Jow ho yay oysters egg-and-breadcrumbed and deep fried

   udang goreng small deep-fried minced shrimp cakes

Kachang bendi goreng okra simmered with shrimp, nuts, chillis, onions and shrimp paste

Kelapa sayur chopped vegetables simmered in spicy coconut milk

Khow muck yue strips of cuttlefish fried with bamboo shoots, mushrooms, pork and other vegetables in a soy sauce

Laksa asam noodles in a sour fish soup flavoured with tamarind

   lemak spicy noodle soup with coconut milk, fish, bean curd, beansprouts, cucumber, lettuce and shrimp

Masak lemak cabbage cooked in coconut milk and a spicy paste with shrimp

Mee goreng fried noodles served with shredded chicken, shrimp and vegetables

Otak otak flaked fish coated with garlic, chillis, ginger, nuts, sugar

and spices and wrapped in banana leaves. Either steamed or grilled over charcoal

Panggang ikan bawal small fish first marinated in coconut milk with onion, garlic and chilli, then wrapped in banana leaves and grilled over charcoal

Pisang goreng banana fritters

Popiah paper-thin pastry rolled up around a variety of vegetables, shrimps, shredded pork, chillis and garlic, and fried

Sambal blachan *sambal* of chillis, shrimp paste and lime leaves

   goreng ikan bilis small dried fish deep fried until crispy and served with a hot chilli and peanut sauce

Satay see *Saté (Indonesia)*

   ayam spiced chicken roasted in coconut milk and tamarind juice

Serikaya egg and coconut custard

Telor dadar omelette spiced with chillis and onions

Udang ubi spicy shrimp with fried potatoes

Useful words

Air water
Bil bill
Daging meat
Gula sugar
Guleng milk
Hidangan menu

Ikan fish
Kopi coffee
Mentega butter
Roti bread
Teh tea
Wain wine

Harap di-nikmati hidangan-hidangan! bon appétit!
Syabas! cheers!

The Philippines

The Philippines have the unusual (for southeast Asia) influence of Spain and, of course more recently, the United States, but their own particular distinctions are palm vinegar and a slightly different fermented fish-paste, which give the food particular sour and salty tastes.

   Beer is good, especially *San Miguel*. Otherwise try *tuba*, a strong drink made from coconut palm sap, or *tapoy*, rice wine.

★**Adobo** pieces of chicken and pork marinated in a mixture of vinegar, garlic, bayleaves, salt and pepper, then fried

Adobong sugpo giant shrimp marinated, then fried in butter

Balut hard-boiled duck's egg with partially developed embryo, considered a delicacy

Bibingka cake of rice, coconut milk and brown sugar, baked

Gulaman fresh fruit jelly

Halo-halo literally "mix-mix"; a liquid dessert of ice and coconut milk with fruit, sweetcorn, etc.

★ **Kari-kari** oxtail stew with onion and garlic, thickened with crushed peanut and rice flour

Lapu-lapu a succulent white fish
Lechon spit-roasted suckling pig
★ **Lumpia** paper-thin pastry rolls,
stuffed with shredded vegetables,
meat and shrimps, and deep fried.
They may also be served fresh
when the filling is first rolled in a
lettuce leaf before being wrapped
in pastry
Makapuno special coconut with a
creamy, tender flesh
Pan de sal small, salted crisp rolls
Pancit guisado noodles with
chopped meats, shrimps and
vegetables
Paksiw a sour dish of fish
simmered with shrimps, bitter
melon, eggplant, ginger, chillis
and vinegar

Pata crispy roast pork hock
Puto sweet steamed rice cake
Rellenong alimango crab shells,
stuffed with crabmeat and
scallions and fried with egg
Sinampalukan thick sour soup
made with tamarind leaves with
fish or chicken and vegetables
Sinigang sour soup with seafood,
vegetables and sour fruits
Suman cigar-shaped cake made
of glutinous rice and wrapped in
coconut leaves
Tapa slices of pork or beef
marinated, dried and quick
fried
Ukoy tiny batter cakes with
chopped shrimps, grated sweet
potatoes and pumpkin

Useful words

Alak wine
Asugal sugar
Cape coffee
Isda fish
Karne meat

Kuwenta, resibo bill
Menú, putahe menu
Tinapay bread
Tsaa tea
Tubig water

Masaganang pagkain! bon appétit!
Mabuhay! cheers!

Thailand

Thai food owes less to European influence than some of its
neighbours and has more in common with India and China,
though appearance and presentation is almost as important
as it is in Japan.

I have not used Thai script in the listings as I felt that it
would be impossible to master casually. With luck, menus
will have a translation and English is quite widely spoken.

The beer is worth trying—either the traditional *singha* or
the new *amarit*. So is the potent *mae khong* whisky.

Haw mok hot dish of chopped
raw fish covered with a paste of
chillis, onions, lemon grass,
garlic, coconut milk and soy
sauce, steamed
Kaeng chued clear soup eaten
with rice and with other dishes
   chued mu ba-chaw clear soup of
ground pork balls and vegetables
   chued pla clear soup with balls
of flaked fish
   chued wun sen clear soup with
vermicelli, Chinese mushrooms
and green vegetables
Kaeng masaman Moslem
curry made with beef or chicken.

The meat is first simmered in
coconut milk then mixed with a
spicy but mild curry paste
   nua beef fried with onions,
garlic and ginger, then simmered
with a mild but spicy curry paste,
coconut milk and tomatoes
   ped kai curry of chicken
simmered in coconut milk
Kai tod chicken coated with a
blend of garlic, coriander and
pepper sauce and fried
   yang marinated, grilled chicken
served with a piquant sauce
Kao lao luk chin clear soup with
meat balls and beansprouts

pud bland fried rice, pieces of crabmeat, chicken, pork, egg and onion with a dash of saffron

tom kai slices of chicken poached with rice in stock

Khai cheow plain omelette

luk kuey literally "son-in-law's egg"; golden-brown deep-fried eggs with a *nam pla* sauce

palo boiled eggs cooked with garlic, pepper, sugar and pork

Kung pao grilled king shrimp served with chillis and *nam pla*

pud prik shrimp fried with chillis

sadung fai king shrimp deep fried with garlic and herbs

Ma hor halved oranges or other fruit stuffed with a spicy, baked, ground pork mixture

Mee krob crisp fried noodles with herbs and spices, garnished with a mixture of shrimp, pork, chicken and vegetables

Muh daeng tenderly roasted pork

Nam pla strong, salty fish sauce

prik very hot pungent sauce that is served as a dip for vegetables or fish. Contains dried shrimps, garlic, *nam pla* and chillis, with a little sugar and lime juice. *Prik* means "chilli"

Nua pud prik beef simmered in a predominantly chilli sauce with garlic, sugar and *nam pla*

Ped yang duck marinated with five-spice powder, pepper, garlic and soy sauce, then roasted

Peek kai namdang fried chicken wings in a sweet and sour gravy

Pla chien steamed fried fish in a sharp chilli and ginger sauce

rad prik crispy deep-fried fish

Poh-taek "fisherman's soup"; seafood and mushrooms simmered in a sour broth

Pra ram long song beef fried with garlic and onions and then simmered with vegetables

Pu ja chunks of crabmeat mixed with ground pork, mushrooms, scallions, chillis, ginger and garlic, stuffed into a crab shell and deep fried

Pud thua ngork stir-fried beansprouts with pork, shrimp, sugar and *nam pla*

Sarim dessert of sweet soya bean noodles in coconut milk

Sen mee rice-stick noodles

Sungkaya dessert made from coconut milk, eggs and sugar

Tod man pla minced freshwater fish mixed with green beans and curry paste and fried

Tom yam kung sour soup cooked with lemon grass, lime leaves, garlic, chillis, scallions, *nam pla* and mint and coriander leaves. Whole shrimp are added before serving

Yam word meaning "to mix with the hands", used as a prefix for any tossed salad

Useful words

Ba-mee noodles
Bai-set bill
Kanom pang bread
Kapi shrimp paste
Karfay coffee
Lao argoon rice wine
Maprao coconut

Nam water
Nam cha rorn China tea
Namtarn sugar
Nom milk
Nua meat
Pla fish
Raikarn-aharn menu

Koh hai im num samran! bon appétit!
Chern-duem krab! *or* **Swadee!** cheers!

Vietnam

Vietnamese food has become better known over the last few years, which is probably the only happy thing to have resulted from the recent history of the country. The cooking is fairly close to Chinese in style, but it is spicier and has been lent a certain extra refinement by French colonial influence.

Ban canh soup with ham, shrimp, *nuoc mam*, vermicelli noodles, scallions and coriander

★ **Bo can quay** squab rubbed with a sauce of honey, soy sauce, five-spice powder, garlic, onion and oil, roasted

nhung dam beef fondue: each diner takes a rice pancake, puts a few pieces of chopped herbs and vegetables on it, then cooks some strips of beef, puts them in the pancake, rolls it up and dips it in *nuoc mam*

Bun a dish of soya beans, vermicelli noodles and meat

bo beef sautéed with onions and garlic, sprinkled with peanuts and mixed with noodles

Ca chien muoi xa fish rubbed with lemon grass, oil, garlic, salt and chillis and fried

Canh chua sweet-and-sour fish soup flavoured with tamarind

Cha gio *or* **nem** (in North Vietnam) deep-fried rice-pastry rolls filled with ground pork or chicken, noodles, beansprouts, Chinese mushrooms, crabmeat, onion and garlic. Wrapped in lettuce and mint leaves and dipped in *nuoc mam*

Chao bao ngu rice, pork and abalone soup

bot ban ground onion and beef with tapioca in consommé

ga chicken and rice soup

tom small balls of minced shrimps with garlic, egg white and oil, skewered on sugar-cane sticks and grilled. Eaten wrapped in mint leaves in a thin rice pancake, and dipped in *nuoc mam*

Chuoi chien fruit fritters

duong thang bananas cooked in a caramel sauce

Com plain rice

dua rice cooked in coconut milk with cloves and cinnamon

ga chicken marinated with onion, garlic, lemon grass and soy sauce and barbecued

rang rice sautéed with onion in oil and served with strips of egg, crabmeat, shrimps, ham, etc.

Cua rang muoi crabs sautéed with garlic and onion

xao chua ngot crab simmered with onion, shallots, garlic, vinegar, sugar and soy sauce

Ga nuong ngu vi chicken highly flavoured with soy sauce, five-spice powder, honey and garlic, grilled

Goi gia salad of beansprouts, sometimes with crab or shrimps

Heo kho chopped onion and pork sautéed in a caramel sauce and then simmered in coconut milk

lui strips of pork marinated in a sauce of onion, *nuoc mam*, garlic and oil and grilled

Hoa qua tron exotic fruit salad

Luon xao mien eel sautéed with onion and vermicelli noodles

Mang cua soup of crabmeat and asparagus tips

Nai nuong venison marinated with lemon grass, chilli, onion, garlic, *nuoc mam* and five-spice powder, skewered and grilled

Nuoc mam salty fish sauce

Pho Hanoi soup; noodles, shrimps, thin meat slices and chopped scallions in consommé

Tom sot cay spicy dish of shrimp sautéed with onion, ginger, chillis, tomato and vinegar

Vit tan duck marinated in ginger and rice wine and stuffed with a mixture of lotus seeds, prunes, mushrooms, chestnuts, ginger, shallots and peanuts, steamed

Useful words

Banh my bread
Bir beer
Ca fish
Caphe coffee
Duong sugar
Hoa don bill

Nuoc water
Qua fruit
Ruou wine
Thit meat
Thuc don menu
Tra tea

Chuc an ngon! bon appétit!
Can chen! cheers!

Spanish cookery is by no means a cuisine—a word which suggests a certain confinement and rigidity, both of place and conduct. Yet it has character and strength and can even surprise one with its delicacy when it comes to some fish or vegetable dishes

Essentially, however, it is a seemingly haphazard piling together of whatever ingredients come to hand. No other nation puts meat and fowl and fish together with such abandon. No two Spaniards cook any named dish in precisely the same way. There are no rules of conduct. That is exuberant.

But to me the real charm of Spanish food is the feeling that it needs no kitchen—a huge pot and an open fire on a beach or in the fields is the spirit of it, the food of picnics and fiestas at which everyone is welcome.

Eating out

Strict quality control is enforced by the Spanish government in most eating-places.

Restaurants (*restaurantes*) are classified according to fork symbols, hence five forks represent a de-luxe establishment and one fork a fourth-class one. Cafeterias, open all day, have three classes, denoted by cup symbols, from one to three. Menus are divided into five groups (*grupos*). Each group will contain a certain number of dishes according to the category of the restaurant. Lower categories may only have three or four groups. All restaurants offer some kind of *menú turístico* (tourist's menu).

Spanish alphabetical order is: a, b, c, ch, d–l, ll, m, n, ñ, o–z

★ *Tapas y entremeses*—*Canapés and hors d'oeuvre*

Human beings, from the purely physical point of view, should ideally eat little and often, but sociability and convenience militate against this academic sanitary arrangement. We like rollicking meals at which to enjoy ourselves with friends. Anyhow who wants to cook eight times a day?

The Spanish eat two large meals at curiously inappropriate times, with the result that they would spend much of the day feeling hungry were it not for the happy invention of *tapas*.

These are delicious little canapés and small dishes, which can be found in any bar at any time of day and which are served in houses and hotels in the long waiting periods before lunch (*el almuerzo*) or dinner (*la cena*).

Some translate the word *tapas* as "blotting paper", rather on the lines of Russian *zakuski*, which always go with vodka. Others say it means "lid", developing from the old Spanish habit of putting a piece of bread over a glass, to keep the flies out. Whatever the truth, they are excellent and sometimes, when dinner does not come till after midnight, positively life-saving.

Alcachofas a la vinagreta artichokes served chilled with vinaigrette dressing

Almejas en salsa de ajo cooked clams served in a garlic, oil and parsley sauce

Almendras tostadas almonds toasted in butter

Anchoas en aceite anchovies in olive oil

Angulas baby eels fried with oil, garlic and chilli

Boquerones fritos fried whitebait

Calamares a la romana squid fried in batter

Caracoles en salsa snails simmered in a sauce of onion, garlic, parsley and tomatoes

Champiñones mushrooms

Chanquetes tiny fish much like whitebait

Chipirones a la plancha baby squid cooked on a hot-plate with oil, garlic and parsley

★Chorizo al diablo (*or* **al infierno**) spicy red sausage flambéed in alcohol

Ensaladilla Russian salad

Gambas a la plancha buttered grilled shrimp, served with lemon

Huevas aliñadas cod's roes

Huevos rellenos a la española halved hard-boiled egg whites stuffed with a variety of mixtures, such as tuna and tomato paste, covered in mayonnaise

Lomo pork fillet, sliced

Mejillones en concha mussels cooked in white wine, kept in their shells, covered with breadcrumbs, lemon juice, butter and parsley and grilled

Pan con tomate y jamón toast rubbed with tomato, covered in olive oil and served with a slice of *jamón serrano*

Pinchitos, pinchos small kebabs

Salchichón type of salami

Sopas—*Soups*

Calderada a Galician fish soup almost as thick as *bouillabaisse*

Caldo de pescado fish broth made with white fish

de pimentón a potato, fish and green pepper soup

Consommé de gallina chicken consommé

Crema sevillana smooth tomato and onion soup with strips of roasted red pepper

Escudilla barrejada de Cataluña vegetable soup with rice and macaroni

Farro vegetable soup cooked in ham stock with vermicelli

★Gazpacho Spain's most famous cold soup, which owes its freshness to the fact that the ingredients are raw. Tomatoes, onions, sweet peppers and cucumber are all chopped, soaked in vinegar and mixed with oil, breadcrumbs and minced garlic. The liquid is provided by ice. In some places the chopped vegetables are served separately with croûtons

Potaje a la riojana salt cod soup thickened with minced turnips, onions and corn flour, flavoured with nutmeg and garlic, sprinkled with croûtons

de col thick, creamy cabbage soup

de habas secas dried bean soup made with bacon

de judías blancas thick white bean and vegetable soup, often with slices of *butifarra* sausage in it

madrileño chick peas and dried cod are mixed with spinach, and flavoured with chilli and saffron to make a thick soup

Pote gallego broth made with white beans, pork, sausage and cabbage, thickened with mashed potatoes. As with so many Spanish soups, the pork and sausage and other ingredients are taken out and served later as a main course

Puré de cangrejos crayfish soup

de garbanzos purée of chick peas

Purrusalda a Basque salt-cod soup with leeks, garlic and potatoes

Sopa a la barcelonesa broth, thickened with toast and added meat balls and thick brown gravy

a la mallorquina thick vegetable purée cooked with a lot of bread

a la valenciana ham, sausage and rice in broth

a la vizcaína haricot bean, pumpkin and cabbage soup

al estilo de Pulgcerdá a north Spanish mountain version of bread and milk

Costa Brava soup of mixed white fish

★ **de ajo** garlic soup. There are many variations of this, but all include an egg per person, often bread, grapes, almonds or whatever and are therefore more filling than you might expect

de ajo blanco slices of melon in a cold garlic and almond soup

de albóndigas a la catalana tomato sauce and toast heated in stock with added meat balls

de Aragón liver and cheese soup

de bolitas fried potato and ham balls in broth

de Cádiz fish soup with rice

de coles a la asturiana cabbage and potato soup poured over bread with grated cheese

de crema de ave cream of chicken soup

★ **de cuarto de hora** fish soup made with oysters, clams, mussels or *ostiones*, some white fish, shrimp, almost always rice, hard-boiled eggs and bacon. The ingredients vary enormously

de empanadillas small fried veal, ham or chicken pies in broth

de galets fried pork balls simmered with celery, saffron and *galets*—shell-shaped pasta—served with grated cheese on top

de gambas shrimp soup with wine and chillis

de macarrones y almejas macaroni and mussel soup

de mandonguilles a la catalana tiny beef balls in chicken stock

de mejillones mussel soup, often with rice

del norte rice in a chicken and meat broth with sliced sausage

de nueces hazelnut and almond soup

de pan con gambas shrimp and vegetable soup with lots of sliced bread in it

de patata rallada potato soup with chopped hard-boiled egg. *Rallada* means "grated"

de picadillo with hard-boiled eggs, ham and rice

de primavera spring soup of fresh young vegetables

de rabo de buey oxtail soup

de rape rich soup of angler fish with ground hazelnuts and peanuts, onions, tomatoes and breadcrumbs, flavoured with garlic and saffron

de vainas green bean and potato soup

de vigilia soup of mixed fish, mussels and rice for fast days

granadina a moderately light soup of tomatoes, sweet peppers and onions, spiced with saffron and garlic, served with cubes of bread

leonesa made with fine wheatmeal, milk and beef dripping, flavoured with cinnamon and lemon, thickened with egg yolk and poured over fried bread

Huevos — Eggs

Greixera d'ous sliced hard-boiled eggs on a bed of mixed vegetables; a Majorcan dish

Huevos a la alicantina poached eggs in hollowed-out potatoes, with a shrimp sauce

a la castellana eggs on a bed of ground beef, covered with béchamel, sprinkled with cheese and baked

a la catalana eggs baked on a bed of ground pork and ham with tomatoes

a la flamenca eggs baked on a bed of peas, beans, sausage and ham, covered with red pepper

a la gitanilla "gypsy eggs", baked on a paste of almonds, garlic, bread, spices and oil

al Jerez eggs baked with kidneys in a sherry sauce

a la marinera eggs with strips of ham and chicken in aspic

a la menorquina hard-boiled eggs in a thick mayonnaise, with shrimp-stuffed hake or halibut

al nido egg yolks, put in a slice of hollowed-out bread, surrounded by beaten egg white and fried

al plato eggs on fried sausage and tomato, sprinkled with cheese and baked

a la riojana eggs baked on a bed of sausage, tomatoes and peppers

a la santanderina eggs baked with peas and asparagus

a la sevillana fried eggs on a bed of tomatoes, onions and ham

a la valenciana fried eggs on a mushroom, cheese and tomato sauce risotto

a la andaluza poached eggs with mussels and cod on a bed of rice

con arroz hard-boiled eggs, stuffed with a mixture of their yolks and ham, flavoured with brandy, served with rice decorated with red peppers

empanados poached eggs, egg-and-breadcrumbed and fried

en panecillos eggs in hollowed-out bread rolls, fried and topped with chopped hard-boiled eggs and parsley

escalfados poached eggs

fritos a la andaluza fried eggs, served with fried sausage, ham and artichoke hearts

mallorquinos fried eggs with fried red pepper sausage, covered in a vegetable purée

primavera eggs baked with string beans, tomatoes and a little ham, sprinkled with cheese

revueltos scrambled eggs

revueltos El Coll a bizarre dish, not much like scrambled eggs, because the yolks are cooked with puréed tomatoes and the stiffly beaten whites added at the last moment, so it looks a bit like a fluffy strawberry mousse

Pastel de tortillas a sandwich of three omelettes, one spinach, one tomato and one onion, placed on top of each other with a layer of béchamel between them

Pisto a la bilbaína beaten eggs fried with zucchini and green peppers

castellanos beaten eggs simmered with zucchini red peppers, onions, tomatoes, potatoes and ham

Tortilla a la barcelonesa chicken liver and ham omelette served with two sauces—one cheese, the other spinach—and tomatoes

Tortilla alcarreña omelette with asparagus, sausage and ham

al estilo de Badajoz sausage and chilli omelette

al sacromonte brains, sweetbreads, potatoes and peas in an omelette

campesina red pepper, mushroom and tomato omelette. In this tortilla the egg whites are beaten separately, so it is fluffier than is usual

coruñesa bacon omelette

española the Spanish omelette. This is no feathery affair, but a serious tough munch, even more solid cold than hot. Often made with potato, always overcooked. Not one of the joys of Spain. An ordinary omelette is called *Tortilla francesa*

madrileña ham and onion omelette served with sweetbreads

murciana red pepper and tomato omelette

primavera with ham, potatoes, carrots, asparagus and peas

riojana ham, sausage and red pepper omelette

Arroz — *Rice*

Rice plays an important part in Spanish cooking and it is thought of as being the main ingredient in dishes which may contain much more fish or meat than rice. This is a sign of increased prosperity. Originally the balance might have been very different and indeed still is in poorer districts. Rice dishes are likely to be filling and in the case of *paella* may be a whole meal. In many cases what we would think of as *paella* is simply called *Arroz a la whatever region*. Even the classic *paella* is sometimes listed as *Arroz a la valenciana*.

Arroz a la alicantina rice with white fish, artichokes and green peppers

★ **a banda** boiled saffron rice, served with stewed angler fish and shellfish. This is a famous fisherman's dish, with many variations, often including as many as six different fish

a la mallorquina rice boiled with squab and mussels, mixed with beans, peas and white fish, covered with sliced pepper sausage (*sobrasada*) and baked

a la marinera rice boiled with shrimp, white fish, cockles and squid, decorated with sweet peppers and asparagus

a la murciana a casserole of rice, pork, red peppers and tomatoes

a la primavera rice boiled with cauliflower, peas, artichoke hearts and asparagus

a la riojana a mould of rice, sausage and ham covered with tomato sauce

a la zamorana rice boiled with pig's foot, ear, cheek and tongue, turnips and onions

gallego rice with mushrooms and onions, served with a tomato sauce

regencia a mould of saffron rice and a little chopped ham, covered with a mushroom and chicken-liver sauce

★**Paella** this is the one Spanish dish which is world famous. In origin it is Arab, for it was the Moors who brought rice to Spain in the eighth century, but it is typically Spanish in that no two people make it in exactly the same way and that almost anything can go into it. There are no rules— even the question of whether the rice or the stock goes first into the frying mixture of meat, shellfish, and vegetables is a matter of keen dispute. The charm of *paella* is its combination of tastes, the consistency of the rice (which is never really quite fried and yet never soggy) and the splendid colour and flavour lent by the saffron. The classic *paella* is *a la valenciana*, but I have listed also a few of the more extreme variations. The name *paella* is the name of the dish in which it is cooked—a heavy iron pan, usually oval, with two handles. It is often served in the pan

a la campesina with ham, chicken, sausage and song birds

a la valenciana see *Paella alicantina* with rabbit, mussels, shrimp and red peppers. This version of *paella* is firm and can be cut in slices

bruta with pork, chicken and white fish

catalana with chicken, snails, beans, peas and artichokes

de mariscos with crayfish, shrimp, squid, angler fish and tomatoes

Pasta and pizza

Pasta is not really a Spanish affair. Nevertheless, various kinds appear on menus and are popular.

The spellings of the usual ones are as follows: *canalones, macarrones, noquis* (gnocchi) and *spagetis*. *Fideos* usually means vermicelli, but can include spaghetti or any long pasta. In Majorca there is a pleasant kind of pizza called *coca Mallorquina*.

Pescado y mariscos — Fish and seafood

Almejas clams, cockles, mussels

Anchoas anchovies

Anguila eel

Arenque herring

Atún tuna

Bacalao al pil-pil salt cod with chillis

Berberechos cockles

Besugo al horno casserole of porgy with pounded garlic, onion and pine nuts, cooked in white wine and lemon juice

Bogavante lobster

Boquerones whitebait

Caballa type of mackerel

★**Calamares en su tinta** young squid fried with onions, served in a sauce made with their ink. It looks black and sinister but is one of my favourite Spanish dishes

Caldereta asturiana a stew of red mullet, porgy, mackerel, flounder and mussels with red peppers, almonds, hazelnuts and sherry

Camarones shrimps

Cangrejo crab

Centolla large sea crab

★**Centollos** these spider crabs are usually minced after cooking, sautéed with tomato sauce, sherry and brandy and put back in their shells for serving, smothered in melted butter

Cigalas variety of crayfish

Chipirones small squid

Chocos squid

Erizos de mar sea urchins

Fritura de pescado mixed fried fish

Gambas shrimp

Lamprea lamprey

★**Langosta a la barcelonesa** spiny lobster sautéed with chicken and simmered with chopped tomatoes and ground almonds

Langostino deep sea shrimp

Lenguado a la andaluza sole rolled up with a red pepper and parsley stuffing and poached, served with rice, eggplant, tomatoes and more red peppers

  a la vasca sole baked with sliced potatoes with a mushroom, red pepper and tomato sauce

★**Marmitako** a Basque stew of tuna fish

Mejillones mussels

Merluza cosquera pieces of hake fried in garlic, then simmered in white wine to which cooked mussels and peas are added

Mújol mullet

Ostiones small shellfish rather like baby oysters, not eaten raw

Ostras oysters

Pastel de pescado cod or hake with tomatoes, flavoured with almonds, baked in a mashed potato pie

Pescadilla a la catalana an assortment of small fish fried with peppers, eggplant and tomatoes

Pescado a la sal a whole fish is packed in damp rock salt, put in the oven and baked. This method of cooking turns up all over the world. The Americans do it with steak (hobo steak), the French with chickens. Only the Spanish, so far as I know, do it with fish

  en escabeche pickled fish

Pez espada swordfish, always over-rated in my view

Pulpo octopus. When cooking, Spanish cooks often put a few corks in the pot. They maintain that they soften the octopus

Salmón con ternera salmon baked with steak. A ghastly dish, particularly as Spanish salmon isn't up to much. The Americans have variations of this mixture of meat and fish, to which they give offensive names on the lines of "surf 'n' turf"

Salmonete red mullet

San Pedro John Dory

Sardinas sardines

Suquet de peix three kinds of white fish sautéed with tomatoes and parsley

Trucha trout

Vieiras a la gallega scallops in a hot chilli sauce

★**Zarzuela** this can range from a simple enough stew of mussels, squid, monk-fish and shrimp with a dash of rough brandy to a grand dish with mullet, turbot, monk-fish, lobsters, large shrimp, wine and liqueur brandy, all arranged in a fancy pattern. The sauce is often quite sharp. The word means light opera or musical comedy, so that the dish is expected to have something of the spectacular about it

Carnes y aves—Meat and poultry

On the whole beef, especially if it is called *vaca, buey, toro* or *carne* is not worth eating. Unless, that is, for the hell of it, you want to go to a restaurant in a bull-fighting town, such as the one I once visited in Jerez, where you eat straight through some six or eight courses, ranging from brains and oxtail, through the testicles and sweetbreads, to cutlets and steaks. If the meat is called *ternera* then it is nominally veal, but the Spanish kill their veal animals much later than we do, so it is half-way to being beef. The pork, if you have no religious restriction, is first rate, but for me the lamb and the kid are the best.

★**Albóndigas** meat balls

Becadas a la barcelonesa woodcock stuffed with their livers and truffles with sherry, wrapped in bacon, roasted and flambéed in brandy

Bistec al natural fried steak as plain as a Spaniard will leave anything

Cachelada sausage and quartered potatoes boiled together

Cadera de toro topside of beef, often overcooked in a casserole

Caldereta de cordero lamb stew

  extremeña de cabrito kid browned in oil, simmered in wine with red peppers, garlic and herbs

Callos a la andaluza tripe stew into which go calf's feet, chick peas, onions, carrots, ham, at least two kinds of sausage, green peppers, tomatoes, herbs, garlic, nutmeg and saffron, to name but a few of the ingredients. In Asturia they put in pig's feet, red pepper and chilli; in Madrid the calf's muzzle, leeks and wine. In short, it's up to you

Capirotada rabbit, chicken or partridge in a thick almond sauce

Capón a la vasca capon with a spiced stuffing of sausage, pork and hazelnuts, doused with sherry and roasted

  ★**relleno a la catalana** roast capon with a really elaborate stuffing of beans, prunes, peaches, pig's ear, sausage, pork, pine nuts and cinnamon

Carne mechada a la andaluza a casserole of beef, stuffed with almonds and olives

  prensada beef and bacon pâté

Carnero verde diced lamb stewed with parsley, mint, lettuce and pine nuts

Cazuela a la catalana a mushy affair of ground beef, carrots, onions and tomatoes with sausages

★**Cocido madrileño** a grand stew of beef, chicken, bacon, ham, sausages, salted pig's foot with chick peas and other vegetables. The meat is served with the chick peas and the vegetables with the sausages. The remaining liquid is thickened with rice and served as soup. This is a regular pattern for stews, which may be called *cocido* or *pote*

Codillo asado roast leg of pork

Codornices asadas roast quails

Conejo "al ram" rabbit and pork rib stew

Cordero al ajillo pastor diced suckling lamb browned in oil and simmered in white wine with paprika, garlic and saffron, served with fried potatoes

  lechal a la chilindrón suckling lamb simmered in a sauce of tomatoes and red peppers

★**Criadillas fritas** fried bull's testicles

Croquetas a la española usually ham and pork croquettes, often flavoured with cinnamon

Chanfaina kid's legs, head, lungs and liver, stewed with green vegetables and silver beet

Chocha a la vizcaína stewed woodcock

Chuletas a la parrilla con ali-oli grilled lamb chops with garlic mayonnaise

  a la riojana lamb chops stewed with tomato paste, diced ham and red peppers

  de cordero a la navarra lamb chops and sausage baked in tomato sauce

  empanadas grilled breaded cutlets

217

★**Churrasco** steak grilled over charcoal, speciality of Cordoba

Empanadillas valencianas small pies filled with minced ham, flavoured with brandy and anise, and baked

Escalopes a la zíngara veal escalopes in sherry

Estofado de vaca beef stew

Fabada asturiana an Asturian white bean dish, which can be elaborate but usually contains sausages. Originally made with salt beef

Faisán al modo de Alcántara pheasant stuffed with duck livers and truffles, then marinated for three days in port. It is cooked in butter, covered with the marinade, cooked a little more and served with a truffle sauce

Filete con especias fillet of beef rolled with bacon and ham strips, browned in oil, simmered in wine and spiced with cloves and cinnamon

Fritura de pechugas de pollo fried chicken breasts

Gallina a la pimienta chicken in garlic sauce (as if they all weren't)

★**en pepitoria** chicken casserole with wine, almonds, saffron, garlic and herbs

★**rellena** ground meat from a carefully skinned chicken, mixed with ground veal and ham, all put back in the chicken skin and stewed with vegetables

Ganso relleno de castañas roast goose stuffed with chestnuts

Guisado a la catalana a beef, sausage and potato stew with masses of herbs, wine and brandy

a la mallorquina mutton and vegetable stew strongly flavoured with almonds

Hígado a la asturiana chopped liver stewed with sliced onions, tomatoes, ground almonds, garlic and wine

Jabalí estofado wild boar, stewed with onions, herbs and spices

Jamón con habas a la granadina sliced, dried Serrano ham fried with fava beans

Lacón con grelos shoulder of pork boiled with turnip tops

Lechazo asado roast suckling lamb

Lechecillas de ternera calf's sweetbreads, simmered in white wine with mushrooms and leeks

Lechona asada vasca roast suckling pig with a stuffing of breadcrumbs, ground pork and veal, herbs and onions, with brandy and wine

Lengua de ternera calf's tongue, often wrapped in bacon and simmered in wine with onions and mushrooms

Liebre en cacerola hare cooked in a casserole with onion, herbs and vinegar, taken out and served with a sauce of its juices

★**estofada con judías** hare and string bean stew; quite sharp as it is cooked with vinegar and chillis

Lomo a la riojana loin of pork simmered in a thin tomato sauce

de cerdo a la aragonesa fried with onions, tomatoes and garlic and then simmered in wine

de cerdo a la catalana with fried white beans and a little gravy

Manitas de cerdo rehogadas boiled pig's feet boned, egg-and-breadcrumbed and fried

Manos de cerdo a la asturiana red peppers stuffed with ground pig's feet, fried and served with chestnut and lentil purée

de ternera a la catalana boiled calf's feet, boned, breaded and fried

Menestra de pollo a la bilbaína chicken stew with vegetables

Menudo gitano see *Callos a la andaluza*

Molde de sesos de corderito a mousse of lamb's brains

Mollejas a la pollensina sweetbreads simmered with onions, carrots and bacon

Morros de ternera a la vizcaína a Basque dish of calf's cheek simmered in a sauce of red peppers, onions and wine

★**Olla podrida** means "rotten pot" —actually much like a *cocido*

Pastel de conejo rabbit pie, baked in potato pastry

de Murcia a pastry case filled with chopped veal, sausage and brains covered with puff pastry and baked

de pichones squab pie—the squab are stuffed with a ham, pork, bacon and gherkin stuffing

Patos de cerdo a la parrilla grilled pig's feet

Pato a la sevillana a complicated

casserole of duck involving onions, tomatoes, oranges, red peppers, olives, garlic and sherry

Pavo adobado turkey marinated in wine, then stewed with onions, tomatoes, garlic and herbs

Pecho de cerdo a la paisana pig's stomach stuffed with ground pork and sausage, boiled and served cold

Pepitoria de gallina, de pollo see *Gallina en pepitoria*

Perdices a la bilbaína partridge stew with vegetables, herbs, spices and chocolate

  a la mallorquina partridge, cabbage and mushroom stew

  ★ **con sardinas** casserole of partridge and tomatoes; during the cooking a sardine is put inside each partridge, but it is removed before serving

  de capellán means "chaplain's partridges", but is actually a Majorcan dish of veal escalopes rolled up with slices of ham and red pepper sausage, fried and then simmered in wine and stock, which makes a thick sauce

  el torero partridge casserole with green peppers and tomatoes

Perdiz estofada partridge stew

Pichones con espárragos squab stuffed with their minced livers and asparagus, stewed in wine and stock; served cold

  en escabeche a la marinera squab simmered in vinegar with ginger, peppercorns and garlic

Pierna de cordero leg of lamb cooked in a pot with carrots, wine and herbs, simmered with garlic and its own sauce

Platito de cordero diced lamb stewed with tomatoes, almonds, saffron and herbs, potatoes and peas

Pollo a la chilindrón chicken simmered in tomato sauce with red peppers

  a la manchega chicken stewed with olives, cabbage and turnips

  a la vizcaína chicken stew with red peppers and tomatoes

  en pepitoria see *Gallina en pepitoria*

Porcella asada roast suckling pig

★ **Puchero de gallina** stuffed boiled fowl with chicken liver sauce

Rabo de toro bull's tail, stewed with vegetables

Riñones al Jerez kidneys cooked in sherry

  en agujas skewered kidneys, ham and bacon, breaded and grilled

Ropa vieja a fry-up of the remains of a *cocido*

Sesos en caldereta calf's brains wrapped in bacon, cooked in white wine and simmered with mushrooms and shallots

Solomillo mechado sirloin steak wrapped in bacon and cooked in the oven, served with mashed potatoes and breadcrumbed, fried artichoke hearts

Ternasco al horno de Aragón lamb chops roasted with garlic

Ternera a la jardinera veal and vegetable casserole

  ★ **borracha** literally "drunken veal"; thick slices of veal, with a hollowed-out dip into which goes ham, parsley and a clove, simmered in white wine and flavoured with cinnamon

  en adobo veal marinated in Madeira and cinnamon, simmered in stock and the marinade, with a lot of ground parsley

  en agujas skewered veal, ham and bacon, breaded and roasted

Verduras — Vegetables

Calabacines rellenos zucchini halves stuffed with onion, garlic and tomato, covered with béchamel sauce and grated cheese, baked in the oven

Cazuela de habas verdes a la granadina casserole of fava beans with tomatoes, artichokes, saffron, herbs and spices finished in the oven with eggs baked on the top

Escalibada catalana sweet peppers, eggplants and tomatoes grilled over a charcoal fire, peeled, cut into strips, and seasoned with olive oil, parsley and garlic

★ **Espárragos al estilo de Málaga** boiled asparagus, covered with a pounded mixture of fried red peppers, breadcrumbs, parsley and garlic, and baked with eggs on the top

Espinacas a la catalana spinach cooked with garlic, anchovies, pine nuts and raisins in oil

Garbanzos salteados chick pea stew

Guisantes a la bilbaína peas, cooked with onion and potatoes

Habas a la asturiana fava beans stewed with carrots, potatoes, onions and ham, flavoured with garlic, wine and paprika

    a la catalana stewed with tomatoes, onions and bacon, flavoured with garlic, nutmeg, herbs, anise and peppermint

    a la montañesa stewed with onion, red peppers, ham, bacon and herbs

Judías encarnadas a la madrileña red beans simmered with bacon, sausage, onion and garlic

    verdes green beans

Menestra de acelgas leaves of silver beet, stuffed with chopped ham, onion, hard-boiled egg and silver-beet stalks, tied in parcels, dipped in egg and flour and fried

    de legumbres frescas a stew of mixed vegetables, often served with poached eggs

Olla cordobesa a stew of chick peas and cabbage

Patatas a la riojana layers of sliced potatoes, tomatoes and onions, sweet peppers and *chorizo* sausage, baked with stock

    catalanas sliced potatoes simmered with paprika, onions, garlic and bay leaf

    y judías a la extremeña potatoes, green beans, tomatoes and green peppers stewed together with plenty of garlic

Pimientos rellenos de manos de cerdo green peppers, stuffed with the meat of boiled pig's feet and baked

Pisto stewed sliced red peppers, tomatoes and zucchini

Postres — Desserts, *Helados* — Ice-cream, *Pasteles* — Pastries, *Frutas* — Fruit

Albaricoque apricot

Arroz con leche rice cooked in milk with cinnamon and lemon

Bizcochos borrachos small sponge cakes soaked in wine, sugared and sprinkled with cinnamon

★**Brazo de gitano** literally "gypsy's arm"; a sponge swiss roll filled with jam, cream, etc.

Buñuelos fritters

Caqui persimmon

Copa helada ice-cream sundae

Churros long sugared doughnuts

Ensaimadas de Mallorca coiled round yeast buns from Majorca

Flan caramelo caramel custard

Frambuesas raspberries

Granada pomegranate

Helado ice-cream

Higos figs

Leche frita custard cut into squares, dipped in egg and breadcrumbs, deep fried and sprinkled with sugar and cinnamon

Macedonia de frutas fruit salad

Mantecado rich golden vanilla ice-cream with added whipped cream

Manzanas asadas asturianas apples baked in white wine, topped with anise-flavoured meringue

Melocotón peach

Naranja orange

Natillas soft custard flavoured with lemon and cinnamon. Served cold

Plátanos fritos fried bananas, sprinkled with sugar, lemon juice and brandy

Polvorones shortbread biscuits, often flavoured with almonds, anise and cinnamon

Rosquillas ring doughnuts flavoured with anise

Sandía watermelon

Semifríos frozen desserts with ice-cream, cream, sponge, candied fruits

Sierra Nevada ice-cream dessert covered in meringue

Tocino de cielo literally "bacon from heaven"; a thick caramel custard

Torrijas small squares of bread, soaked in milk, dipped in egg and fried. They are then baked in the oven with honey and water

Turrón de Jijón soft nougat with honey, ground nuts and cinnamon

Uvas grapes

Spanish wine

Spain is a grand country for drinking, the more so perhaps because the Spaniards do not approach the matter too reverentially. Sherry (a corruption of the name Jerez—pronounced "Hereth"—the centre of sherry) is, of course, one of the world's great drinks. However, you would never catch the French calling one of their finest clarets "Uncle Bill", which is, after all, the rough equivalent of *Tio Pepe*. *Sangría* is a popular iced drink, made of wine, fizzy lemonade, fruit juice and brandy. It is a marvellous picnic invention, but hardly the concoction of wine snobs.

This is not to say that Spain does not produce good wines. The Riojas, from Old Castile, which have various subdivisions, are the best table wines, although they can range from fairly rough stuff from the Rioja Baja to expensive fine wines, like *Viña Vial* from the Bodegas Paternina or *Castillo Ygay* from the *bodega* of Marqués de Murrieta.

For the rest, there are reasonable enough regions—e.g., Alella, Las Campanas, Panadés, Priorato and Valdepeñas, but unless you see these names the best thing is to drink the local wine. It is particularly good in the north-west, where the "green" wine comes from, or on the Mediterranean coast.

Strength is often given priority over finesse in Spain. A few barmen, if one is feeling low, will give one a *sol y sombra*, a mixture of Fundador brandy (there are incidentally some quite delicate Spanish brandies of which this is not one) and *anís* (something like Pernod). It is a knock-out, always reminding me of the Kingsley Amis hero Bowen who, when dreaming of owning a brewery, decided that his no-nonsense advertising slogan would be "Bowen's beer makes you drunk". Bowen and the Spaniards, it seems to me, have a certain amount in common in their approach to drink.

Useful words

Aceite oil
Aceitunas olives
Agua water
Azúcar sugar
Buey beef
Café exprés espresso coffee
  con leche white coffee
  solo black coffee
Caliente hot
Caza game
Cerveza beer
Cuenta bill
Dulce sweet
Ensalada salad
al Estilo de in the style of
Frío cold
Frito fried

Jamón ham. *Jamón serrano* is cured and sliced
Leche milk
Lista menu
Mantequilla butter
Pan bread
Platos combinados selection of *tapas* and/or main dishes
Queso cheese
Reserva good-quality mature wine
Salchichas sausage
Seco dry
Té tea
Vino wine
  blanco, dulce, espumoso, rosado, seco, tinto white, sweet, sparkling, rosé, dry, red wine

¡ **Buen provecho!** bon appétit!
¡ **Salud!** cheers!

Sri Lanka — *See* India
Sweden — *See* Scandinavia

Switzerland

The art of hotel-keeping lies in the ability to do everything correctly, which is why the Swiss are the world's best hoteliers and why the world's most famous catering college is in Lausanne. It takes a particular cast of mind not to jumble the bookings, to remember to change the soap, to check that the shower doesn't drip, to notice the dust on the wardrobe shelf. Alas, it is not an inventive mind (no, it was the Germans who invented the cuckoo clock), which means that those same hoteliers have never created a national cuisine. It does, however, mean that you will never eat badly in Switzerland, for in their correct manner they have taken over the very proper dishes of each of the countries of which the nation is comprised and they serve them correctly, albeit mostly without flair.

The geography of the country, in a rather contradictory way, has meant that individual localities and even valleys have preserved their own particular way of doing various dishes. This would make a definitive list of Swiss dishes repetitive and useless for the traveller going to only one place. The following selection is made up of the most typical dishes which are less likely to appear in any other country. Most menus are printed in at least two of Switzerland's three official languages—German, French and Italian. It is possible that you might come across one in Romansch but it will certainly have a second language list as well. If you cannot find a dish in the Swiss section, look for it in the French, German or Italian section. *Spätzle* (or *Spätzli*, in Swiss-German), for example, is a common Swiss accompaniment to meat dishes. It appears in the German word list. I have purposely not included a useful word list here since the other relative sections are fairly comprehensive.

In order to have a more interesting meal and to learn what the Swiss like to eat, it might be better to work the other way round. Find a dish in this section which you think you would like and ask for it.

Aargauer Rüeblitorte the main ingredients of this famous cake from the German part of Switzerland are carrots and almonds glazed with sugar. The canton of Aargau, an area important for farm products, is also known as "Rüebliland"

Basler Lummelbraten a whole fillet of beef roasted with bacon and served with fresh vegetables. Used to be a speciality of the more wealthy old Swiss families and was served on festive occasions

Mehlsuppe a flour-based soup served with cheese. This is traditionally eaten in the early morning of carnival (the week before Ash Wednesday) together with the equally famous *Zwiebelwähe* (onion tart)

★**Berner Platte** a casserole of mixed cooked meats and sausages served with sauerkraut or dried beans. A typical winter dish

Topf a soup made from yellow split peas and pig's feet

Birchermüsli one of the permanent results of the "reform" school of cookery introduced at the Bircher-Benner clinic in Zurich in 1897. The basic mixture should be oat flakes, milk, grated apples and chopped nuts, to which any fresh fruits in season are added. Eaten either for breakfast or as a snack lunch mixed with yoghurt. Infinitely better than the packets of sawdust sold with similar names

Brunsli biscuits made with sugar, almonds, dark chocolate, spices, egg whites and kirsch. Usually made at Christmas time

★**Bündnerfleisch** thin slices of beef dried in Swiss mountain air at an altitude of 1,500 metres, but surprisingly tender with an aromatic flavour

Bündner Gerstensuppe very creamy soup with vegetables, plenty of barley and *Bündnerfleisch*. A speciality of Engadine

★ **Busecca alla Ticinese** multi-vegetable soup with small strips of tripe

Cervelat, Chlöpfer a popular smoked sausage used in many sausage dishes as well as for grilling

Coppa air-dried neck of pork. Tastes best when eaten in a *grotto* (a typical small Ticino restaurant) with a glass of Merlot wine

Käseschnitten toast covered with Emmental cheese and a dash of white wine and glazed

Käseschnitte Oberländer Art toast with butter and mustard and a slice of ham coated with Emmental cheese, which is allowed to melt in the oven. Often served with a fried egg

Käsewähe cheese flan

Leckerli honey biscuits with dried fruit and almonds, a speciality of Basle

Potée vaudoise leeks and potatoes stewed in white wine and served with *saucisson vaudoise* on top

Quiche au fromage see *Käsewähe*

★ **Raclette** *raclette* parties are a

He . . . ordered champagne, three bottles of Mumm and Co., *Cordon rouge*, extra dry, with *petits fours*, toothsome cone-shaped little dainties in lace frills, covered with coloured frosting and filled with chocolate and *pistache* cream . . . coffee followed the champagne, "Mocha double," with fresh rounds of "bread" and pungent liqueurs: apricot brandy, chartreuse, crême de vanille, and maraschino for the ladies. Later there appeared marinated *filets* of fish, and beer; lastly tea, both Chinese and camomile, for those who had done with champagne and liqueurs and did not care to return to a sound wine, as Mynheer himself did; he, Frau Chauchat and Hans Castorp working back after midnight to a Swiss red wine.

Thomas Mann *The Magic Mountain*

Egli freshwater perch from the Swiss lakes

Felchen white fish found in large quantities in the Swiss lakes

Filets de perche à la vaudoise fillets of freshwater perch fried in butter and served with mushrooms and tomatoes

★ **Fondue** a hot cheese dip made from different cheeses depending on the region. Eating *fondue* is something of an event and is appropriately accompanied by various rituals. Anyone losing his cube of bread in the bubbling pot, for example, is expected to buy a bottle of wine or a round of kirsch. Only the women of the company are exempt, but they must forfeit a kiss per cube

bourguignonne a modern dish from the French part. Cubes of raw meat which you dip into hot oil and then into any of a selection of sauces

custom of the Valais. This is what happens: a mature *raclette* cheese is cut in half and the sliced end is placed facing the heat of the fire until it begins to melt. The liquefied cheese is quickly scraped on to a warm plate and served with potatoes boiled in their jackets, pickled gherkins and onions

Ramequins small cheese tarts

Rehpfeffer there is plenty of game in the Swiss woods and mountains so many restaurants will serve it in some form or other. This highly seasoned deer stew is a well-known one and may also be made with hare (*Hasenpfeffer*) or roe deer (*Hirschpfeffer*) but during the season—October to December—each locality produces its own speciality

Rohspeck raw smoked or air-cured bacon

★ **Rösti** potatoes boiled in their

223

skins, then peeled, grated and fried in butter until golden brown. Used to be eaten for breakfast

Salm nach Basler Art salmon steak fried in butter with plenty of fried onion. Salmon was at one time so plentiful and cheap that a law was introduced in Basle forbidding masters feeding it to their servants more than twice a week

Salsiz small air-dried sausages from the Grisons

Saucisson vaudois smoked pork sausage

St Galler Festbratwurst grilled veal sausage

Schwyzer Käsesuppe more of a cheese and bread pudding than a soup. Prepared with fresh farmer's bread and alpine cheese. Used to be eaten mainly by Swiss farmers

Trippa minestra see *Busecca alla Ticinese*

Viande des Grisons see *Bündnerfleisch*

★ **Wähen** large tarts filled with fruits, cheese or vegetables. Somewhere between a French quiche and an Italian pizza

Zuger Rötel a kind of trout in season in the winter months, poached in white wine with plenty of fresh herbs and cream

★ **Zürcher Leberspiessli** skewered, sautéed cubes of calf's liver wrapped in bacon strips, flavoured with sage. Served with green beans and boiled potatoes

Ratsherrentopf a mixture of small beef, veal and pork fillets with calf's liver and kidneys, served on a bed of fresh peas with carrots and potatoes

Züri Gschnätzlets thinly sliced veal, veal kidneys and mushrooms in a cream sauce, usually served with *Rösti*. Just eat it—don't worry about the pronunciation, it takes years of practice

Käse, fromage, formaggio — Cheese

All those alpine pastures with their rich flush of spring grass make for wonderful dairy products. Swiss cheeses in particular are some of the best in the world. Everyone knows Emmental and Gruyère, but even these taste better in their own country. But in the hope that you will experiment a bit, here is a list of some marvellous varieties hardly ever heard of outside Switzerland: Appenzeller, Entlebucher, Hobelkäse, Raclettekäse, Saanen, Sbrinz, Schabziger, Schafkäse, Tête de Moine, Urseren, Vacherin fribourgeois, Vacherin Mont d'Or, Ziegenkäse.

Incidentally, the German and Italian names for Gruyère are Greyerzer and Groviera.

Swiss wine

The great thing about Swiss wine is that it isn't good enough for anyone to start mucking it about in order to pretend that it is something else. It is never so distinguished that it could be worth anyone's while to stick a false label on a *Dorin* from Vaud and pretend it is a *Fendant* from Valais. Nor is it ever rough or cheap enough for someone to grind a quantity of carrots into it and pass it off as local plonk.

What you will get is genuine wine, carefully made, which will go well enough with what you are eating. Most Swiss wine is white. The names to look out for are *Sion*, *Domaine du Mont d'Or*, *Fendant Dézaley*, and *Epesses*. The best reds come from Ticino, the Italian part of Switzerland. Look for Viti and anything with the grape name Merlot.

Syria—*See* **Arab food**
Thailand—*See* **Southeast Asia**
Tunisia—*See* **Arab food**

Turkey

Gastronomically speaking, Turkey is a sort of buffer between Europe and Asia. Its food is a wonderful jumble and its customs are a matter of enormous confusion. Originally a nomadic people, they have food with the hallmarks of all wandering cookery—small packages of food such as *börek*, *mantı* and *köfte*, easily cooked over a camp fire or baked in a pit dug in the ground (the *tandır*: a relation of India's *tandoori*). Then comes the influence of ancient Greece, descending through Rome and the Byzantine empire. Next, the food adopted from the Balkans and other countries occupied by the Ottoman empire—borsch, for instance, is a common dish in Turkish restaurants. Finally, there is the religious influence from their Islamic heritage.

Officially, as Muslims, the Turks do not drink. Despite this they have a lively wine, beer and spirit industry. Turkish wine can be extremely good. The names to look for are *Buzbağ, Doluca, Kavaklidere* and *Trakya*. *Anis* is a popular drink and comes in three types, in varying strengths—*yeni*, the weakest, *kulüp*, and *altinbas*, a real knock-out drop. They also make a reasonable vodka and a near-lethal brandy (*kanyak*). The sweet liqueurs can be very good if you like that sort of thing, in particular the orange and the rose-petal.

Turkish alphabetical order is: a, b, c, ç, d, e, f, g, ğ, h, i, ı, j, k, l, m, n, o, ö, p, r, s, ş, t, u, ü, v, y, z

Meze — Hors d'oeuvre

Arnavut ciğeri fried pieces of lamb's liver with paprika, parsley and sliced onions

Beyaz peynir white goat's milk cheese

Beyin tavası lamb's brains fried and sprinkled with lemon juice and paprika

★**Börek** small pastry envelopes or rolls (*cigara börek*) filled with a meat, vegetable or cheese mixture. Served also as a main course and there is even a sweet version for dessert

Cacık sliced cucumber in yoghurt flavoured with garlic, mint and a little salt. Sometimes olive oil is poured on top

Dolmalar means "stuffed things", usually vegetables, but may be fish, especially shellfish, or even chicken. With rice stuffing they will be served cold, with meat, hot. Like *börek*, they may appear at any time during a Turkish meal

Fasulye pilâkısı navy beans stewed with onions. Served cold

Havyar caviar, comparatively cheap from the Black Sea

Humus a purée of chick peas flavoured with garlic and sometimes sesame paste and paprika

Kavun melon, very popular, eaten with *beyaz peynir* and *raki*

Köfte ground lamb or mutton meat balls, served hot or cold

Marul cos lettuce, often eaten with a glass of *raki*. The whole lettuce is served with the heart upright in a glass of lemon juice

★**Midye dolması** mussels minced with rice and onion and served in their shells

tavası mussels dipped in yeast batter and fried in olive oil

Pastırma dried beef spiced with cummin, garlic and paprika. Fried, baked or served cold, thinly sliced

Patlican salatası a purée of eggplants with garlic and olive oil, eaten with bread

tavası yoğurtlu fried eggplants with yoghurt

Pohaça yoghurt dough rolled into balls and stuffed with a mixture of cream cheese and parsley, baked and served hot

Sardalya tavası fried sardines

Yalancı dolma stuffed vine leaves

225

Çorbalar— Soups

Bezelye çorbası split pea soup
Düğün çorbası "wedding soup"; made with mutton, beaten eggs and lemon and garnished with sticks of raw carrot, cinnamon and paprika
Erişteli çorba clear soup with noodles
Havuç çorbası soup made with chicken stock and carrots and thickened with egg yolks
İrmik çorbası semolina soup
★ **İskembe çorbası** thick tripe soup containing red peppers, egg

and lots of garlic. Eaten by Turks as hangover cures
Mantı çorbası pastry envelopes stuffed with ground lamb in mutton stock. Served with tomato paste or yoghurt
Mercimek çorbası lentil soup flavoured with paprika
Tarhana çorbası soup made from yoghurt, tomatoes and peppers
Tavuk çorbası chicken soup
Yayla çorbası beef soup with chopped onions, parsley, mint and yoghurt

Balıklar— Fish

Alabalık trout
Ancuez anchovies
Barbunya red mullet
Dil balığı sole
İstakoz lobster
İstiridye oysters
Kalkan turbot
Karagöz porgy
Karides shrimp
Kefal grey mullet
★ **Kılıç** swordfish, in season from September to November
Kırlangıç gurnard
Levrek fırın sea bass stuffed with a mixture of onion, celery, parsley, breadcrumbs and butter, baked and served with an onion and tomato sauce
Lüfer fish similar to bass
Mercan porgy
Mersin balığı sturgeon

Midye pılâkısı mussels stewed with vegetables and served cold with parsley and lemon juice
Palamut tuna fish
Pilâki fish and vegetable stew
Pisi brill
Sardalya sardines
Sazan carp
Ton balığı, torik tuna
Uskumru mackerel
★ **dolması** the mackerel skin is carefully separated from the body in one piece and stuffed with a mixture of the flesh, chopped onions, nuts, raisins, spices and herbs, rolled in egg and breadcrumbs and fried
  papaz yahnisi mackerel baked in foil with garlic, tomatoes, onion and parsley. Served cold
Yengeç crab

Etler— Meat

Bahçivan kebabı a stew of diced mutton, onions, carrots, garlic, tomatoes, sweet peppers and dill
Beyin lamb's brains
Bobrek kidney
★ **Çerkez tavuğu** "Circassian chicken"; shredded chicken in a sauce of crushed walnuts, garlic, breadcrumbs, paprika and chicken stock
Ciger liver
Dana veal
Domuz pork
★ **Döner kebab** slices of lamb marinated in oil, herbs and spices, then stacked on an upright spit with layers of ground lamb mixed with herbs and beaten eggs.

This is slowly turned before the grill and, as the outside layer of meat cooks it is cut off the spit on to a waiting plate. Served with salad or with *pide* and yoghurt
Etli fasulye string beans cooked with onions and meat
Etli yaprak dolması vine leaves stuffed with ground lamb and served hot
Fusulyeli paça calf's feet stewed with navy beans
Güveç a casserole of meat and vegetables baked in small individual dishes and served with yoghurt
Hindi turkey

Hünkâr beğendi literally "His Majesty enjoyed it"; cubes of lamb braised with onions and tomato, served on an eggplant purée
İç pilâv sliced goose livers fried in butter with rice, pine nuts, raisins, spices, tomato and onion
İşkembe tripe
 nohutlu tripe stewed with chick peas, garlic and onions
Kadın budu literally "ladies' thighs"; meat balls made with ground lamb, rice, eggs and herbs, first poached then dipped in beaten egg and flour and fried
Kağıt kebabı lamb and vegetables cooked in paper bags
★ **Keşkec** a traditional dish of shredded chicken meat and cracked wheat simmered together until they have the consistency of porridge. Served sprinkled with paprika and melted butter
Kıyma ground meat
Köfte meat balls
Kokoreç a street snack common throughout Turkey, consisting of sheep's intestines grilled over charcoal. Served sprinkled with herbs and sandwiched between two slices of bread
Konya a speciality of Konya. Pieces of lamb baked very slowly with scallions, lettuce and tomatoes
Lâhmacun slice of dough covered with ground meat

Mantı pastry envelopes stuffed with meat, poached and served with tomato sauce or yoghurt and garlic
Pirzola a chop, usually lamb
Parça kuslar slices of lamb rolled and stuffed with a mixture of ground lamb, onions and tomatoes and baked
Piliç see *Tavuk*
Sığır beef
Şiş kebab cubes of lamb marinated and grilled on skewers. The word *şiş* derives from the Turkish for "sword"— originally the cubes of meat were spiked on swords and grilled over the camp fire
Sülün pheasant
Tandır kebab only prepared for special occasions since the dish involves cooking a whole sheep or lamb. The animal is placed on a bed of charcoal in a specially dug pit then covered with earth and baked for several hours
Tauşan hare
Tavuk, piliç chicken
 ızgara chicken grilled or spit-roasted over charcoal
 jölesi a layer of boned chicken inside a clear jelly, decorated with nuts and chopped parsley
Yoğurtlu kebab cubes of lamb on a bed of toasted bread, puréed tomatoes and yoghurt
 paça calf's feet stewed with yoghurt

Sebze — Vegetables

Bamya okra
Biber sweet peppers
 dolması stuffed peppers
Domates tomatoes
Domatesli fasulye stewed navy beans covered with thick tomato paste. A very popular dish often eaten hot for breakfast
Fasulye beans
Hıyar, salatalık cucumber
★**İmam bayıldı** literally, "the priest fainted", whether at the taste of this delicacy or its cost nobody knows. Eggplants, stuffed onion, tomato, garlic and parsley cooked in lots of olive oil. Served cold
İspanak spinach
Kabak zucchini or squash
Karnabahar cauliflower

Karışık salata mixed vegetable salad
Kuru fasulye pujaz butter-bean salad
Marul cos lettuce
Patates potatoes
Patlıcan eggplants
Pirinçli ispanak layers of rice and spinach cooked with tomato paste
Sebze bastısı a stew of eggplants, tomatoes, sweet peppers, zucchini and green beans served with yoghurt
Soğan onion
Turlu haricot beans, potatoes, onion and garlic, stewed in oil
Yalanci, yaprak vine leaves
Yeşil salata green salad
Zeytin olives

Tatlilar—Sweets, *Meyve*—Fruit

Aşure traditional pudding made from an unusual mixture of navy beans, chick peas, rice, dried fruit, sugar and nuts

Baklava sheets of flaky pastry stuffed with nuts and soaked in syrup

Bülbül yuvası a nest of shredded wheat containing pistachios and soaked in syrup, served with water ice

Çilek-kaymali sieved strawberries mixed with beaten egg whites, sugar and cream and a few drops of orange-flower water

Dondurma ice-cream

Elmalı börek apple pastries

Halva, helva a sweetmeat usually made in a slab. It is very sweet and stiff and crumbly in consistency. There are many different variations on the basic flour, honey, sugar and butter mixture, including nuts and even cheese

★**Helvaci kabaği kompostosu** a delicious pudding from Kastamonu; a purée of pumpkin with sugar, chopped nuts and coconut

Kadayıf, kedayıf rolls of shredded wheat filled with cream or nuts and soaked in syrup

flavoured with orange-flower water

Kadın göbeği literally "ladies' navels". Round balls of sponge baked and soaked in syrup. The extraordinary name presumably derives from the "dimple" made on the tops of them before baking

Karpuz watermelon

Kavun melon

Kazan dibi similar to cream caramel

Keşkul pudding made from ground almonds, sprinkled with pistachios and coconut

Lokum Turkish delight

Muhallebi a very popular cold pudding of milk, ground rice, sugar and rose-water. Quite unlike our idea of rice pudding, but very good

Nar pomegranate

Portakal orange

Seftali peach

★**Tavuk göğsü** a curious moulded pudding made of milk, ground rice, sugar and finely shredded chicken breasts, served chilled and sprinkled with cinnamon

Üzüm grape

Yoğurt tatlısı yoghurt cake soaked in syrup, served hot with cream

Useful words

Ayran a yoghurt drink

Bademli süt almond-flavoured milk

Bal honey

Bira beer

Boza a drink made from fermented millet

Buz ice

Çay tea

Ekmek bread

Hesap bill

Kahve coffee, Turkish of course, served *sade* (unsweetened), *az şekerli* (slightly sweetened), *orta* (medium sweet) or *şekerli* (very sweet). The waiter will ask you which you would like when you order

Peynir cheese

Pide flat bread

Pirinç rice

Rakı aniseed spirit, usually diluted with water and drunk with meals

Salep a sweet milk drink

Seker sugar or sweets

Simit rings of bread sprinkled with sesame seeds

Su water

Süt milk

Şarap wine

Tereyağı butter

Tursu mixed pickles

Yahni stew or casserole

Yerli yemekler local dishes

Yufka unleavened bread

Zeytinyaği olive oil

Serefe! cheers!
Afiyet olsun! bon appétit!

USSR

Russian cuisine, in one sense, does not exist. Russia is an agglomeration of countries in which the basic peasant foods vary from Mongolian through Turkish to Polish. There is in fact very little truly Russian food. Dishes we associate with Russia, like *borsch*, are often Polish; others with grand names like Soubaroff, Demidoff or Stroganoff are usually called after princely employers of inventive Frenchmen.

This is not to say that people may not eat well in Russia for what is derivative is often excellent. Tourists, on the other hand, are less likely to eat so well. If they are in a group they will very seldom be given any choice, but simply have their food dumped in front of them after an appropriate wait of an hour or so. Independent tourists will be shown a menu, again after an hour's lugubrious waiting. I have, therefore, made a selection of those dishes which appear most frequently.

It pays to be very precise in ordering. A friend of mine once took his wife to a Moscow hotel for their wedding anniversary. She wanted caviar. They waited their hour and he ordered caviar, toast, butter, chopped onion, chopped egg, lemon slices—all the trimmings which he knew he would not get unless he specified them. After another half-hour, the waiter brought the toast, butter, chopped onion, chopped egg and lemon slices. "Where's the caviar?" "Sorry, no caviar tonight."

A further problem is to get the wine waiter and the food waiter synchronized. The odd thing is that it is absolutely in order to make a fantastic fuss. Indeed waiters only respect those who throw their weight around. Almost the first act in any restaurant is to ask for the *administrator* (head waiter).

Wine in Russia is inclined to be too sweet for our taste. The Russian Republic itself produces some good Rieslings. Moldavia and the Ukraine have some drier wines. On the whole you will have to take a chance. The words for red and white are **красное вино** (krasnoye vino) and **белое вино** (byeloye vino). Dry is **сухое вино** (sukhoye vino). A tip when eating in Georgia: the wine waiter will ask you how many bottles you want—it is normal to order one each to start with.

Russian alphabetical order is: А, Б, В, Г, Д, Е, Ж, З, И, Й, К, Л, М, Н, О, П, Р, С, Т, У, Ф, Х, Ц, Ч, Ш, Щ, Ъ, Ы, Ь, Э, Ю, Я
а, б, в, г, д, е, ж, з, и, й, к, л, м, н, о, п, р, с, т, у, ф, х, ц, ч, ш, щ, ъ, ы, ь, э, ю, я

★ Закуски *(zakuski)* — Hors d'oeuvre

The main meal of the day always begins with *zakuski*, however modest the household or restaurant. The tradition was brought from Scandinavia by Rurik—the first Viking Prince of Kiev—and was later introduced to France by the Russians as hors d'oeuvre. The Russians always drink vodka with *zakuski* and usually have *zakuski* with vodka.

Анчоусы с яйцами (anchoussi s yaitzami) anchovies on eggs, with lettuce, tomato and parsley
Баклажан с овощами (baklazhan s ovoshami) cubed eggplant fried with chopped onion, carrots, tomatoes and squash. Served cold
Блины (bliny) buckwheat pancakes served hot with bowls of melted butter and sour cream and red or black caviar

229

Заливное из рыбы (zalivnoye iz rybi) fish in aspic

из языка (iz yazika) tongue in aspic

★**Икра (ikra)** caviar. Black is sturgeon's roe and red is salmon's

Картофельный салат (kartofelni salat) potato salad with sliced onion, eggs and sour cream

  салат с селедкой (salat s selyodkoi) herring and potato salad with dill pickles, eggs, onions and oil

Огурцы в сметане (ogurtzi v smetane) cucumbers in sour cream

Паштет (pashtet) liver paste

Печенка в сметане (pechyonka v smetane) chicken livers fried with onion in sour cream

Помидоры с мясом (pomidori s myasom) tomatoes stuffed with a mixture of cold meat, ham, chopped egg and mayonnaise

Редиска в сметане (rediska v smetane) finely chopped radishes mixed with sour cream

Рыбная икра (rybnaya ikra) skinned soft roe of mackerel or herring mixed with oil and lemon

Салат из копченой рыбы (salat iz kopchenoi rybi) cold smoked fish salad with onion, oil and mustard

с курицей (s kuritzei) diced cooked chicken mixed with boiled potatoes, carrots, apple, olives, cucumber, egg, lettuce and dill

★**Селедка (selyodka)** salted herring which may be served in many different ways—with eggs on black bread, with salads or with hot boiled potatoes sprinkled with dill, chives or scallions

Фаршированные артишоки (farshirovaniye artishoki) artichokes stuffed with mushrooms or with shrimp and veal

  баклажаны (baklazhani) eggplants stuffed with ground chicken or other leftovers, bread, egg, parsley and cream

  перцы (pertzi) green peppers stuffed with fried onion, carrot and tomato sauce

  яйца (yaitza) hard-boiled egg white halves filled with caviar and decorated with sliced tomatoes, chopped dill and scallions

Черные оливи (chorniye olivi) stoned olives chopped with hard-boiled eggs, onion and garlic and mixed with oil and vinegar

Яйца с хреном (yaitza s khrenom) hard-boiled egg halves covered with a mayonnaise, horseradish and sour-cream sauce

Супы *(supi) — Soups*

Абрикосовый суп (abrikosovi sup) cold soup made from boiled apricots, sugar and cornstarch, served with rice and sour cream

Бозбаш (bozbash) Armenian mutton soup, with chunks of mutton, apples, potatoes, peas, onions and tomato paste

Борщ (borsch) this famous soup varies from region to region. It generally contains beef, beets, carrots, potatoes and other vegetables. See *Barszcz* (Poland)

★**Ботвинья (botvinya)** cold soup made with spinach, *kvass* and stock, to which a small glass of sherry or a little champagne can be added before serving. Also used as a fish sauce

Вишневый суп (vishnovi sup) cold cherry soup

Клюковый и яблочный суп (klukovi i yablochni sup) cold soup made with cranberries, sugar, apples and cornstarch

Креветкий суп (krevetki sup) large shrimp, onion, dill rice and sour-cream soup

Малекий суп (malyoki sup) with whitebait, parsnips, leeks, celery, onion and buckwheat

Окрошка (okroshka) cold soup with *kvass*, potatoes, radishes, cucumber, diced meat, chives and sour cream

  Рассольник (rassolnik) kidney and cucumber soup with carrots, onions, potatoes and sour cream

Солянка (solyanka) soup with boiled or roast meat, cucumbers, onions, tomato paste and olives or with boned white fish, cucumber, carrots and olives

Уха (oukha) a very popular soup made from fresh white fish, carrots, onions and potatoes

Харчо (kharcho) Georgian beef soup made from brisket, tomatoes, tomato paste, tart plums, coriander leaves, parsley, garlic and rice

Холодец (kholodetz) cold soup made with *kvass* or cider, stock, beet cucumber and scallions

Чихиртма (chikhirtma) Georgian mutton soup with onion, saffron and coriander

★ **Шампанский суп (shampanski sup)** extravagant soup made with salmon boiled in fish stock, doused with champagne. Served with caviar

Шурпа (shurpa) Turkmenian mutton soup with mutton, onions, carrots, potatoes and tomato purée

★ **Щи (shchi)** fresh cabbage soup with sauerkraut, carrots, tomato paste and sour cream

Яблочный суп (yablochni sup) cold apple soup with raspberry jam, sweet white wine, cloves and breadcrumbs

Ягодный суп (yagodni sup) fresh berry soup with sugar, cream and egg yolks

Пироги и пирожки (pirogi i piroshki) — Pies

Вареники (vareniki) similar to *pelmeni*

Ватрушки (vatroushki) small open patties with a cottage cheese filling

★ **Кулебяка (kulibyaka)** patties filled with salmon, rice, onion, hard-boiled eggs, dill and mushroom

★ **Пельмени (pelmeni)** similar to Chinese *dim sum*. They are small yeast envelopes filled with ground beef and onion and boiled in stock or water. Eaten with soya sauce, butter, mustard and vinegar

Пирог с мясом (pirog s myasom) meat pie with yeast pastry

Пирог с рыбой (s riboi) fish pie

Пирожки с луком и яйцами (piroshki s lukom i yaitzami) pies with scallion and egg filling

Расстегай (rastegai) patties made of yeast dough with onion and fresh salmon or herring filling

Сырники (syrniki) fried patties made of cottage cheese and mashed potato, served hot with well-chilled sour cream

Хачапури (khachapuri) Georgian savoury bun filled with sheep cheese and yoghurt

Хинкали (hinkali) large Georgian patties filled with ground pork, beef and onions

Рыба (ryba) — Fish

Fish is an important element in Soviet cookery, because of the large number of inland seas, lakes and rivers and because of the frequent fasts of the Russian Church.

Зразы (zrazy) fish fillets stuffed with mushrooms, onion and parsley

Камбала с шпинатом (kambala s shpinatom) flounder fillets with spinach and chopped eggs

Рыбные котлеты с грибным соусом (rybniye kotletki s gribnym sousom) fish cutlets with mushroom sauce

Сациви (satsivi) a Georgian dish of cold fish in a sauce of ground walnuts, garlic, coriander, cloves, cinnamon and black pepper

Семга в мадире (syomga v madire) salmon cooked in Madeira and served with a crayfish sauce

Соте из трески (soté iz treski)

sautéed porgy or flounder cooked in garlic, onion and tomato sauce

★ **Стерлядь по-русски (sterlyad po russki)** boiled sturgeon with a sauce of fried onion, mushrooms, carrots, parsnips, capers, tomato and cooked cucumber

Угорь в вино (ugor v vino) pieces of eel cooked in red wine, onion and lemon juice

Фаршированная камбала (farserovaniya kambala) flounder stuffed with breadcrumbs, butter, chopped parsley and shrimps, mixed together with beaten egg and nutmeg

Форель в вино (forel v vino) trout cooked in white wine

Мясо, птица и дичь *(myaso ptitza i dich)* — Meat, poultry and game

Азу (azu) steak and vegetable stew

★ **Аштарак толма (ashtarak tolma)** a Caucasian dish of apples or quinces stuffed with lamb

Бефстроганов (bef stroganoff) named after Count Stroganoff whose chef discovered, when stationed in northern Siberia, that his beef was frozen so hard that it could only be cut into paper-thin strips. It now consists of thin strips of good quality beef, mushrooms and onions served with sour cream and rice

Буженина (buzhenina) ham baked in beer

Голубцы (golubtzi) cabbage leaves stuffed with ground beef, onion and rice. Served with sour cream

Грузинский плоф (gruzinscki plof) rice pilaff with mutton, onions and pomegranates

Заяц жаренный в сухарях (zayetz zharini v suharyakh) hare fried in breadcrumbs

Индушка с каштанами и яблоками (indushka s kashtanami i yablokami) roast turkey with chestnut and apple stuffing

★ **Киевские котлеты (kievskiye kotleti)** chicken fillets stuffed with fingers of butter, egg-and-breadcrumbed and fried

Котлетки из свинины (kotletki iz svinini) fried cutlets of ground pork and breadcrumbs

Кучч (kchouth) casseroled lamb with dried apricots

Мясной рулет с кашей и грибами (myas noi rulet s kashei i gribami) meat roll with a mushroom and buckwheat filling

Мясные ролики (myasniye roliki) slices of beef, bacon, carrot and onion rolled together and fried

Поросенок с кашей (porosyonok s kashei) suckling pig stuffed with apples. Served with a buckwheat and horseradish sauce

Рагу (ragu) a very popular stew in all Russian households

Рулеты (ruleti) rolls of ground meat or mashed potato with various fillings

Свинина отбивная с яблоками (svinina otbivnaya s yablokami) pork fillets cooked with apples

Тефтели (tefteli) braised meat balls

Узбекский плоф (uzbekski plof) a rice dish with mutton, carrots, onions, red peppers and apple

Утка с капустой (utka s kapustoi) duck casseroled with cabbage, onions and apple

★ **Фазан с грибами в сметане (faizan s gribami v smetane)** pieces of pheasant in a mushroom and sour-cream sauce

Форшмак (forshchmak) ground beef, herring, potatoes and onion mixed together with egg yolks and whites, sprinkled with breadcrumbs and cheese

★ **Цыплята табака (tsyplyata tabaka)** boned chicken, halved and flattened, covered with sour cream and butter. It was originally pressed between two hot stones and fried

Чакапули (chakapuli) a thick Georgian lamb stew

Чанахи (chanakhi) braised lamb with potatoes, tomatoes, beans, diced eggplant and coriander

Шашлык (shashlyk) consists of pieces of meat, mushrooms and onions on a skewer, either grilled or barbecued and served with pomegranate juice or *tkemali*

Овощи и салаты *(ovoshchi i salati)* — Vegetables and salads

★ **Баклажан с орехами (baklazhan s orekhami)** eggplant in a walnut, garlic, coriander, chilli and pomegranate sauce

Вареные картошки в сметане (vareniye kartoshki v smetane) baked potatoes with sour cream and scallions

Грибы в сметане (gribi v smetane) mushrooms in sour cream

Жареные огурцы (zharini ogurtzi) cucumbers fried with onions

Кабачок жареный (kabachok zharini) fried vegetable squash

Капуста с ромом (kapusta s romom) cauliflower and rum sauce

Картофельное кольцо с яйцом (kartofelnoye koltzo s yaitzom)

eggs in mashed potato rings

Квашеная капуста с грибами (kvashenaya kapusta s gribami) sauerkraut with mushrooms

Лобио (lobio) a Georgian dish of white beans with walnuts

Плоф (plof) pilaff;

арарат (ararat) pilaff with white raisins, apricots, almonds, apples and quinces

Салат из зелени (salat iz zeleni) green salad with sour cream

из яблок и сельдерей (iz yablok i seldere) apple and celery salad

Спинат с орехами (spinat s orekhami) spinach with walnut sauce and pomegranate seeds

Фаршированные картошки (farsherovaniye kartoshki) potatoes stuffed with mushrooms, leeks and breadcrumbs

огурцы в сметане (orgutzi v smetane) stuffed cucumbers in sour cream

Хморопатик (khmoropatik) Caucasian asparagus fritters

Сладкое, печеные и торты *(sladkoye, pecheniye i torti) — Desserts, biscuits and cakes*

Бублики (boubliki) yeast dough rings either eaten hot with butter or halved and toasted

Вафля (vaflya) waffle

Галушки (galushki) Ukrainian fried cakes, served with large helpings of sour cream

Гозинах (gozinakh) Armenian honey and walnut sweetmeat

Каштановый пудинг (kashtanovi pudding) chestnut pudding

Кисель (kisel) dessert made with tart fruit juice

Кулич (kulich) tall, cylindrical loaf for special occasions. Made with fruit, almonds and saffron

Наполеон торт (napoleon tort) a light cake with sour cream in

the dough, baked in layers, filled with cream

Ореховый пудинг (orekhovi pudding) walnut pudding

★ **Пасха (paskha)** traditional pyramid-shaped Easter cake, usually made with unsalted cream cheese, fruit and almonds

Пряник (prianik) spiced honey cake

Пудинг из маков (pudding iz makov) poppy-seed pudding with almonds

Торт из меринги (tort iz meringi) meringue and cream cake with walnuts and brandy, decorated with nuts and chocolate

Тянушки (tyanushki) soft fudge

Useful words

Барашек (barashek) lamb

Брага (braga) mead

Вино (vino) wine

Вода (voda) water

Водка (vodka) vodka

Говядина (govyadina) beef

Каша (kasha) a dry sort of buckwheat porridge

Квас (kvass) a drink made from fermented rye bread and yeast. Also used as a stock base

Кофе (kofe) coffee

Курица (kuritsa) chicken

Лаваш (lavash) flat Armenian bread

Масло (maslo) butter

Меню (menu) menu

Молоко (moloko) milk

Пиво (pivo) beer

Рис (ris) rice

Сахар (sakhar) sugar

Сметана (smetana) sour cream

Счет (schyot) bill

Сыр (syr) cheese

Телятина (telyatina) veal

Ткемали (tkemali) Georgian sauce of sour plums, garlic and coriander

Чай (chai) tea

За ваше здоровье! (za vashe zdorovye) cheers!
Приятного аппетита! (pryatnovo appetita) bon appétit!

The United States

The United States is maligned on two counts. Firstly it is abused for its fast food, secondly it is said to have no food of its own. If fast food is so dreadful, one wonders why the rest of the world has seized upon it so eagerly. American ingenuity has devised perfectly palatable ways of eating swiftly prepared food and we should be grateful for the hamburger, the hot dog, even Kentucky fried chicken, all of which can be pleasant, nutritious and far better than the lugubrious alternative of a sandwich. And think what America did with that, turning it into the club sandwich. Too many days of eating fast food is gravely constipating, but we have no right to sneer, except when "milk" has never seen a cow or "meat" has been coaxed from a soya bean.

The second accusation is preposterous. American cuisine may not have a clearly identifiable style, but the waves of immigrants over the centuries have brought their own cuisines and adapted them to the climate and the land and produced, regionally, a diverse collection of original dishes.

It is these dishes I have concentrated on in the listings—the Creole cooking of the South, the amalgam of Puritan with Indian of New England, the Spanish adaptations in the southwest, the "Dutch"-Swiss in Pennsylvania. There are even more obscure enclaves which could be studied, such as the Basques in Idaho, Oregon and Nevada, and the Danish in California. In some cases, especially the Mexicans in Arizona and California, I have left out dishes as they can be found in the appropriate sections on whatever country. Indeed, it may surprise travellers in the States how often they will have to look in the Chinese, British, Polish, Jewish, French, German and Scandinavian chapters.

Soups

Black bean soup a purée of beans, vegetables and ham served with sliced lemon and hard-boiled eggs

★Clam chowder this famous soup from New England is traditionally eaten while the *clambake* is cooking. It consists of clams, salt pork or bacon, potatoes and onion, seasoned with black pepper and thinned with clam juice. It may also contain milk, tomatoes and chopped leeks or, in New York, garlic, and in the south, okra, celery, and cayenne pepper

Corn chowder paprika-flavoured soup of sweetcorn, potato and salt pork with, in the south, tomatoes and, in New England, cheese

Garbanzo soup a very thick, filling soup made from chick peas simmered in water with ham bones, onions, green pepper, oil, garlic, Spanish *chorizo* sausages

and potatoes

Gumbo the highlight of Creole cuisine, the name derives from the Congolese word for okra. A soup-stew consisting of any of a variety of ingredients including game, poultry and seafood. The best gumbos are those made with shellfish, such as crab and shrimp gumbo. There is also *gumbo z'herbes* made with quantities of mixed greens and herbs. Other basic elements are rice, okra and tomatoes but the most essential is *filé*, powdered young sassafras leaves

Philadelphia pepperpot soup tripe, onions, potatoes and herbs in a rich stock made from veal knuckle. Served with dumplings

She-crab soup crab meat and crab eggs mixed with cream and chopped onion and flavoured with mace, Worcester sauce and dry sherry. A dish from South Carolina

234

Fish

Cape Cod turkey cod fish balls
Cioppino a Californian seafood casserole containing lobster, crab, shrimps, mussels, white fish meat and clams
Clam fritters spoonfuls of batter containing chopped clams, breadcrumbs and herbs, stiffened with beaten egg whites and fried
★**Clambake** part of the great American tradition of outdoor eating where the ritual of preparation is almost as important as the food itself. Rocks are heated with piles of burning brushwood, then spread with seaweed and layers of food —lobsters, green corn and clams alternating with layers of seaweed. The lobsters go at the bottom, the corn in the middle and the clams at the top, all covered with a tarpaulin. Ideally, after an hour and a half you start eating from the top. Each ingredient, as you reach it, should be perfectly cooked
Crab imperial a mixture of crab meat, mustard, Worcester sauce, mayonnaise and hard-boiled egg heated and served in crab shells
Hangtown fry a Californian dish of oysters dipped in flour and egg and fried
★**Jambalaya** the Creole version of a pilaff. Rice mixed with shellfish, beans, meat or any other available ingredients
La médiatrice bread rolls hollowed out and stuffed with sautéed oysters, hot cream and Tabasco. Originally, it is said, errant New Orleans husbands on their way home when the bakers

were baking used to pop oysters into the fresh rolls and take them home to pacify their wives
★**Lobster Newburg** lobster in cream sauce flavoured with wine and paprika or cayenne pepper. A speciality of Delmonico's— the Mecca of fashionable New York in the late 19th century— and originally named after a Mr Wenburg but changed after the erstwhile customer had displeased the restaurant owners
Lomi lomi salmon a Hawaiian dish consisting of cooked salmon mixed with tomatoes and scallions and serve chilled
Lox and bagels a favourite New York breakfast of Jewish origin. Smoked salmon on toasted *bagels* (see *Bread*). Served with scrambled eggs and cream cheese
New England boiled cod boiled salt cod served with béchamel sauce and hard-boiled eggs
Oysters farcis chopped oysters in a thick sauce of onions, celery, herbs and breadcrumbs seasoned with cayenne pepper and served in their shells
★**Oysters Rockefeller** a speciality of Antoine's, the famous restaurant in New Orleans— poached oysters with anise-flavoured spinach purée, served in their shells
★**Soft shell crabs** crabs caught just as they shed their shells and before new ones have grown. Usually breadcrumbed and fried or sautéed. The whole crab can be eaten
Steamed clams clams steamed in their own juice

Meat

Brunswick stew a thick chicken and veal stew with lots of vegetables. Originally containing squirrel
Chicken à la King Delmonico's, the Waldorf, and Claridges in London are among the distinguished contenders for the origin of this dish. It is diced chicken in a rich creamy mushroom sauce flavoured with dry sherry and cayenne pepper

Chicken hash a breakfast dish of chopped chicken in a cream sauce
Chilli con carne a Texan dish, the responsibility for which is firmly denied by the Mexicans, ground beef laced with quantities of chilli powder. The original version is without the usual accompaniment of kidney beans
Chitillins, chitterlings deep-fried pig's intestines

Grillade panée strips of veal marinated in beaten egg, onion and hot pepper, "breaded" with cornmeal and deep fried. A Creole dish

Hobo steak fillet steak completely embedded in sea salt and baked. The salt forms a solid casing round the meat which is cracked open and the steak emerges, beautifully roasted and perfectly seasoned. Quite how tramps afford it I don't know, as I have paid $50 for it

Hog's head cheese pork brawn

Kentucky burgoo a stew of mixed meats, originally including goat, squirrel and any game that could be found

Lau lau a Hawaiian dish of steamed salt fish, pork and greens

Maryland Easter ham boiled ham cooked with herbs, cooled and served with vinegar

Maryland fried chicken chicken pieces fried in butter and bacon fat and served in a thick cream sauce with bits of bacon

Neckbones and corn mush a meat loaf made with cornmeal and pork and then sliced and fried

★ **New England boiled dinner** corned beef boiled with cabbage, turnips, potatoes, carrots and beets, and served with freshly grated horseradish and beets

Puaa Kalua a Hawaiian feast, a whole pig cooked in a pit oven

Red flannel hash beef, potato, beet (to give it the characteristic red colour) and onions all fried together and made into a flat cake

Schnitz-un-gnep a speciality of Pennsylvania Dutch cooking, sliced dried apples cooked with ham or pork and served with dumplings

Scrapple called *ponhaws* by the Pennsylvania Dutch, pieces of pork meat mixed with onions, spices, herbs and cornmeal, simmered slowly then cooled, sliced and fried

Smothered chicken cut up chicken cooked with milk

Son-of-a-gun stew calves' offal stewed with onion and chilli

Southern fried chicken chicken pieces dipped in batter or buttermilk and fried

Surf 'n turf a monstrous intruder on modern menus. A mixture which doesn't mix of steak and shellfish

Tamale pie an Amerindian-influenced dish, layers of cornmeal, ground beef, onions and tomatoes baked in the oven

Virginia ham the hams from pigs fed on peanuts and sweetcorn are smoked over oak, apple and hickory wood fires and aged for at least a year. They are often served baked, covered with molasses and studded with cloves

Vegetables

Boova shenkel literally "boy's leg", a Pennsylvania Dutch dish, potato pies cooked like dumplings in a stew

Boston baked beans Bostonian Puritans were strict observers of the Sabbath so this dish was prepared in bulk on Saturday night for supper, eaten with fish cakes for breakfast on Sunday and again at lunch time. Any left-overs appeared in various guises throughout the week. The basic dish was beans baked slowly in an earthenware pot with salt pork, onions, mustard and molasses

Caesar's salad cos lettuce leaves in a dressing made of coddled eggs tossed in the salad with salt,

pepper, anchovy paste, olive oil and lemon juice. Served with garlic flavoured croûtons and Parmesan cheese

Calas fried spiced rice cakes

Candied sweet potatoes cooked sweet potatoes sliced and baked in brown sugar, water, butter and lemon juice

Coleslaw a genuine Dutch dish, originally "kool sla", shredded cabbage in a cream, sugar and vinegar dressing

Dutch potatoes potatoes hollowed out, stuffed with sausage, wrapped in bacon, braised then browned under the grill

Fried green tomatoes slices of unripe tomatoes dipped in cornmeal and fried

Hash brown potatoes diced potatoes fried in bacon fat and turned out in one piece like a cake. Sometimes milk, cream, butter and chopped bacon are added. From the mid-West
Hominy hulled corn, a food introduced to the early settlers by the Indians. Simmered slowly until tender and eaten with butter, fried or baked. Usually served with meat instead of potatoes but also made into bread and fritters

    grits ground hominy boiled, mixed with butter and served for breakfast in the south

pudding boiled hominy grits mixed with eggs, cream and seasoning and baked in the oven
Hopping John black-eyed peas and rice cooked with ham or bacon. See also *The Caribbean*
Saratoga chips thin potato chips
Succotash originally an Indian dish, a mixture of lima beans and corn kernels, nowadays cooked with cream and possibly salt pork. The Indians used bear fat and called it *misickquatash*
Waldorf salad chopped apple, celery and walnuts with mayonnaise, served on lettuce leaves

Desserts and cakes

Ambrosia layers of thinly sliced oranges, sugar and coconut
Baked Alaska a layer of sponge cake and ice-cream sealed into a meringue coating and baked
Blueberry slump blueberry dumplings with cream
Boston cream pie two layers of cake sandwiched with custard
Brownies chocolate nut squares
Chess pie a southern tart filled with custard made of butter, sugar, corn syrup and pecan nuts
Crab lanterns fried pastry turnovers filled with peaches, apples, mincemeat or jam
Grunt stewed fruit topped with steamed dumplings
Haupia Hawaiian coconut pudding
Ice-cream this is a universal American treat and it is impossible to list all the varieties. Many restaurants advertise scores of "flavors"
Indian pudding a milk pudding made with molasses, brown sugar, spices and cornmeal, served with cream and nutmeg

Key lime pie from Key West in Florida, a pastry case filled with a mixture of condensed milk, lime juice, eggs and sugar, covered with meringue and baked. Served cold
Molasses pie tart filled with custard, molasses and buttermilk
Pecan pie a pastry case filled with rich custard and pecan nuts
Persimmon pudding a mixture of persimmon purée, nuts and crackers. Served cold
Pumpkin pie puréed pumpkin, brown sugar, egg yolks, cream and spices baked in a pastry case
Shoofly pie a biscuit crumb case filled with a mixture of molasses, sugar and spices
Snitz Kloes a highly spiced steamed fruit pudding from Pennsylvania
Strawberry shortcake two layers of shortcake sandwiched together with fresh strawberries and sugar and covered with whipped cream
Waffles rich egg batter cooked in a waffle iron and served with maple syrup or honey and butter

Bread

Anadame bread a simple bread made from yeast dough with cornmeal and molasses
Bagels circular rolls with holes in the middle made from dough which is first boiled then baked
Beaten biscuits one of the hot breads characteristic of mealtimes in the south. A simple

dough beaten up to a thousand times with a wooden mallet before baking. Served with smoky southern hams
Blueberry muffins sweet rich muffins served for breakfast or accompanying *New England boiled dinner*
Buckwheat cakes yeast, molasses,

buckwheat and wheat flour
baked on a griddle and eaten
with maple syrup for breakfast
Hoe cake cornmeal bread
originally baked on a shovel over
an open fire
Hominy bread hot bread made
from *hominy grits*. See *Vegetables*
Hush puppies simple cornmeal
and water griddle-baked bread
Johnny cake another hot
breakfast bread of Indian origin
baked on a griddle, served with
butter or maple syrup. The name
may be a corruption of "journey

cake" possibly because of its
associations with pioneer food
or, as seems more likely,
"Shawnee cake"
Poor boy French bread sandwich
with beef, cheese and mustard
Pretzels lengths of sweet dough
twisted into knots and baked
Shortnin' bread a rich bread
including flour, sugar and butter
Spoon bread a cornmeal mixture
spooned out of a dish and eaten
hot with butter as a side dish to
meat. From the Indian word
suppawn—a kind of porridge

As American as apple pie

There are innumerable versions of apple pie. The classic New
England pie has two crusts and a filling spiced with cloves,
cinnamon and nutmeg. This is the pie that was reputedly
served at Yale every night for a hundred years and in hundreds
of ordinary homes for breakfast. It is traditionally eaten with
Cheddar cheese or ice-cream. Then there is apple pandowdy,
apple Jonathan or apple Betty, all names for a deep apple pie
covered with sponge mixture rather than pastry. Apple slump
is a North-eastern mixture of spiced apples covered with soft
dough, pan-cooked and served hot with cream. Green apple
pie is made with small sour apples. Cob apple pie is a one-
crust pie served upside down. McGintie's pie is the Californian
version made with dried apples. Yet another from Connecticut
has spiced apples in pastry with more apples on top.

American wine and other drinks

American wine is now extremely good and there is a lot of it.
That being so, it is worth sticking to Californian wine, rather
than bothering with any of the less good eastern wines. The
Americans use the grape name on bottles and in descending
order the best six are: *Cabernet Sauvignon* (for red), *Chardonnay* (for white), *Johannisberg Riesling, Zinfandel, Gewürtz-
traminer* and *Muscat*.

The names of wine-makers to look for are: Beaulieu, David
Bruce, Christian Brothers, Hacienda, Heitz, Inglenook,
Charles Krug, Louis Martini, Robert Mondavi, Joseph
Phelps, Martin Ray, Ridge, Sonoma Vineyards, Stag's Leap
Wine Cellars, Stony Hill and Wente.

American whiskey—bourbon—is made from corn and is
first-rate (and much stronger than we are accustomed to).

The Americans have always specialized in mixed drinks
starting probably with the mint julep (made with bourbon,
soda, ice, sugar and mint leaves). While cocktails are rather
despised in Europe, they are often quite stunning (in every
sense) in their homeland.

Venezuela—*See* South America
Vietnam—*See* Southeast Asia
Yugoslavia—*See* Eastern Europe
Yemen—*See* Arab food

Glossary of culinary terms

Bain-marie (Fr.) a method of cooking where the food stands in its own container within another larger receptacle which holds boiling water

Bard cover meat, poultry, game or fish with thin slices of fatty bacon to prevent flesh drying out

Baste moisten meat etc. with the pan juices during cooking

Beurre manié (Fr.) mixture of butter and flour used as a thickening agent

Blanch boil briefly (to remove bitterness, loosen skin, set colours)

Bouquet garni (Fr.) selection of herbs (usually thyme, parsley, bay leaf) tied together or in a bag, for flavouring

Braise brown in fat and then cook very slowly in a covered dish with vegetables and a little liquid

Brine salt and water mixture for preserving, etc.

Broiling (US) grilling

Canapé (Fr.) appetizer of biscuits etc. topped with savoury mixtures

Casserole ovenproof cooking pot with lid, hence also the stew cooked slowly in it

Chaud-froid (Fr.) poultry or game cooked, covered in a cream sauce and glazed with aspic. Served cold

Clarify make soups, jellies, etc. absolutely clear (e.g. by filtering)

Compote (Fr.) fruit, fresh or dried, cooked in a syrup and served cold

Consommé (Fr.) concentrated clear broth of meat or poultry

Court-bouillon (Fr.) liquid in which vegetables and herbs have been cooked. Used mostly for poaching fish

Croûtons (Fr.) tiny bread shapes, fried or toasted. Used as a garnish, or when larger, as a base

Deglaze dilute pan juices (with wine, stock, etc.) to make gravy

Escalope (Fr.) thin slice of meat, usually veal, from the fillet or leg

Fines herbes (Fr.) mixture of finely chopped parsley, tarragon, chervil and chives

Flambé (Fr.) literally "flamed"; alcohol is poured over food during cooking, lit and stirred until the flames die out

Fumet (Fr.) concentrated meat, fish or vegetable stock

Fricassée (Fr.) "white" stew of chicken, rabbit or veal with vegetables, fried, then cooked in stock and thickened with cream and egg yolks

Garnish decoration of a dish, such as croûtons, vegetables, etc.

Glaze glossy finish to a dish, achieved by grilling, painting with egg white, icing sugar, etc. *or* much-reduced stock used to enhance certain sauces

Gratiné (Fr.) topping of browned breadcrumbs or cheese

Julienne (Fr.) matchstick-like slices of raw vegetables

Lard insert fatty strips of bacon with a needle into lean meat to prevent it from drying up

Liaison (Fr.) thickening or binding agent

Marinate tenderize and flavour meat, poultry, game or venison, by steeping in a *marinade*, usually wine or alcohol with oil, vinegar and spices

Pilaff rice cooked in stock with added fish, meat, etc.

Poach cook in simmering liquid

Ramekin individual ovenproof dish or small pastry case

Reduce concentrate and diminish a liquid by boiling

Render obtain fat by cooking meat trimmings, etc.

Risotto (It.) rice, first fried, then cooked in liquid and served with other savoury ingredients and sometimes cheese

Roux (Fr.) mixture of fat and flour used as a sauce base

Salmis (Fr.) stew of game first roasted then cooked in wine

Salpicon (Fr.) mixture of diced ingredients bound with a sauce

Sauté (Fr.) stir fry in shallow pan, making ingredients "jump", until uniformly browned

Sear brown meat rapidly to seal in the juices

Simmer cook in liquid just below boiling point

Steam cook food in the steam rising from boiling water below

Stew simmer in closed container

Truss tie bird or cut of beef with string

Acknowledgements

I would like to thank the following people and organizations for their help, varying from gentle suggestions to salvation from total disaster: Algerian Embassy; Bridget Ardley; Australian High Commission; Belgian Embassy; Eva and Joseph Berkmann; Bulgarian National Tourist Office; Canadian High Commission; Sandy Carr; Czech National House; Danish Food Centre, London; Zelfa Draz, Sheba; Fiona Duncan; Arab Republic of Egypt Embassy; Finnish Embassy; Christine Forth; George Foster; Pamela Gagliani; Gaylord of India Restaurant, London; The Great Britain-U.S.S.R. Association; National Tourist Organization of Greece; Lily Greenham; Lady Harlech; Marie-Monique Huss; Icelandic Embassy; India Club; Government of India Tourist Office; Israel Government Tourist Office; Italian Institute of Culture; Catherine Jackson; Japanese Embassy; Kaya Korean Restaurant; Korean Embassy; Willie Landels; Lebanese Food Centre; Dinah Lee; George Lesov; Bernard Levin; Kenneth Lo; Lady Maclean; Malaysian High Commission; Ingrid Mason; Melati Restaurant; Moroccan Tourist Office; Royal Netherlands Embassy; New Zealand High Commission; Royal Norwegian Embassy; Embassy of the Philippines; Portuguese Embassy; Mme. Rochon, Chez Solange; Embassy of the Socialist Republic of Romania; Evelyn Rose; Michel Roux; Rumwong Restaurant, Guildford; Don Jaime Saldívar; Salvat Editores; Victor Sassie, The Gay Hussar; Caroline Schuck; Shezan Restaurant; Sol e Mar Portuguese Restaurant; Uitgeverij het Spectrum bv; Sri Lankan High Commission; Swedish Embassy; Swiss Centre Restaurants; Syrian Arab Republic Embassy; The Royal Embassy of Thailand; Information Service of Thailand; Tunisian National Tourist Office; Embassy of the Socialist Republic of Vietnam; Penelope Wacks; Tarja Wilson; Yugoslav National Tourist Office.